Statistics and the German State, 1900–1945

J. Adam Tooze provides an interpretation of the dramatic period of statistical innovation between 1900 and the end of World War II. At the turn of the century, virtually none of the economic statistics that we take for granted today were available. By 1944, the entire repertoire of modern economic statistics was being put to work in wartime economic management. As this book reveals, the Weimar Republic and the Third Reich were in the forefront of statistical innovation in the interwar decades. New ways of measuring the economy were inspired both by contemporary developments in macroeconomic theory and the needs of government. The Weimar Republic invested heavily in macroeconomic research. Under the Nazi regime, these statistical tools were to provide the basis for a radical experiment in economic planning. Based on the German example, this book presents the case for a more wide-ranging reconsideration of the history of modern economic knowledge.

J. ADAM TOOZE is University Lecturer in Economic History in the History Faculty, University of Cambridge. He directs studies in history at Jesus College. He has published in the *Economic History Review*. Articles and reviews have also appeared in French and German.

Cambridge Studies in Modern Economic History

Series editors

Charles Feinstein (All Souls College, Oxford)
Patrick O'Brien (London School of Economics and Political Science)
Barry Supple (The Leverhulme Trust)
Peter Temin (Massachusetts Institute of Technology)
Gianni Toniolo (Università degli Studi di Venezia)

Cambridge Studies in Modern Economic History is a major new initiative in economic history publishing, and a flagship series for Cambridge University Press in an area of scholarly activity in which it has long been active. Books in this series will primarily be concerned with the history of economic performance, output and productivity, assessing the characteristics, causes and consequences of economic growth (and stagnation) in the western world. This range of enquiry, rather than any one methodological or analytic approach, will be the defining characteristic of volumes in the series.

Statistics and the German State, 1900–1945

The Making of Modern Economic Knowledge

J. Adam Tooze

Jesus College and the Faculty of History
University of Cambridge

CAMBRIDGE
UNIVERSITY PRESS

CAMBRIDGE UNIVERSITY PRESS
Cambridge, New York, Melbourne, Madrid, Cape Town, Singapore, São Paulo

Cambridge University Press
The Edinburgh Building, Cambridge CB2 8RU, UK

Published in the United States of America by Cambridge University Press, New York

www.cambridge.org
Information on this title: www.cambridge.org/9780521803182

First published 2001
This digitally printed version 2007

A catalogue record for this publication is available from the British Library

Library of Congress Cataloguing in Publication data
Tooze, J. Adam.
Statistics and the German state, 1900–1945: the making of modern economic
knowledge / J. Adam Tooze.
    p.   cm. – (Cambridge studies in modern economic history; 9)
Includes bibliographical references and index.
ISBN 0 521 80318 7
1. Germany–Economic conditions–1888–1918. 2. Germany–Economic
conditions–1918–1945. 3. Economics–Germany–Statistical methods.
I. Title. II. Series.

HC285.T668 2001
330.943´08–dc21   00-067609

ISBN 978-0-521-80318-2 hardback
ISBN 978-0-521-03912-3 paperback

For Sarah, John
and
Becky

Contents

Figures

Tables

Acknowledgements

This book has been a long time in the making and I have accumulated very many debts.

The idea that became this book germinated in my final year as an economics undergraduate. Paul Ryan, my Director of Studies at King's, and Solomos Solomou of Peterhouse got me started and pointed me in the right direction. The project took shape in Berlin (1989–91), during which time I am particularly grateful for the advice and encouragement I received from Jürgen Kocka, Bernd Dornseifer, Rolf Krengel, Ralf Rogowski and Jakob Vogel. The PhD on which this book is based was completed at the LSE between 1991 and 1996. It was generously funded by the ESRC and supervised by Alan Milward. At the LSE I would like to thank Les Hannah, Paul Johnson, Peter Howlett, Mary Morgan and Dudley Baines for their support. It would not have happened without Linda Sampson. The last year of graduate work was supported by a Scouloudi grant from the Institute of Historical Research in London for which I am profoundly grateful. Thanks, in particular, to Patrick O'Brien.

In graduate school one needs good friends. The LSE graduate students were a good bunch especially Max Schulze and Roy Edwards. Most thanks of all to Francesca Carnevali. For friendship and comradeship in Germany I owe a great deal to Kati Koerner, Kirsten Poutros, Brigitte Preissl, Fritz Betz, Dorothea Moltke, Leoni Schroeder and her parents. During this period I was lucky enough to acquire the support of Helena Rainsford, who has helped me through some bad times.

To write this book I spent a long time in many different archives. I would particularly like to thank the staff of the former Bundesarchiv, Zweigstelle Potsdam. I have fond memories of the place!

Early versions of various chapters were commented upon by seminars at the Institut für Vergleichende Gesellschaftsgeschichte in Berlin, the European University in Budapest, the DIW, a joint seminar of the Departments of Economic History and Accounting at the LSE, the German History seminar and the graduate student seminar at the Institute of Historical Research, the Centre for History and Economics at Cambridge, the economic history seminar at the University of Birmingham and the economic history seminar at the University of Cambridge. I would particularly like to thank an impromptu colloquium of graduate students at the University of Michigan including Don LaCoss and Warren Rosenblum. The best questions of all came from an audience at my job talk at the University of Oregon, Eugene. I would like to thank everyone involved in that search for their professionalism and courtesy. Though I was not lucky enough to be offered the post, I learned an enormous amount.

Richard Overy and Richard Bessel read and reread the manuscript and I thank them for their help both times. A special thank you to Keith Tribe who received a draft in the mail and provided me with much-needed encouragement and criticism. Thanks also to the anonymous referees of the *Economic History Review* who provided excellent comments on an early article.

In 1995 my life was changed for a second time by Cambridge. Gareth Stedman Jones and Emma Rothschild at the Centre for History and Economics offered me a Research Fellowship. Their support has continued long after I have moved on. They deserve all my thanks. Thank you also to the Fellowship of Robinson College for their welcome, in particular to Deborah Thom. The second set of doors was opened by the Cambridge History Faculty. Thank you for taking a chance! In particular, I owe a great deal to Jonathan Steinberg and to Celia Hewetson who made me welcome from the first. Jesus College has proved a wonderful new home. I would like to thank my friends and close colleagues at Cambridge, James Thompson, Chris Clark, Max Jones and Martin Daunton, for making the last few years such a pleasure.

I might have finished this book on my own, but it would have been even less satisfactory without the help of all these people. I cannot even begin to imagine what it would have been like without the presence in my life of Becky E. Conekin. I am truly blessed to have found someone with such intelligence, such strength and such capacity for love. This book is dedicated to her and to my parents, who set me on my way.

Glossary and abbreviations

ADGB	Allgemeiner Deutscher Gewerkschaftsbund: Federation of German Trade Unions associated with the SPD
ASA	*Allgemeines Statistisches Archiv*, journal published by German Statistical Association
Auskunftspflicht	Obligatory Reporting Decree introduced in 1917 to formalize and expand the state's powers of enquiry, renewed in 1923
Betriebszählungen	Workplace censuses
Cambridge circus	A small group of young economists in Cambridge who read and critiqued early drafts of Keynes' *General Theory*
DAF	Deutsche Arbeitsfront: Nazi labour organization that replaced the free trade unions
DANAT	Darmstädter und National Bank
DIW	Deutsches Institut für Wirtschaftsforschung, *see* IfK
DSZ	*Deutsches Statistisches Zentralblatt*, fortnightly bulletin of the German Statistical Association (DSG)
Gau	Regional sub-division of Nazi party organization
GBW	Generalbevollmächtigter für die Wehrwirtschaft: General Plenipotentiary for the War Economy, office created in 1935 to give the RWM (q.v.) responsibility for the civilian side of military-economic planning
General equilibrium analysis	The generalization of marginalist analysis to the entire economy; the aim is to establish the possibility of an equilibrium not just in one market, but simultaneously across all markets
Gesamtplan	Statistical overview of the German economy

	which the Planungsamt (q.v.) struggled to create in 1944
Gewerbezählungen	Trade Surveys (nineteenth century)
Gleichschaltung	'Coordination', euphemism to describe the process through which organizations declared loyalty to the Nazi regime
GNP	Gross National Product: measure of total output attributable to economic activity of nationals
GRA3	Statistical section of Kehrl's staff in the RWM (q.v.), est. 1942
IfK	Institut für Konjunkturforschung: Institute for Business-Cycle Research founded in 1925; since the 1940s known under its present name as DIW
Konjunkturforschung	Business-cycle research
Konzerne	Corporations or trusts
Kreislauf	Circular flow
KSA	Kaiserliches Statistisches Amt: Statistical Office of Imperial Germany
Kuratorium	Governing Board of the IfK (q.v.)
Länder	Member states of the German federation
Lenkungsbereiche	Lb: Streamlined planning organizations for civilian production est. 1942–3 on the basis of Reichsstellen (q.v.)
Machtergreifung	(Nazi) seizure of power; term coined by the Nazis to describe the events of 1933
Macroeconomics	The study of economies in the aggregate
Marginalist economics	A brand of economics that dates to the 1870s; it describes the economic process in terms of the rational decision-making of individual actors, which is modelled as a mathematical process of maximization and involves the behaviour of variables 'at the margin'
MB	Maschinelles Berichtswesen: Title given to the army Hollerith organization in 1942
Microeconomics	The study of rational decision-making by individual economic actors in particular markets; the twentieth-century descendant of marginalism
Mittelstand	Middle class
National Revolution	Nationalist euphemism for the Machtergreifung (q.v.)
Neoclassical	A brand of monetary theory, which emerged in

monetary theory	the 1870s, concerned to revamp the classical Quantity Theory of Money
NEP	New Economic Policy, comparatively liberal period in Soviet economic policy between 1921 and 1928
Net product	The value of final output calculated from total turnover by excluding the value of all intermediate stages of production
NSBO	Nationalsozialistische Betriebszellenorganisation: Nazi shopfloor organization
Physiocrat	Eighteenth-century French economic doctrine
Planungsamt	Economic staff of the Zentrale Planung (q.v.) established by Kehrl during the reorganization in the summer of 1943
Polizei	In seventeenth- and eighteenth-century German the term embraced not merely police, but the entire field of absolutist policy
Public choice analysis	Brand of political science which treats bureaucrats as self-seeking, utility-maximizing actors
RdI	Reichsverband der deutschen Industrie: peak association of German industry, succeeded after 1934 by the RgI (q.v.)
Reichsbank	German Central Bank
Reichsbeauftragten	Heads of the Supervisory Agencies, Reich's Agencies and Lenkungsbereiche (q.v.)
Reichsindex	National cost of living index that came into operation in spring of 1921
Reichsstellen	Reich's Agencies: New title given to Supervisory Agencies in 1939
Reichstag	German parliament
Reichswehr	Name given to the German armed forces between 1918 and 1935
Reichswirtschaftsrat	Reich's Economic Council: Corporatist revising chamber of the Weimar Republic
RgI	Reichsgruppe Industrie: Industry organizations within the Nazi system of business organizations
RPI	Retail Price Index
Ruhr	North-Western heartland of German heavy industry
RWM	Reichswirtschaftsministerium: Reich's Ministry of Economic Affairs

RwP	Reichsamt für wehrwirtschaftliche Planung: Reich's Office for Military–Economic Planning, est. 1938
Sonderweg	Shorthand for the idea that Germany followed a predetermined 'special path' through modern history
Sozial Marktwirtschaft	Social market economy, a concept developed by German liberals opposed to the Weimar Republic and the Third Reich
Sparkommissar	Reich's Savings Commissioner
SPD	Social Democratic Party
SRA	Statistisches Reichsamt: Reich's Statistical Office
State Secretary	Highest civil service rank in German Ministry
SZA	Statistischer Zentralausschuss: Central Statistical Committee, est. 1939 to cull redundant surveys
Time-series	Data arrayed along a time axis, as opposed to cross-sectional snapshots
Überwachungsstellen	Supervisory Agencies: est. 1934 under the 'New Plan' to implement control of German imports
Value added	*See* net product
VdMA	Verein deutscher Maschinenbauanstalten: , Industrial organization for mechanical engineering
Verein für Sozialpolitik	Association for Social Policy, the most important association of German economists from the late nineteenth century
Volksgemeinschaft	Nazi utopia of a racially unified community
Volkswirtschaft	The national economy, a term used in German from the mid-nineteenth century
Vorwärts	Social Democratic daily
VzK	*Vierteljahrshefte zur Konjunkturforschung*: quarterly bulletin of the IfK (q.v.)
WuS	*Wirtschaft und Statistik*, fortnightly bulletin of the Statistical Office, first appeared in 1920
ZAG	Zentrale Arbeitsgemeinschaft (Central Working Group): Corporatist assembly of major interest groups formed in 1918
Zentrale Planung	Central Planning Committee est. in the spring of 1942 by Speer

Introduction

Today, statistics define our knowledge of the economy. The countries of the world rank themselves in terms of their gross national product (GNP). Indicators such as the Retail Price Index (RPI) are used routinely in the regulation of everyday life. New numbers are news. The calendar of statistical publications provides grist to the mill of financial speculation and business planning. Numerical representations shape our conception of the economy in subtle but profound ways. Statistics reinforce our sense of the economy as a realm apart from other spheres of life. The economy has assumed the status of a substantive entity, even an actor: an actor, however, who moves in one dimension. We speak of unemployment as 'going up' or 'down', 'rising' or 'falling'. In large part, this is surely because we think of unemployment as a statistic or a graph plotted over time. It would be eccentric to describe unemployment as 'spreading'. Whereas an earlier language spoke of economic expansion, or progress, the master term in our vocabulary is 'growth'. Statistics also shape our understanding of economic history. The reconceptualization of the economic past in terms of macroeconomic data has come close to obliterating the 'industrial revolution'.[1] The dramatic story of Arkwright and the dark satanic mills has been replaced by a narrative of undramatic growth in large statistical aggregates such as industrial production. This book is driven by the desire to understand how this peculiar structure of economic knowledge came into existence. In pursuit of this larger question, it explores the making of modern economic statistics in Germany in the first half of the twentieth century. How to justify this narrow focus in time and place?

When we scratch the surface we discover that modern economic statistics are of surprisingly recent origin. The first recognizably modern statistical projects in Europe date to the birth of the modern state in the

---

[1] D. Cannadine, 'The Present and Past in the English Industrial Revolution', *Past and Present*, 103 (1984), pp. 131–172 and M. Berg and P. Hudson, 'Rehabilitating the Industrial Revolution', *Economic History Review*, 45 (1992), pp. 24–50.

seventeenth century.[2] The intrusive policies of absolutism made censuses a regular event in the eighteenth century. But it was the revolutions of the late eighteenth century, which gave shape to official statistics in the form we know today. In 1787 the constitution of the newly independent United States called for a regular census to establish the membership of the House of Representatives. In 1800 revolutionary France established the first 'Bureau de statistique'.[3] This was enough to persuade counter-revolutionary Britain. In 1753 the Houses of Parliament had rejected a census as an unwanted intrusion upon 'English liberty'. In 1801 the first modern census of population went ahead almost entirely unopposed. Statistical offices were established in Prussia in 1805, in Bavaria in 1806, in 1810 in Habsburg Vienna, in 1820 in Württemberg, in 1826 in the Netherlands and in 1831 in the newly independent Belgium. The British Board of Trade established its statistical department in 1832. Five years later demographic statistics were placed under the control of the Registrar General.[4] Russian administrative statistics were put on an institutional footing in 1834. In 1833 Denmark set up a Central Statistical Commission, followed by Norway in 1837. Finland was the last of the Scandinavian countries to establish a statistical office in 1865. The constitution of the 'double-monarchy' was shortly followed in 1867 by the formation of an Hungarian statistical bureau. The provisional Republic put Spain on the statistical map in 1873. Inspired by the ideas of Saint-Simon the fledgling Greek state had set up a statistical section as early as 1834. In 1850 funds were finally appropriated to establish a semi-permanent office of the census for the United States. By this time, no self-respecting state administration did without some kind of statistical equipment.

This early history of statistics is a field that has recently begun to attract historians.[5] We have studies of social statistics, demography and the techniques of mathematical statistics. But, strangely enough, despite their obvious importance, the history of economic statistics remains

[2] M. Rassem (ed.), *Statistik und Staatsbeschreibung in der Neuzeit* (Paderborn, 1980). For a general discussion see S.J. Woolf, 'Statistics and the Modern State', *Comparative Studies in Society and History*, 31 (1989), pp. 588–604.

[3] J.-C. Perrot and S.J. Woolf, *State and Statistics in France, 1789–1915* (London, 1984); M.-N. Bourguet, *Déchiffrer la France: la statistique départementale à l'époque napoléonienne* (Paris, 1988) and J. Dupâquier and M. Dupâquier, *Histoire de la Démographie* (Paris, 1985), pp. 256–274.

[4] P. Corrigan and D. Sayer, *The Great Arch: English State Formation as Cultural Revolution* (Oxford, 1985), pp. 124–125.

[5] T.M. Porter, *Trust in Numbers. The Pursuit of Objectivity in Science and Public Life* (Princeton, 1995); S. Patriarca, *Numbers and Nationhood: Writing Statistics in Nineteenth-Century Italy* (Cambridge, 1996); A. Desrosières, *La politique des grands nombres. Histoire de la raison statistique* (Paris, 1993).

underexplored. We do have a number of excellent studies of econometrics.[6] They trace the development of the mathematical techniques used to manipulate data and to test economic theories. These studies are fascinating in their own right. For the uninitiated they provide an excellent historical introduction to an arcane discipline. However, they are largely orientated towards the preoccupations of the discipline of econometrics itself. At their heart is the conversation between a series of canonical figures: Slutsky, Frisch, Tinbergen and Haavelmo. This book pursues an agenda which is different but complementary. It is concerned not with statistical techniques but with the production of factual economic knowledge. It makes a first attempt to map out the development of the repertoire of modern economic statistics. Its subject matter is therefore more mundane in all senses of that word: more commonplace, but also more popular and widespread. The history of statistical facts cannot be written without reference to the history of statistical techniques, but the history of factual economic knowledge demands a wider approach. The statistical data discussed here are treated not as the sole property of academics but as an integral part of the economic and social world, which they seek to describe. As is suggested by the title, this book analyses how the *German state* set about *making* a modern form of economic knowledge. Statistics are not neutral reflections of social and economic reality. They are produced by particular social actors in an effort to make sense of the complex and unmanageable reality that surrounds them. The most fundamental aim of this book is to show that historical statistics should not therefore be relegated to footnotes, encapsulated within tables or consigned to appendices. They should be treated like other cultural artefacts, texts or images. Their history should be integrated within the wider history of the society that produces them.

To historians of the medieval or early modern periods, in which the practices of quantification first became established, this need to treat statistics as cultural artefacts will be entirely obvious. For modern economists and economic historians the effect of contextualization may be somewhat more jarring: the independent status of our disciplines is founded to such a large extent on the authority of statistics. Perhaps it is therefore worth adding a few words of reassurance. By showing that statistical facts are produced by particular actors, in particular contexts, with particular interests, this book does not aim to 'debunk' the efforts of economic statisticians; on the contrary. The attitude of this book is pragmatic. Over the last couple of centuries the usefulness of statistics

[6] M. Morgan, *The History of Economic Ideas* (Cambridge, 1990) and J.L. Klein, *Statistical Visions in Time. A History of Time Series Analysis 1662–1938* (Cambridge, 1997).

has surely been demonstrated beyond reasonable doubt. They are now so ubiquitous in the everyday practices of economic life that the idea of writing modern economic history without reference to statistics amounts to romantic nostalgia. Whether or not statistical facts can claim the status of 'truth' or 'objectivity' in some metaphysical sense is irrelevant for all practical purposes. This book, in any case, is not concerned with questions of philosophy. If there is a critical edge to the argument, it is political. The questions with which we will be concerned are about the relationship between practical knowledge and power – and, in particular, the relationship between efforts to govern the economy and efforts to make the economy intelligible through systematic quantification.

I

The systems of economic statistics, that we take for granted today, emerged across the industrialized world as the result of a dramatic burst of innovation. This began tentatively in the 1870s and gathered momentum around the turn of the century. The most intense phase of activity was unleashed by World War I. Three decades later, in the 1950s, the process culminated with the global standardization of the modern repertoire of macroeconomic statistics.[7] In less than a century, the state of empirical economic knowledge was radically transformed. The result was a new empirical image of the economy. We can solidify this chronology with a brief comparative history of four key elements in this new matrix of statistical knowledge: the balance of payments, unemployment, prices and national income.

Trade statistics are the oldest economic statistics. It might therefore be argued that they fit least well with the modern chronology set out here. Records of goods crossing the borders of states and statelets go back to the early modern period. However, these data were compiled for administrative purposes. When did customs records become trade statistics as we know them today? In the British case, which may be taken as representative of the first generation of nation-states, systematic records of trade began to be collected in the seventeenth century.[8] But, at first, no attempt was made to record the value of exports and imports in current terms. Throughout the eighteenth century the unit prices of

---

[7] The term 'macroeconomics' is used to distinguish aggregative economic analysis of all kinds from microeconomics, which focuses on individual economic agents and their interactions.

[8] R. Davis, *The Industrial Revolution and British Overseas Trade* (Leicester, 1979), pp. 77–86 and A. Maizels, 'The Overseas Trade Statistics of the United Kingdom', *Journal of the Royal Statistical Society*, 112 (1949) II, pp. 207–223.

imports and exports were fixed at so-called 'historic values' set in the 1690s. By the late eighteenth century these were wildly inaccurate. It was only in 1798 that export figures began to be compiled in current values. Of course, it was possible for economists and journalists to make their own estimates of the balance of trade, but these were unauthorized interpretations of the official data. Official import figures were not finally valued in current prices until the 1850s. The modern procedure for calculating the trade balance from customs declarations for both exports and imports was instituted only in 1869. From this point onwards one can definitely speak of an official estimate of the balance of trade. On closer inspection, the history of British trade statistics thus falls into line with the chronology for late-developing European nation-states, such as Germany. The trade accounts of the Zollverein set up in the 1830s were really no more than spin-offs of the customs system.[9] They covered only those goods on which duty was charged. It was only in 1879 that all goods crossing the borders of the new German Empire were systematically registered, classified and valued. Between the 1840s and 1880 24 countries established reliable trade statistics. By 1913 this number had increased to 33 and by the 1920s the trade between 90 countries could be monitored in statistical terms.[10] The inter-national economy was thus defined as a space of trading relationships between more or less clearly defined national economic units tied together by the well-monitored movements of goods.

In statistical terms, however, the monitoring of this inter-national economy was still incomplete. The trade balance was only one part of an increasingly complex network of international economic transactions. Trade in services, earnings on foreign investments and international borrowing and lending matched visible trade flows. The practice of international finance was, of course, well understood by contemporaries. However, it was not until the 1870s that economic theorists began to systematically integrate the balance of payments into their models, embracing both trade transactions and capital movements. It was the arguments over international finance and reparations in the 1920s that gave birth to international economics in the form that is still taught today.[11] During that turbulent decade, the state of statistical information on the balance of payments remained, in the words of John Maynard Keynes 'deplorably deficient . . . in search of facts of vital

---

[9] W. Heimer, *Die Geschichte der deutschen Wirtschaftsstatistik von der Gründung des Deutschen Reichs bis zur Gegenwart* (Frankfurt, 1928), pp. 10–33.
[10] E. Wagemann, *Wagen, Wägen und Wirtschaften. Erprobte Faustregeln – Neue Wege* (Hamburg, 1954), p. 72.
[11] M.J. Flanders, *International Monetary Economics, 1870–1960. Between the Classical and the New Classical* (Cambridge, 1989).

national importance, we . . . continue to grope in barbaric darkness'.[12] In response to this situation, the League of Nations began to compile estimates of the balance of payments for the leading nations in the early 1920s. And in 1926 the United States Commerce Department issued the first official estimates of the US foreign account. Germany followed suit later in the decade. But Britain did not finally begin a regular series of official estimates until after World War II.[13] One of the first tasks of the International Monetary Fund (IMF) in the late 1940s was to formulate global standards for the measurement of the balance of payments.[14] Despite the early development of trade statistics, the modern system of international economic statistics took shape between the mid-nineteenth century and the 1950s.

The statistical definition of unemployment falls in the same broad period. In the late nineteenth century, unemployment was viewed primarily as an issue of social policy. Analysts were primarily concerned with 'the unemployed' rather than 'unemployment'. Joblessness was attributed to the feckless character of the jobless, or to the peculiar problems of casual labour markets. By contrast, the concept of unemployment that emerged in the aftermath of World War I was defined primarily in economic terms. This has been a common finding of historical research on Britain, France, the United States and Germany.[15] Unemployment was reconceived as a mismatch between the demand for and the supply of labour. Its primary explanation therefore lay not in individual behaviour but in wider economic problems. Of course, the social concern for the unemployed remained. Moral denunciations of the work-shy were never completely silenced. But the fundamental cause of unemployment was now seen as economic. This new understanding was underpinned by the increasing organization of the labour market, which in turn permitted the creation of new unemployment statistics. In Britain and Germany the innovations bunch around World War I. Unified labour exchanges were established by Act of

[12] J.M. Keynes, 'The British Balance of Trade, 1925–27', *Economic Journal*, 37 (1927), pp. 551–565.

[13] C.F. Carter and A.D. Roy, *British Economic Statistics. A Report* (Cambridge, 1954), pp. 79–93.

[14] F. Machlup, 'Three Concepts of the Balance of Payments and the So-Called Dollar Gap', *Economic Journal*, 40 (1950), pp. 46–68.

[15] On Britain see J. Harris, *Unemployment and Politics* (Oxford, 1972) and W. Walters, 'The Discovery of "Unemployment": New Forms for the Government of Poverty', *Economy and Society*, 23 (1994), pp. 265–290; on the United States see A. Keyssar, *Out of Work. The First Century of Unemployment in Massachusetts* (Cambridge, MA, 1986); on France R. Salais, N. Bavarez and B. Reynaud, *L'invention du chômage* (Paris, 1986); on Germany A. Faust, *Arbeitsmarktpolitik im Deutschen Kaiserreich. Arbeitsvermittlung, Arbeitsbeschaffung und Arbeitslosenunterstützung 1890–1918* (Stuttgart, 1986).

Parliament in Britain in 1909 and unemployment insurance followed in 1911. In Germany a unified national system of labour exchanges was established in 1915, which was brought fully under state control in 1922. Unemployment insurance followed in 1927. The insurance system generated data on the numbers in work and the numbers receiving benefits. The exchanges registered job seekers and vacancies. France and the United States monitored the labour market less closely but here too there was increasingly regular and intensive statistical measurement from the turn of the century. By the interwar period the masses of men and women unsuccessfully seeking work had been established as a phenomenon demanding economic analysis.

The history of price statistics and national income accounting help further to solidify our chronology. In 1922, Irving Fisher, the foremost exponent of index numbers, wrote as follows: 'index numbers are a very recent contrivance . . . although we may push back their invention a century and three quarters, their current use did not begin till 1869 at the earliest, and not in a general way till after 1900. In fact, it may be said that their use is only seriously beginning today.'[16] In the 1860s and 1870s mathematicians and economists including Jevons, Paasche and Laspeyres experimented with the construction of index numbers. The weekly periodical *The Economist* published the first regular price index in 1869.[17] But the really dramatic upsurge in interest came in the late 1890s when generalized deflation of prices gave way to creeping inflation. The response, this time, came not just from private investigators and journalists but also from the state. The US Bureau of Labor published the first official index of wholesale prices in 1902. Retail price figures and a cost of living index followed in 1907 and 1919, respectively. The British Board of Trade was also a pioneer, producing the first wholesale price index for Britain in 1903. The inflations of World War I triggered a boom in index numbers. By 1927 Fisher was able to list 120 price indices covering no less than 30 countries, published by official statisticians, business periodicals, daily newspapers and large corporations. And it is not just the proliferation of numbers that should interest us. The new indices had a new economic content. The earliest indices were simple averages of commodity prices; by contrast, the wholesale indicators produced by the United States and Britain after the turn of the century were far more sophisticated. They were weighted averages, giving greater significance to some prices rather than others. And there was a clear economic logic behind their construction. The weights

[16] I. Fisher, *The Making of Index Numbers. A Study of their Varieties, Tests and Reliability* (Boston, 1927, 3rd edn), p. 460.
[17] *The Economist 1843–1943* (Oxford, 1943), pp. 138–154.

Table 1. *Date of first publication of official estimate of national income*

Year	Country
1886	Australia
1925	Soviet Union and Canada
1929	Germany
1931	Netherlands
1931	New Zealand
1934	United States
1935	Turkey
1937	Yugoslavia
1939	Switzerland and Mexico
1941	United Kingdom
1944	Sweden and Norway
1947	France

Sources: P. Studenski, *The Income of Nations* (New York, revised edn. 1958), I, pp. 151–153; F. Fourquet, *Les comptes de la puissance. Histoire de la comptabilité nationale et du plan* (Paris, 1980).

attached to the Board of Trade's wholesale price index were calculated to reflect the total consumption of key commodities by the economy as a whole. More specific indices covered the cost of living and retail prices. These were the first attempts to make visible Adam Smith's 'invisible hand'.

National income statistics are the last and really conclusive piece of evidence.[18] As with the other statistics, one can find early attempts at national income estimation as far back as the seventeenth century. But the early twentieth century witnessed a sudden explosion in activity with new estimates being produced by academics and journalists and then increasingly by official agencies. Studenski's pioneering study provides a truly extraordinary overview (see table 1). In 1900 estimates of national income had been prepared for no more than eight countries. By 1946 there were figures – official and unofficial – for 39 countries. Ten years later, there were more than 80. And here, too, the qualitative change in the data was dramatic. Estimates of national income produced up to the late nineteenth century tended to be crude extrapolations from fragmentary tax records. The questions they sought to answer were distribu-

---

[18] They are also the one branch of economic statistics to have attracted sustained historical attention. See F. Fourquet, *Les comptes de la puissance. Histoire de la comptabilité nationale et du plan* (Paris, 1980) and M. Perlman, 'Political Purpose and the National Accounts', in W. Alonson and P. Starr (eds.), *The Politics of Numbers* (New York, 1987).

tional. What share of income was attributable to the 'unearned' rents of landowners? How was the remainder divided between capital and labour? Economic statistics were thus orientated towards 'social' questions. The 1920s saw the emergence of a more purely 'economic' interpretation of national income. With the advent of comprehensive censuses of production it became possible to match the figures for national income with estimates of national product. As a result, the interpretative focus began to shift away from issues of distribution towards primarily 'economic' concerns, such as the comparative level of productivity in different sectors and the fluctuations over the business-cycle of total economic activity, as measured by national income or national product. This shift was completed in the late 1920s and early 1930s with the first estimates of total expenditure, divided principally into consumption, investment and government expenditure. It now became possible to picture the economy, in statistical terms, as a self-contained 'circular flow' of production, income and expenditure. This image, first made real in the interwar years, has since occupied the first pages of every textbook in macroeconomics.

Taken together these interrelated statistical innovations constituted a new matrix of economic knowledge, which gave substance to a new conception of the economy.[19] First of all 'the economy' was envisioned as a separate system, distinct, for instance, from 'the social', 'the cultural', or 'the political'. It was a measurable entity, a 'thing'. This conception of 'the economy' as an autonomous social system was more restricted than that embodied in eighteenth-century ideas of a commercial society, or Marx's totalizing conception of the mode of production. But it was also more concrete than those earlier formulations. Linguistic changes signal this shift to a more reified idea of the economic world. In German it was already possible in the mid-nineteenth century to speak of the 'Volkswirtschaft', or national economy.[20] In England, true to its liberal heritage, 'the economy' as a term with which to refer to the entire system of production and exchange did not come into common use until the 1930s.[21] What defined this entity was the relationship between a limited number of key variables: national income, physical production, employment, the balance of payments, the volume of money in circula-

[19] P. Miller and N. Rose, 'Governing Economic Life', *Economy and Society*, 19 (1990), pp. 1–31.

[20] J. Burckhardt, 'Wirtschaft', in O. Brunner, W. Conze and R. Koselleck (eds.), *Geschichtliche Grundbegriffe. Historisches Lexikon zur politisch-sozialen Sprache in Deutschland* (Stuttgart, 1992), 7, pp. 511–594.

[21] M. Emmison, '"The Economy": Its Emergence in Media Discourse', in H. Davis and P. Walton (eds.), *Language, Image, Media* (Oxford, 1983), pp. 139–155.

tion and the aggregate price level. As we have seen, the measurement of each one of these variables had its separate history. The distinctively modern conception of the economy emerged when they began to be articulated with each other as an interconnected system. The interrelationships were established through the revival in the last decades of the nineteenth century of two of the founding metaphors of modern economics. The most fundamental of these was the conception of the economy as a self-reproducing, circular flow of production and consumption, of expenditure and income. A second key metaphor was the so-called Quantity Theory of Money, which also enjoyed a major revival in the late nineteenth century.[22] This expressed the value of money (the inverse of the aggregate level of prices) as a function of the quantity of money, the rate of its circulation and the level of real economic activity. This relationship was recast in the 1880s as an algebraic equation and acquired canonical status in 1911 with Irving Fisher's *The Purchasing Power of Money*. We shall have much more to say about both these representations of the economy. Suffice to say at this point that they allowed the key economic variables to be brought together as elements in a systematic, aggregative model of the economy. The result was a conception of the economy which since the 1930s has become known as 'macroeconomic'.

This new conception of the economy was emphatically national. This, too, was an option that had been left open by earlier theorizing. For liberals any boundaries imposed on the free operation of markets were artificial intrusions. Similarly, Marx's conception of the mode of production was potentially global in scope. By contrast, the new economic statistics measured the economy as a national unit. And in doing so they constituted it as an obvious field of government action. The creation of the new economic statistics was inseparable from the appearance of a new set of practices known as 'economic policy'. As Donald Winch has put it, our modern conception of 'economic policy' emerged 'out of elements that had previously been treated separately as questions of social administration on the one hand or narrow technical matters of banking and fiscal management on the other'. The new purpose of economic policy was precisely to manage the 'connections between employment levels and monetary, exchange rate, and fiscal conditions'.[23] Winch dates the emergence of this new field of government to the interwar period, which of course coincides with the appearance of

---

[22] D. Laidler, *The Golden Age of the Quantity Theory* (Princeton, 1991).

[23] D. Winch, 'Economic Knowledge and Government', in B. Supple and M. Furner, *The State and Economic Knowledge. The American and British Experiences* (Cambridge, 1990), pp. 62–63.

the new economic statistics. Economic policy presupposed the existence of a new object of government: an economy conceived of not as an amorphous mass of individuals and markets, but as a holistic entity constituted by the relationship between a limited number of highly aggregated variables. The task of the new economic statistics was to measure these variables and thus to make them governable.

II

How does this book relate to the existing literature on the history of economics? In particular, some readers may be wondering whether this is simply a retelling of the familiar story about the so-called 'Keynesian revolution'. For a long time this has been the mainstay of the history of modern economic thought. *The General Theory of Employment, Interest and Money* published by John Maynard Keynes in 1936 is generally taken to be the founding text of modern macroeconomics. Its intellectual genesis through the 1920s and 1930s has been an obvious starting point for historians. It is impossible to adequately summarize this enormous literature in a few lines.[24] However, the gist of most recent writing is that Keynes' central contribution was theoretical. *The General Theory* explained how an economy suffering from a shortfall in aggregate demand could find itself in a state of heavy unemployment, from which it had no tendency to recover. The low level of activity brought on by a depressed level of investment became self-sustaining.[25] It was this theoretical analysis of an unemployment equilibrium which gave Keynes' heretical policy prescriptions their originality and force. When the economy was seriously depressed monetary policy would be ineffective. Lowering interest rates would not be enough to raise investment. Government spending was essential to raise aggregate demand and to lift the economy out of recession. It was Keynes' long-running struggle with the Treasury that, in the British case, defined the new field of economic policy. In the United States the battle for demand management was fought out within the New Deal administration. In the aftermath of World War II Keynes' ideas were carried across the globe, establishing the common sense of the postwar period.[26]

---

[24] For two excellent summaries see G.C. Peden, *Keynes, The Treasury and British Economic Policy* (London, 1988) and P. Clarke, *The Keynesian Revolution and its Economic Consequences* (Cheltenham, 1998b).

[25] Technically speaking this is the 'theory of effective demand', see D. Patinkin, *Anticipations of the General Theory. And other Essays on Keynes* (Chicago, 1982), pp. 5–17.

[26] P.A. Hall (ed.), *The Political Power of Economic Ideas. Keynesianism across Nations* (Princeton, 1989).

The almost obsessive focus on Keynes has produced a historiography of a remarkably high standard. But it has also served to obscure the wider context.[27] As we have progressively sharpened our understanding of the specificities of Keynes' theoretical innovation and the complexities of his own intellectual biography, it has become ever more clear that Keynes' work must be situated within a broad sweep of new macroeconomic theorizing that can be traced back to the 1870s. It is more conventional to see the 1870s as the origin of modern marginalist economics. It was in this period that the building blocks of neo-classical economics were first formulated by Jevons, Menger and Walras: the attribution of factor incomes to marginal productivity, the reformulation of demand theory in terms of consumer preferences and subjective utility, and the consistent linkage of the structure of production to the structure of demand through general equilibrium analysis. However, as David Laidler has shown in his study of neo-classical monetary theory, the 1870s can also be seen as the origin of twentieth-century macroeconomics.[28] It was in the decades after 1870 that theorists such as Alfred Marshall, Irving Fisher and Knut Wicksell elaborated the Quantity Theory of Money into a consistent and powerful tool for understanding movements in the aggregate price level. Building on this analytical framework a second generation of theorists, notably in Britain and Austria, began, around the turn of the century, to elaborate what became known as monetary business-cycle theory. Their models were emphatically macroeconomic, their purpose being to explain the interaction between monetary fluctuations and movements in total production and employment.[29] As Laidler has pointed out, it is quite possible to see even Keynes' *General Theory* as an extension of this tradition. Certainly, Keynes' earlier work can be seen as a linear development of Marshallian monetary macroeconomics.

The development of mathematical techniques for analysing statistical data and testing theory – the so-called econometric revolution – was heavily influenced by these early developments in monetary economics and business-cycle theory. It was interest in the fluctuations of prices that stimulated Jevons and Juglar to undertake the first time-series analysis of price data in the 1860s. As has already been mentioned, it was the switchback of deflation in the 1870s and 1880s followed by inflation from the late 1890s that stimulated the development of index

---

[27] For a powerful summary see R. Middleton, *Charlatans or Saviours? Economists and the British Economy from Marshall to Meade* (Cheltenham, 1998).

[28] Laidler, *The Golden Age*, pp. 193–199.

[29] In the British case the outstanding examples are A.C. Pigou, *Wealth and Welfare* (London, 1912), R. Hawtrey, *Good and Bad Trade* (London, 1913) and D.H. Robertson, *A Study in Industrial Fluctuations* (London, 1915).

numbers designed to accurately reflect the movements in the general purchasing power of money. By the 1920s the basic techniques for estimating trends and removing seasonal variations were well established. In the 1930s it was the desire to test monetary explanations of the business-cycle that stimulated Tinbergen and the Dutch statistical office to construct the first genuine mathematical model of an entire economy. And it was the econometrician, Ragnar Frisch, who first introduced the term 'macro-dynamics' into the literature, thus giving rise to the more familiar term macroeconomics.[30] Again, this is a story which can be told almost entirely without reference to the Keynesian revolution.

It is these twin 'revolutions' in macroeconomic theory and in econometrics that provide the intellectual context for this book, not the Keynesian revolution *per se*. The explosion of new economic statistics between the 1870s and the 1950s deserves to be treated as a 'statistical revolution' in its own right.[31] As will be shown here, the development of the infrastructure of data-gathering had its own distinct history. But one gets a proper sense of the transformation of economic knowledge in this period only if one understands how the three revolutions were interrelated. The concepts that informed practical efforts at data collection were developed in dialogue with economic theory. And it was the new data produced by the statisticians that provided the material for the econometricians. The interweaving of these three separate strands constituted modern macroeconomic knowledge.

To analyse this process of multiple innovation we need a new analytical model. The existing literature describes the Keynesian revolution in terms of a process of diffusion. At its core are Keynes and his intimates in the 'Cambridge circus'. Out of this incestuous milieu sprang *The General Theory*. The central question for historians is to understand how economists and policy-makers across the world 'reacted' to the provocation of this revolutionary book. In the language of the literary scholar Franco Moretti, this is a 'tree model' of cultural development.[32] Branches, stems and shoots sprout from the Cambridge trunk. By contrast, Moretti suggests that comparative cultural historians

---

[30] See J.C. Andvig, 'Ragnar Frisch and Business Cycle Research during the Interwar Years', *History of Political Economy*, 13 (1981), p. 713. Frisch applied the label 'macrodynamics' to those studies of the business-cycle that focused on national aggregates, as opposed to those that focused on disequilibria in specific industries. The broader term, macroeconomics, was introduced in 1941, see Clarke, *The Keynesian Revolution and its Economic Consequences*, p. 213.

[31] By contrast with Patinkin, *Anticipations of the General Theory*, pp. 223–260, who collapses the production of new economic statistics and the development of statistical techniques into a single 'econometric revolution'.

[32] F. Moretti, 'Conjectures on World Literature', *New Left Review*, II, 1 (2000).

should adopt the metaphor of the wave. And this certainly seems a more appropriate concept on which to base the study of modern economic knowledge. In the first half of the twentieth century, innovations in the conceptualization and measurement of the economy swept across the globe.

Britain and the United States are well established as independent sites of theoretical and empirical innovation in the interwar years.[33] But the war and the revolution of 1917 also ushered in a feverish period of innovation in Communist Russia.[34] This included the construction of models of economic growth and elaborate and entirely unprecedented systems of national accounting.[35] These experiments were terminated between 1928 and 1930 by the Stalinist crackdown. But, while they lasted, they formed an integral part of an international process of innovation. The Soviet economists followed developments in the West closely. Their work, in turn, had a considerable impact abroad. As will be discussed in chapters 3 and 5, the Weimar Republic appears to have played a strategic role in this transmission of ideas, through the rapid translation into German of Russian publications. Simultaneously, there emerged in Sweden a powerful line of macroeconomic business-cycle analysis – known as the Stockholm school. Unfortunately, discussion of the Stockholm school has, until recently, centred around one question: did Wicksell, Lindahl, Myrdal and Ohlin anticipate Keynes' theory of effective demand, as set out in *The General Theory*?[36] Probably not. But from the broader point of view adopted here, this matters little. The Stockholm school undoubtedly included some of the most sophisticated exponents of the new macroeconomics. Their concern was to account for fluctuations in overall economic activity. Like most of the early generation of macroeconomists their focus was on the aggregate price level. But during the 1930s the younger Swedish economists also turned to the questions of output and employment that were preoccupying Keynes.[37] Accompanying this theoretical work was a parallel pro-gramme of empirical enquiry. Most notably a large grant from the

---

[33] On the United States see G. Alchon, *The Invisible Hand of Planning. Capitalism, Social Science, and the State in the 1920s* (Princeton, 1985), W.J. Barber *From New Era to New Deal. Herbert Hoover, The Economists, and American Economic Policy, 1921–1933* (Cambridge, 1985).

[34] See L. Smolinski, 'Planning Without Theory 1917–1967', *Survey. A Journal of Soviet and East European Studies*, 64 (1967), pp. 108–128.

[35] N. Spulber (ed.), *Foundations of Soviet Strategy for Economic Growth. Selected Soviet Essays, 1924–1930* (Bloomington, 1964) and V. Barnett, *Kondratiev and the Dynamics of Economic Development: Long Cycles and Industrial Growth in Historical Context* (London, 1998).

[36] Patinkin, *Anticipations of the General Theory*, pp. 36–57.

[37] L. Jonung (ed.), *The Stockholm School of Economics Revisited* (Cambridge, 1991).

Rockefeller Foundation enabled Swedish statisticians to compile one of the longest series for national income available in the 1930s.[38] The steady pace of Swedish expansion, untroubled by major wars, provided the ideal case study of stable, long-run growth trend. The history of econometrics reveals two other sites of innovation. In Norway Ragnar Frisch was pivotal to the development of the theory of modern econometrics.[39] He formed a crucial link between the theoretical work of the Russian statistician Slutsky, who was one of the few survivors of the Stalinist purges, and the Cowles Commission in Chicago that was to set the agenda for postwar econometrics. In the Netherlands, meanwhile, Jan Tinbergen and the Dutch Statistical Office began work on the world's first macroeconomic model.[40] With the assistance of the League of Nations his techniques were later to be extended to modelling the US economy.

This book aims to establish the existence in Germany of another major strand of 'new economics'. Germany has hitherto played a shadowy role in debates about interwar economics. It has always been tempting to seek out precursors of Keynes amongst the German advocates of work-creation in the 1930s.[41] However, this line of enquiry has proven an intellectual dead-end. The foundation for a more adequate understanding has now been provided by a number of important studies.[42] These provide a panoramic reconstruction of the intellectual field of German economic theory in the interwar period. The result, as in the United States, Sweden and Britain, has been to reveal a broadly based tradition of monetary macroeconomics. This originated in the decades before World War I, and by the 1920s had reached a considerable level of sophistication. This book hopes to consolidate this reassessment of economics in interwar Germany. It reveals how the new macroeconomic theory formed the basis for an innovative programme of

---

[38] E. Lindahl, E. Dahlgren and K. Koch, *National Income of Sweden 1861–1930* (Stockholm, 1937).

[39] Andvig, 'Ragnar Frisch'.

[40] A. Wilts, 'Changes in Dutch Economics in the 1930s', in P. Fontaine and A. Jolink (eds.), *Historical Perspectives on Macroeconomics. Sixty Years after the General Theory* (London, 1998), pp. 105–132.

[41] G. Garvy, 'Keynes and the Economic Activists of Pre-Hitler Germany', *Journal of Political Economy*, 83 (1975), pp. 391–405 and G. Bombach, K.-B. Netzband, H.-J. Ramser and M. Timmermann (eds.), *Der Keynesianismus III. Die geld- und beschäftigungstheoretische Diskussion in Deutschland zur Zeit von Keynes* (Berlin, 1981).

[42] R. Vilk, *Von der Konjunkturtheorie zur Theorie der Konjunkturpolitik* (Wiesbaden, 1992), H. Janssen, *Nationalökonomie und Nationalsozialismus. Die deutsche Volkswirtschaftslehre in den dreißiger Jahren* (Marburg, 1998) and H. Hagemann, 'The Analysis of Wages and Unemployment Revisited: Keynes and Economic "Activists" in Pre-Hitler Germany', in L.C. Pasinetti and B. Schefold (eds.), *The Impact of Keynes on Economics in the 20th Century* (Cheltenham, 1999), pp. 117–130.

statistical investigation, heavily sponsored by the Weimar state. Germany must thus be counted alongside the United States, the Soviet Union, Britain, Sweden and the Netherlands as an important site in the development of modern macroeconomic statistics. This, in turn, should consolidate the more general shift in perspective being advocated here. The development of new forms of economic knowledge was too wide-spread to be described helpfully in terms of a process of diffusion. German-speaking economists read the theoretical and statistical work being published in Britain as a matter of course. But these influences were seen as part of a more general move towards an aggregative conception of the economy. In the 1920s, when German macroeco-nomics began to be articulated most forcefully, Cambridge, England commanded no outstanding place in its intellectual universe. From a German perspective the emergence of the new economics appeared to be a truly global phenomenon.

And the breadth of this development also implies that its end-point was uncertain. Teleology is one of the characteristic weaknesses of the literature on 'proto-Keynesian' and 'pre-Keynesian' economic thought. A case study of Germany provides a powerful antidote. The first half of this book traces the development of Germany's precocious macroeco-nomic statistics to familiar intellectual origins in the quantity theory of money. After World War I this aggregative understanding of the economy was embodied in an innovative system of official national accounts. Germany might therefore be seen as travelling along a path that led to the 'Keynesian consensus' of the postwar period. However, after 1933 Germany took a radically different direction. The Reich's statisticians placed themselves at the service of the Nazi regime. As a result, the system of macroeconomic statistics created in the 1920s began to mutate into something quite different. By the final stages of the war German statisticians were beginning to elaborate a system of comprehensive surveillance that resembled a full-blown system of Stali-nist planning. The German case thus forms a bridge between the development of new techniques of economic governance in the capitalist West and that other great experiment in modern government in the East. Interwar modernity was multi-faceted, its ultimate destination uncertain. A case study of Germany provides a powerful reminder of this contingency.

Understanding the development of modern economic knowledge as a wave of innovation rather than a process of diffusion requires us to stretch the chronological frame and expand our geographic range. It also requires us to problematize the postwar 'Keynesian consensus' as the inevitable conclusion of our story. More generally it requires us to rethink our analytical strategies.[43] Local accounts need to be controlled by being set against a broader backdrop. Hitherto, the diffusionist story of the Keynesian revolution has tended to focus on the interactions between economists and state elites – 'experts', civil servants and politicians. This nexus must undoubtedly be central to each national story. But, given the ubiquity of new forms of economic knowledge, particular stories that focus on the interactions between small groups of individuals can hardly suffice. We must always bear in mind the role played by more general explanatory factors. The rest of this introduction will be concerned with four general influences that have helped to frame this German case study: the transformation of the industrial economies themselves in the period between the 1880s and the 1930s; the crisis-ridden development of the 'big state'; the development of new information technologies; and the cultural and intellectual tendencies encapsulated within the term 'modernism'.

III

The decision to make real economic change the first point on the list may require some justification. In recent years it has been fashionable to adopt a constructivist approach to the study of knowledge. The literature has tended to emphasize the autonomy of the knowledge producers from the object they are observing. It has stressed the discursive construction of new forms of economic knowledge rather than the influences of 'real' economic changes.[44] In the 1980s there was a parallel shift in the political sciences towards stressing the autonomy of the state. As a result, we have an important collection of essays on *The State and Economic Knowledge*, but no equivalent volume on 'the economy and economic knowledge'.[45] This is not to advocate a return to crude determinism. An engagement with the broader currents of economic history follows naturally from studying statistics like other forms of practical economic knowledge, such as accountancy. Statisticians, after all, generate their data not through abstract speculation but through interactions with economic actors themselves, through questionnaires returned by businesses or households, or indirectly by harvesting the data generated by other branches of the state in their dealings with the private sector. Changes in economic life thus have a direct impact on the

---

[43] See the remarks in P. Hall 'Introduction', in Hall, *The Political Power of Economic Ideas*, pp. 3–26.

[44] A particularly radical example is P. Mirowski, *More Heat than Light. Economics as Social Physics: Physics as Nature's Economics* (Cambridge, 1989).

[45] M.O. Furner and B. Supple (eds.), *The State and Economic Knowledge. The American and British Experiences* (Cambridge, 1990).

activity of data-gathering. In recent years this has been brought home very forcibly by discussions of the so-called 'weightless economy'. How are statisticians to measure an economy that is increasingly driven by the rapid product cycle of microelectronics and the intangible products of the service sector?[46] This book provides the historical backdrop to these present-day concerns. It shows how we learned to measure the 'heavy economy'.

By the turn of the twentieth century, economic and social development had transformed the conditions for economic data-gathering. For generations, statisticians and economists had dreamed of imposing an orderly scheme of measurement on the world. What distinguished early twentieth-century planners and social engineers from their predecessors was that they could actually do it! In the advanced economies of the world the vast bulk of productive activity was directed towards the market. Most production was separated from the domestic sphere and organized in businesses – farms, industrial firms or commercial businesses – with a clear-cut legal identity. Communication across the territory of nation-states was eased by the revolution in transport and communication technologies. These in turn encouraged the spread of literacy and numeracy, supported by the extension of formal education. These fundamental processes made the economy countable in a new way. In fact, as Marx pointed out, the economy was quantifying itself in an apparently unstoppable and profoundly alienating fashion. Liberals saw the same process as the progress of rationality; Max Weber, characteristically, saw both sides of the coin: the all-encompassing rationalization of the world and the disenchantment it inevitably entailed. Statisticians and accountants were part of the army of bureaucrats who were the agents of this process. Whereas eighteenth- and early nineteenth-century statistics had relied on impressionistic accounts provided by local notables, statisticians in the early twentieth century could hope to directly enumerate the entire economic process. Questions could be addressed to firms and businesses and they could be expected to provide a verifiable account of themselves in a mutually intelligible language. The fringes of the formal economy, such as the homeworkers who had so plagued nineteenth-century enquiries, were shrinking to extinction.[47] Counting an economy dominated by a few thousand substantial firms presented immense new opportunities. The commanding heights could be surveyed with relative ease. By the

[46] J. Madrick, 'The Cost of Living', *The New York Review of Books*, 44, 4 (1997), pp. 19–23.

[47] R. Meerwarth, 'Die Erfassung der Hausindustrie durch die gewerbliche Betriebsstatistik', *Jahrbücher für Nationalökonomie und Statistik*, III, 42 (1911), pp. 313–330.

interwar period one could survey the vast majority of industrial activity by addressing questions only to firms with more than 10 employees, 'reasonable' entities with at least a sense of modern managerial habits. Such firms could be asked to supply more information, more regularly and more quickly. Not, of course, that all was simple. Large firms posed their own problems of enumeration. As production became more complex and more integrated it became increasingly difficult to obtain information on separate processes. And this was not just a problem for statisticians looking in. Firms were far from transparent to themselves. Only through elaborate cost accounting systems was it possible for large corporations to 'see inside' their own operations. The wave of new economic statistics rode in on the spring tide of modern bureaucracy and scientific management.

The broad processes of economic and social change thus created new conditions for enumeration. But economic change, like every other aspect of reality, requires interpretation. What sense the statisticians made of economic change was not determined by the process itself. Spokesmen of various kinds played a creative role in naming and interpreting the profound economic transformations going on around them.[48] Over the course of the nineteenth century official statisticians came to occupy a particularly important role as interpreters of economic and social change. The German statisticians who are the subjects of this book were convinced that with the boom of the 1890s Germany had entered a new phase of corporate capitalism. Their ambition was to reorganize the system of economic statistics to match this challenge. And the descriptions they produced were not neutral. Statistics and economic research were a weapon of choice in the interest group struggle. Was the future agrarian or industrial? How might small-scale production survive alongside the giants of industry? Which were the industries of the future? People turned to statistics for answers. The statisticians did more than describe; they defined the parameters for interest group formation and political argument. In the process, they contributed to the shaping of social reality.

IV

The growth of modern economic statistics was thus linked to the emergence of the modern economy. But it also clearly belongs to the history of the state. The quantum leap in the production of economic knowledge that is the subject of this book was due largely to the

---

[48] P. Bourdieu, *Ce Que Parler veut Dire. L'économie des échanges linguistiques* (Paris, 1982), pp. 135–161.

involvement of the state. Modern economic statistics are an integral part of 'big government'.[49] The expansion of public sector activity was a general phenomenon observable across the globe from the late nineteenth century. Again, this can be interpreted as an incremental process driven by the demands of a complex civil society for services and regulation. The emergence of 'labour statistics', for instance, was clearly a systematic response to the emergence of capitalist labour markets and organized forms of industrial relations. The revival of interest in national income estimation around the turn of the century can also be related to the pressures of 'mass politics'. Imperialist nationalism was one factor. A national income estimate allowed one to compare one's position to that of other industrial powers. But the estimates also addressed common domestic concerns. The increasingly intense interest group struggles fermenting within industrializing societies made the language of productivism attractive to both intellectuals and politicians.[50] Across the political spectrum the promotion of higher production and greater material welfare as ends in themselves was a characteristic feature of the early twentieth century. Productivism, as a politics of quantity, naturally spoke the language of statistics. How big was the cake that was to be divided? How fast was it expanding? How much did each group contribute? And how many people did it have to feed? These were crucial questions for the new democratic politics. And it was these questions that stimulated efforts to estimate national income in the United States, in the United Kingdom and in Germany.[51] In due course it was the state that took responsibility for producing the figures that defined the parameters of social and economic policy.

But the example of national income estimation also points to the independent momentum of state expansion. The production of new statistics was sustained by the growth in other branches of the state. It constituted a form of second-order state expansion. Statistical divisions sprang up to make the most of the paperwork accumulating within the official bureaucracy. Tax records were the fundamental source for most of the early estimates of national income. As the share of national income going through the state coffers increased, it became easier to assemble the data from which to compile a national income estimate. The crucial threshold was the imposition of comprehensive income

[49] For a very helpful discussion see R. Middleton, *Government versus the Market. The Growth of the Public Sector, Economic Management and British Economic Performance, c. 1890–1979* (Cheltenham, 1996).
[50] C.S. Maier, *In Search of Stability. Explorations in Historical Political Economy* (Cambridge, 1987b), pp. 19–69.
[51] J.A. Tooze, 'Imagining National Economies: National and International Economic Statistics, 1900–1950', in G. Cubitt (ed.), *Imagining Nations* (Manchester, 1998).

taxes. But national income estimates were not the only branch of statistics to benefit from an administrative free ride. Trade statistics, the earliest national economic statistics, were generated by the customs posts strung along the state's frontier. Many of the earliest industrial statistics were compiled from the reports of factory inspectors. Unemployment statistics were a spin-off of the labour administration. As the state expanded it generated within itself multiple reflections of economic life.

But official statisticians did not simply react to societal demands. The official statisticians discussed in this book were self-conscious bureaucratic actors seeking to expand their administrative province, struggling to find an advantageous position for themselves within the newly extended state. In this minimal sense they enjoyed autonomy from the demands of interested civil society. More generally, it was official statisticians who in many areas took the initiative, acting in advance both of interested groups in civil society and of the rest of the state apparatus.[52] Measuring a social or economic phenomenon, be it unemployment or the size of the Jewish population, was often the first step towards defining a 'problem'.[53] This in turn might trigger interventionist activity from within the state or, by exposing the issue to the public gaze, it might generate public pressure for a remedy. As this book will show, the leaders of the Reich's Statistical Office (SRA) pursued this role in a self-conscious fashion. Indeed, their historical self-consciousness blurs the distinction between structure and agency. The strategic action of the Reich's statisticians was motivated by their broader vision of economic development. According to the stage models that many of them espoused, the current phase of capitalism demanded a systematic role for the state in coordinating economic activity. The Reich's statisticians were not merely administrative empire-builders of the type beloved of analysts of 'public choice'. They believed themselves to be accomplishing a historic mission in constructing an apparatus of expertise that would mediate between the state and the growing complexity of civil society. The accumulation of state expertise was thus multiply determined. On the one hand it can be traced to the actions of specific state elites. But their actions were inspired by a belief in the structural necessity of state expansion. And the existence of the activist elite itself was a product of the general proliferation of state bureaucracy that began in the late nineteenth century.

The expansion of official statistics as part of the general expansion of

[52] M. Furner and B. Supple, 'Ideas, Institutions, and State in the United States and Britain', in Furner and Supple (eds.), *The State and Economic Knowledge*, pp. 3–39.
[53] I. Hacking, *The Taming of Chance* (Cambridge, 1990), pp. 189–199.

state activity thus had a degree of inescapability. But it was also an uneven process prone to crises and interruptions. Particularly in the aftermath of World War I, it was a contested and complex process.[54] Conventionally this tends to be conceived of as a battle in which the remnants of private autonomy succumbed to public interference. Certainly, this is how economic historians describe the growth of the state.[55] The share of private incomes taken in taxes increased. The scale of transfers and public procurement rose. Free markets were hedged around with regulations. But this is simplistic. 'Big government' was not merely a threat to private freedom. It also called into question the identity of the state.[56] The 'big state' was a state without the clear contours and the undisputed sovereignty of the nineteenth-century model. Having involved itself in so many aspects of economic and social life the state could no longer claim to stand apart from, let alone above, civil society. To many, the new state appeared overextended, colonized by the conflicts and tensions of civil society. Nowhere was this crisis more pronounced than in interwar Germany. The myth of the Prusso-German State as the guiding light of the nation was shattered by defeat in World War I and revolution.[57] In the aftermath, the Reich's civil service struggled to reinvent itself. The Weimar Republic experimented with a combination of parliamentary government and technocratic corporatism. Meanwhile, forces on the right demanded the restoration of a 'strong state', which in practice actually meant a novel form of authoritarian, militarist dictatorship. And it was this vision that seemed to have triumphed with the 'National Revolution' of 1933. But authoritarian conservatives were to be disappointed. The Nazis did not allow themselves to be corralled by the conservative political establishment, the army and the civil service. By the late 1930s they had overcome the resistance of traditional elites and had embarked on a radical project of political and social reconstruction. The Nazi answer to Germany's political crisis was not the creation of a 'strong state'. Their goal was the

---

[54] S. Skowronek, *Building a New American State. The Expansion of National Administrative Capacities, 1877–1920* (Cambridge, 1982), P. Clarke, 'The Twentieth-Century Revolution in Government: The Case of the British Treasury', in Clarke, *The Keynesian Revolution and its Economic Consequences*, pp. 175–189 and K. Burk (ed.), *War and the State. The Transformation of British Government 1914–1919* (London, 1982).

[55] H. James, *The German Slump. Politics and Economics 1924–1936* (New York, 1986).

[56] C.S. Maier, *Recasting Bourgeois Europe. Stabilization in France, Germany, and Italy in the Decade after World War I* (Princeton, 1988, reprint), M. Geyer, 'The State in National Socialist Germany', in C. Bright and S. Harding (eds.), *Statemaking and Social Movements: Essays in History and Theory* (Ann Arbor, 1984), pp. 193–232, D. Melossi, *The State of Social Control. A Sociological Study of Concepts of State and Social Control in the Making of Democracy* (Cambridge, 1990).

[57] J. Caplan, *Government Without Administration. State and Civil Service in Weimar and Nazi Germany* (Oxford, 1988).

purified race-nation. In this struggle the state was no more than a means to an end. The existing structure of the German civil service was cast aside along with the conventions of ordinary government and the restraints of the law. When in 1941 the political theorist Franz Neumann spoke of an 'Un-state' emerging in the Third Reich, he was not merely pointing to the administrative incoherence and disorder of Nazi politics. His point was that the order that was emerging in the Third Reich could no longer be described in terms of the categories of conventional political theory.[58] German civil society had been destroyed but so had the fragile structure of the German state. The boundary between state and civil society that was so fundamental to modern conceptions of politics had dissolved.

As this book will show, official statistics in Germany were deeply affected by this crisis of the state. The expansion of official economic statistics in the first half of the twentieth century certainly involved the exploration of hitherto uncharted realms of private economic activity. As one might expect, this extension of official enquiries encountered substantial resistance, particularly from within the German business community. But it also raised fundamental questions within the statistical establishment. The practice of official statistics, as it developed over the course of the nineteenth century, was built around the liberal distinction between state and civil society.[59] Unlike the extractive agencies of the state, such as the tax office and the bureaucracy of military conscription, the statisticians did not resort to coercion. They did not employ threats to obtain responses to their questionnaires and they did not check the accuracy of the returns in an intrusive fashion. The 'objectivity' of official numbers was founded on a supposed bond of trust between the official statisticians and the citizenry. This trust in turn was based on self-limitation on the part of the statisticians. They refrained from making enquiries on issues likely to provoke resistance. And they guaranteed respondents the protection of anonymity and confidentiality. In particular, they promised never to reveal statistical returns to the tax office. These guarantees, emblazoned on the official questionnaires, implied an acknowledgement of the right to 'privacy'. At

---

[58] F. Neumann, *Behemoth. The Structure and Practice of National Socialism 1933–1944* (New York, 1963, reprint) and K. Tribe, *Strategies of Economic Order. German Economic Discourse, 1750–1950* (Cambridge, 1995), pp. 169–202.

[59] See paradigmatically the vision of official statistics outlined by Ernst Engel, chief statistician of first Saxony and then Prussia in the mid-nineteenth century, E. Engel, 'Die Volkszählung: ihre Stellung zur Wissenschaft und ihre Aufgabe in der Geschichte', *Zeitschrift des königlich preußischen statistischen Bureaus (ZKPSB)* 2 (1862), pp. 25–31 and E. Engel, 'Über die Organisation der amtlichen Statistik mit besonderer Beziehung auf Preussen', *ZKPSB* 1 (1860), pp. 53–56.

the same time, the technology of large-scale censuses symbolically positioned 'the state', represented by the bureau of official statistics, outside and 'above' civil society. The mass of particular, self-interested individuals were submerged in large aggregates. The accumulation of millions of individual returns would produce a true image of society as a whole. Official statistics thus sustained the idealistic image of the civil service as a disinterested 'general class' presiding wisely over the social consequences of industrialization and urbanization.

This liberal order of power and knowledge did not survive the expansion of state activity. And it is the collapse of this nineteenth-century understanding of official statistics that is the starting point for this book. In the first half of the twentieth century Germany's official statisticians were forced to renegotiate their relationship with civil society. Private businesses had to be coaxed or coerced into answering more questions and returning questionnaires more frequently. This expanded the range of economic data, and enhanced the role of official statistics in government. But it also implied a new relationship between the statisticians and civil society and thus a new identity for official statistics. In the 1920s the Reich's Statistical Office was reinvented as a clearing house for information, a corporatist centre of data-sharing between the state and the powers of civil society. In the 1930s, in the early years of the Nazi regime, this mutated in an authoritarian direction. The statisticians began to imagine themselves at the centre of state-controlled economy. But, this statist fantasy was not to last. It was swept away in the late 1930s by the radicalization of the Nazi regime. Combining the Nazi ideal of the Volksgemeinschaft with visionary technology, a radical faction within the Statistical Office sought to reconstruct German official statistics as a seamless system of surveillance. They would record not the economic and social aggregates but every single firm, every single worker and every single machine tool, indeed the movement of every single product throughout the economy. This totalitarian vision clearly had profound implications for the 'freedom' of the individual. But it also redefined the practice of official statistics. An integrated system of surveillance would make no distinctions between statistical questionnaires, tax records or private accounts. They all fed into the common database. Statisticians would thus forfeit their separate identity as guardians of a unique form of official knowledge. But as managers of the unified information system of the Reich, their reach would be extended beyond the wildest dreams of conventional official statistics. In pursuit of omniscience, statisticians in Nazi Germany extinguished the practice of official statistics itself.

V

Such fantasies were fuelled by new information technologies. The development of large-scale bureaucracy in the late nineteenth and early twentieth century propagated an astonishing range of new techniques for handling and processing data. Many of these were mundane, but as historians of business administration have made clear, they were crucial to managing the increased flow of information and to the rationalization of administrative activity.[60] The new technologies of the office included the telegraph, the telephone and the typewriter. But there were also great breakthroughs in the handling of paper records. Carbon paper eliminated the copy book. Vertical filing allowed random access to material. The conventions of business correspondence were adapted to the new filing systems. The invention of the card index revolutionized the control of very large quantities of information. All of these technologies found their applications in the business of official statistics, but the real buzz word of the early twentieth century was 'mechanization'. The key date here is 1890 when the first machines produced by the German–American inventor Hermann Hollerith were put to work on the US census. His target was to finish the count in three years rather than seven.[61] From our present-day perspective it is hard to avoid seeing the introduction of this primitive form of digital data-processing as a breakthrough of fundamental importance. But we need to be cautious here. Hollerith's machines did not revolutionize the production of statistics. A prior division between different classes of human labour prefigured mechanization.

In the compilation of the first official statistics in the early nineteenth century, the basic operations – observing, recording, classifying the individual observations, counting the totals – were merged into a single process. Local notables simply returned an account of their surroundings to the new statistical bureaux.[62] The only element of central control were the questionnaires, issued as templates for the local reports. The development of statistical technology over the course of the nineteenth century involved separating each one of these operations – observing, recording, classifying and counting – allowing the entire process to be

---

[60] J. Yates, *Control through Communication. The Rise of System in American Management* (Baltimore, 1989).

[61] H. Petzold, *Rechnende Maschinen. Eine historische Untersuchung ihrer Herstellung und Anwendung vom Kaiserreich bis zur Bundesrepublik* (Düsseldorf, 1985), pp. 195–290.

[62] B. Curtis, 'Administrative Infrastructure and Social Enquiry: Finding the Facts about Agriculture in Quebec, 1853–4', *Journal of Social History*, 32 (1998), pp. 308–327 and S. Woolf, 'Statistics and the Modern State', *Comparative Studies in Society and History*, 31 (1989), pp. 588–604.

controlled from the centre while keeping costs to a minimum. The first step was to dispense with the mediating role of local notables and to have the questionnaires filled out directly by households and businessmen. It was still important to have reliable local census-takers, but their task was now limited to checking the accuracy of the individual returns and compiling preliminary tables of local results. The next move was to centralize the entire process of tabulation. After checking by the census-takers, the original returns were despatched to the central statistical office. This, for the first time, gave the statisticians control over the process of classification, but it also posed enormous practical problems. Coordinating the movement of millions of bulky statistical returns was dependent on a modern infrastructure of transport and communications. And once the returns were gathered in, how were the statisticians to cope? Initially, the returns were classified and counted in a single process. A mark was made in a tabular form for every return of a particular type, the returns being discarded in the process of counting. For simple classifications, this was a quick procedure. But classifying and counting in a single operation made it impossible to check for errors or to make any retrospective changes to the system of classification. Any second thoughts necessitated a complete recount. Furthermore, if errors were to be avoided, trained staff had to perform both the intellectual labour of classification and the routine business of counting. It was therefore expensive. The final stage in the development of nineteenth-century enumeration was the separation of classification, sorting and counting. This was achieved by numbering each return and matching it with a numbered counting card. In effect, the statisticians created a paper double of the census, an image of the image. As each return was classified, a code was inscribed on a counting card, which was then added to the appropriate pile. If the final results appeared dubious one could move back from the classified counting cards to the numbered originals. Reclassifications could be performed simply by reviewing the relevant returns identified by the counting cards. Finally, the counting operation itself was speeded up. The cards were far easier to handle than the bulky questionnaires and pre-sorting increased reliability. But the major saving came from the division of labour. The staff of expert statisticians were concentrated on the process of classification while women and unskilled homeworkers were hired to count the batches of cards. The European censuses of the late nineteenth century thus came to resemble the putting-out operations of early industry. A core of trained assistants performed the business of classification under the supervision of professional statisticians who were also responsible for preparing the final volumes of tables and text. Meanwhile, a temporary army of human 'computers' accomplished the sorting and counting. The intelligent work of classification was thus separated from the rest of the process. The path was cleared for mechanization.

Hollerith's machines slotted neatly into this division of statistical labour. The codes marked on the counting cards by expert officials were transferred to a third set of cards, which recorded the information as a pattern of punched holes. These cards were then fed through the machines, which sorted and counted them mechanically or electro-mechanically. The Hollerith Company made bold claims for its machines. In practice, however, it took years to perfect a really useful technology. It proved very difficult to find paper of sufficiently high quality to withstand the beating in the machines. The early models lacked printing mechanisms. The entire operation had to be halted to allow results to be read off and recorded by hand. In the 1920s the fastest sorting machines were rated at 20,000 cards an hour. Experience in Germany suggested that they could in fact handle no more than 12,000 cards per hour. Tabulating machines with a nominal capacity of 7,500 cards were actually capable of producing the results from no more than 2,500 cards per hour.[63] For enumerations of less than 5,000 cards the machines were actually less cost-effective than manual processing. The expensive equipment needed to be fed with very large batches of cards. The machines were useful for carrying out the rough classification of large collections of data, but became increasingly inefficient as the classification was refined.[64] Nevertheless, their use became increasingly common in both the public and business world before World War I and their spread was encouraged by the intense competition between Hollerith and its main rival, Powers. Classically, the machines were employed in the compilation of urgent trade returns or in the processing of large batches of financial data. In these roles, they did deliver substantial savings of labour. The Reich's Statistical Office estimated in the late 1920s that its extensive use of machines made possible a 25 per cent saving in its labour budget, which was the largest part of its costs.[65] The conclusion is clear: mechanization of data-processing facilitated the statistical revolution. It enabled the accelerated production of large volumes of data at reduced cost. But it was not necessary in the strict sense of the word.

However, such a rationalist appraisal may lead one to underestimate

[63] GStA 1. HA Rep. 77 3893 no. 151 ff, Niederschrift der Verhandlungen der Statistiker des Reichs und der Bundesstaaten zu Bremen am 29. bis 31. Mai 1913, pp. 21–29.
[64] P. Quante, 'Die Erfahrung mit elektrischen Zählmaschinen in Preußen bei der Volks- und Berufszählung vom 16. Juni 1925', *Allgemeines Statistisches Archiv* (*ASA*), 20 (1930), pp. 82–112.
[65] See chapter 3.

the importance of technical change. The vision of mechanical data-processing held a powerful fascination in its own right. One perceptive commentator spoke of the 'suggestive power of the concept of "centralization"' peddled by suppliers of business machines.[66] Across the world, bureaucrats were inspired to dreams of omniscience. Arguably it was through these fantasies of total control that the technology of mechanical data-processing had its most profound impact on the history of statistics. For the first time it became possible to conceive of an entire nation recorded in a single database instantly accessible by means of mechanical handling equipment. This fantasy seems to have occurred independently in at least three different European countries in the interwar decades. In France it began to be realized in the early 1940s under the Vichy regime.[67] In Britain it dated back to an abortive scheme for national identity cards initiated during World War I.[68] In Germany, too, it had its origin in police plans for personal identification but took a sinister twist after 1933 in the form of an SS databank.[69] As this book will demonstrate, the 'romance of information technology' was also to have a dramatic impact on the history of economic statistics. New technologies of data-processing inspired contemporaries to believe that the economy might be most effectively controlled, not by manipulating national aggregates, but by a comprehensive system of individualized surveillance.

VI

As this discussion of information technology makes clear, it is not enough to understand the emergence of modern economic statistics simply as an effect of bureaucratization in the broadest sense of the word. It also needs to be understood as an intellectual and cultural phenomenon. To understand particular statistical projects one cannot avoid the detailed reconstruction of their particular intellectual context. But are there ways of generalizing about such cultural processes? As the sub-title claims, this book is about the emergence of a specifically

---

[66] A. Busch, 'Zur Frage der Verwendung von Lochkartenmaschinen', *ASA*, 20 (1930), pp. 260–265, in response to a puff from a representative of the Deutsche Hollerith Maschinen GmbH, K. Koch, 'Die Verwendung von Speziallochkartenmaschinen bei der Volkszählung 1930', *ASA*, 19 (1930), pp. 560–568.

[67] G. Chevry, 'Un Nouvel Instrument de travail statistique: Le Fichier des établissements industriels et commerciaux?', *Journal de la Société de Statistique de Paris (JSSP)*, 89 (1948), pp. 245–262 and 'Nécrologie: René Carmille', *JSSP*, 86 (1945), pp. 145–148.

[68] J. Agar, 'Modern Horrors: British Identity and Identity Cards', in J. Caplan and J. Torpey (eds.), *Documenting Individual Identity* (Princeton, 2001).

[69] G. Aly and K.H. Roth, *Die restlose Erfassung. Volkszählen, Identifizieren, Aussondern im Nationalsozialismus* (Berlin, 1984).

modern form of economic knowledge. Not that 'modern' is a term to use without caution. Its meanings are contested and bewilderingly various. However, handled with care it can serve as a useful framework within which to generalize about intellectual and cultural trends. It helps us to place our particular stories of intellectual genesis in a broader context.

A first helpful distinction is between 'modernity' and 'modernism'. The term 'modernity' is commonly used to refer to the processes of social, economic and technical change that have already been discussed: the development of modern industry and services, the ever-expanding role of bureaucracy in both corporate capitalism and the public sector, the development of new technologies of data handling, data-processing and communication. We can certainly describe the new economic statistics that began to emerge in the late nineteenth century as a form of economic knowledge peculiar to modernity. They were part of the deliberate effort by powerful social actors to exercise conscious control over the development of the national economy. In this sense they were an integral part of the institutionalized, social self-reflexivity that numerous authors have identified as characteristic of modernity.[70]

But what about 'modernism' or 'the modern'? The first problem is to disentangle the multiple meanings of these words.[71] On the one hand there is the usage favoured in debates surrounding postmodernism.[72] In this context, 'the modern' refers to the dominant continuity of Western rationalist, scientistic thought stretching back to the Enlightenment. This is the way in which Keith Tribe has used the term in his fascinating volume, *Strategies of Economic Order. German Economic Discourse, 1750–1950*. Tribe constructs a grand arch of continuity connecting the rationalist economic thought of the Enlightenment to the visionary projects of twentieth-century technocracy. According to Tribe they share the same 'dream of reason', the compulsion to subject the world to the order of reason.[73] The history of statistics certainly witnessed the compulsive recurrence of such dreams. Utopian rationalists of the eighteenth and early nineteenth century sketched numerous schemes for comprehensive statistical enumeration. In 1805, the first head of the Prussian statistical office, Leopold Krug, drew up an ambitious scheme for a complete enumeration of the incomes of the

---

[70] A representative example is A. Giddens, *The Nation-State and Violence*, 2, *A Contemporary Critique of Historical Materialism* (Cambridge, 1985), pp. 180–181 and 308–310.

[71] The following discussion owes much to Dorothy Ross (ed.), *Modernist Impulses in the Human Sciences 1870–1930* (Baltimore, 1994).

[72] A. Eysteinsson, *The Concept of Modernism* (Ithaca, 1990), pp. 3–4, 103–142.

[73] Tribe, *Strategies*, p. 1.

Prussian population.[74] Needless to say, this plan never left the drawing board. Krug shortly lost his job to a more liberally inclined University Professor of Smithian persuasion. But, the dream returned. In 1870, Ernst Engel the director of the Prussian bureau launched a plan for a comprehensive system of national economic statistics.[75] He, too, was to be disappointed. As we shall see, the Reich's Statistical Office, established in 1872, was hedged around with restrictions. It was not until the 1920s that the dream was finally to be realized. The Statistical Office of the Weimar Republic set about creating a comprehensive system of national accounts. By the 1940s Germany's statisticians were embarked on a minute enquiry into the structures of German industry, that would have satisfied even the most ambitious advocates of absolutist 'police' (Polizei).

And these continuities were not lost on contemporaries. As will be discussed in chapter 3, the upsurge of interest in macroeconomic questions around the turn of the twentieth century was often described as the revival of an Enlightenment tradition. The metaphor of the circular flow, which was so central to the understanding of the economy in the 1920s, was commonly attributed to the eighteenth century French physiocrat Quesnay. It was Quesnay's *Tableau économique*, which had inspired Krug in 1805. Maintaining the memory of Quesnay's work into the twentieth century was one of the great achievements credited to Karl Marx's *Das Kapital*. The other theoretical inspiration for twentieth century macroeconomics, the Quantity Theory of Money, was also understood as a theory of ancient pedigree. Its first modern expression was commonly credited to David Hume, the philosopher of the Scottish Enlightenment, and its earliest origins could be traced to classical antiquity. Together these two metaphors provided the building blocks for an aggregative and macroeconomic conception of the economy. Whether or not there was a real continuity between the Enlightenment and the technocratic experiments of the early twentieth century, there was certainly an 'invented tradition' of rationalist economics.

But this is not the only meaning of the words 'modern' and 'modernist'. The term may also refer more specifically to the highly sceptical and corrosive intellectual currents of the turn of the century. H. Stuart Hughes in his classic, *Consciousness and Society. The Reorientation of European Social Thought 1890–1930* showed how artistic modernism radiated powerfully onto the social sciences through such figures as Max

---

[74] L. Krug, *Ideen zur einer Staatswirthschaftlichen Statistik* (Berlin, 1807).

[75] E. Engel, 'Die Notwendigkeit einer Reform der volkswirtschaftlichen Statistik', *ZKPSB* 10 (1870), pp. 141–408.

Weber and Sigmund Freud.[76] More recently, Dorothy Ross has provided us with a helpful encapsulation. In the era of high Victorian optimism, she writes, 'thinkers in Europe and the United States believed that scientific and historical knowledge would provide synthetic and normative foundations for modern life of the kind that philosophy and religion had traditionally provided. By the end of the century that hope could no longer be sustained.'[77] The early twentieth century was thus marked by a new understanding of the subjectivity of knowledge, scepticism about rationality as a general guide to life, a turn to aesthetics and a radical stress on historicity and contingency. For the United States Ross has described how the crisis of the historical narrative of American exceptionalism led, in the last decades of the nineteenth century, to a search for new models for the social sciences. She uses the term 'scientism' to describe the effort by American economists, sociologists and political scientists to refashion their disciplines in the image of the natural sciences. 'Social science was to be an autonomous body of knowledge . . . directed at and constituted in accordance with the technological capacity for control.'[78] It would thus legitimate itself in the face of modernist doubt.

Germany is another country in which the development of twentieth-century economics bears the scars of an encounter with modernism. The statisticians and economists that are discussed in this volume no longer enjoyed the self-confident authority commanded by the so-called 'Historical School' of late nineteenth-century Germany.[79] Figures such as Professor Gustav von Schmoller claimed an Olympian detachment from the fray of private interests. Schmoller's chosen audience was the civil service, the Hegelian guardians of the fate of the nation. Moral judgements were an indispensable component of his economic analysis. This self-confident model of academic politics (Gelehrtenpolitik) did not survive the turn of the century. Its intellectual foundations were subject to devastating methodological criticism by the younger generation, led by Max Weber. The impossibility of establishing a neutral vantage point from which to view society was brutally exposed by the bitter political divisions within the academy. Some professors were

[76] H. Stuart Hughes, *Consciousness and Society. The Reorientation of European Social Thought 1890–1930* (London, 1974).

[77] Ross, 'Introduction: Modernism Reconsidered', in *Modernist Impulses*, p. 1.

[78] D. Ross, *The Origins of American Social Science* (Cambridge, 1991), p. 400.

[79] Various stages in this process are described in D. Lindenlaub, *Richtungskämpfe im Verein für Sozialpolitik* (Wiesbaden, 1967), D. Krüger, *Nationalökonomen im wilhelminischen Deutschland* (Göttingen, 1983), F. Lenger, *Werner Sombart 1863–1941* (Munich, 1994), R. vom Bruch, *Wissenschaft, Politik und öffentliche Meinung. Gelehrtenpolitik im wilhelminischen Deutschland (1890–1914)* (Husum, 1980).

drawn into party-political engagements. Others preached the need for support of the labour movement. And the reformist consensus was rejected altogether by an increasing number who embraced capitalism and sought to foster close links with industry and commerce. If the Historical School ever existed as a coherent body of knowledge, it was certainly dead by 1914. It was buried by war, revolution and defeat. This devastating experience destroyed the idealized image of the German state to which men like Schmoller had addressed their appeals for social reform.

By contrast with their Wilhelmine forebears, the new experts of interwar Germany spoke a disillusioned language. The role models for Ernst Wagemann, the head of the Weimar Statistical Office, were the immensely successful chemists and physicists. What economics had to offer was not moral leadership but specific expertise for the making of economic policy. The German statisticians discussed in this book were committed empiricists. But theirs was no longer the triumphant positivism of the mid-nineteenth century. They were acutely aware that they did not have access to reality in any fundamental sense of the world. Their first ambition was to register symptoms, proxies for processes that were too complex to be grasped in the totality of their detail. They were cautious about making causal claims, conceiving their task more modestly as the sifting of evidence with a view to projecting stable patterns from the past into the future. In the early 1920s the leaders of the Reich's Statistical Office hoped that this disillusioned empiricism might form the basis for a new relationship with academic economics. An attempt was made to turn the Statistical Office into a coordinating centre around which economics in Germany could be reconstructed as an empirical, policy-orientated discipline. However, the strategy of scientism that was so hegemonic in the United States commanded no consensus in interwar Germany. It was unacceptable to those who sought to maintain a role for the economist as moral authority and spiritual guide. It was also unacceptable to the minority of mainly younger economists, who devoted themselves to the elaboration of abstract economic theory. The result was a widening gulf between the Statistical Office and the increasingly divided field of academic economics.

Culture wars of this sort clearly have highly specific, national dynamics. However, the outcome appears to have been quite generic. In both the United States and Germany, economics was subject to a process of institutional and intellectual differentiation. Empirical, practical economic knowledge prospered by placing itself at the service of power. Theoretical economics in the Universities, on the other hand, developed as an ever-more arcane and mathematized discipline, driven by its own intellectual logic. And both forms of economic knowledge insulated themselves institutionally and intellectually against the other social and human sciences, which were far more powerfully affected by modernism and its discontents. Statistics thus provided one of the foundations for a peculiarly self-contained, indeed isolated, form of modern economic knowledge.

VII

The development of modern economic statistics in the first half of the twentieth century can thus be understood as the product of a number of quite general influences. But what about the specifically German aspects of this story? Much more will be said about the German historiography in the following chapters. However, there are some basic interpretative issues that should be addressed from the start: first of all the question of the Sonderweg. Since the late nineteenth century it has been common to accord the German state an exceptionally important role in guiding national economic development.[80] It would not be surprising, therefore, to find in Germany a strong tradition of official economic statistics. The peculiarly dramatic expansion in the interwar period could thus be seen as an outgrowth of a deep German tradition.[81] This is not the line followed in this book. The history of economic statistics, in fact, reveals the limits of the supposedly 'strong' German state. The German nation-state established by Bismarck in 1871 had no national structures of economic intervention. And, over the following decades, despite the extraordinary development of the German economy, it did not acquire any. Of course, in the nineteenth century, states such as Prussia and Saxony played an active role in promoting local industrial and commercial development. Municipalities also performed a key function in providing economic infrastructure. However, it is fanciful to suppose that they pursued anything remotely akin to modern macroeconomic policy, in the sense described by Winch.[82] It was World War I that finally forced the creation of national Ministries for the economy, for labour and for agriculture. The emergence of modern economic policy dates to the 1920s and it was this which set the stage for the sudden explosion of statistical innovation in interwar Germany. The new statistics of the

---

[80] For a critical discussion see G. Herrigel, *Industrial Constructions. The Sources of German Industrial Power* (Cambridge, 1996).

[81] For a history of Nazi economic policy constructed in these terms see A. Barkai, *Das Wirtschaftssystem des Nationalsozialismus. Ideologie, Theorie, Politik 1933–1945* (Frankfurt, 1988, 2nd edn.).

[82] V. Hentschel, *Wirtschaft und Wirtschaftspolitik im wilhelminischen Deutschland. Organisierter Kapitalismus und Interventionsstaat* (Stuttgart, 1978).

1920s and 1930s were the creation of the new national economic administration. They were established as a self-conscious break with tradition and they were opposed by those Länder which still had pretensions to independence. As will be shown, the new statistics of the Weimar Republic were emphatically macroeconomic in orientation.

The innovative activity of the Reich's Statistical Office in the 1920s and 1930s was part of a wider effort to reinvent the German state. The threat of revolution in Germany may have been exaggerated, but the depth of the crisis affecting the German state is hard to exaggerate.[83] The civil servants of the Weimar Republic struggled to create a new system of national economic administration in a peculiarly hostile environment. The statistical projects that are the subject matter of this book were a response to this crisis. Radical discontinuity rather than continuity is our theme.

In stressing the genuinely innovative character of the Weimar Republic this book follows the flow of recent historical writing.[84] The revolution of 1918 was certainly incomplete. It left intact certain key elites such as the conservative judiciary. However, one should not make simplistic assumptions about continuities with the Wilhelmine era. As Michael Geyer has shown, even the German armed forces were far from conservative. The commanders of the Reichswehr may have been hostile to democracy but to think of them as reactionary hangovers is to ignore the modernity of militarism.[85] In the 1920s and 1930s the German officer corps led a restless search for new means with which to conduct war. In non-traditional fields of government this tendency to innovate was even more pronounced. The state apparatus of the Weimar Republic was a laboratory of modern government, a conclusion strongly reinforced by a wealth of recent literature on areas of social work and welfare policy.[86] One of the aims of this book is to incorporate the sphere of economic government into this new picture of the Republic. In practice, economic policy was of course conditioned by a variety of institutions and pressures. However, policy was not simply a reflex of interest group preserves. By sponsoring economic statistics and economic research the new national Ministry for Economic Affairs was

[83] For a spectacular overview see G.D. Feldman, *The Great Disorder. Politics, Economics, and Society in the German Inflation, 1914–1924* (Oxford, 1993).

[84] Led by the influential work of Detlev Peukert above all. D. Peukert, *Die Weimarer Republik. Krisenjahre der Klassischen Moderne* (Frankfurt, 1987). For a critical appreciation of Peukert's contribution see D.F. Crew, 'The Pathologies of Modernity: Detlev Peukert on Germany's Twentieth Century', *Social History*, 17 (1992), pp. 319–328.

[85] M. Geyer, 'Etudes in Political History: Reichswehr, NSDAP and the Seizure of Power', in P.D. Stachura (ed.), *The Nazi Machtergreifung* (London, 1983), pp. 101–123.

[86] For a critical survey see Y.-S. Hong, *Welfare, Modernity, and the Weimar State, 1919–1933* (Princeton, 1998).

seeking to lay the foundations for an innovative programme of government founded on empirical data and systematic analysis. By 1927 the
Ministry had developed concrete plans for economic stabilization that
gave a key role to the Statistical Office and the state-sponsored Institute
for Business-Cycle Research (IfK). What destroyed this optimistic
scenario was the cataclysm of the Great Depression.

The Weimar Republic thus makes an ideal case study for a history of
modern economic knowledge. But what about the Third Reich?
Surely, Hitler's regime was an atavistic dictatorship with little or no
interest in questions of rational economic management. Its barbarity
surely makes it a case so special as to be irrelevant to any wider
discussion. One response to such objections is to make a distinction
between means and ends. The ends of Nazi ideology may have been
genocidal and reactionary. Hitler may have dreamed of returning to an
agrarian, Aryan utopia. However, as was argued long ago by David
Schoenbaum, to achieve its goals, Hitler's regime had to make use of
the technology and managerial resources provided by industrial modernity.[87] At the very least the Third Reich required a supply of up-to-
date military technology with which to fight its war. And Hitler
certainly had no difficulty in rallying professional and technical elites
to the National Revolution.[88] Indeed, as historical research has revealed the full extent of elite collaboration our perception of the Nazi
regime has changed.[89] This has been amplified by our increasing
awareness of the ambiguities of modernity and modernism. Is it, in
fact, true that the regime's aims were atavistic or reactionary? Hitler's
conception of the Volksgemeinschaft certainly contained many elements normally associated with programmes of social modernization
and modernity.[90] He was a bitter opponent of old-fashioned class
divisions and provincialism. Even his anti-Semitism was of a modern
variety. Hitler's hatred of the Jews was couched in terms of race not
religion and the SS was generous in its sponsorship of 'racial science'.
Furthermore, Nazi ideology more generally can clearly be related to
currents in modernist culture. The movement's anti-materialism, its

---

[87] D. Schoenbaum, *Hitler's Social Revolution: Class and Status in Nazi Germany 1933–1939*
(New York, 1966).
[88] For German economics in National Socialism see C. Kruse, *Die Volkswirtschaftslehre im
Nationalsozialismus* (Freiburg, 1988) and W. Krause, *Wirtschaftstheorie unter dem
Hakenkreuz. Die bürgerliche politische Ökonomie in Deutschland während der faschistischen
Herrschaft* (Berlin, 1969).
[89] For a survey see M. Roseman, 'National Socialism and Modernization', in R. Bessel
(ed.), *Fascist Italy and Nazi Germany. Comparisons and Contrasts* (Cambridge, 1996),
pp. 197–229.
[90] R. Zitelmann, *Hitler. Selbstverständnis eines Revolutionärs* (Stuttgart, 1990, 2nd edn.).

obsessions with the idea of national rebirth, its emphasis on subjective will, all had a wider resonance.[91]

But, it is not the re-evaluation of Nazi ideology that most concerns us here. Far more important from the point of view of this book is the parallel re-evaluation of the relationship between means and ends, between technology, expertise and Nazism. Schoenbaum's formulation pivoted on a distinction between the atavism of Nazi ideology and the modern technology that provided its weapons. But this comforting distinction was never stable. In the 1940s it had already been called into question by Horkheimer and Adorno.[92] In the *Dialectic of the Enlightenment* they presented fascism not as a counter-reaction to modernity but as an outgrowth of alienated, objectifying reason. In the 1960s Hannah Arendt's commentary on the Eichmann trial provided an explanation of how bureaucratic banality made mass murder possible.[93] These early interpretations have had a profound effect on the recent literature. Far from being counterposed to Nazi racial ideology, modern bureaucracy and technology have come to be seen as conducive to genocide.[94] Bureaucracy enabled mass murder in a technical sense. It also had moral and political effects. Far removed from the consequences of their decisions, the Nazi elite and their servants could coolly order the destruction of Europe's Jews. At a deeper level, it was the rationalist dream of remodelling society that was, itself, the root of evil. The hubristic fantasies of social engineers inspired many of the disasters of the twentieth century.[95] It was modern medicine and genetic theory that gave rise to the idea of the national body and the associated policies of eugenics and racial cleansing. In a Nietzschean twist, Detlev Peukert located the spirit of science at the origin of the genocidal murder of Europe's Jews.[96] Far from there being a conflict between Nazi ideology and modernity, there was a natural complicity between the two.

This kind of interpretation has also been applied to our subject. In the 1980s Götz Aly and Karl-Heinz Roth published a short book on the history of German statistics.[97] As an intervention in the popular protest against the German census of 1983, their aim was to cast doubt on the claim that statistics were a harmless technology of social administration.

[91] R. Griffen, *The Nature of Fascism* (London, 1991).

[92] T. Adorno and M. Horkheimer, *Dialektic der Aufklärung* (Frankfurt, 1980, 7th edn.).

[93] H. Arendt, *Eichmann in Jerusalem. A Report on the Banality of Evil* (New York, 1963).

[94] Most notably Z. Bauman, *Modernity and the Holocaust* (Cambridge, 1991).

[95] J.C. Scott, *Seeing Like a State. How Certain Schemes to Improve the Human Condition have Failed* (New Haven, 1998).

[96] D. Peukert, 'The Genesis of the "Final Solution" from the Spirit of Science', in T. Childers and J. Caplan (eds.), *Reevaluating the Third Reich* (New York, 1993), pp. 234–252.

[97] Aly and Roth, *Die restlose Erfassung*.

To make their point, Aly and Roth exposed the willing collaboration of German official statisticians in the system of Nazi tyranny. As active proponents of eugenics, Directors of the Statistical Office such as Dr Friedrich Burgdörfer helped to provide the intellectual foundations for policies of sterilization, euthanasia and ultimately genocide. Other statisticians collaborated with the SS in creating systems for registering the entire population in cardfile databases. Aly and Roth even went so far as to suggest that it was administrative technologies of this kind that allowed the regime to maintain its grip so effectively for so long. Statisticians are thus presented as key agents of the regime. And this collaboration was no accident. It followed from the objectifying, de-humanizing logic of the statistical technology itself. Once people were reduced to numbers it was a short step to cancelling them out.[98] In answer to the question raised above, Aly and Roth would contend that it is precisely by studying Nazism that we can comprehend the real potential of statistics as a tool of oppressive, dehumanizing reason.

Though it is not a study of racial policy or genocide this book is indebted to these recent reinterpretations of the Third Reich. The Third Reich is discussed here in a contextualized way, situated both in relation to the Weimar Republic and contemporary developments outside Germany. In this fundamental respect Nazism is treated as an outgrowth of modernity rather than a sudden departure from historical continuity. This is an important advance in our understanding, made possible by the latest generation of research. As has been stressed in this introduc-tion, the structures of national government inherited from the Weimar Republic were a work in progress. For many bureaucrats the early years of the Nazi regime, at least, were an exhilarating period of liberation from the fetters of parliamentarianism. The Third Reich appeared as an opportunity to realize the experiments in national government initiated by the Weimar Republic. This book, however, is also the result of learning in a negative sense. It rejects the simplistic equation drawn by authors such as Aly and Roth between Nazism and technocracy. Studying statistics as an infrastructure of modern power has its attrac-tions. It opens a new window on the business of government. It also allows one to uncover new parallels and continuities across time and space between superficially dissimilar regimes. But this approach is also associated with certain intellectual risks, risks that are starkly revealed by the work of Aly and Roth.

First, there is the problem of critical distance. Government tends to

---

98 This line of argument has subsequently been extended into a general analysis of the genesis of the Holocaust in G. Aly and S. Heim, *Vordenker der Vernichtung. Auschwitz und die deutschen Pläne für eine neue europäische Ordnung* (Hamburg, 1991).

present a monolithic visage to the outside world. And it is tempting to take this at face value, particularly if one is seeking to establish the importance of administrative and technical history for our more general historical understanding. Aly and Roth, for instance, are remarkably uncritical of the technical achievements of Nazi technocracy. And they have little incentive to be otherwise. Their purpose, after all, is to warn us of the dangers posed by statistics in an age of electronic data-processing. Why not, therefore, let the Nazi technocrats indict themselves? Their bold claims to have delivered a functioning system of totalitarian surveillance provide precisely the evidence that Aly and Roth are looking for. The result, however, is a shallow and instrumentalized interpretation of the Third Reich. This book, by contrast, attempts to provide a realistic assessment of the contribution made by economic statistics to the functioning of the Nazi dictatorship. The facade of the Reich's Statistical Office may have been monolithic. However, it hid a multiplicity of competing visions of the statistical future. The result, in practice, was a shambles. Successive waves of bureaucratic initiative produced an information system fundamentally incapable of satisfying the needs of wartime economic government. The grandiose schemes for individualized personal surveillance, on which Aly and Roth concentrate their attention, were the least successful of all. By focusing on the more ominous technocratic initiatives, they misunderstand the role played by Germany's statisticians in the functioning of the Nazi regime. By the later stages of the war the ideologues of totalitarian surveillance had been sidelined. It was the statistical apparatus created by the Weimar Republic that really provided the underpinnings for the Nazi war effort. Aly and Roth fail to understand this because they take the propaganda of technocratic totalitarianism at face value.

Aly and Roth's work however suffers from more than just a lack of critical distance. Its most fundamental problem is its technological determinism. The alliance between the Reich's Statistical Office and the Third Reich is not seen as the contingent product of the crisis of the German state. Rather, it is presented as the necessary result of the dehumanizing logic of statistical technology. This in turn underpins Aly and Roth's reductive account of the Federal Republic as a direct descendant of the Third Reich. If any form of quantifying social discourse is inherently dehumanizing and oppressive, then the political and legal framework in which it is situated makes little difference.[99] Statisticians in the Weimar Republic, the Third Reich and the Federal

---

[99] For a powerful critique of overly deterministic approaches to social policy in the Third Reich see D. Peukert 'Zur Erforschung der Sozialpolitik im Dritten Reich', in H.-U. Otto and H. Sünker (eds.), *Soziale Arbeit und Faschismus* (Frankfurt, 1989), p. 39.

Republic were all pursuing the same basic objective. The Statistisches Bundesamt in Wiesbaden, the statistical office of the Federal Republic, may appear to be an innocuous centre of social administration. But according to Aly and Roth it in fact served as a sinister haven for the racial scientists of the Third Reich and their intellectual descendants. In their portrayal of the Federal Republic, Aly and Roth push the logic of their argument to absurd extremes. However, this tendency towards determinism is inherent in any study which addresses itself to technologies of government such as statistics. After all, this introduction began in a similar vein, blurring conventional distinctions and insisting that we should view the development of modern economic knowledge as an interconnected process, stretching across more than half a century and a surprising variety of countries. Unlike Aly and Roth, however, this book insists on the need to differentiate. The statistical systems developed in Nazi Germany, the Soviet Union, Scandinavia, the Netherlands, Great Britain and the United States were indeed related. They shared certain common intellectual origins, certain technical preconditions and they were marked by their simultaneous appearance at a particular moment in time. But they were not identical. They were differentiated in technical terms. But, more fundamentally, they were distinguished by their relationship to politics. The most serious side-effect of technological determinism is that it makes it impossible to take politics seriously. One ends up, like Aly and Roth, equating the Third Reich and the Federal Republic simply because they shared certain administrative practices. This is a reductionism reminiscent of the crudest forms of Marxism. By contrast, this book shows how the development of new forms of economic knowledge was combined in the interwar decades with an intense argument over the appropriate political and legal framework for economic government. In Germany, this argument was taken to extremes. It is this which makes the study of the Third Reich so important. It reveals the potential inherent in common technologies of economic knowledge when combined with a peculiarly racist brand of collectivism.

1   Official statistics and the crisis of the Wilhelmine state

In May 1900 the Imperial Statistical Office of the Wilhelmine Empire put the finishing touches to its first major publication of the twentieth century, a volume proudly entitled *The German National Economy at the End of the 19th Century*.[1] The book celebrated a century of completely unprecedented economic and social development. The volume also marked the first century of German official statistics, the Prussian statistical bureau having been established in 1805. The Imperial Statistical Office (Kaiserliches Statistisches Amt, KSA) itself dated to 1872. The commemorative volume drew particularly heavily on the last great census of the nineteenth century, the occupational and workplace census of 1895, which was the most sophisticated national survey ever to have been attempted in Germany. The commemorative volume struck a resolutely nationalist tone, with the preface giving pride of place to his Imperial Highness Kaiser Wilhelm II. The Emperor hailed the census of 1895, 'as an outstanding achievement, which by far outdid the statistical work of other countries in this area both in completeness and precision'. However, the 18 remorseless volumes of census results had strained even the Kaiser's lively interest. In the hope 'that the results might be made useful to the general public', both the Kaiser and the Reichstag had requested a compact, popular summary.[2] And the Statistical Office was happy to oblige. Indeed, Hans von Scheel, the Director, went further.[3] He set himself the task of collecting together 'everything

---

[1] Kaiserliches Statistisches Amt (KSA), *Die Deutsche Volkswirtschaft am Schlusse des 19. Jahrhunderts. Auf Grund der Ergebnisse der Berufs- und Betriebszählung von 1895 und nach anderen Quellen* (Berlin, 1900).

[2] KSA, *Die Deutsche Volkswirtschaft*, p. iii.

[3] Hans von Scheel (1839–1901) was Professor for Economics, Finance and Statistics at the University of Bern before moving to Berlin. His principal interests were in the area of social policy. He joined the statistical office in 1877, becoming its Director in 1891. He took a leading role in instigating the Reich's labour statistics. For his views on the field of economics see H. von Scheel, 'Die politische ökonomie als Wissenschaft', Handbuch der Politischen Ökonomie, ed. G. von Schönberg (Tübingen, 1896, 4th edn.), I, pp. 77–118. He counted himself amongst the 'reformist, anti-Smithian' mainstream of German economics.

that German statistics has to contribute to an assessment of the state of our national economy'. The result was a 220-page volume packed with text and tables, summarizing the state of statistical knowledge about the German economy.

The German National Economy was divided into five broad sections, which tell us much about the official view of the German economy. The first section dealt with population as an economic force, drawing on the occupational census of 1895 to trace the division of labour in the national economy. The following three sections addressed agriculture, industry and commerce, the classic sub-divisions of economic activity. In 1895 agriculture was still the largest employer of German labour. It was also the sector most thoroughly covered by German official statistics. There were periodic assessments of land use, annual estimates of the harvest, censuses of livestock, surveys of agricultural machinery and even a regular compilation of agricultural prices. It was thus possible to assemble a working image of the economics of agriculture. By contrast, the information collected on trade and industry was scanty. By far the most important source were the workplace censuses (Betriebszählungen) of 1882 and 1895. They provided a comprehensive overview of German trade and industry, classifying establishments into no less than 300 branches. They also provided information on the social composition of the workforce. A rough image of the German class structure divided the population three ways, into employers, white-collar staff and blue-collar manual workers and then by sex and age. Special attention was paid to the use of mechanical power sources in the workplace. But, unlike in agriculture, there were no questions either about the value or volume of production. The only production figures were those generated as a by-product of special excise duties or regulations on beer, brandy, salt, sugar, starch and tobacco. But these trades were hardly the heartbeat of German industry. For information on more important sectors such as mining, iron and steel, textiles and paper the official statisticians had to draw on unofficial sources. Some of the better-organized trade associations published annual returns. The records of imports and exports provided the most comprehensive official information on economic activity outside agriculture. The quantity and value of German imports and exports finally began to be recorded in 1879. Indirectly, these figures illuminated the structure of industry. They were suggestive of a pattern of industrial development dependent on the import of food and raw materials. One could also make comparisons between Germany's pattern of trade and that of other countries. However, since there was no figure for the value of domestic production, there was no way of assessing the overall significance of foreign trade.

Despite the limits of the sources, *The German National Economy* presented an impressive picture. Since 1871 the German population had increased from 41 million to an estimated 56 million in 1900 and yet the supply of the basic commodities of life had more than kept pace. Germans had definitely grown richer. But, the Imperial statisticians also sounded a note of anxiety. While the population had expanded, the Reich's territory had not. Significantly, the statisticians remarked that Germany was far more densely populated than France. This concentration of humanity was a source of both strength and vulnerability. In a country as tightly packed as Germany, there was no room for dissent. According to the official statisticians, Germany's fertile population could be maintained only by 'disciplined work [strenge Arbeit] and a firm collaboration [fester Zusammenschluss] of economic forces': a thinly veiled warning to advocates of class war.[4] The unity of the national economy was a persistent theme. 'For reasons of economy', the Statistical Office allocated no space to a comparative discussion of the member states of the Reich. The great divide between Protestant and Catholic Germany was similarly downplayed. In fact, the relationship between religion and economic activity was dismissed as a question not worthy of further investigation, at least insofar as the Christian denominations were concerned.[5] Max Weber, famously, thought otherwise.

With its endorsement by the Kaiser, its invocation of national unity and its ideological conclusions, the centennial volume was clearly aimed at a nationalist audience. It was thus very much of the moment. And yet the picture of the German economy the official statisticians chose to present was curiously archaic. We do not find in this volume the familiar image of German industrial power, giant corporations and 'great banks'. The economy pictured by the Imperial statisticians was small-scale, made up largely of artisanal businesses and medium-sized farms. According to *The German National Economy*, land and labour were still the driving forces of production at the end of the nineteenth century. And these resources were under the direction of no less than five million independent businessmen of all shapes and sizes. More than 60 per cent of the workforce in trade and industry was employed by small or medium-sized businesses. Only 5 per cent of workers were concentrated in truly 'gigantic plants' of more than 1000 employees. Mining, iron and steel were the only industries where one could speak of true social polarization. Large-scale industry and commerce were given short shrift by the Imperial statisticians. Germany's industrial giants received no special mention. Indeed, capital as an independent economic force had

[4] KSA, *Die Deutsche Volkswirtschaft*, p. 3.
[5] KSA, *Die Deutsche Volkswirtschaft*, p. 18.

no place in the account at all. The great accumulators, the Berlin banks, the insurance funds, the savings banks were absent. And technology, that other motor of industrial growth, was also accorded a modest role. According to the official statistics, steam had overtaken water as the main motive force of the German economy only in 1895. Only 6 per cent of workshops were powered by 'motors' of any kind and the greatest concentration of industrial power was to be found in grain milling.

The aim of this chapter is to show how in the first two decades of the twentieth century, this traditional image of the German economy was shattered, along with the statistical system that sustained it. By 1918 the statistical apparatus of the Wilhelmine Empire was in tatters. The surveys that provided the sources for the centennial volume were no longer working. Problems of statistical organization had been apparent even before 1914. The statistics of Imperial Germany were widely criticized for their archaism. But there were powerful forces constraining the repertoire of official economic knowledge. It took the dramatic impact of World War I to unleash a radical process of change. In its aftermath Germany's official statisticians faced up to the challenge of industrial capitalism. This meant adopting new techniques, but it also meant a deep conceptual shift from an artisanal model of the economy to one centred on the capitalist corporation.

I

The 1900 commemorative volume marked a moment of transition in German history. Around the turn of the century, the political nation was embroiled in an impassioned debate about the country's future socio-economic order.[6] Was Germany predestined to become an urbanized, industrial state? Were the traditional estates doomed to extinction? Was there an alternative to the development of capitalism as foretold by Marxism? This argument ran right across the political landscape from right to left and it involved the entire spectrum of academics, journalists, politicians and civil servants. The development of German official statistics in the early twentieth century is inseparable from this complex intellectual and political scene. The official statistics were produced quite self-consciously as interventions in this debate. And it is by examining the way in which they were taken up and criticized that we can gain vital clues to the underlying conceptual structure of Wilhelmine official statistics. It is also to these debates that we must look for the first impulses for change.

[6] K.D. Barkin, *The Controversy Over German Industrialization 1890–1902* (Chicago, 1970).

Conservatives had traditionally located the popular basis of social stability in the *Mittelstand*, the mass of small and medium-sized farmers and the traditional estate of skilled, self-employed artisans. And *The German National Economy* certainly fits this mould. The Imperial statisticians celebrated the traditional social order, founded on the unbroken strength of agrarian and *Mittelstand* interests. Farmers were the backbone of the nation and the beneficiaries of tariff protection. They were also, as the statistics revealed, an expanding social group. Similarly, the censuses illustrated the survival of the artisanate, representatives of robust independence and the higher values of craft labour. And the Empire, of course, was their friend as well. Craft chambers and new guild regulations would help them to sustain their precious traditions.

By the turn of the century, however, this traditionalist rhetoric was beginning to wear thin. The Kaiser himself, around whom politics increasingly revolved, found it hard to resist the excitement of dynamic commerce and new-fangled industrial technology. On closer inspection, it is clear that 'social protection' was largely an exercise in propaganda. The tariffs on agricultural imports were modest and David Blackbourn has labelled the protection offered to the artisanate a 'sham'.[7] Particularly at the local level, the apparatus of the German state was highly supportive of industrial and commercial development.[8] In this sense, the title of the centennial volume is very apt. It marked not the beginning of the twentieth century but the end of the nineteenth.

Already in the 1890s, Kaiser Wilhelm had entertained a brief flirtation with the idea of 'social imperialism' – an alliance between the Empire and the proletariat. One of the few lasting products of this short-lived 'new course' was the creation of a Commission for Labour Statistics.[9] In 1902 this was established as a separate Department of the Statistical Office. Its development, however, was held back by the refusal of the Reich and Prussia to extend recognition to Germany's burgeoning trade unions. Significantly, the results of the Commission's enquiries made no impact at all on the centennial volume. By the late 1890s the Imperial government was espousing a more aggressive brand of anti-socialism. Short of a violent *coup d'état*, however, the Kaiserreich needed a popular political base. Where to look for a social counter-weight to the working class? Only diehards clung to the old *Mittelstand* as the last bastion of a

[7] D. Blackbourn, *Fontana History of Germany 1780–1918. The Long Nineteenth Century* (London, 1997), pp. 313–350.

[8] G. Steinmetz, *Regulating the Social. The Welfare State and Local Politics in Imperial Germany* (Princeton, 1993) and G. Herrigel, *Industrial Constructions. The Sources of German Industrial Power* (Cambridge, 1996).

[9] H.-J. von Berlepsch, *'Neuer Kurs' im Kaiserreich? Die Arbeiterpolitik des Freiherrn von Berlepsch 1890 bis 1896* (Bonn, 1987), pp. 200–205.

healthy social order. A more promising answer was provided by Gustav von Schmoller, Professor of Economics at Berlin, and undoubtedly the most influential economist of the Wilhelmine era. In 1897 Schmoller identified a new base for stability in the so-called 'new middle-class' (*neuer Mittelstand*), the army of white-collar, salaried employees who staffed the offices of big business and the state.[10] Unlike the old artisanate and peasantry the white-collar class was itself the product of modern industrial and commercial development. Economic development would thus produce from within itself a counter-weight to the proletariat.

Again, the centennial volume marks a moment of transition. It showed no awareness of Schmoller's new interpretation. The white-collar salariate were described as an insignificant social group confined to industries with large number of specialist technicians.[11] In fact, rather than treating white-collar staff as a separate, intermediate class, the official statisticians lumped them together with the workers, implicitly, in opposition to their employers. A few years later, Schmoller's thesis was to become the guiding idea of official social analysis.[12] The new *Mittelstand* were at the centre of the last great census of Wilhelmine Germany in 1907. The statistician largely responsible for the counts of both 1895 and 1907 was Dr Friedrich Zahn. Zahn can quite unhesitatingly be described as a propagandist of the Wilhelmine regime. He was subsequently to gain a degree of notoriety as a passionate supporter of the Tirpitz naval programme and the Reich's fiscal reform of 1909.[13] Comparing the results for 1895 and 1907 Zahn was only too happy to conclude that:

The insertion of a middle stratum between the business-man and the small self employed on the one hand and the workers on the other is proceeding at a fast pace and on a considerable scale . . . the effect of industrial concentration on the independent producers is finding a counter-weight in the rapid emergence of a stratum of technically and commercially trained staff (Beamten).[14]

By contrast, the growth of the working class between 1895 and 1907

---

[10] G. von Schmoller, 'Was verstehen wir unter dem Mittelstand?', *Verhandlungen des 8. evangelischen Kongresses* (Göttingen, 1897), cited in J. Feig, 'Deutschlands gewerbliche Entwicklung seit dem Jahre 1882', *Zeitschrift für die gesamte Staatswissenschaft*, 56 (1900), p. 665.

[11] KSA, *Die Deutsche Volkswirtschaft*, p. 83.

[12] KSA, *Statistik des Deutschen Reichs*, 211, *Berufs und Betriebszählung vom 12. Juni 1907. Berufsstatistik Abteilung X, Die berufliche und soziale Gliederung des deutschen Volkes* (Berlin, 1913), pp. 169–175.

[13] BHStA MInn 79425, Präs KSA to the Staatssekretär des Innern 8.12.1905, pp. 2–3 and BHStA MInn 79425, 30. Protokoll der Sitzung des Steuerausschußes vom 13.2.1909. Entwurf eines gewerbesteuergesetzes 1. Lesung.

[14] *Statistik des Deutschen Reichs*, 211, p. 278.

was less than expected. According to Germany's official statistics, capitalist development did not lead to the inevitable dominance of the proletariat but to a well-organized corporate economy directed by a new class of salaried 'intellectual workers'.

Schmoller thus provided a conveniently optimistic model for official social analysis. Other academic commentators were less obliging. The younger generation of German economists, in particular, were drawn to Marx. In 1894 the publication of the final volume of *Das Kapital* sparked a major revival in the academic reception of Marx throughout central Europe.[15] For a generation that included the Weber brothers, Werner Sombart, Joseph Schumpeter and many others, Marx established capitalism as the central object of analysis. In 1903 Max Weber, Werner Sombart and Edgar Jaffee dedicated the *Archiv für Sozialwissenschaften und Sozialpolitik* specifically to the 'historical and theoretical analysis of the cultural significance of capitalism'. For this generation, there was no doubt that the extension of the market and the rational accumulation of capital were the central dynamics of modern economic development. Over the course of the nineteenth century the pursuit of profit had combined in new ways with the logic of technology and bureaucracy. Alongside the massive bulk of the modern state had emerged the giant capitalist corporation, a spectacle that inspired analysis and critique but also awed excitement and fantastic projection. Max Weber foresaw a new era of bureaucratic rationalization, whether in capitalist or socialist form. Sombart, on the other hand, espoused a more conventional stage theory, describing 'high capitalism', as a transitional phase on the evolutionary path towards socialism.[16] The increasing scale of capitalist production and the impersonality of property relationships prepared the way for socialization. But, if capitalism was destined to be superseded, was Marx right in predicting that it would end in apocalyptic crisis? And if socialism was indeed capitalism's natural successor, what form would it take?

On these questions there was disagreement and not just between 'bourgeois' authors such as Weber and Sombart. In the late 1890s the Social Democratic Party (SPD) itself was thrown into intellectual turmoil by the debate over 'revisionism'. In the 1880s the leadership of the party, backed by the aged Friedrich Engels, had worked on the assumption that the final crisis of capitalism was imminent.[17] This

---

[15] D. Lindenlaub, *Richtungskämpfe im Verein für Sozialpolitik. Wissenschaft und Sozialpolitik im Kaiserreich* (Wiesbaden, 1967), pp. 272–373.

[16] F. Lenger, *Werner Sombart 1863–1941* (Munich, 1994), pp. 78–110.

[17] R. Walther, '. . . *aber nach der Sündflut kommen wir und nur wir.' 'Zusammenbruchstheorie', Marxismus und politisches Defizit in der SPD, 1890–1914* (Frankfurt, 1981) and

seemed a realistic possibility in light of the prolonged depression of profits and prices that had afflicted the European economies since the early 1870s. Perhaps the era of capitalism was destined to be short-lived. Instead, in the 1890s, the world economy entered into an extra-ordinary boom, with Germany in the forefront. New technologies such as electrical engineering and synthetic chemistry promised a second industrial revolution. Germany emerged as an international economic power. And yet, in the midst of this capitalist *belle époque*, the SPD as a political movement was on the rise. The lifting of Bismarckian persecu-tion was followed by a series of stunning electoral successes. The party emerged as the most popular political force in Wilhelmine Germany. It was these 'new realities' that prompted the exiled socialist journalist Eduard Bernstein to call for a fundamental revision of party doctrine.[18] Capitalism was not heading for an inevitable crisis. Capital was not simply being concentrated in the hands of the few at the expense of the majority, far from it. Increasingly large numbers of small and medium-sized businessmen were acquiring property. The skilled working class enjoyed an unheard of prosperity. Economic development was produ-cing not polarization and simplification, but a complex social and economic system. Fantasies of immediate, wholesale collectivization were unrealistic and irresponsible. Rather than fixating on the final goal of socialism the party should concentrate on using its new political muscle to initiate immediate reform. The ensuing debate in the socialist press and at the Stuttgart Party Conference of 1898 was fierce. The party leadership around Kautsky was embarrassed by a violent assault on Bernstein, led by Rosa Luxemburg and Alexander Helphand (Parvus). There were deep philosophical differences between Bernstein and his opponents. But the issue that occupied centre stage was the state of capitalism in Germany. Whereas Bernstein painted a rosy picture of steady progress, Parvus insisted on the stark reality of the concentration of capital and the immiseration of the vast majority. Rosa Luxemburg, for her part, argued that it was only imperialist expansion that was saving capitalism from collapse. The final crisis remained an inevitability.

From the point of view of this book, what is important about these classic debates is the empirical questions they generated. In their efforts to assess the state of the German economy the participants had no

---

F.R. Hansen, *The Breakdown of Capitalism. A History of the Idea in Western Marxism, 1883–1983* (London, 1985), pp. 32–67.

[18] Tudor, *Marxism and Social Democracy. The Revisionist Debate 1896–1898* (Cambridge, 1988) and P. Gay, *The Dilemma of Democratic Socialism. Eduard Bernstein's Challenge to Marx* (New York, 1952), pp. 157–212.

option but to refer to the anodyne productions of the Imperial Statistical Office. What resulted were a series of fascinating methodological critiques, which judged Wilhelmine official statistics in terms of their ability to represent the emerging structures of German capitalism. Eduard Bernstein's argument relied heavily on both German and British official statistics.[19] Certainly the figures supported his case, but there was also a methodological point to make. The need for empirical testing was central to Bernstein's critique of the emerging Marxist orthodoxy. In his view, the treatment given to the German census results of 1895 by the Party press was indicative of the growing unwillingness to 'face facts'. The figures on the distribution of employment had been wilfully misconstrued. The advocates of orthodoxy had produced a simple image of the inevitability of capital concentration by treating all firms with more than 50 employees as 'large firms'. On this reading, the petty bourgeoisie was doomed. The polarization of class relations was inescapable. But, as Bernstein sought to show, a very different picture of German social development could be made to appear from the same data. By contrast with the Imperial statisticians, Bernstein did not seek to minimize the development of modern capitalism. The development of the very largest corporations was phenomenal. And there was no doubt either that artisans and small shopkeepers were being driven out of business. But this dichotomous model was not the whole story. Between the two extremes there was a prosperous mass of medium-sized firms living happily alongside the giants. In 1895, firms with between 6 and 200 employees accounted for no less than 40 per cent of employment. Read with an open mind the official statistics revealed a more differentiated picture than the Party ideologues were willing to allow. Bernstein's main criticism of the official statistics was that they were slow and patchy in their coverage. In particular, they failed to provide information on capital accumulation and ownership. From 1900 the Statistical Office did begin to record the deposits in Germany's savings banks, the most popular form of capital accumulation. Then, in 1906, in response to the widening debate about capitalist high finance, the Office began registration of all German companies that issued shares or enjoyed limited liability status. In statistical affairs as well, there was thus hope of reform.

To Bernstein's critics on the left, notably Parvus and Luxemburg, his handling of the official data was woefully 'unscientific'. He was able to arrive at his conclusions only by taking official ideology at face value:

Bernstein . . . had forgotten that the relationships revealed in the official

[19] E. Bernstein, *Evolutionary Socialism* (New York, 1961).

statistics were purely formal and abstract and that, as such, they gave at best an incomplete picture of the relationships that actually obtained in bourgeois society. Statistics might provide useful material for social and economic analysis, but only if they were interpreted from the standpoint of social and economic reality. Bernstein, in short, had fallen into the trap of 'formalism'. He had mistaken the appearance for the reality, the form for the content.[20]

Parvus illustrated Bernstein's misperception with an example. One of the industries benefiting from the boom of the 1890s was shipbuilding. German yards mounted a serious challenge to Britain's global dominance.[21] The result, as any good socialist should have known, was an enormous agglomeration of capital and labour in the northern port cities of Hamburg and Bremen. As companies such as Blohm and Voss concentrated thousands of workers to construct gigantic liners, they created an urban proletariat that provided the SPD with some of its most solid support. And yet, according to the official statistics, the German shipbuilding industry was a typical example of *Mittelstand* prosperity. The census of 1895 counted 22,731 workers employed by just over 1,000 firms: barely more than 20 workers per employer. As Parvus commented, these figures entirely missed the essential dynamic of the sector, '. . . the statistical picture is obscured by a few hundred manufacturers of barges and small boats, . . . Bernstein sees only the fleet of small fishing smacks and overlooks the great fleet of German ocean-going ships'.[22] The bland statistical averages failed to register the economy's shifting centre of gravity.

Helphand and Luxemburg were not alone in criticizing the false image of social balance presented by Wilhelmine official statistics. Werner Sombart, in his widely read account of the economic history of Germany in the nineteenth century, harshly criticized the inadequacies of the official data.[23] His central theme was the displacement of needs-orientated craft production by the all-embracing, profit-driven system of capitalism. In his view there was, by the turn of the century, not a single sector of the German economy that was untouched by capitalist business practices. Trades that appeared in the census returns as bastions of the artisanate, such as tailoring or cabinet-making, were in fact entirely dominated by capitalist merchants. The millions of independent entre-

[20] H. Tudor, summarizing the views of Parvus and Luxemburg, see 'Introduction' to *Marxism and Social Democracy*, p. 20.

[21] N. Ferguson, *Paper and Iron. Hamburg Business and German Politics in the Era of Inflation, 1897–1927* (Cambridge, 1995), pp. 31–92.

[22] Parvus, '2. Further Forays into Occupational Statistics', *Sächsische Arbeiter-Zeitung* 1 February 1898, reprinted in Tudor, *Marxism and Social Democracy*, pp. 177–181.

[23] W. Sombart, *Die Deutsche Volkswirtschaft im neunzehnten Jahrhundert und im Anfang des 20. Jahrhunderts. Eine Einführung in die Nationalökonomie* (Berlin, 1927, 7th edn.), pp. 283–298.

preneurs celebrated by the Statistical Office were for the most part dependent sub-contractors, 'small cogs in the giant clockwork of capitalist commerce'.[24] Adding up the nominally independent producers told one nothing about the real structure of the economy. Legal independence by itself was meaningless. For Sombart, too, 'the facts' as presented and authorized by official statistics served only to obscure the central dynamic of contemporary social development.

Max Weber, who might well have had a thing or two to say about these methodological questions, did not himself comment on the official statistics. However, a powerful 'Weberian' critique actually emerged from within the statistical establishment itself, a critique that was to have a direct practical influence on the subsequent development of the German census. The author of this critique, Rudolf Meerwarth, embodied many of the contradictory tendencies of the period. By training he was a classic product of the liberal school of so-called Historical Economics, gaining his PhD under the supervision of Lujo Brentano with a dissertation on the impact of protective legislation on the condition of home workers.[25] In 1906, he joined the Imperial statistical service where he was employed both in the Labour Statistics Department and in the preparation of the results of the 1907 census. In 1914, Meerwarth departed the service of the Reich for a new post in the Prussian Statistical Office, which he combined with a teaching position at the Technical University in Berlin. Meerwarth thus followed the career path of many of the most distinguished German statisticians of the nineteenth century, combining the practice of official statistics with academic teaching. In the early twentieth century, however, this involved straddling worlds that were increasingly out of joint. The growing gap between the practice of official statistics and the intellectual preoccupations of the younger generation of academic economists is a recurring theme in Meerwarth's publications.[26] In Meerwarth's view this disjuncture was damaging to both economics and official statistics. Academic economics was left without adequate empirical underpinnings, while the practice of official statistics was diminished by its lack of conceptual clarity. Deploying the neo-Kantian methodological language pioneered by Max Weber, Meerwarth argued that all statistical enquiries were implicitly or explicitly based on ideal types – simplified models that embodied salient features of reality in a refined and heightened form.[27]

---

[24] Sombart, *Die Deutsche Volkswirtschaft*, p. 286.

[25] P. Quante, 'Rudolf Meerwarth zum Gedächtnis', *ASA*, 35 (1951), pp. 157–162.

[26] R. Meerwarth, 'Die Berufs- und Betriebszählung im Deutschen Reich vom 12. Juni 1907 und ihre Literatur', *Deutsches Statistisches Zentralblatt (DSZ)*, 5 (1913), pp. 97–106.

[27] R. Meerwarth, *Einleitung in die Wirtschaftsstatistik* (Jena, 1920), pp. 1–6.

The task for the social scientist was to choose the most appropriate ideal type for the situation in hand and to apply it as self-consciously as possible. Meerwarth, like the other economists of his generation, was convinced that an adequate understanding of the contemporary economy had to be built around an ideal type of capitalist enterprise. What made Meerwarth distinctive was the precision with which he diagnosed the deficiencies of Wilhelmine official statistics. As Meerwarth showed, the archaic image of the German economy presented by the Statistical Office in its centennial volume was no accident, nor was it merely ideological window-dressing. It reflected the fundamentally artisanal conception of economic activity that had informed German statistics of trade and industry since their emergence in the mid-nineteenth century.

II

To understand how the artisanal ideal type was embodied in the Wilhelmine statistical system, we need to follow Meerwarth into the workshop of official statistics.[28] In particular, we need to understand the organization of the centrepiece of Wilhelmine statistics, the censuses of workplace and occupation. The German Empire carried out censuses of this type in 1882, 1895 and 1907. Until the interwar period these complex enquiries were the defining events in the working lives of most professional statisticians. They were enormous projects, involving millions of households and firms, armies of census-takers, hundreds of temporary staff hired by the statistical bureaux to mark up and to count the millions of returns and the entire resources of the statistical profession. They were hugely expensive. Even the German system of using 'volunteer' civil servants as census-takers could not keep the cost below many millions of marks.[29] They were accomplished through a collective effort involving the Reich in collaboration with the statistical bureaux of all the member states of the federation. Not surprisingly, therefore, they were the chief topic of discussion at the statistical 'summits', held annually after 1890 to coordinate statistical affairs in the Reich. Furthermore, unlike most of the other major statistical systems, such as trade statistics, the censuses were free-standing statistical enquiries. They were divorced from all other branches of state administration. Above all,

---

[28] For the following see Meerwarth, *Einleitung*, pp. 6–83.

[29] The census of workplaces and occupations in 1895 cost a total of 3.6 million marks. By comparison the US census of the 1890s, which was based on a far more elaborate questionnaire and employed paid census-takers, cost the equivalent of 48 million marks, see KSA, *Die Deutsche Volkswirtschaft*, p. 74.

they were carefully preserved from any entanglement with the fiscal authorities. Respondents were assured that the census returns would be used exclusively for 'statistical purposes'. The censuses were under the sole control of professional statisticians, and they reveal most clearly the profession's understanding of German economic and social life.

The twin censuses of personal occupations and workplaces were conceived as an integrated system for registering the nation's social and economic structure. This is itself worthy of comment. Wilhelmine official statistics made no clear distinction between 'the economic' and 'the social'. As we shall see, this demarcation was to assert itself forcefully after World War I with the application of a new brand of systematic economic theory to the practice of official statistics. This created a separate system of economic statistics on the one hand and on the other a new alignment between social and demographic statistics, but this split belongs to the 1920s. Before World War I there was no separate department for economic statistics within the Statistical Office. The statistics of foreign trade were the closest thing to purely economic statistics, but they were little more than an elaboration of administrative records generated by Germany's customs posts. In the censuses, the most authentic products of 'statistical science', the social and the economic were integrated. The occupational census aimed to link the profile of occupations to a variety of 'social' variables such as age, sex, marital status, religion and family size. The questionnaires were directed to heads of households. The workplace census, by contrast, was directed to employers. It captured the workplace and its technical equipment. But it also registered the social structure of the workforce; employers returned the number of employees divided into a variety of social 'positions', ranging from proprietor to unskilled hands.

Ultimately, the entire elaborate edifice of the census hung on the definition of its basic objects. How did the Wilhelmine censuses define 'occupation' and 'workplace'? What was remarkable about the occupational censuses of the Wilhelmine period was the full meaning they attributed to the concept of occupation. The canonical definition was supplied by the doyen of Bavarian statistics, Professor von Mayr. To paraphrase, Mayr defined occupation in vocational terms as a person's 'permanent task' (dauernde Aufgabe), which also conditioned a 'certain consolidation of their economic circumstances'.[30] Mayr's definition established an intimate relationship between occupation and social status. Accordingly, the occupational census did not ask people to

---

[30] G. von Mayr, *Statistik und Bevölkerungslehre*, II, p. 133, quoted in BAP 39.01 10559, Grundsätze für die Aufstellung des Berufsverzeichnisses Anlage II. Entwurf B. (Meerwarth).

record their actual occupation on the day of the count. It asked them to record what they considered their normal or proper occupation. The census thus embodied a static view of the economy according to which people acquired skills at an early age and then lived out careers and social lives shaped around this well-defined vocation. The commitment to an artisanal conception of the economy was revealed by a further characteristic of the occupational census. The questionnaires and the evaluation of the census made no distinction between personal occupation and industry of employment. The former was assumed to define the latter. Painter-decorators were classed as a single occupation, regardless of whether they worked on their own account or for the maintenance department of a giant industrial corporation. Classification by industry of employment was reserved for those without clearly defined occupations. The guiding assumption was that the work of the vast majority of the population was defined principally by a distinctive craft skill. Following from this, as in *The German National Economy*, the entire economy might be depicted as an assemblage of human labour of different qualities.

By the early twentieth century the results produced by this conceptual scheme were increasingly unsatisfactory. The census of 1907 allocated no less than 60 per cent of the workforce to ill-defined industrial categories, such as 'semi-skilled worker, chemicals'. The artisanal, skills-based conception of occupation was losing touch with the realities of work life. As a result, the census yielded no consistent image of the German industrial workforce. The skilled minority were classified by craft independently of their industries of employment. The majority could not be fitted into the hierarchy of crafts, and had to be lumped into rough, industrial groupings. The results provided neither a clear occupational picture, nor a straightforward count of employees by industry. The assumption that each person could be assigned to a 'proper' craft occupation had nostalgic appeal, but as an image of the current experience of work it was entirely misleading.[31]

The same artisanal vision also underpinned the census of workplaces. The workplace surveys of the Second Empire originated in the Gewerbezählungen (Trade Surveys) of the early nineteenth century. And German statisticians clung doggedly to the ancient vocabulary of 'trade' (Gewerbe), despite its increasing irrelevance in the more modern sectors of the economy. The overriding interest of these surveys was to capture the proliferating multiplicity of the division of labour. At every census, Germany's statisticians added new trades to the classification.

---

[31] Sombart, *Die Deutsche Volkswirtschaft*, pp. 424–425.

And the ideal type informing the workplace census remained artisanal. In line with its vocational definition of occupation, the Imperial statisticians defined the workshop, a self-contained, technical unit of production, as their basic unit. Following this definition integrated industrial plants were simply agglomerations of dozens, or even hundreds, of specialized workshops. The job of the workplace survey was to record each node in this network of workshops, to count individually the 'real' sites of production. Proprietors were asked to declare not just the main business of their firm, but every discrete technical unit under their control.

The results obtained by applying this artisanal scheme in the workplace survey were as ambiguous as those produced by the occupational census. The vast majority of German workplaces were small. And for them the guidelines presented no problem. However, it could not be denied even by the most stubborn defenders of the *Mittelstand* that such firms accounted for a dwindling share of both output and employment. Increasingly, it was medium and large firms that dominated German industry. For them, the official questionnaires presented insuperable problems. How was a complex industrial corporation to sub-divide its activities into workshops? If the official statisticians believed that there was a universal technical logic determining the organization of production, they were out of touch with the realities of modern industry. As Meerwarth pointed out, even a medium-sized industrial firm had its own distinctive commercial and technical organization. In one firm workshops might be closely integrated and controlled by a single accounting office, in another the organization might follow technical lines. In large corporations different organizational logics might apply to different lines of production or different stages of the same production process. The official questionnaires were oblivious to this complexity. The guidelines they offered belonged to a bygone era. Pub landlords were encouraged to make a separate declaration if they also operated a shop. Complex industrial brewers were left to their own devices.

A fundamental lack of consistency thus obscured the results of the workplace censuses. Comparing 1895 and 1907, it appeared that the agglomeration of 'workshops' within larger firms had increased. In the 1895 the census counted 2.109 million firms and 2.147 million technical units. In 1907 2.9 million firms were reported as controlling a total of 3.45 million technical units. However, given the imprecision of the guidelines it was unclear whether this reflected 'real' changes in economic organization or simply a change in statistical procedures. What was certain was that the figures for both years grossly underestimated the complexity of German industry. If one took seriously the idea of sub-dividing industry into 'technical units of production', there should have been vastly more technical units. Meerwarth was able to demonstrate the degree of underreporting with case studies. In the German sewing machine industry there were 25 medium-sized producers with 200–500 workers. Of these, no less than 23 had declared their operations as single, technical units. In fact, production of sewing machines on this scale involved at least 10 clearly distinct technical operations. Instead of 23 workplaces the census, according to its own criteria, should have counted at least 230! On the other hand, there were some firms that had attempted to satisfy the demands of the statistical questionnaire. Meerwarth reported the case of a mechanical engineering firm with 1,200 employees that had made 15 separate returns including one for its baths department, with a staff of four. But, for lack of guidance, this diligence was misdirected. Despite its far-reaching subdivision the firm in question had made no separate declaration for either its sales department or its drawing office.

In practice, Meerwarth considered these problems insoluble. If the technical sub-division of industry were to be consistently applied, there would need to be hundreds of tailor-made questionnaires. And, in any case, this was more than a question of practicalities. A technical subdivision of industry obscured what for Meerwarth and many of his contemporaries was the essential feature of contemporary economic change: the capitalist agglomeration of giant industrial complexes. An image of the German economy as a variegated mass of tiny workshops, even if it could be made accurate, was beside the point. The old categories were failing because they were fundamentally at odds with the dominant trend of economic development. To make sense of the modern economy, what was required was a new ideal type of modern capitalism.

III

Meerwarth's critique of Wilhelmine official statistics was penetrating, but it was also one-sided. In his view the problems of German economic statistics were conceptual. The unwillingness of the official statisticians to relinquish the artisanal ideal type explained their failure to adequately register economic reality. But he had nothing to say about the concrete material obstacles that stood in the way of a more adequate statistical system. After all, if the object of statistical enquiry was a capitalist economy, this begged the question of the knowing subject. The Imperial Statistical Office was part of the state bureaucracy of Wilhelmine Germany. How did this state apparatus relate to the capitalist economy? Was it an independent force? Or did it enjoy only a relative degree of autonomy? What material constraints did the context and the particular traditions of the German state impose on the business of data-gathering? As Meerwarth himself was to discover, understanding these real constraints was crucial, both to understanding the peculiar structure of Wilhelmine official statistics and to overcoming the obstacles that were to stand in the way of reform.

First of all, would profit-seeking capitalists allow their affairs to be inspected by official statisticians? On the basis of past experience there were few grounds for optimism. German tradesmen and merchants jealously guarded their secrets.[32] Over the course of the nineteenth century official statisticians had learned to limit their enquiries to inoffensive areas. Rationalizing this experience they espoused a rather forced brand of liberalism. If the state acknowledged the right of its citizens to freely conduct business, it was not reasonable for official statisticians to enquire into the more intimate aspects of their business dealings. If pushed, respondents would simply make false returns. Intrusive enquiries, therefore, came to be seen as unsound statistical practice. Ultimately, reliable official statistics were thought to rest on a peculiar relationship of trust between the citizen and the dedicated statistical agencies of the state. By the end of the nineteenth century this imagined relationship of trust came to be a defining preoccupation of official statisticians. It founded their claim to a distinctive position within the state apparatus, in particular *vis à vis* the apparatus of military conscription and the extractive administration of taxes. But, it also demanded self-restraint.

The reality of this constraint was forcefully illustrated by the struggle over statistics of industrial production. Following Germany's return to protectionism in 1879, tariffs and trade policy became the symbolic focus of public economic debate in Germany. Fierce argument preceded each of the tariff rounds. These battles pitted agriculture against industry, heavy industry against manufacturing, commerce against both industry and agriculture, consumers against producers, workers against business men. In the run-up to the new tariff of 1902 (the Bülow Tariff) the Reich's Office of the Interior decided to discipline the debate by carrying out a series of production surveys in the industries most affected by trade policy. These enquiries went well beyond the 1895 census with questions about the value and quantity of production, the quantity of raw materials consumed, the number of workers, the number of hours worked and the wage bill. Significantly, these data were considered too sensitive to be shared with the public through the

[32] W. Sombart, *Der moderne Kapitalismus* (Munich, 1927a), 3, 2, pp. 60–61, 411–414.

Imperial Statistical Office. Instead, the Office of the Interior carried out the production survey itself. Their results were shrouded in secrecy, and were withheld from the Reichstag.[33]

Behind the scenes, state and business were bitterly at odds about the legitimate extent of official enquiries. When confronted with the new questionnaires, German heavy industry engaged in a systematic campaign of obstruction.[34] The Ruhr Revier was deeply suspicious of Berlin civil servants, whom they suspected of harbouring sympathies for the dangerous doctrines of the 'socialists of the lectern'.[35] The questionnaires were returned only after all references to the wage bill and the cost of raw materials had been removed. In this edited form, the surveys were transferred to the Statistical Office in 1910. Year by year the statisticians engaged in a cat and mouse game with recalcitrant firms and the surveys of production remained limited to a small number of industries.[36] The workplace census of 1907, which did cover all of German industry, respected the traditional limits of official statistics. Questions about production were strictly off limits. Germany's official statisticians could only admire from afar the comprehensive censuses of production being pioneered in the United States and the British Empire.[37] Given the secretiveness of the business community, detailed enquiries into the actual operations of German industry were simply not feasible in the Wilhelmine era.

The crippling effect of business opposition was also visible in the area which contemporaries referred to as 'labour statistics'. In Britain and the United States this was one of the most active fields of statistics in the prewar decades. 'Labour statistics' were a fluid category, reflecting the emerging contours of organized industrial relations. The term embraced all information relevant to the management of the labour market, statistics of employment, unemployment, wages, prices and household consumption. Despite Germany's venerable tradition of social statistics, the Statistical Office was late in joining the band-wagon. As we have already mentioned, the civil service of both the Reich and Prussia refused to extend official recognition to the trade union movement. The Commission for Labour Statistics was not integrated into the Imperial

---

[33] See the indignant comments by M. Weber, *Wirtschaft und Gesellschaft* (Tübingen, 1972, 5th edn.), p. 573.

[34] The archive of the Gute Hoffnungshütte documents the role of Paul Reusch (Gutehoffnungshütte) and Springorum (Hoesch) in organizing resistance to the 1909 production survey, see HA 3001322/6.

[35] D. Krüger, *Nationalökonomen im wilhelminischen Deutschland* (Göttingen, 1983), pp. 117–141.

[36] GStA 1. HA Rep. 77 3853 no. 71.

[37] O. Nerschmann, 'Die Englische Produktionserhebung von 1907', *ASA*, 8 (1914/1915), pp. 53–71.

Statistical Office until 1902. However, its work lagged far behind that of its counterparts abroad.[38] Ten years of fruitless negotiations failed to persuade German employers to participate in a survey of industrial earnings.[39]

The exceptions to this pattern of resistance suggest the terms under which business *was* willing to cooperate in official enquiries. Before 1914 agriculture was by far the most intensively monitored sector of the German economy. And this was owed in large part to the cooperation of rural elites. The harvest estimates were based on information supplied by networks of local informants. Agricultural communities saw a direct benefit in having advanced information on the likely balance between demand and supply. When it was no longer in their interest to cooperate, as during the war, the local reporting network broke down. But even before 1914 the coverage of the food supply chain was far from complete. To assess the state of national supplies it was not enough to combine the harvest estimates with figures for imports and exports. One also needed to have information on the level of grain stocks held by merchants. However, the grain trade vigorously resisted any investigation of its holdings. Despite the anxieties of the Prussian military, this was enough to block statistical enquiries until July 1914.[40]

The other area of economic activity that was subject to detailed statistical monitoring was foreign trade. Here, too, it proved possible to recruit business support. Representatives of Germany's main trading firms sat on the consultative committee on trade statistics. As far as they were concerned the primary purpose of the trade statistics was to provide information on the success of German exporters and the competitive pressure of foreign imports. This interest was reflected in the extremely detailed commodity classification of German trade statistics. But trade statistics were also a political weapon. Gaining a place in the trade statistics was a first step towards defining an industry's identity and staking its claim for consideration by the political authorities.[41] The most striking instance of the statistical construction of an economic 'interest', was the mechanical engineering sector. 'Mechanical engineering' did not have the obvious coherence and economic size, which gave coal and steel such prominence in public life. It was through the action of their industrial association, the VdMA (Verein deutscher

[38] KSA, 'Gebiete und Methoden der amtlichen Arbeiterstatistik in den wichtigsten Industriestaaten', *Beiträge zur Arbeiterstatistik* 12 (Berlin, 1913).

[39] W. Gerß, *Lohnstatistik in Deutschland. Methodische, rechtliche und organisatorische Grundlagen seit der Mitte des 19. Jahrhunderts* (Berlin, 1977).

[40] BAP 15.01 18524 no. 89, Reichskanzler to Kriegsministerium November 1912.

[41] L. Boltanski, *The Making of a Class. Cadres in French Society* (Cambridge, 1987).

Maschinenbauanstalten), that machine builders and engineering firms of all kinds were brought together in a fragile coalition, to challenge the might of heavy industry.[42] For the VdMA, reform of the trade statistics was a priority. The association campaigned to have all the exports of German engineering grouped together under a single broad statistical category, rather than dispersed across a variety of archaic categories such as 'instruments and automata' or 'agricultural implements'. By recategorizing the statistics, the VdMA was able to demonstrate that mechanical engineering contributed more to German exports than either coal or steel. In future it should be the true economic importance of industries that decided policy. Statistical measurement, not influence-peddling in Berlin, would decide the issue.[43]

The entire repertoire of Imperial statistics was thus moulded around the interests of German business. Enquiries to which business objected were boycotted. And the threat of resistance was enough to forestall any statistical penetration into vast swathes of economic life. In those cases in which surveys did go ahead, business was able to impose limits on the range of questions or channel enquiries in directions favourable to their sectional interests. And it has to be said that the bureaucracy of Wilhelmine Germany showed little willingness to challenge this constraint. In 1911, the Statistical Office floated the idea of a general statistical law to enforce surveys even against the will of respondents.[44] Such laws were available to statisticians in a number of other countries.[45] However, the statistical establishment was divided. The Bavarian statistical office was satisfied that it could achieve better results by cooperating with the local business community.[46] The Prussian office, which had to deal with the most recalcitrant sectors of German industry, was more enthusiastic. But it was also painfully aware that coercive legislation stood no chance of passing the Prussian parliament, which

---

[42] VdMA, 'Statistik half, die Branche zu formen' (manuscript), pp. 2–3.

[43] In 1909 the liberal Handelsvertragsverein, which lobbied for low tariffs, proposed that trade policy should be decided by a committee weighted according to export shares, see D. Stegmann, *Die Erben Bismarcks. Parteien und Verbände in der Spätphase des Wilhelminischen Deutschlands. Sammlungspolitik 1897–1918* (Cologne, 1970), p. 137.

[44] GStA 1. HA Rep. 77 3853 no. 71, Minutes of the Meeting of German Official Statisticians 15.-16.2.1911, p. 69.

[45] In 1911 Norway was the only country with a general statistical law covering all surveys. Austro-Hungary and Belgium had general laws providing sanctions to enforce the larger censuses. The United States, Italy, Switzerland and France had general laws governing statistical surveys, which did not provide for sanctions. The only country with a practice similar to that of Germany was Great Britain, but even in Britain, the census of production was backed by strong legal measures. See GStA 1. HA Rep. 77 3853 no. 71, p. 69.

[46] GStA 1. HA Rep. 77 3853 no. 71, p. 70.

was packed with the interests most likely to oppose it.[47] The archaic, artisanal ideal type identified by Meerwarth no doubt reinforced the conservatism of German statistics. But, even if Wilhelmine officials had espoused a more innovative approach, it is unlikely that they would have got far. In the field of statistics, the Wilhelmine Empire was very far from being a 'strong state'.

Whilst the statistical bureaucracy thus accommodated itself with powerful business interests, it was also shaped by the particular traditions of the German civil service and the peculiar structure of the Bismarckian state. Above all it was constrained by the decentralized, federal constitution of the Reich. Federalism imposed severe limits on the range of economic questions that could be addressed by national government. Despite presiding over one of the most dynamic, industrializing economies in the world, the German nation-state created in 1871 possessed only the most rudimentary infrastructure of national economic administration.[48] The Reich, as the inheritor of the Zollverein, was restricted to the sphere of trade policy. The individual states making up the Empire jealously guarded the prerogatives of their local Ministries of Trade and Commerce. Other than the Reichsbank, there was no national agency with responsibility for the affairs of the economy as a whole. By the end of the century, German business was beginning to appeal for the creation of a national office. However, the Reich's civil service displayed a remarkably casual attitude towards the economy. In the late nineteenth century it was 'social policy issues' rather than 'economic' issues that dominated the political agenda. The term 'national economy' (Volkswirtschaft) entered the official language of the Reich only in the 1880s with the creation of a Department for National Economy in the Reich's Office of the Interior and Bismarck's initiative for a National Economic Council (Volkswirtschaftsrat). But this burst of bureaucratic enthusiasm did not last. The civil service department was soon swamped with social policy issues and in 1890 its title was changed accordingly. Bismarck's National Economic Council was still-born. Not until 1899 was a dedicated Department of National Economic Affairs finally established within the Reich's Office of the Interior. A truly independent administration for the national economy did not come into existence until World War I. There was thus little pressure from within

[47] GStA 1. HA Rep. 77 3893 no. 14, 'Niederschrift der Verhandlungen der Statistiker des Reichs und der Bundesstaaten zu Danzig vom 9.-13.6.1911', p. 12.
[48] W. Hubatsch, *Entstehung und Entwicklung des RWM 1880–1933. Ein Beitrag zur Verwaltungsgeschichte der Reichsministerien. Darstellung und Dokumentation* (Berlin, 1978) and F. Facius, *Wirtschaft und Staat die Entwicklung der staatlichen Wirtschaftsverwaltung in Deutschland vom 17. Jahrhundert bis 1945* (Boppard, 1959).

the Reich's bureaucracy for the production of more extensive economic statistics.

Federalism was also at the root of the financial difficulties that constrained government activity in Wilhelmine Germany.[49] The acceleration of the arms race and the escalation of social costs demanded higher spending. However, Prussia's inequitable political system brought enormous pressure to bear on any politician brave enough to suggest the need for a widening of the tax base. By the turn of the century, financial constraints were beginning noticeably to restrict the development of official statistics in Wilhelmine Germany. At the national level both budgets and staffing expanded. In 1913 the office employed 27 senior civil servants, 349 lower-grade permanent staff and 346 temporaries.[50] However, these resources were not sufficient to keep up with the rising costs of monitoring the expanding economy. The financial crunch was most severe in the member states which were responsible for the vast bulk of domestic statistical work, Prussia and Bavaria.[51] Of course, there is always an element of choice in any budget. Next to the costs of the arms race, official statistics were a trivial item. However, given the prevailing culture in the Reich's bureaucracy, statistics did not enjoy a high priority. In fact, in the decade prior to 1914, the Reich's Office of the Interior made statistics – symbol par excellence of government red tape – into a scapegoat for the financial crisis afflicting the Empire. State Secretaries trumpeted their successes in saving thousands of marks by cancelling the publication of statistics.[52] This was indicative of the general lack of appreciation for statistics shown by the hide-bound caste which dominated the upper reaches of the Reich's administration.[53] As Meerwarth himself acknowledged, the shortage of funds powerfully reinforced the conservatism of Germany's statistical establishment. Rather than pursuing exploratory 'research', senior statisticians found themselves having to concentrate on routine number-crunching.[54] Material constraints thus helped to widen the gulf

[49] P.-C. Witt, *Die Finanzpolitik des Deutschen Reiches von 1903 bis 1913. Eine Studie zur Innenpolitik des Wilhelminischen Deutschland* (Lübeck, 1970) and N. Ferguson, 'Public Finance and National Security: The Domestic Origins of the First World War Revisited', *Past and Present*, 142 (1994), pp. 141–168.

[50] E. Hölder and M. Ehling, 'Zur Entwicklung der amtlichen Statistik in Deutschland', in W. Fischer and A. Kunz (eds.), *Grundlagen der Historischen Statistik von Deutschland. Quellen, Methoden, Forschungsziele* (Opladen, 1991), pp. 15–31, p. 22.

[51] K. Saenger, 'Das Preußische Statistische Landesamt 1805–1934. Ein Nachruf', *ASA*, 24 (1935/1936), pp. 445–460.

[52] 'Statistik und Reichstag', *Der Tag* 133, 9.6.1911.

[53] R. Jaeckel, *Statistik und Verwaltung. Mit besonderer Berücksichtigung der Preussischen Verwaltungsreform* (Jena, 1913).

[54] R. Meerwarth, 'Die Berufs- und Betriebszählung im Deutschen Reich vom 12. Juni 1907 und ihre Literatur', *DSZ*, 5 (1913), pp. 97–106.

between contemporary economic thought and the practice of official statistics.

Given limited budgets, the agenda of Wilhelmine statistics could be expanded only if means were found to economize on the cost of existing surveys. The obvious place to look for cuts was the census. The census of 1907 was not just an intellectual failure; it was also an administrative albatross around the necks of Germany's statisticians. The giant survey overran its budget and processing the returns took much longer than expected. Work dragged on to such an extent that all plans for new statistics had to be cancelled, the fledgling Department of Labour Statistics being one of the most prominent casualties.[55] And here again federalism was the root cause of the problems.[56] The performance of the national system was limited by the performance of its largest and slowest element – Prussia. Though the design of the census questionnaire and the broad outline of the practical organization was agreed at the national level, the execution of the census lay entirely in the hands of the member states. The Imperial Statistical Office was restricted to a supervisory role. It resumed control only at the final editorial stage in the compilation of national figures. Given the lop-sided structure of German federalism, this meant that the vast burden of work fell on the severely underfunded Prussian office. It lagged years behind the smaller member states in the production of its results. Decentralization not only slowed up the completion of the census, it also introduced a large element of uncertainty. As Meerwarth had shown, the basic concepts of both the occupational and workplace censuses were imprecise and subject to arbitrary interpretation. This placed a premium on consistency. The decentralized system of processing virtually guaranteed that the categories were not uniformly applied. This became apparent when the national results for 1907 were finally compiled. The Länder returned wildly inconsistent figures for the agricultural workforce, skilled and unskilled industrial workers, the small-scale self-employed and home workers.

As far as the staff of the Imperial Statistical Office were concerned, the solution was obvious. Centralization would cut down costs, speed up processing and improve reliability. It would also allow the large-scale employment of the new-fangled Hollerith punch-card technology. Hollerith machines were actually used in the processing of the population

[55] BAP 39.01 506 no. 42, Zacker, Direktor of SRA/Arbeiterstat to Staatssek. Bauer, Reichsarbeitsamt 30.12.1918.
[56] GStA 1. HA Rep. 77 3853 no. 71, Minutes of Meeting of Statisticians 15.-16.2.1911 and GStA 1. HA Rep. 77 3853 no. 55, Prussian Statistisches Landesamt to Min. des Innern, 21.3.1911, pp. 9–10.

census of 1910 in Württemberg, Baden, Elsaß and Lothringen.[57] And the Imperial Statistical Office was in the process of mechanizing the trade returns.[58] Centralization and mechanization thus appeared to offer a way out of the statistical impasse.[59] However, in the context of Wilhelmine federal politics, such proposals were naive. The statistics of population size, occupations and workplaces were bargaining counters in the negotiations between the member states and the Reich over tax and trade policy. The influential statisticians of Prussia and Bavaria led a public outcry against the proposed centralization of the census. In the face of a concerted press campaign, the Reich's statisticians were forced to back down. Centralization was shelved. Even in 1925 the census was to be organized on the decentralized model.

IV

The intellectual conservatism identified by Meerwarth was one side of a triangle of forces constraining German official statistics in the prewar period. The opposition of German business and the bureaucratic inertia of the Wilhelmine State completed the geometry. The outbreak of war in 1914 smashed this conservative equilibrium.[60] The initial assumption was that the war would be short and would therefore require no economic planning. Statistics were an administrative dead-weight that could be dispensed with for the duration. The younger staff of the Reich's statistical offices joined the ranks. All but the core of basic statistical surveys were cancelled. Only a handful of prescient observers realised the risk of a long war and the need for urgent measures to maintain industrial production.[61] They found a spokesman in Walther Rathenau, the technocratic Director of AEG, one of the two giant

[57] GStA 1. HA Rep. 77 3893 no. 68, Minutes of Meeting of Statisticians 30.5.-1.6.1912, p. 45 and GStA 1. HA Rep. 77 3893 no. 151, Minutes of Meeting of Statisticians 29.-31.5.1913, pp. 21–29.
[58] *Festschrift zur 25. Jahresfeier der Deutschen Hollerith Maschinen Gesellschaft* (Berlin, 1935), pp. 68–69.
[59] For these proposals and the ensuing battle see GStA 1. HA Rep. 77 3853.
[60] The major source for the history of the Statistical Institute during World War I is the report, BAP 31.01 6031 no. 109, 'Das SRA in der Kriegswirtschaft. Kriegswirtschaft Bericht für das Reichsamt des Innern, Prof. Dr Spiethoff 25.9.1919'. This was intended as a contribution to an official history of the economic war effort to be compiled, on behalf of the Reich's Office of the Interior, by Professor Arthur Spiethoff. The history was designed to serve as a guide in case of future mobilization. The statisticians' report must therefore be read as a piece of advocacy. C. Lorenz, *Die Statistik in der Kriegswirtschaft* (Hamburg, 1936) provides an outsider's survey written with an eye to the next war.
[61] G.D. Feldman, *Army, Industry and Labour* (Providence, 1992, reprint) and L. Burchardt, 'Walther Rathenau und die Anfänge der deutschen Rohstoffbewirtschaftung im Ersten Weltkrieg', *Tradition*, 15 (1970), pp. 169–196.

corporations that had carved up the electrical engineering industry. With the cooperation of the military, Rathenau established an improvised system of controls to ensure the supply of raw materials to German industry. A year later Walther Rathenau described his rescue of the German war effort to the influential Berlin club, the Deutsche Gesellschaft. Significantly, he chose to begin his account with an anecdote about official statistics:

It was the middle of August [1914] . . . The first question facing us was the question of supply. We needed to know for how many months the country was supplied with essential materials. On this hung every measure. The opinions of industrialists contradicted each other and in some cases differed by a factor of ten.' 'I asked an important official agency: Is it possible to get statistics on this question? 'Certainly' I was told, 'such statistics can be made'. When? [Rathenau asked] 'In about six months'. And if I need the numbers in fourteen days, because the matter is urgent? To this, I received the reply: 'Then you will have to do without [the statistics].'[62]

In Rathenau's narrative this bureaucratic failure serves as a dramatic turning-point. The organization of the war economy could not be left to the existing state apparatus. Instead, Rathenau turned to the military. At the centre of his system stood the War Raw Materials Office (Kriegsrohstoffamt) attached to the Prussian War Ministry. It exerted loose control over a network of so-called War Corporations (Kriegsgesellschaften), which were in the hands mainly of managers on secondment from leading firms. Their principal task was to manage the acquisition and distribution of critical raw materials. This hybrid organization dominated the German industrial war effort in the first years of the war. Of course, the civil service was not entirely excluded. Later in his speech to the Deutsche Gesellschaft, Rathenau found space to acknowledge their role in providing the administrative underpinnings for his system. However, the initiative and energy came from the general staffs of German business and the officer elite. A new alliance was forged between the army and 'the productive nation', which marginalized the civil service bureaucracy.

As retold in anecdotes such as Rathenau's, the war represented a profound crisis of legitimacy for Germany's civil servants, a crisis that ushered in the revolution of 1918. Whereas the military continued to be held in high esteem by at least a large minority of the population, the civilian structure of the Wilhelmine State was bankrupt, literally and figuratively. It was rejected by both the elites and the wider population. Jürgen Kocka has aptly described the revolution as the product of an

---

[62] W. Rathenau, *Deutschlands Rohstoffversorgung* (Berlin, 1918), pp. 11–13.

'anti-administrative coalition'.[63] Of course, stories similar to Rathenau's were told everywhere in Europe.[64] Why was the German sense of crisis so acute? Was the Wilhelmine state any less competent than its allies and opponents? On the basis of comparative administrative history, there is reason to believe that the German home front was less well managed than in Britain and France.[65] In particular, the management of the food supply was disastrously botched, seriously undermining civilian morale. But the crisis of legitimacy that destroyed the Wilhelmine Empire was as much a product of disappointed expectations as of real failure. There can be little doubt that the gap between expectations and reality gaped wider in Imperial Germany than elsewhere. The performance of civil servants in Britain, France and the United States was certainly not flawless, but much less was expected of them. The national self-image was in no way damaged by the need for business men, trade unionists and other outsiders to take a hand in government. By contrast, the historic leadership of the strong state was one of the founding myths of the German nation.[66] When measured against this high standard the failure of the Wilhelmine civil service was undeniable. There was surely no country where the shock of wartime disillusionment was greater.

The fate of official statistics is emblematic of these wider political developments. The Imperial Statistical Office was cut off from the heart of the economic war effort. As Rathenau's initial enquiry had suggested, the management of the industrial economy demanded unprecedented volumes of information, far more than was available from the Statistical Office. But Rathenau's account also illustrated the way in which business mistrust of official statisticians extended into the war. The War Corporations under the instructions of the War Raw Materials Office collected vast quantities of statistics from the firms under their control. However, these were kept a closely guarded secret. The staff of Rathenau's corporations were drawn from the head offices and trade associations of German business. No more than before the war were they willing to allow outside interference. Within the shell of the state, German industry governed itself. The War Raw Materials Office provided the official front. During the war, the Deutsche Statistische

[63] J. Kocka, *Klassengesellschaft im Krieg. Deutsche Sozialgeschichte 1914–1918* (Frankfurt, 1988, 2nd edn.), p. 178.

[64] C. Wrigley, 'The Ministry of Munitions: An Innovatory Department', in K. Burk (ed.), *War and the State. The Transformation of British Government 1914–1919* (London, 1982), pp. 32–56 and J.F. Godfrey, *Capitalism at War. Industrial Policy and Bureaucracy in France 1914–1918* (Leamington Spa, 1987).

[65] J. Winter and J.-L. Robert (eds.), *Capital Cities at War: Paris, London, Berlin 1914–1919* (Cambridge, 1999), pp. 305–341.

[66] J. Caplan, *Government Without Administration. State and Civil Service in Weimar and Nazi Germany* (Oxford, 1988), p. 1.

Gesellschaft (German Statistical Association, DSG) – the professional association of German statistics – sought to document the statistical contribution to the war effort.[67] With the help of the civilian authorities it compiled a complete annual register of all wartime surveys. However, the core of the war effort, the organization of German industry, would not be included. On instructions from the War Raw Materials Office, the War Corporations refused to provide even cursory information on their statistical activities. Industrial statistics remained a matter for business not official statisticians.

Though Rathenau's organization dissociated itself from German official statistics, it could not escape the problems which had bedevilled statistical surveys before 1914. The improvised organization headed by the Raw Materials Office was staffed by a self-selected group of managers, who were far from representative of German industry.[68] In most branches it was only the largest firms that could afford to second their staff to the corporations, or who were invited to do so. The entire system was shot through with conflicts of interest. To build relations of trust between the War Corporations and their industrial constituencies, efforts were made to separate data-gathering from the functions of requisitioning and allocating raw materials. In effect, Rathenau's organizations were forced to invent their own distinct organizations of 'official statistics'. However, this was never enough to overcome the suspicion of the excluded majority. And as resources ran increasingly short, the potential for conflict multiplied. They reached their height in 1917, when the industrial organizations embarked on a brutal programme of rationalization, involving the closure of thousands of smaller, less efficient plants. Faced with this challenge, the system of voluntary reporting broke down altogether. Prompt and reliable statistical returns could be obtained only by coercion.

Given the breakdown of trust between the authorities of the wartime state and German civil society, the need to provide a compulsory foundation for statistical enquiries could no longer be avoided. The skirmishes of the prewar period escalated into pitched battle. The first priority at the beginning of the war was to requisition the available

---

[67] 'Die amtliche Statistik und der Krieg, insbesondere im Deutschen Reiche', *DSZ*, 8 (1916), pp. 1–18.

[68] A. Schroeter, *Krieg – Staat – Monopol: 1914–1918. Die Zusammenhänge von imperialistischer Kriegswirtschaft, Militarisierung der Volkswirtschaft und staatsmonopolistischer Kapitalismus in Deutschland während des ersten Weltkrieges* (Berlin, 1965), H. Cron, 'Die Kriegswollwirtschaft', in Reichsarchiv, *Kriegswirtschaftliche Organizationen* (Potsdam, 1932, manuscript), Heft 5 Serie II, O. Goebel, *Deutsche Rohstoffwirtschaft im Weltkrieg. Einschließlich des Hindenburg-Programms* (Stuttgart, 1930) and A. Müller, *Die Kriegsrohstoffbewirtschaftung 1914–1918 im Dienste des deutschen Monopolkapitals* (Berlin, 1955).

stocks of raw materials and food. Obligatory surveys of food stocks marked out the baseline for the rationing system. Through a series of ad hoc measures these obligatory surveys were progressively expanded from agriculture to the entire economy.[69] Penalties were steadily increased to match the profits that beckoned on the black market. To provide a check on the accuracy of statistical returns, firms and individuals were required to keep detailed accounts. Finally, in the summer of 1917 the powers of enquiry were codified and dramatically expanded with the introduction of the so-called Auskunftspflicht (Decree on the duty to provide information). In the context of the massive Hindenburg armaments programme and the drive to shut down inefficient capacity, this decree was designed to ensure the 'subordination of the individual economic unit to the whole economy'.[70] The innovation was twofold. First, the decree empowered unrestricted enquiries. Firms might be asked to report not only stocks of raw materials but also current levels of production, past levels of output and the future capacity of their plants. Secondly, the decree for the first time arrogated to the Reich the right to empower compulsory enquiries throughout the national territory, independently of the member states.

Predictably, this enormous extension of central powers did not go unopposed. The Bavarian and Saxon authorities responded with indignation. However, the Prussian War Ministry waved their protests aside.[71] Far more serious was the opposition of German business. By 1917, the planning authorities, despite the close involvement of certain major corporations, were increasingly at odds with the wider business community. The shape of the postwar economy was at stake.[72] Both industry and commerce were growing weary of the intrusive discipline of the war effort and demanded a return to genuine industrial 'self-government'. By contrast, Rathenau and Moellendorff, the original architects of wartime self-government, advocated the continuation of planning into the peace. They envisioned a new system of 'German socialism', emerging from the wartime symbiosis of state and industry. To suspicious businessmen, the new Auskunftspflicht, with its wide-ranging administrative powers, was a sign of things to come. The

---

[69] The gradual extension of the legal measures is chronicled in BAP 30.01 film 22607/ 8017.

[70] BAP 31.01 6042 no. 33, Staatssek des Innern circular 25.6.1917, draft 'Auskunftspflicht Decree' discussed at meeting on 23.6.1917.

[71] BHStA MH 15516 and BAP 31.01 6042 no. 50, Bundesrat Nr. 195 Session 1917, Helferrich Stellvertretender Reichskanzler to the Bundesrat, 30.6.1917 and BAP 31.01 6042 no. 53, 'Bekanntmachung über Auskunftspflicht 12.7.1917'.

[72] F. Zunkel, *Industrie und Staatssozialismus. Der Kampf um die Wirtschaftsordnung in Deutschland 1914–1918* (Düsseldorf, 1974).

centralization of economic knowledge was the first step towards economic dictatorship. In the last year of the war the Auskunftspflicht became an object of bitter contention between the military authorities and the representative body of German industry, the so-called War Committee of German Industry (Kriegsausschuß der deutschen Industrie). The industrialists accused the military of seeking to 'acquire powers over industrial firms that completely suspend the rights of the proper owner'.[73] The Decree, with its unlimited powers of enquiry, threatened German industry with 'the disclosure of its entire intellectual property'.[74] It could serve only 'to provide advocates of state socialist doctrines with insight into the particular circumstances of [individual] firms'.[75] But, despite this broadside, the planning authorities were unrelenting. Statistical enquiries were essential to the management of the war economy. And, what was more, the Auskunftspflicht might well be required beyond the end of the hostilities.

The willingness of the War Office to insist on the Auskunftspflicht, in the face of industrial protests, certainly illustrates the growing alienation between business and the bureaucratic managers of the wartime planning apparatus. However, given the balance of political influence in the final stages of the war, the battle over the Auskunftspflicht was of largely symbolic importance. In practice, it was only small firms in civilian industries that were at risk of prosecution. To major military contractors, the Decree presented no real threat. Despite the flurry of anxiety over 'state socialism', the hold of heavy industrialists over the Army High Command remained unbroken. The sternest critics of industry and the toughest advocates of cost control were kept silent. Rathenau and his friends might dream of a Spartan regime of German socialism, but so long as the Wilhelmine Empire remained in existence, they presented no real threat to the profits of big business.

V

The war was a process of creative destruction. It brought into the open the latent struggle over the control of economic information. It also broke the deadlock within the Wilhelmine state. The Länder were weakened. The Reich's bureaucracy was finally forced to establish a comprehensive, national system of economic administration. In the

[73] BAP 31.01 6042 no. 72, Kriegsausschuß der deutschen Industrie to Staatssekretär des Innern 3.8.1917, p. 2.
[74] BAP 31.01 6042 no. 115, Kriegsausschuß der deutschen Industrie to Staatssekretär des Innern 8.10.1917, p. 3.
[75] BAP 31.01 6042 no. 172, Kriegsausschuß der deutschen Industrie to Reichstag, 25.3.1918, pp. 1–2.

management of the industrial war economy, Rathenau's organization forcibly centralized power. And a similar process of centralization also took place in civilian government. In 1916 a Kriegsernährungsamt (War Food Office) was finally established to organize the national food supply. In 1917 the Reichswirtschaftsamt (Reich's Economic Office) was set up to make national preparations for the transition to a peace-time economy. And finally in 1918, as one of the last administrative acts of the Empire, the demands of the labour movement were satisfied with the creation of a Reichsarbeitsamt (Reich's Labour Office). All three national agencies were immediately faced with the problem of acquiring adequate supplies of statistical information. First in the field, the Food Office established its own Economics Department. It was responsible for coordinating the wartime price control measures and liaising between the Food Office and the official statisticians.[76] As we shall see, the staff of this first national economic agency were to have a formative influence over the future of German economic statistics. During the war, however, they fought a losing battle.

The administration of agriculture and food supplies was the cardinal weakness of the German war effort. In wartime, Germany's situation was bound to be precarious.[77] Industrialization had led to a heavy dependence on imported food. Self-sufficiency was attainable only through drastic adjustments in patterns of production and consumption. The situation was rendered impossible very early on in the war by the short-sighted failure of military and industrial planners to appreciate the vital significance of agriculture. To make matters worse, the Reich's Office of the Interior was criminally slow to realize the need for comprehensive state regulation. Only in 1916 was the War Food Office established with the necessary powers to control production, purchasing and distribution.[78] Statistics played an inglorious role in this administrative fiasco. The inability of the Reich's statisticians to arrive at an accurate assessment of the nation's food stocks symbolized the bungled administration of the German war effort.[79] Statistics were fundamental to the entire 'system' of food planning. The target level of requisitioning from each administrative district was based on the annual harvest estimate. At the other end of the supply chain, the allocation of food to each municipality was based on estimates of

[76] BAP 36.01 26 no. 2, Präs. des Kriegsernährungsamtes to Staatssekretär des Reichs-schatzamtes 26.8.1916.
[77] A. Skalweit, Die Deutsche Kriegsernährungswirtschaft (Stuttgart, 1927).
[78] A. Roerkohl, Hungerblockade und Heimatfront. Die kommunale Lebensmittelversorgung in Westfalen während des Ersten Weltkriegs (Stuttgart, 1991).
[79] Haselberger, 'Erntefeststellung und Bewirtschaftung des Getreides', ASA, 11 (1918/19), pp. 50–68.

population. Without reliable and accurate data, the system was doomed. And the failure of the statistical system was no surprise. The farming population was well aware that the statistical reports determined the level of state exaction.[80] As a result, all returns made by farmers or by any other reporters with close ties to the local community were chronically unreliable. The initial estimate for the 1915 harvest was 25 per cent below the actual out-turn, leading to an unnecessary reduction in food rations. Attempts to correct this downward bias failed to produce a reliable estimate in the next year. For the grain harvest of 1916 the Imperial Statistical Office produced three estimates, diverging by as much as 13 per cent. The final figure was an overestimate.[81] And there was no improvement in the following year. The worst discrepancies in 1917 were as large as 20 per cent. In the final years of the war, military commandos had to be despatched to check the accuracy of the statistical returns. But, by 1918, this was not enough to prevent collapse. Colloquially, the reports of the Food Office became known as the 'tables of lies' (Lügentabellen).[82]

While the War Food Office struggled from day to day, the Reich's Economic Office and the Reich's Labour Office looked to the future. The task of the Reich's Economic Office was to prepare plans for the return to peacetime conditions. It owed its existence to the German business lobby, which hoped to use the Office as a bulwark against the 'state socialists'. To define a common business platform, the new Office began a process of extended consultation involving the major trade associations. Plans were drawn up to secure the necessary raw materials for key industries and to prepare for the revival of consumer industries. German reparation demands were much to the fore. To assist in these investigations, the Imperial Statistical Office was reassigned to the Economic Office. This move heralded a bright future for economic statistics. However, in 1918 the Economic Office was not the only organization with an interest. The war had enormously increased the influence of Germany's trade unions. On their prompting, the Reich had, as we saw above, established a national Labour Office, as a counterweight to the business lobby. It came too late to take any active part in the war. However, in the confused aftermath of the war the Labour Office moved aggressively to acquire a statistical capacity of its own. Backed up by the political clout of the trade union leader, Carl Legien,

---

[80] BAP 31.01 6031 no. 109, 'Das SRA in der Kriegswirtschaft', p. 17.
[81] BAP 36.01 25 no. 15, 'Sitzung des Vorstandes des Kriegsernährungsamts vom 21.5.1917'.
[82] BAP 39.01 film 37081/10550, 'Referat Dr Platzer bei der Besprechung über die Reorganisation der Statistik des Deutschen Reiches 13.8.1920', pp. 31–32.

it wrested control of the Department for Labour Statistics away from the Statistical Office.[83] For the Economics Ministry and the Statistical Office this was a major setback; labour statistics were the only branch of official statistics to have done well out of the war.

Before 1914 the Department for Labour Statistics had been the step-child of official statistics, squeezed by the shortage of resources and obstructed by business. The demands of war gave it a new significance. Manpower was the essential basis of the war effort. However, in August 1914 no system existed for planning its allocation. That autumn, the unfettered recruitment of farm labour threatened to leave the harvest rotting in the fields. More waste followed in the winter as hundreds of thousands of seasonal workers were thrown into unemployment. By the early summer of 1915 the Reich had finally established a national system of labour market reporting.[84] A long-held ambition of German social reformers was finally fulfilled. Out of this embryonic system emerged the more comprehensive regulations of the Auxiliary Service Law (Hilfsdienstgesetz), which universalized conscription as of December 1916. From the summer of 1917 labour exchanges across the country were tied into a single chain of command, that ended with the Labour Statistics Department in Berlin. For the trade unions the Department was thus of strategic importance in their bid to entrench the influence of organized labour within the postwar state. A comprehensive system of employment statistics was the first step towards a wider role for the state in managing the labour market. For the Statistical Office the amputation of the Department of Labour Statistics was a setback. But, the removal of an important branch of 'social statistics' set the stage for the reorientation of German statistics around the concerns of the new Reich's Economic Office.

VI

Despite the new importance of statistics in wartime government, the war sparked surprisingly little intellectual debate about the future of German official statistics. In light of the mystique, which surrounds the German war economy, this may come as something of a surprise. Rathenau's system of industrial organization was the archetype for the twentieth-century idea of economic planning. His system appeared to vindicate the possibility of comprehensive state control. Lenin certainly viewed Rathenau's system of wartime industrial controls as a warrant for the practical possibility of centralized planning. In Germany and

[83] BAP 39.01 506.
[84] BAP 31.01 6031 no. 109, 'Das SRA in der Kriegswirtschaft', p. 9.

elsewhere, academics were inspired to flights of fancy about the future of state socialism. In the war's aftermath German-speaking economists fiercely debated the possibility of 'socialist calculation'.[85] Was it possible to elaborate a new form of economic rationality independent of the price system? Assuming that a socialist government had the power to dictate production, what were the criteria it would follow? Even if it were possible to establish a clear hierarchy of social priorities, how could one weigh the relative costs of different programmes? These were the abstract questions raised by the experience of the war economy, which were to be debated amongst economists throughout the interwar period.

If the gulf between official statistics and economic theory had been wide before 1914, it became even wider in the course of the war. The analysis of the German war economy in terms of ideal types of rational planning stood in stark contrast to the wartime experience of German statisticians. Historians who have looked behind the impressive facade of Rathenau's organization have found only a chaotic proliferation of organizations, without central direction or plan. In neither the civilian nor the military sector of the economy was there an overarching scheme for the allocation of crucial raw materials, labour or transport capacity. In any case, if central planning had in fact been attempted, the Imperial Statistical Office would have had little to contribute. We have seen the limits of its prewar repertoire. And the official history of German statistics during the war mentions not a single statistical initiative that involved conceptual innovation. Given the conservative intellectual attitude prevailing among German official statisticians this is hardly surprising: there was much bickering about who should take responsibility for the many disasters of wartime statistics. But there was nothing in the periodicals of the German Statistical Association to compare with the feverish debate over the future organization of the German economy. Economists debated the pros and cons of planning, and drew up grand schemes that implied an entirely new order of empirical economic knowledge. Meanwhile, the establishment of German official statistics hoped for nothing more than a speedy return to prewar 'normality'.

The only statistical author in the German-speaking world to have embraced the radical vistas opened up by the war was an Austrian – Karl Pribram. During the war Pribram published a number of articles in which he heralded a fundamental break with the prewar order of

[85] K. Tribe, *Strategies of Economic Order. German Economic Discourse 1750–1950* (Cambridge, 1995), pp. 140–168.

liberalism and sought to spell out the fundamental implications for official statistics.[86] According to Pribram:

The mirror image of the liberal view of the state is, of course, the citizen's holy right to freedom, designed to protect him, to render him invisible to the curious gaze of officials. Can there be any more forceful expression of the fundamental demand that the state should respect the special interests of the individual, than the state's willingness to do without any obligation [on the citizen] to supply it with information?[87]

It was this liberal self-restraint that had excluded official statisticians from vast tracts of social and economic reality. In particular, it had made it impossible for them to penetrate the sphere of production. It was liberalism, therefore, that was to blame for the failure of official statisticians in wartime. According to Pribram, the war was an opportunity to shake off these shackles. In the post-liberal future, the individual would be subordinate to a new state that would be empowered to make compulsory enquiries into every aspect of social and economic life. A new statistical law would impel a profound extension of official statistics. The basis would be created for a genuinely totalizing overview of economy and society.

In practice, the Kriegsamt (War Office) was the closest approximation to a control centre for the German war economy. And the closest the Kriegsamt ever came to assembling a total overview of the German war economy were the botched censuses of 1916 and 1917. The need for a complete overview of the home front first became apparent with the introduction of comprehensive food rationing in 1916. The last census of population dated to 1910. These figures would have been out of date even if the war had not added to the movement of the population. Given the difficulty of carrying out a comprehensive enumeration in wartime, the Statistical Office proposed a simple head count.[88] However, at the last moment, the so-called Scientific Commission of the Kriegsamt intervened, insisting that it also needed information on current and prewar occupations for purposes of labour force planning. The Commission was originally appointed to write a celebratory history of the war economy. But under the aggressive leadership of the right-

[86] K. Pribram, 'Die Zukunft der amtlichen Statistik', *DSZ*, 9 (1917), pp. 129–138 and responses in the same journal. For Pribram's perspective on later developments in German statistics see the illuminating article K. Pribram, 'European Experiences and New Deal Statistics', *Journal of the American Statistical Association*, 30 (1935), pp. 227–236.

[87] K. Pribram, 'Die Zukunft', p. 132.

[88] BAP 31.01 6031 no. 109, 'Das SRA in der Kriegswirtschaft', pp. 5–13. There are no sources from the War Ministry or the Scientific Commission against which to check the story told by the Reich's statisticians.

wing economist Max Sering it aspired to a wider and more practical role.[89] It sought to establish itself as the statistical Directorate of the War Ministry. On its behest the simple head count was transformed into a full-scale occupational census. The official statisticians knew this was entirely unrealistic, but they were powerless to resist the imperious demands of the Scientific Commission, which could invoke the full authority of the Prussian Ministry of War.

The result was a disaster. The hastily extended census was carried out on 1 December 1916. After much double-checking, the population returns were made usable for the War Food Office. However, the occupational data were worthless. By the early summer of 1917, Sering's Scientific Commission had lost interest. Work on the occupational returns was stopped. Instead, Sering and the Commission decided that what they in fact needed was not an occupational survey but an overview of Germany's industrial establishments and their workforce. And, this time, Sering decided to side-line the official statisticians altogether. The Commission set about independently planning its own census. As part of the bureaucratic empire of the Kriegsamt, Sering operated under a cloak of secrecy. The Imperial Statistical Office and most of the rest of the statistical establishment first got wind of the Commission's activities from newspaper reports.[90] In any case, the wartime census of workplaces was doomed to failure. A complete census of industrial workplaces was a hugely ambitious project that would normally have required many years of intense preparations. The questionnaires, rushed out to German firms in August 1917, were hopelessly imprecise. The official statisticians were left with their Schadenfreude and a vast collection of uncounted returns mouldering in the cellars of the Imperial Statistical Office.

VII

The war blew away the world described by the centennial volume of the Imperial Statistical Office. The Kaiser was dethroned. The very survival of the German nation-state was cast into doubt. The Wilhelmine Empire collapsed. And the Statistical Office was convulsed by its own catastrophic loss of legitimacy. The attempts by the Prussian Ministry of War to carry out two censuses against the advice and without the

---

[89] For the conflicts between Spiethoff and Sering see BAP 15.01 8987 and 8993. For the membership of Sering's Kommission see BAP 15.01 8987 no. 35.

[90] Lorenz, *Die Statistik in der Kriegswirtschaft*, p. 20. The Prussian office may have had some access to Sering's Kommission, see BAP 31.01 6031 no. 109, 'Das SRA in der Kriegswirtschaft', p. 4 and *DSZ*, 8 (1917), pp. 209–214, 255–260.

assistance of the official statisticians marked the nadir of Wilhelmine official statistics. The statisticians had lost control of the centrepiece of nineteenth-century official statistics. More fundamentally, the war shattered the image of the German economy enshrined in the centennial volume. The war vindicated the prophets of high capitalism. In the struggle for survival the small businesses lauded by the propagandists of the *Mittelstand* had proved disposable. It was corporate Germany with its capital, technology and labour that dominated the war economy. In November 1918 the forces of capital and labour were to prove themselves more durable even than the German state itself. The pressing task facing Germany's official statisticians was to define a role for themselves in relation to this new reality. New surveys were required to satisfy the interests of Germany's new rulers. Old surveys needed to be redesigned. And, if they were to have any future at all, Germany's statisticians had to find new ways of extracting information from the recalcitrant interests of civil society.

2   The Republic's new numbers, 1918–1923

The Weimar Republic has long suffered the condescension of posterity. The left traditionally bewailed the unfinished revolution. Timid Social Democrats were accused of having brutally choked off the popular movement of 1918–19.[1] The established order survived. The development of a truly democratic political culture was stunted at birth. Reactionary elites maintained an unbroken grip on such major institutions as the army, the judiciary and large parts of the civil service. In German business the authoritarian Wilhelmine style prevailed, making democratic control of the economy impossible, either by the state or the workforce. The Republic was doomed to counter-revolution. In recent years, comment from right-wing historians has been no less critical. In their view, Weimar's inexperienced political elite failed to confront social conflict.[2] Fearful of working-class unrest, the first governments of the Republic drifted irresponsibly into ruinous hyperinflation. The infrastructure of bourgeois life was sacrificed to short-term political expediency. And fiscal incontinence did not end with the inflation in 1924. Unjustifiable social spending, facilitated by foreign loans, progressively tightened the financial constraints on the German state.[3] When the world tumbled into depression in 1929, Chancellor Brüning had no option but to pursue a harsh policy of expenditure cuts and price deflation. His undemocratic style of government was a logical response to Weimar's factious and ineffective parliamentary system. Some form of authoritarianism, if not the savage dictatorship of the Nazis, was inescapable.

Since the 1970s a generation of scholarship has challenged these one-sidedly critical interpretations. From a variety of perspectives historians have sought to reconstruct the enormously difficult circumstances of the

[1] S. Haffner, *Die Deutsche Revolution* (Munich, 1979) and R. Rürup, *Probleme der Revolution in Deutschland 1918/19* (Wiesbaden, 1968).

[2] For a recent statement of this view see N. Ferguson, *Paper and Iron. Hamburg Business and German Politics in the Era of Inflation, 1897–1927* (Cambridge, 1995).

[3] H. James, *The German Slump. Politics and Economics 1924–1936* (New York, 1986).

Republic's birth, challenging simplistic attributions of blame from either left or right.[4] The refusal by the Social Democrats to make 'revolutionary' change, reflected above all their democratic desire to avoid civil war. The failure to halt the slide into hyperinflation had as much to do with the intransigence of German business as the recalcitrance of labour. It was not the working class that withheld precious tax revenue and hard currency from the impoverished state. The ill-fated stabilization in 1924 was largely on terms set by German capitalists. The radical programme of fiscal redistribution was halted in its tracks. Nevertheless, the Weimar state was not paralysed. Recent work on the 'golden twenties' has emphasized the formidable 'modernity' of much government activity in the Weimar Republic.[5] The German state apparatus was by no means the exclusive preserve of backward-looking traditional elites. Nor was the new public expenditure simply a 'blind', incremental response to the pressure of special-interest groups. The Weimar welfare state and labour administration embodied radical, technocratic schemes for social rationalization. The crisis of the Weimar Republic was not the product of a reactionary backlash. It resembled far more the crises suffered by welfare states since the 1970s. It revealed the tensions inherent within the reformist project of the modern welfare state. The following chapters seek to place the history of economic statistics in Weimar Germany as part of this still-contested narrative.

I

The driving force behind economic statistics in the Weimar Republic was the Reich's new economic administration. The new Republic established the national economy for the first time as a regular object of government. Of course, the greater degree of 'state intervention' under the Weimar Republic is a cliché of the literature. However, talking simply in terms of an increased share of government expenditure in national income obscures the qualitative changes that took place within the German state and in its relations with civil society. The German state in the aftermath of World War I suffered a profound crisis of authority and emerged from this crisis transformed. The most dramatic symptom was, of course, the collapse of the Empire and its replacement with a Republic. Simultaneously, a 'soldiers' strike' paralysed the mili-

---

[4] For a magisterial summary of the revisionist literature see G.D. Feldman, *The Great Disorder. Politics, Economics, and Society in the German Inflation, 1914–1924* (Oxford, 1993).

[5] D. Peukert, *Die Weimarer Republik. Krisenjahre der Klassischen Moderne* (Frankfurt, 1987) and for a critical discussion Y.-S. Hong, *Welfare, Modernity, and the Weimar State, 1919–1933* (Princeton, 1998).

tary arm of the German state. Encroachment from both East and West threatened Germany's external boundaries. Separatist movements flourished on the frontier with France, threatening to tear the Reich apart from within. Meanwhile, the integrity of the national economy was jeopardized by the collapse in the value of the national currency, raising the ominous prospect of a foreign economic invasion. Into the vacuum left by the disintegration of the Wilhelmine Empire rushed the powerful forces of German civil society. With the terrifying spectre of Bolshevism before them, Germany's industrialists and their counterparts in the official trade unions organized themselves in the so-called Zentrale Arbeitsgemeinschaft (Central Working Group), or ZAG.[6] As the immediate representatives of the 'working nation', the ZAG claimed the right to govern the national economy according to its own rules. At their most radical the members of the ZAG denied the institutions of the new Republic any independent role in economic policy. Industrial self-government would dispense with the state. Given the reduction of Germany's military power, self-governing industry would emerge as the pre-eminent representative of the nation and the fulcrum of both domestic and foreign policy. It soon became clear, however, that the ZAG's authority was as precarious as that of the political authorities. The ZAG was never a legitimately constituted body. It was unrepresentative of business. Furthermore, the business associations and the trade unions soon discovered that their hold over their constituencies was fragile. To maintain credibility with their membership they were increasingly tempted to break the fragile truce between capital and labour on which the authority of the ZAG was founded. In a society on the edge of civil war the problem of representation was not limited to the state.

Over the course of the early 1920s, the politicians and the state bureaucracy gradually reasserted themselves. But this was no longer the same political elite or the same state structure as before the war. There was a fundamental centralization of power at the level of the nation-state. Money and information now began to flow to Berlin. In the economic sphere a new national system of economic administration was assembled out of the embryonic structures created in the final stages of the war. The Reich's Offices for Economic Affairs, Labour and Food were transformed into Ministries of the new Republic. In this field of government there was no possibility of continuity with the Wilhelmine past for the simple reason that there had been no national system of economic administration before 1914. The new Republic took on

---

[6] E. Kolb, *Die Weimarer Republik* (Munich, 1984), p. 14 and G.D. Feldman and I. Steinisch, *Industrie und Gewerkschaften 1918–1924. Die überforderte Zentralarbeitsgemeinschaft* (Stuttgart, 1985).

fundamentally new responsibilities for managing the national economy. Within six days of his appointment as Reich's President Friedrich Ebert, the new head of state, requested monthly reports on the state of the economy from the Reichswirtschaftsministerium (Reich's Ministry for Economic Affairs, RWM) and the Agriculture Ministry.[7] The contrast with the Wilhelmine era could hardly have been more stark.

The RWM in the immediate aftermath of World War I was a Ministry in turmoil.[8] Amid the general confusion, Wichard von Moellendorff, one of the leading advocates of 'state socialism', managed to establish himself as second in command. Under his influence the RWM turned against the business lobby to which it owed its existence. Moellendorff hoped to exploit the revolutionary situation to develop his scheme for a state-managed economy (Gemeinwirtschaft). However, his grandiose project found little support in the ruling coalition of Social Democrats and Liberals. By June 1919 both Moellendorff and 'his' Minister Rudolf Wissell had resigned. The RWM was taken in hand by the Social Democratic Minister for Agriculture, Robert Schmidt, and his Secretary of State, Professor Dr Julius Hirsch. Hirsch was a veteran of the wartime food administration. Formerly a Professor at the Cologne business school, he had cut his teeth on problems of price control.[9] With Hirsch and Schmidt came a selection of other veterans from the War Food Office, most notably Ernst Wagemann, the new head of official statistics.[10] Between 1919 and 1922 the RWM was to promote a policy of productivism, prioritizing output, employment and consumption over price stability. Unlike Moellendorff, Hirsch was no doctrinaire advocate of state control, but to revive the economy he did not shrink from direct regulation and high state spending. Not surprisingly, given his background, Hirsch was also a strong advocate of economic statistics.

For German official statistics the interventionist RWM opened a new era. In the aftermath of the Revolution the Imperial Statistical Office was renamed the Statistisches Reichsamt (Reich's Statistical Office,

---

7 P.C. Witt, 'Bemerkungen zur Wirtschaftspolitik in der "Übergangswirtschaft" 1918/19, zur Entwicklung von Konjunkturbeobachtung und Konjunktursteuerung in Deutschland', in D. Stegmann, B.J. Wendt and P.-C. Witt (eds.), *Industrielle Gesellschaft und politisches System. Beiträge zur politischen Sozialgeschichte. Festschrift für F. Fischer zum 70. Geburtstag* (Bonn, 1978), pp. 79–96.

8 H.G. Ehlert, *Die Wirtschaftliche Zentralbehörde des Deutschen Reiches 1914 bis 1919. Das Problem der 'Gemeinwirtschaft' im Krieg und Frieden* (Wiesbaden, 1982), p. 155.

9 On Hirsch's role in the war food agency see BAP 36.01 14, 15, 16, 25, 26. On his spell at the Reich's Ministry of Economic Affairs see G.D. Feldman, *The Great Disorder*, pp. 165–188.

10 On Wagemann see chapter 3. Another recruit was H. Staudinger, *Wirtschaftspolitik im Weimarer Staat. Lebenserinnerungen eines politischen Beamten im Reich und in Preußen 1889 bis 1934* (Bonn, 1982), pp. 17, 37–38.

SRA) and the break with the Wilhelmine past was more than titular. Over the following decade German official statistics were reshaped into a recognizably modern form of economic knowledge. The most spectacular phase of innovation began in 1924, and will be the subject of chapter 3. It was initiated by Professor Dr Ernst Wagemann who had served with Hirsch at the Food Office and was appointed by him in 1919 to manage statistical affairs at the RWM. Wagemann forged a tie between official statistics and a novel form of economics known as Konjunkturforschung (business-cycle research). The argument of this chapter is that Konjunkturforschung was preceded by a less spectacular but nonetheless influential episode of statistical innovation, beginning in the immediate aftermath of World War I. This first wave of reform can be understood as a direct response to the problems of the Wilhelmine era discussed in chapter 1. Though less dramatic than the initiatives instigated after 1924, this early stage of reform was to have a profound and lasting impact on the development of German statistics. Both projects initiated in the first half of the 1920s had in common that they sought to make German official statistics into a tool for monitoring the capitalist economy. In this sense they were two branches of the same intellectual current originating in the mid-1890s. They both represented a fundamental break with the artisanal conception of the economy that had informed Wilhelmine statistics. However, the two projects of reform differed in the way in which they conceptualized capitalism. Konjunkturforschung adopted a holistic approach to understanding the economic process, basing itself on the metaphors of the equation of exchange and the circular flow (Kreislauf). By contrast, the reforms initiated in the immediate aftermath of World War I were informed by a more concrete, organizational vision. They aimed to register statistically the basic building block of the modern economy: the capitalist firm. The relationship between these two projects, both emerging from the turmoil of World War I, will form a thread running throughout the chapters of this book.

II

The RWM's plans for a reform of German official statistics were announced at an inter-ministerial conference in Berlin on 13 August 1920.[11] The meeting drew an impressive crowd. The Ministry, as the parent of the Reich's Statistical Office, sent no less than ten representatives, including State Secretary Hirsch and two Ministerial Directors.

[11] BAP 39.01 film 37081/10550 RWM, 'Besprechung über die Reorganisation der deutschen Reichsstatistik im RWM 13.8.1920'.

All the branches of the Reich's new national economic administration were represented – the Reich's Ministry for Food and Agriculture, the Reich's Labour Ministry and the Reich's Labour Administration – as was the Prussian Ministry for Commerce. Both the Foreign Office and the Reich's Health Office were on the list. For official statisticians this was an unmissable event. The Reich's Statistical Office was represented by its President, Dr Ernst Delbrück, and by the up-and-coming young statistician Dr Hans Wolfgang Platzer. The Presidents of all the Länder Offices were in attendance, as was the head of Berlin's municipal office. This gaggle of officials mingled with representatives of some of the most important interest groups in Weimar politics. Karl Brandt of the ZAG represented the joint interests of business and labour. From the business side there were the Association of German Iron and Steel Industrialists (Verein deutscher Eisen- und Stahlindustrieller) and the Association of German Engineers (the Verein deutscher Ingenieure, VDI). Not to be outdone the Federation of German Trade Unions (Allgemeiner Deutscher Gewerkschaftsbund, ADGB) sent its chairman, Carl Legien, a well-known statistical enthusiast. This list by itself gives some indication of the importance attached to statistics by Weimar's ruling elite. Never before had there been such an assembly. In the Second Empire, statistics were a technicality well beneath the dignity of senior civil servants. Now, they concerned some of the most influential men in the land.

Hirsch set the agenda by openly acknowledging the failure of Germany's existing official statistics: 'the need for a reform of the Reich's statistics [has] been clear for a long time.'[12] The State Secretary did not mince his words: 'During the war the Reich's statistics were unable to meet the demands placed on them by the central authorities.'[13] Alongside social policy, which had been a preoccupation of policy-makers since the 1870s, the German nation-state was now faced with the task of formulating a national economic policy. This was a novel responsibility faced under extremely difficult circumstances. And it demanded a new type of governmental knowledge: national economic statistics. Hirsch's speech underlined the energetic, experimental mood prevailing at the RWM and the SRA. His outspoken criticism of the wartime performance of German statistics clearly indicated the break with the past. There was no hallowed Wilhelmine tradition for the national economic administration of the Weimar Republic to draw on. The new apparatus of national economic government was not an extension of some long-

---

[12] BAP 39.01 film 37081/10550 RWM, 'Besprechung', p. 3.
[13] BAP 39.01 film 37081/10550 RWM, 'Besprechung', p. 3.

standing tradition of state interventionism. On the contrary, it was created as an answer to the disastrous failure of the Wilhelmine state.

The President of the Reich's Statistical Office, himself a hangover from the Wilhelmine era, made no response to this challenge. Ernst Delbrück was one of the less inspiring offspring of his illustrious clan.[14] He was close to retirement and was to play no constructive role in the statistical affairs of the Weimar Republic. Instead, Dr Platzer, the most promising young statistician in the Reich's Office, took the lead. Platzer was to be remembered by a later generation as the first of a new breed.[15] In the early years of the Republic he was the driving force behind the new agenda of economic statistics. Earlier in the year Platzer had launched the new periodical of the Statistical Office, a fortnightly bulletin entitled *Wirtschaft und Statistik* (Economy and Statistics, *WuS*). In August 1920, Platzer held the comparatively lowly rank of Regierungsrat. However, within a year he was to be promoted to a Directorship with control of his own Department, only one step away from the Presidency. Following Hirsch, it was Platzer who set out specific proposals for a new, national system of economic statistics.[16] What was required were national figures indicating the price level, the level of wages, the production of key industries, the state of Germany's foreign trade and the Reich's financial accounts.[17] The state of German agriculture was a matter of life or death. However, given the level of resentment and mistrust in the countryside, there was simply no hope of obtaining reliable information by conventional statistical means. Government would have to rely on more forceful administrative enquiries.

The situation in agriculture dramatically illustrated a more general problem. As Platzer emphasized, the new statistical initiative needed to be more than an official effort. The war had forced into the open the latent conflict over the control of economic information between the state and business. Unlike their Wilhelmine predecessors, Weimar's statisticians did have at their disposal the Auskunftspflicht. But this continued to be bitterly contested. Questions were asked in the Reich-

---

[14] Delbrück headed the Statistical Office between 1913 and 1923. However, he receives no mention in the official history, G. Fürst, *Bevölkerung und Wirtschaft 1872–1972* (Stuttgart, 1972), nor does he appear in the *Deutsche Biographische Enzyklopädie* (Munich, 1998).

[15] A. Jacobs, 'Hans Wolfgang Platzer obit.', *ASA*, 46 (1962), pp. 192–193 and A. Jacobs, 'Der Weg bis zum Ende der Reichsstatistik', *Jahrbücher für Nationalökonomie und Statistik*, 185 (1971), pp. 289–313.

[16] BAP 39.01 film 37081/10550, 'Referat Dr Platzer bei der Besprechung über die Reorganisation der Statistik des Deutschen Reiches, im RWM am 13.8.1920'.

[17] Platzer might also have mentioned labour statistics but these were disputed between the RWM and the Labour Ministry and were kept off the agenda in August 1920. See BAP SRA 31.02 3573 and BAP 39.01 film 33203/896, film 37081/10550 and 10422.

stag.[18] Trade associations petitioned and lobbied against the Decree.[19] Individual businessmen appealed against convictions under its provisions and sought to obtain judgements fundamentally constraining its practical application.[20] The Reich took these signs of discontent seriously, but stuck doggedly to its new powers.[21] They were a vital element in the fragile system of price controls and trade regulations with which Weimar's economic administration sought to retain some measure of control over the national economy.[22] The RWM encouraged agencies empowered under the Decree to make use of its penalties.[23] When convictions were successfully appealed, the Länder pursued the cases through the higher courts.[24] The powers of the wartime Auskunftspflicht were renewed on 13 July 1923 under the emergency powers granted to the Reich's government to deal with the Ruhr crisis and the final burst of hyperinflation.[25] But whatever its political significance, the Auskunftspflicht was not a practical means of obtaining reliable or timely statistics. The national authorities desperately needed the collaboration of German business. Platzer therefore appealed directly to both business and labour for their cooperation in the SRA's new enquiries. In the Weimar Republic the Reich's statisticians would have to accustom themselves to haggling for information. Reverting to the standoff of the prewar period was not an option.

In the early 1920s, the need for information was too acute. The outlines of the economic calamity facing the Weimar Republic were clear enough. Industry and trade were undergoing a drastic process of demobilization. Supplies of coal and fuel were at critically low levels. There was a desperate need to reintegrate Germany into world trade, to revive commerce and to stave off starvation. The Allies were making exorbitant demands for reparations. Meanwhile, a fiscal crisis was threatening to suck the country into hyperinflation. But in Berlin the

[18] BHStA MH 15516 nr. 3086, Reichstag 1. Wahlperiode 1920/21. Anfrage Nr. 1236 Sikovich 29.11.1921.
[19] BHStA MH 15516, *Sächsiche Staatszeitung* 263 11.11.1921 and BAK R 43 I/1173.
[20] BHStA MJu 15548, *Bayerischer Kurier* 21 21.1.1920, 'Handel und Volkswirtschaft, die Auskunftspflicht gegenüber den Preisprüfungsstellen'.
[21] BHStA MH 15516, RWM circular 17.2.1921.
[22] For the role of Auskunftspflicht in price control see BHStA MH 15516, Bayerische Landespreisstelle (Zahn) to Bayerisches Staatsmin. für Handel Industrie und Gewerbe 18.11.1921. For its role in trade controls see BAK R 43 I/1173, A. Goldschmidt, *Revisionsbefugnis und Ausfuhrsperren* (1922).
[23] BHStA MH 15516, RWM circular 24.12.1920.
[24] BHStA MJu 15548, Der Staatsanwalt bei dem Landgericht München I to Bayerischen Staatsmin. der Justiz 22.10.1920 and Der Staatsanwalt bei dem Landgericht München I to Bayerischen Staatsmin. der Justiz 24.1.1921.
[25] K.E. Thomä, *Auskunfts- und Betriebsprüfungsrecht der Verwaltung, seine rechtstaatlichen Grenzen* (Heidelberg, 1955), pp. 17–18.

ministries lacked any precise information as to the state of the economy. The early presidential reports contained virtually no useful information. They simply listed the administrative actions of the ministries over the preceding month. The state of the economy remained an unknown. Even in 1920 the RWM could provide only impressionistic comments on a limited range of industries. The report for the 'Chemical Industry' in February 1920 consisted of a single paragraph patched together with scraps of information about the match industry![26] Economic histories of the period, with their neat tables of statistics, convey an entirely misleading impression of the state of contemporary information. Ironically, the Reich's Statistical Office is in part to blame for this misperception. After the event it compiled a helpful handbook of data on the inflation years, which has become a standard reference.[27] In 1920, however, the vacuum of knowledge was almost complete. There was no working indicator of inflation, the national trade statistics were in disarray, the unemployment figures were regarded with suspicion even by the Labour administration, the level of employment, production and earnings were unknown.[28] The Weimar Republic was attempting to make economic policy for the first time, without knowledge of the basic parameters.

III

The programme outlined by Platzer at the meeting in August 1920 was no more than a common-sense minimum. However, to informed observers it was clear that it involved a major break with Wilhelmine tradition. This was most clear with respect to the census, the traditional centrepiece of German official statistics. Apart from the disastrous experiments of the war years, there had been no general survey of occupations and workplaces in Germany since 1907. A new census to establish the parameters of economic life within the new, restricted territory of the Reich was urgently needed. If the fiascos of wartime were not to be repeated, this would require a collective mobilization of Germany's statistical resources. In general, after World War I, it was the Reich that took the lead in the organization of German official statistics. However, the organization of the census followed Wilhelmine tradition.

---

[26] BAK R 43 I/1147 no. 102, RWM report on economic situation in February submitted to the Reichskanzlei 25.3.1920.

[27] SRA, *Zahlen zur Geldentwertung in Deutschland 1914 bis 1923* [Sonderheft 1 zu *Wirtschaft und Statistik*, Bd. 5] (Berlin, 1925).

[28] On the unreliability of unemployment data see H. Knortz, 'Der Arbeitsmarkt in der frühen Weimarer Republik. Ein Beitrag zur "Vollbeschäftigungsthese" der Inflationsforschung', *Jahrbuch für Wirtschaftsgeschichte* (1997), pp. 119–134.

It was a federal affair. Fortunately for Platzer and the reformers in Berlin, they could count on the support of the Prussian Statistical Office, where Rudolf Meerwarth now occupied a key position.

The census of the 1920s was the first opportunity for the critics of Wilhelmine statistics to make their mark. Platzer and Meerwarth were exact contemporaries.[29] They both had graduated from the doctoral seminar of Lujo Brentano in 1905. They both joined the Imperial Statistical Bureau in 1906. And they cooperated in pushing through the reforming agenda that had been spelled out by Meerwarth in his monograph on economic statistics published in 1920.[30] The artisanal conception of the economy embodied in the Wilhelmine censuses was obsolete. If there had been any residual doubt at the turn of the century, World War I had decided the issue. 'High capitalism' was triumphant. The economy of small-scale agricultural and artisanal production was a thing of the past. Skilled, artisanal labour was no longer the basic building block of the economy. The fundamental dynamic force within the twentieth-century economy was the capitalist firm. It was within the firm that labour, capital and technology were harnessed in systematic pursuit of profit. It was within large, capitalist corporations that a new division of labour was taking shape, an organization that rendered the artisanal model obsolete. Of course, capitalist business was not completely dominant. Different forms of economic organization coexisted. There was still a substantial constituency of small-scale producers, who remained bound within traditional, craft norms. For them, trade constituted a way of life rather than simply a means to the end of profit. However, in economic terms these elements were of dwindling importance. If official statistics were to register the new economic reality, they had to be reconstructed around the ideal type of the modern capitalist enterprise. As Meerwarth had stressed since before the war, this was essential if official statistics was to re-establish a dialogue with contemporary economics.[31] But this was no mere academic matter. Whatever the statisticians might think or say, the power of organized capital and labour was inescapable in the aftermath of World War I. It weighed heavily on the German state. Continuing to ignore the reality of organized, capitalist power would condemn official statistics to irrelevance. Impelled by this grand historical logic, Platzer and Meerwarth

---

[29] On Meerwarth see chapter 1. On Platzer see obit. by Alfred Jacobs in *ASA*, 46 (1962), pp. 192–193 and the 70. birthday note in *ASA*, 33 (1949), pp. 397–399.

[30] R. Meerwarth, *Einleitung in die Wirtschaftsstatistik* (Jena, 1920).

[31] R. Meerwarth, 'Die Berufs- und Betriebszählung im Deutschen Reich vom 12. Juni 1907 und ihre Literatur', *DSZ* 5 (1913), pp. 97–106.

embarked on a campaign to redefine the basic concepts of the German census.[32]

In reorganizing the census of workplaces it was the Reich's Office that took the initiative, represented by Platzer and his junior Dr Walter Grävell. As was discussed in chapter 1, the censuses of both 1895 and 1907 had been based on the ideal type of the artisanal workplace, the self-contained workshop. As Meerwarth's investigations had revealed, the application of this concept to an increasingly complex industrial economy yielded increasingly confused results. Many large firms simply ignored the instructions. Those firms that were willing to undertake a technical sub-division of their activities were provided with no specific guidelines on how to proceed. The result, as far as the reformers were concerned, was an ambiguous mess. The solution pushed by the Reich and Prussia was to reorganize the workplace survey around the economic unit of the firms. It was in the head office of the capitalist firm that power and control were concentrated. The economic unit of the firm was, at least in principle, unambiguously defined and would thus yield more consistent results. It would also provide a true image of the agglomeration of economic power. Using information gleaned from business reports, trade association literature and academic accounts the statisticians would devise a map of the basic forms of vertical and horizontal integration in German industry.[33] Combined categories would be provided to take account of the giants of German industry, the 'integrated producers of coal and steel', 'heavy engineering corporations' and 'integrated textiles firms'.

The Prussian Office proposed a parallel set of changes to the organization of the workplace census.[34] As we have seen, the prewar occupational census had matched the workplace survey in its artisanal conception of occupation. And, like the artisanal concept of the workshop, the craft concept of occupation as vocation was losing its grip on reality in the years before the war. High capitalism was revolutionizing the world of work. And in the wake of World War I, the artisanal model was even less applicable. Technical change, deskilling, increased mobility of employment and mass unemployment rendered the vocational concept of occupation unworkable. In future, Meerwarth argued that the census should simply register a person's occupation on the day of the count. Furthermore, it was necessary to make a clear distinction

---

[32] For the following discussion of the census see the material in BAP 39.01 10559 and 10560.

[33] BAP 39.01 10560, SRA, 'Volks, Berufs und Betriebszählung, Das Gewerbeschema' 4.9.1922.

[34] BAP 39.01 10559, Meerwarth, 'Grundsätze für die Aufstellung des Berufsverzeichnisses Anlage II. Entwurf B. Neues Schema', April 1921.

between personal occupation and industry of employment. Again, this had been a subject of confusion in 1907. The solution proposed by Meerwarth was obvious, but its implications were far-reaching. Each worker would in future be identified both in terms of personal occupation and industry of employment. Personal skill was no longer identical with industry of employment. The map of skills was no longer a guide to the structure of production.

The changes pushed by the Reich's Statistical Office and the Prussian Office were highly controversial in statistical circles. In particular, they were opposed by Friedrich Zahn. In the confrontation between Zahn and the 'new men', there was something of a generational conflict. As we have seen, Zahn had been personally responsible for the organization of the censuses of both 1895 and 1907. He was rewarded with the Directorship of the Bavarian Statistical Office, a prestigious post previously held by such luminaries of the Historical School as Rümelin and von Mayr. World War I and the ensuing transformation of German political life threatened Zahn's career trajectory. The new Republic centralized power and money at the national level. Statistical information was bound to follow. Given the straitened circumstances of Bavaria and the ambition of the new Reich's ministries, the Munich office began to look like a dead-end. In the early 1920s, Zahn made no secret of his ambition to return to the service of the Reich.[35] Given his seniority, there was only one job for him in Berlin, the Presidency of the Reich's Office. And according to the standards of the Wilhelmine era, there was no one better qualified than Zahn. However, would those be the criteria on which the succession to Delbrück was decided? In light of the fierce criticism of Wilhelmine statistics voiced by Hirsch, Platzer and Meerwarth, there was reason for doubt. For Zahn, the battle over the census thus took on a vital personal significance. The reforms advocated by the Reich and Prussia threatened radically to devalue the work of his youth and to jeopardize his future.

At the meeting of August 1920, Zahn sought to position himself as the advocate of a new statistics capable of calming the waters of democratic politics. Statistics were required to wean Germany's new rulers away from dogma and to sharpen their sense of reality. 'This was the only way to achieve the desirable goal of economizing politics and depoliticizing the economy.'[36] However, in his confrontation with Platzer and Meerwarth over the census, he pursued a doggedly tradi-

---

[35] BAP 39.01 506 no. 9, Walter Abelsdorf to Staatssekretär RAa 3.1.1919 and Bayerisches Hauptstaatsarchiv MInn 79425, Zahn to Bayerisches Königliches Staatsmin. des Innern 30.7.1919.

[36] BAP 39.01 film 37081/10550, 'Besprechung', p. 7.

tional line.[37] In his view their programme of reform was based on a caricature of Wilhelmine statistics. Much of what was now being presented as innovation had been discussed and rejected a generation ago. Meerwarth's critique of the occupational census was misplaced. The survey of personal occupations was never intended to provide information on the composition of each industry's workforce. That was the job of the workplace census. Meerwarth's proposal to ask workers to declare both their personal occupation and industry of employment confused the two types of enquiry. It was straightforward in theory, but would never work in practice. Characteristically, Zahn doubted whether the majority of the workforce could be trusted to supply reliable information on their industry of employment.[38] In opposing the changes to the workplace survey, Zahn enlisted the support of the other Länder offices. From a federal point of view, the Wilhelmine surveys had the advantage of presenting a decentralized image of the German economy. The proposal to count firms as economic units threatened to radically redraw the economic geography of Germany. The losers would be the South German states. The largest German firms tended to site their head offices in Berlin, whereas production was located in the low-wage South. A strictly economic definition of the firm would attribute a disproportionate share of economic activity to Prussia. The Southern statistical offices thus lobbied for a compromise conception of the plant as an integrated physical unit. This would allow local production facilities to be counted separately from the administrative headquarters that controlled them. An elaborate network of paper traces would satisfy Meerwarth and Platzer's desire to count economic units, allowing dispersed facilities to be agglomerated into a single firm.

Throughout 1919 and 1920 the statistical establishment withheld final approval from Platzer and Meerwarth's plans. On the organization of the workplace survey, the strength of the Länder lobby was too strong to be ignored. A compromise was finally reached involving a combination of spatial and economic definitions of the workplace unit.[39] However, on the occupational census, it was the intervention of the interest groups and the RWM that decided the issue. At the meeting of official statisticians in Erfurt in October 1920, the representative of the ZAG spoke in favour of Meerwarth's scheme. What the industrial

[37] The argument began at the Erfurt meeting of statisticians in October 1920, and then continued in Coburg in June 1921, Göttingen in October of the same year and Magdeburg in September 1922, see BAP 39.01 10559 and 10560.

[38] BAP 39.01 10560, Beratungen des Ausschusses für die Volks-, Berufs- und Betriebszählung in Coburg 14.-15.6.1921, p. 9.

[39] BAP 39.01 10560, Besprechung des Ausschusses für Volks-, Berufs- und Betriebszählung in Magdeburg am 15.-16.9.1922.

relations system needed to know was the number of workers in each industry.[40] This information could not be obtained from the existing occupational census. Zahn's condescending claim that workers could not be expected to provide reliable information on their industry of employment was out of touch with reality. The advent of collective bargaining and more formal employment practices rendered Wilhelmine experience obsolete. Through the use of formal wage scales, workers were now perfectly familiar with their industrial affiliation.[41] In the spring of 1922, the Reich's Ministry of Economic Affairs weighed in to decide the issue.[42] State Secretary Hirsch wrote personally to the Bavarian government expressing his regret at Zahn's opposition to the proposed changes.[43] Not only did his opposition undermine the authority of the national census, it was futile. The changes were necessitated by fundamental changes in economic organization, which meant 'that the economy is given its peculiar structure less by the composition of occupations than by the composition of its firms'.[44] The issue was finally settled at the Magdeburg statistical meeting in the autumn of 1922. There was to be no return to the artisanal conception of the economy that had for so long dominated the central institution of German official statistics. Personal occupation and industry of employment would be separated in all cases. Conservative continuity, personified by Friedrich Zahn, was defeated. With Delbrück's retirement imminent, the stage was set for further radical change at the Reich's Statistical Office.

IV

From the point of view of the professional community, the census was undoubtedly the major item on the agenda in August 1920. However, the industrial parties and the ministries had other priorities. Most urgent was the demand for statistics of earnings and prices. These were vital to the regulation of the emerging system of industrial relations. In Britain and the United States they had been collected as a matter of routine since before World War I. By contrast, the statisticians of the Weimar Republic had to scramble to make good Wilhelmine neglect.

---

[40] BAP 39.01 10560, Verhandlungen des Statistikerausschusses in Erfurt 25.-26.10.1920, p. 7.
[41] BAP 39.01 10560, Beratungen des Ausschusses für die Volks-, Berufs- und Betriebszählung in Coburg 14.-15.6.1921, p. 12.
[42] BAP 39.01 10559, SRA memorandum for Coburg meeting 10.6.1921.
[43] BAP 31.01 20361, no. 56 RWM, Hirsch to the Regierung des Landes Bayern 8.4.1922.
[44] BAP 31.01 20361 no. 74 RWM, Hirsch to Zahn 2.2.1922.

The new Republic had neither an official national index of the cost of living, nor any reliable indication as to the level of industrial earnings.

Demands for a survey of earnings in the Reich had been made in the Reichstag as early as the 1880s.[45] For years prior to 1914, the Department for Labour Statistics, including the young Dr Meerwarth, engaged in long-winded discussions with German metal industrialists in the hope of establishing a system of wage statistics.[46] But this proved fruitless; the industrialists refused to supply any information that might serve as ammunition for the Social Democrats. During the war the Imperial Statistical Office, on its own initiative, began to improvise a system of wage statistics based on a sample of a few hundred cooperative firms. These gained wide currency despite their suspect reliability.[47] The end of the war provided the opportunity to produce something more authoritative. In early 1919 the Labour Statistics Department established an 'archive' of collective wage agreements.[48] However, the relationship between the rates of pay fixed in collective contracts and actual earning in industry remained obscure. A sample survey of earnings was the only technically satisfactory solution. This was to become a test case for the new collaboration between the Reich's Statistical Office and the ZAG. The original plan was to carry out a simultaneous survey of earnings and the cost of living in December 1919.[49] Meetings with the ZAG began in August. The cost of living survey went ahead as planned. However, owing to foot-dragging by the ZAG and protests from the Finance Ministry, the earnings survey was delayed. Finally, in January 1920, despite the concerns about cost, agreement was reached on a vast survey. It was to cover the wages and salaries earned by each individual employee in no less than 10,000 workplaces.[50] Down to the last detail this was a matter of corporatist compromise, including the provision that every individual return should be counter-signed by the works council of the firm.

The creation of an official index of the cost of living followed a similar

[45] F. Huhle, *Statistik als ein Erkenntnismittel der Wirtschaftspolitik* (Jena, 1938), p. 12.

[46] W. Gerß, *Lohnstatistik in Deutschland. Methodische, rechtliche und organisatorische Grundlagen seit der Mitte des 19. Jahrhunderts* (Berlin, 1977), pp. 29–30.

[47] BAP 39.01 10668 no. 14, SRA Report on Wage and Price Statistics to RAM 9.8.1919, p. 2. See the expressions of interest in BAP 39.01 film 32893 no. 25, 27 and 159.

[48] BAP 39.01 10668 no. 218, Präs. SRA to RAM 25.11.1919. Interested parties were forced to actually visit the premises of the Statistical Office, see BAP 39.01 10668 no. 227, DIHT to RAM 5.12.1919.

[49] BAP 39.01 10668 no. 29, 'Kommissarische Besprechung' 5.8.1919.

[50] BAP 39.01 10669 no. 92, SRA circular to SLa 2.2.1920. For a technical discussion see R. Scholz, 'Lohn und Beschäftigung als Indikatoren für die soziale Lage der Arbeiterschaft in der Inflation', in G.D. Feldman, C.-L. Holtfrerich, G.A. Ritter and P.-C. Witt (eds.), *Die Anpassung an die Inflation* (Berlin, 1986), pp. 278–322.

pattern. It was the Prussian military in 1912 who had first taken the initiative in demanding a minimal system of national price statistics. But the Länder were not able to agree on a common set of standards before 1914.[51] At the end of the war, the issue could no longer be dodged. The pay bargaining system was increasingly centralized and the Reich's Labour Ministry could not do without an authoritative guide to price movements.[52] Interest in an official cost of living index both within the state bureaucracy and amongst the wider public was intense.[53] Statisticians inside and outside government responded by producing a bewildering array of price statistics and indices. Local index numbers appeared for Berlin, Magdeburg, Leipzig, Cologne, Nürnberg, Mannheim and other major industrial towns.[54] By 1922 a municipal statistician commented: 'not without justification one speaks of index number mania . . . Such numbers, . . . have shot out of the ground like mushrooms after a mild summer's rain, and the volume of comment on index numbers, their value, or otherwise, in the specialist press, in daily newspapers and in the associational literature, not to mention what is said at public meetings, has become quite unmanageable.'[55] For the Labour Ministry the proliferation of competing indices was a problem in its own right. The Reich needed to restore order to what was becoming a chaotic scene.

What was required was an up-to-date official figure for the Reich as a whole. Lacking all experience of price enquiries, the SRA made a slow start. For four months, in the late summer and autumn of 1919, the Reich's statisticians, the Ministries and the representatives of labour and business puzzled over the mechanics of the new survey. The main problems were to choose a representative sample of reporting towns, to decide on the goods that were to be included in the index and to allocate weights to each item in the basket.[56] Finally, on 18 November 1919 the Reich's Statistical Office despatched copies of the official questionnaires to the Statistical Offices of the Länder.[57] The survey was to cover the prices of the most important foodstuffs, the cost of fuel for heating and lighting and rents. For lack of any more up-to-date information, the weighting scheme was based on surveys of working-class budgets taken

[51] GStA 1. HA Rep. 77 3893 no. 101–220.
[52] BAP 39.01 10668 no. 3, RAM report on Tarifamt und Lohn (Preis-) Statistik, 31.7.1919.
[53] See the requests for information from Ministries, firms and interest groups in BAP 39.01 10668 no. 142–152 and BAP 39.01 10658 no. 145–146 and no. 212.
[54] BA 39.01 14–17.
[55] BA 39.01 15 no. 13, *Mitteilungen des Statistischen Amtes der Stadt Leipzig*, NF, Heft 4, p. 4.
[56] BAP 39.01 10668 no. 14, 45, 57, 103.
[57] BAP 39.01 10668 no. 145, SRA to SLa 18.11.1919.

in 1907. The questionnaires were to be completed by all towns with more than 10,000 inhabitants, slightly over 600 in total. The local magistrates were to report the prices as of 10 December 1919 to the Statistical Office of their Land. To guard against accusations of fraud, the returns from the municipal officers were to be counter-signed by local committees representing employers and labour in each town. The aim was to plug the price reporting system into the local corporatist networks which had grown up during demobilization.[58] This procedure for agreeing the return was vital, since the overriding priority at the municipal level was to obtain a consensual basis on which to make local wage adjustments. The Länder Statistical Offices were given the job of checking the returns and compiling regional aggregates. The results were to be transmitted to Berlin by 28 January 1920. By early February 1920 the Reich's Statistical Office was in possession, for the first time, of a national figure for the cost of living. The survey was then repeated for 10 February 1920 and monthly thereafter.[59] But despite enormous public interest,[60] questions in the National Assembly[61] and pressure from the interest groups[62] the Labour Ministry refused to allow the price figures to be released.[63] It was not finally convinced of the reliability of the survey until August 1920 when the national price figures for February 1920 were released to the German public.[64] It was not until April 1921 that the SRA was able to publish an up-to-date monthly index of the national cost of living based on the prewar standard.[65] According to the so-called Reichsindex the cost of living stood at 13 times its prewar level![66] The first disastrous phase of inflation thus went unrecorded in the Reich's statistics.[67]

[58] R. Bessel, *Germany After the First World War* (Oxford, 1993), pp. 110–111.

[59] BAP 39.01 10669 no. 135, SRA to SLa 29.1.1920 and BAP 39.01 10658 no. 5, RAM to SRA 15.5.1920.

[60] See the requests for information from employers in BAP 39.01 10669 no. 237, BAP 39.01 10658 no. 1, 16, 19, 94.

[61] BAP 39.01 10669 no. 221, *Stenographische Berichte der Nationalversammlung*, 152. Sitzung, 9.3.1920, p. 4786.

[62] BAP 39.01 10658 no. 4, Vereinigung der Deutschen Arbeitgeberverbände to RAM 7.4.1920.

[63] See the reply of the Ministry to the National Assembly, BAP 39.01 10669 no. 221, *Stenographische Berichte der Nationalversammlung*, 152. Sitzung, 9.3.1920, p. 4786, and the Employers' Federation, BAP 39.01 10658 No 4, RAM to Vereinigung der Deutschen Arbeitgeberverbände 15.5.1920.

[64] BAP 39.01 10658 no. 98, SRA to RAM 10.8.1920 and no. 108 and 109, RAM, Press Release 'Teuerungsstat' 25.8.1920.

[65] *WuS* 1 (1921), 1, 20.1.1921, p. 20.

[66] *WuS* 1 (1921), p. 170.

[67] Quite by contrast with the view expressed in S.B. Webb, *Hyperinflation and Stabilization in Weimar Germany* (Oxford, 1989), p. 10.

V

The publication of the Reichsindex satisfied one of the major objectives set out by Platzer and Hirsch in August 1920. An authoritative official index of the cost of living and a survey of earnings were important additions to the new repertoire of official economic statistics. And at the meeting there appeared to be no disagreement about the other priorities. All present – officials, trade unions, industrialists and academics – concurred with Platzer's basic agenda.[68] Legien expressed the enthusiastic support of the trade union movement for the plan to carry out surveys of earnings. And even the representative of heavy industry signalled his willingness to cooperate in government data-gathering. Economic statistics appeared to be a consensual objective of Weimar's ruling elite. In practice, however, this was far from the truth.

The plans for extensive surveys of industrial earnings ran into obstacles from the start. In fact, by the time of the meeting in August 1920 the first attempt to collect data on earnings had already ended in failure. Though the ZAG had approved the questionnaire and the procedure for the earnings survey, major employers across Germany mounted a concerted boycott. A list of recalcitrants compiled by the Prussian statistical office included many of the giants of German industry: GHH (steel and engineering), Benz und Cie (engineering), Gebr. Siemens und Co. (electrical engineering), Hansa-werke (shipbuilding), Friedr. Klöckner (engineering), Simson und Co. (engineering) and practically all of the major heavy industrial corporations of the Ruhr.[69] In March 1920 the government was forced to resort to the wartime Auskunftspflicht to enforce the survey. This made it possible to pursue firms through the courts. However, under inflationary conditions, the inevitable delay rendered the returns worthless. The first results for the February survey began to trickle out of the Reich's Statistical Office only in late November 1920.[70] As the Reich's Association of Industry pointed out gleefully, such statistics were of little more than historic interest.[71] Plans were drawn up for a second attempt. To provide effective powers of enforcement, the Reich's administration even embarked on the arduous process of passing a law specifically to enforce wage statistics. At every stage, the employers and their political allies resisted the bill. It did not

---

[68] BAP 39.01 film 37081/10550, 'Besprechung', pp. 14–16.
[69] BAP 39.01 10670 no. 89, 'Verzeichnis der Firmen die auf das Rundschreiben des preussischen SLa v. 4.2.1920 . . . und das Erinnerungsschreiben v. 24.3.20 nicht geantwortet haben.'
[70] The first sector to be evaluated completely was construction, see BAP 39.01 10671 no. 9, SRA to RAM 15.11.1920.
[71] BAP 39.01 10670 no. 81, RDI to RAM 2.6.1920 and no. 82, RAM to RDI 24.6.1920.

finally reach the Reichstag until the summer of 1922, by which time inflation had accelerated to such an extent that a complex and slow-moving survey stood no chance of providing useful information.[72]

Inflation allowed German industrialists to escape the bothersome surveys of earnings, and the fiscal crisis that was the root cause of the inflation killed the census. By the autumn of 1922, when the arguments over the design of the census had been finally resolved, it was virtually impossible to provide sensible costings for a project that would extend over a number of years. The rate of inflation was too high and too erratic. The first estimate in 1920 had been 50 million. By the autumn of 1922 this had risen to 1 billion marks and the figure went up by the day.[73] These cost increases were real. During the inflation, the price of unskilled labour and paper, the two basic ingredients for any census, increased substantially in relative terms. The financial situation of the Länder was precarious and it was they who would have to pay for the data-processing. In any case, the expense of the census was only half the problem. The German economy was in flux. The precious census results would be out of date before they could be processed, let alone published. There was no prospect of producing information of any practical value. In December 1922 the decision was taken to postpone the census until stability had returned. Dr Walter Grävell, who was serving as Platzer's assistant, recounted the sorry story in the official bulletin of the German Statistical Association.[74] Given the apocalyptic circumstances, Grävell's conclusions were dramatic. The days of giant, nineteenth-century censuses were over. The costs were too high and the procedures too ponderous. Only by means of new-fangled techniques such as sampling could official statisticians hope to keep up with events. As we shall see, this hostility towards the census was to stay with Walter Grävell for the rest of his career.

The Reichsindex of the cost of living, which was based on rudimentary sampling, did finally begin to appear in April 1921. However, it too was to prove extremely fragile. It was vulnerable to criticism precisely because it provided only a very partial representation of working-class expenditure. In particular, it did not include the cost of clothing. The more complete indices compiled by municipal statisticians revealed this to be a particularly volatile component of inflation.[75] The Reichsindex thus came under attack for understating the true rate of increase in the

---

[72] BAP 39.01 10676 no. 241, RWM to RAM 9.6.1923.
[73] BAP 39.01 10561, RAM circular 27.12.1922.
[74] W. Grävell, 'Die Not der Statistik und die Repräsentativ-Methode', ASA, 13 (1921/1922), pp. 345–353.
[75] WuS 1 (1921), pp. 20–21.

cost of living, biasing wage settlements in favour of the employers.[76] The Statistical Office was fully aware of these lacunae. However, again, it was business that was the problem. The German textile trades refused to assist the statisticians in selecting a representative working-class wardrobe.[77] In February 1922 the Reich was forced to initiate a survey of textile prices without the cooperation of the trade.[78] The textile association even called upon its members to make false returns.[79] The statisticians persevered and from May 1922 the cost of clothing was finally included in the Reichsindex.[80] As the trade unions had predicted, the index was found to be almost 10 per cent higher.

In the third quarter of 1922, however, these slow-moving adjustments were overtaken by events. Annualized inflation, as measured by the Reichsindex, leapt to 467 per cent and then shot up to 1030 per cent in February 1923. The accuracy of the figures was now a secondary issue. Immediate information was the overriding concern. Private agencies and local statistical offices responded by publishing fortnightly or even weekly indices.[81] But the Labour Ministry refused to give permission for the Reich's Office to follow suit;[82] the labour market administration was terrified of accelerating the spiral of wages and prices. In both March and May 1923, lulled by the illusion of a temporary stabilization in prices, the Reich's cabinet voted to stick with the monthly publication of the Reichsindex.[83] Right up to the final astronomic burst of inflation in the summer of 1923 the Statistical Office was forced to stick to a monthly rhythm. The Reichsindex was thereby reduced to an irrelevance. It was mid-June 1923, before the Labour Ministry finally

---

[76] BAP 39.01 10659 no. 162, Gewerkschaftsbund der Angestellten to RAM 10.9.1921.

[77] See the discussions with industry representatives in BAP 39.01 10658 no. 41, 42, 87–93 and BAP 39.01 10659 no. 185.

[78] BAP 39.01 10659 no. 218, RWM to RAM 19.12.1921, BAP 39.01 10660 no. 23, Sitzung im SRA 5.1.1922, BAP 39.01 10660 no. 24–27, 'Erläuterungen zur Besprechung 5.1.1922 im SRA' and BAP 39.01 10659 no. 225, RAM to RWM 9.1.1922.

[79] BAP 62 DAF 3 8819 no. 126, *Der Deutsche*, 137, 18.6.1922 'Krasse Verfälschung von statistischem Zahlenmaterial. Die "Herstellung" von Textilpreisen'.

[80] *WuS* 2 (1922), p. 370.

[81] *WuS* 1 (1921), p. 364.

[82] BAP 39.01 10661 no. 40, RAM/III/A Vermerk 20.10.1922. The RAM was internally divided on the issue, see BAP 39.01 10661 no. 28, 44, 48.

[83] In early 1923 the Länder resorted to publishing their own weekly indices, thereby undermining the authority of the Reichsindex, see BAP 39.01 10661 no. 112, RWM to RAM 19.2.1923, p. 1. However, the RAM refused to accept more frequent publication and insisted on a cabinet decision. See: BAP 39.01 10661 no. 116, RAM/III/A Meldung to Staatssekretär 2.3.1923; BAP 39.01 10661 no. 117, RAM note 14.3.1923 and BAP 39.01 10661 no. 219, 'Auszug aus dem Protokoll der Sitzung des Reichsministeriums 25.5.1923'.

accepted the need for automatic wage indexation.[84] With no time for careful preparation, the statisticians were ordered to produce a weekly index to which the national wage level could be pegged.[85] The result was a fiasco.[86] In its desperation to keep up to date, the Statistical Office adopted a flawed estimation procedure. Cumulated over a number of weeks this led to contradictory results. In the third week of August 1923 the Statistical Office announced first a weekly inflation rate of 50 per cent and then, a few days later, corrected the figure to 75 per cent. The press comment was scandalous.[87] The only escape was to call in the interest groups. Trade unions and employers were already responsible for vetting the returns at a local level. Now they were appointed to a national commission for price statistics.[88] For the time being, the Reich's Statistical Office had forfeited its authority as a reliable source of information. The legitimacy of official data could be secured only through the complete corporatist integration of both capital and labour.

VI

Official statistics purported to impose an external, neutral measure on socio-economic reality. What the period of 'the Great Disorder' revealed was that this effect of detached objectivity was itself a product of social and economic order. It depended on a number of interrelated conditions: an authoritative state, a minimum level of consensus in civil society and a degree of stability in the economy to be measured. Before 1914 these factors limited the operation of official statistics. In the aftermath of World War I, they became prohibitive. By 1923 it was virtually impossible to collect statistics in Germany. The new economic administrators of the Weimar Republic were ambitious. The SRA was elaborating a new conception of the capitalist economy. However, in

[84] J. Bähr, *Staatliche Schlichtung in der Weimarer Republik. Tarifpolitik, Korporatismus und industrieller Konflikt zwischen Inflation und Deflation 1919–1932* (Berlin, 1989), pp. 66–67; H.A. Winkler, *Von der Revolution zur Stabilisierung. Arbeiter und Arbeiterbewegung in der Weimarer Republik 1918 bis 1924* (Berlin, 1984), pp. 608–609; G.D. Feldman and I. Steinisch, *Industrie und Gewerkschaften 1918–1924. Die überforderte Zentralarbeitsgemeinschaft* (Stuttgart, 1985), p. 110.
[85] BAP 39.01 10661 no. 277–283.
[86] BAP 39.01 10662 no. 110, Der Präs. SRA report on weekly index numbers 3.9.1923 and BAP 39.01 10662 no. 17, RAM note 8.9.1923.
[87] BAP 39.01 10662 no. 23, *Vorwärts*, 399, 28.8.23 'Indexwirrwarr', BAP 39.01 10662 no. 22, *Industrie und Handelszeitung*, 198, 29.8.23, BAP 39.01 10662 no. 27, *Industrie und Handelszeitung*, 201, 1.9.23, BAP 39.01 10662 no. 103, Verband der Deutschen Schuh- und Schäftefabrikanten to RAM 31.8.1923.
[88] See BAP 39.01 10662 no. 132, RWM to Verband der deutschen Schuh- und Schäftefabrikanten e.V. 5.10.1923 and BAP 39.01 10662 no. 188, SRA to RAM 22.10.1923.

practical terms it could achieve little. Statistical surveys were delicate instruments. They could operate only in a society not deeply riven by political, social and economic conflict. In a state of massive fiscal crisis and hyperinflation statistical surveys were both unaffordable and inoperative. In a situation of open confrontation between the nation's political institutions and the forces of civil society, official statisticians could not hope to organize effective enquiries. Nor could they expect their hard-won results to be treated with respect.[89]

Between 1923 and 1924 the Weimar Republic entered a period of conservative consolidation. The Reichswehr imposed domestic order by suppressing the paramilitaries of both right and left. The collapse of the inflationary boom and rising unemployment dramatically weakened the trade unions. Business made peace with the Republic largely on its own terms. The United States and Britain forced French withdrawal from the Ruhr, restoring the integrity of the German nation-state. An injection of US capital following the 1924 Dawes Plan provided the necessary lubrication for the reparations machinery. And, as political and economic order was restored, the instruments of official statistics began to function again. In short order, the Reich's Statistical Office was able to make good on the promises of the August 1920 meeting.

June 1925 saw the plans for the census at long last put into effect. The first results began to appear in 1926. But, as in 1907, the preparation of national figures was held up by the slow progress of the underfunded Prussian Office. The results, unsurprisingly, confirmed the central claims made by Meerwarth, Platzer and the other advocates of reform. The expansion of employment and mechanical power since 1907 was concentrated almost entirely in plants with more than 50 staff and disproportionately in the very largest plants with more than 1,000 staff.[90] The picture was even starker if one broke down the workforce by economic units (firms) rather than by individual sites of production. The increasing concentration of ownership meant that 60 per cent of the German industrial workforce and 40 per cent of the workforce in commerce and transport services were concentrated in firms with 50 staff or more.[91] Furthermore, these large undertakings increasingly took the form of anonymous, public limited companies. Their share of employment in trade and industry rose from one-eighth in 1907 to one-

[89] This conclusion extends the argument of P.-C. Witt, 'Staatliche Wirtschaftspolitik in Deutschland 1918–1923: Entwicklung und Zerstörung einer modernen wirtschaftspolitischen Strategie', in G.D. Feldman, C.-L. Holtfrerich, G.A. Ritter and P.-C. Witt (eds.), *The German Inflation Reconsidered. A Preliminary Balance* (Berlin, 1982), pp. 151–179.

[90] *WuS* 7 (1927), pp. 158–173, 446–457 and *WuS* 8 (1928), pp. 46–49.

[91] *WuS* 10 (1930), pp. 122–125.

fifth in 1925.[92] The onward march of corporate capitalism could not be denied.

Indeed, by the mid-1920s this had become such a commonplace that the belated publication of the census results attracted practically no public attention. By contrast, the Reichsindex remained very much in the public eye. After the shambles of 1923 it took secret tripartite negotiations involving the employers and the trade unions to re-establish the Reichsindex as an authoritative measure of the national cost of living. The revised index, released in 1925, could count on solid support in the political mainstream.[93] When it came under attack in the Communist press, the Social Democratic daily *Vorwärts* sprang to its defence.[94] With the full backing of the trade unions, critics of the Reichsindex could now be dismissed as ignorant troublemakers. No such consensus could be achieved on industrial earnings. A further attempt to carry out a voluntary survey in the textiles industry failed.[95] The survey had to be imposed under the provisions of the law of 1922. The results, which were released in December 1927, revealed a very considerable gap between actual earnings and the collectively agreed wage rates. The obvious value of this information was enough to convince even sceptical employers. Between 1927 and 1933 the Statistical Office was able to push through surveys in 18 other industries without encountering resistance.[96]

It was not until the mid-1920s that German official statistics began to move beyond the limits of the agenda set in August 1920. The new concept introduced by Meerwarth and Platzer had been to register the real decision-making unit of the capitalist economy, the firm, as an economic unit. In practice, however, the census of 1925 was forced to count something rather less interesting: the legal entity of the firm. As the official statisticians frankly acknowledged, this did no justice to the increasing complexity of German corporate life. The largest firms were making increasing use of trusts, and holding companies to cloak their ownership of ramified economic empires. A large number of separate legal entities might effectively constitute a single economic unit. In the aftermath of the inflation, social democrats and liberals engaged in an anxious debate about the nature of ownership and control in the

---

[92] *WuS* 10 (1930), pp. 186–189.
[93] BAP 39.01 10664 no. 105–106, no. 156–158, 163.
[94] The problem was the large weight given to rent-controlled housing that depressed the index, see BAP 39.01 10664 no. 245, 280 and BAP 39.01 10664 no. 273, *Vorwärts* 419, 5.9.1925 'Der mißverständliche Index'.
[95] BAP 39.01 10676 no. 321 and BAP 39.01 10677 no. 24, 89–136 and 306.
[96] BAP 39.01 10679 no. 181 RAM Note 5.5.1933.

modern economy.[97] The key demand was for greater publicity, to hold corporate management and the controlling minority of shareholders to account. Secrecy was the central obstacle. In the words of a representative of the SRA, there was no hope, using a standardized questionnaire, of obtaining accurate information on the true relations of 'capitalist domination'.[98] Investigative journalism and patient, case-by-case reconstruction were the only ways to unveil what was deliberately hidden from the public, the trade unions and the taxman. In the spring of 1925, the Statistical Office was prompted to take its own investigations a step further, when the Committee for Economic Affairs of the Reichstag requested an enquiry into the economic importance of Konzerne.[99]

Since 1906 the Statistical Office had maintained an up-to-date register of all German public companies. Under the provisions of the Commercial Code of 1900 firms were required to publish regular accounts and to publicize any change to their capital base. The Statistical Office combined this routine information with regular clippings from the financial press. From this archive the Statistical Office set itself the task of reconstructing the networks of ownership in German business. The research was painstaking. In some cases telephone books had to be consulted to identify groups of 'independent' firms that were in fact registered at the same address. Once a network of trusts had been established the analysis was despatched to the putative headquarters for verification. A compilation of the results appeared in February 1927 as the first of a new series of statistical monographs.[100] In total the Statistical Office was able to identify 330 Konzerne controlling 3,500 German firms and 500 foreign affiliates. As the statisticians acknowledged, the list was far from complete; 15 per cent of corporations had refused all cooperation and this number included such giants as the Vereinigte Stahlwerke, Stinnes, Wintershall, Zeiß and Schultheiß-Patzenhofer. Many others had provided no more than perfunctory or misleading replies. However, the Office was not deterred. A section of the Statistical Office was henceforth dedicated to monitoring the struc-

[97] C.W. Bajak, 'The Third Reich's Corporation Law of 1937', PhD thesis, Yale University (1986), pp. 7–60.

[98] BAP 39.01 10559, Beratungen des Ausschusses für die Volks, Berufs und Betriebszählung, Göttingen 21.-22.10.1921, p. 5.

[99] U. Roeske, 'Die bürgerliche Wirtschaftsstatistik insbesondere von Großbanken, Monopolen und Wirtschaftsverbänden. Organisations- und Strukturprobleme vom Beginn des Imperialismus bis zum Beginn der II. Weltkrieges', Diplomarbeit. Sektion Geschichte. Bereich Archivwissenschaft, University of Berlin (1974) and M. Vogelsang, 'Die deutsche Konzernstatistik. Ein geschichtlicher, kritischer und technischer Beitrag', ASA, 19 (1929), pp. 29–46.

[100] SRA, Konzerne, Interessensgemeinschaften und ähnliche Zusammenschlüsse im Deutschen Reich Ende 1926. Einzelschriften zur Statistik des Deutschen Reichs Nr. 1 (Berlin, 1927).

ture of corporate ownership. By 1931 it had on its files no less than 1,688 Konzerne or trust-like organizations. This information was used for a variety of internal purposes, including the estimation of industrial investment. However, it was withheld from the public. A second edition of the Konzern monograph was discussed in the early 1930s. But representatives of German industry vetoed the idea.

The work on corporate ownership was not the only extension of the Meerwarth and Platzer programme. In the course of the 1920s other, even more visionary, proposals surfaced from both official and unofficial sources. Between 1927 and 1929 the German Statistical Association hosted a Commission to investigate the possibility of closer collaboration between business statistics and national economic statistics.[101] The details of the Commission's history need not concern us here. However, its work is significant for the way in which it extended the thinking of Meerwarth and Platzer and connected it to trends in German business economics. If capitalism from the point of view of national economic statistics could be pictured as a collection of capitalist firms, then surely it should be possible to assemble an image of the totality of the capitalist economy by working upwards from the accounts and management statistics of the firms. To realize this vision, the Commission recommended a new form of business statistics and accounts that would allow them to serve as the building blocks of an aggregative system of national statistics. What this, of course, ignored was the interest of concealment, which had been such a persistent obstacle to more comprehensive economic statistics.

Nevertheless, the idea of a single, integrated system of economic information stretching from the accounts of the firm to the accounts of the nation retained its seductive technocratic charm. And in 1932, Walter Grävell took the first practical steps towards its realization. As we have seen, the young Dr Grävell had been driven during the inflation to heretical conclusions about the future of the census. After this turbulent apprenticeship, Grävell had followed a patchy career. He was seconded to the Reichschancellory to help in establishing its economic advisory section. He was then loaned to the Chilean government as a statistical advisor. He returned to the SRA in 1929 as Director of trade statistics, a position that gave him control of his own substantial Department.[102] He inherited a system which had gone through a decade of administrative

[101] C. Eisfeld, 'Die wissenschaftliche und praktische Entwicklung der Betriebsstatistik', *ASA*, 17 (1927/1928), pp. 432–440, A. Isaac, 'Die betriebswirtschaftliche Statistik im Dienste der Konjunkturforschung', *ASA*, 18 (1928/1929), pp. 558–565, A. Isaac, 'Zusammenarbeit der volkswirtschaftlichen und privatwirtschaftlichen Statistik', *ASA*, 19 (1929/1930), pp. 347–360.
[102] 'Walter Grävell 65, *ASA*, 40 (1956), p. 176 and *ASA*, 46 (1962), pp. 81–83.

transformation.[103] Reform legislation in 1928 had finally put in place a system of record keeping that guaranteed the accurate registration of import and export values. In the summer of 1931 Grävell oversaw what on the surface appeared to be a further round of minor administrative improvements. Bulk importers and large exporting firms were permitted to make monthly 'group registrations' for all their foreign business. Instead of recording each individual shipment at the customs post, the importing or exporting firms would send a monthly account of their foreign business direct to the Statistical Office. This represented a considerable saving of paperwork. More importantly, however, it suggested the possibility of a new kind of statistics. All existing systems of trade statistics concentrated on registering the physical movement of goods across national boundaries. By contrast, Grävell aimed to carry out a monthly survey of importing and exporting firms. The movement of goods would thus be connected directly to the businesses involved. This would make it possible to identify the domestic origin of German exports and the first destination of the country's imports. In the spirit of Meerwarth and Platzer, national statistics would be traced directly back to the firm as an economic unit. Grävell was not naive enough to believe that under current conditions this system could be made to work as a comprehensive replacement for conventional trade statistics. The accounts of the vast majority of firms were not adequate to allow for the separate registration of foreign business. Furthermore, there was no way of knowing, *a priori*, which firms would conduct foreign trade in a particular month. One certainly could not rely on the willingness of private firms to make returns unprompted. The Statistical Office would have to compile and maintain an up-to-date register of all trading firms. In the early 1930s, this was technically impractical and excessively expensive. But there were obvious opportunities for cooperation in those sectors where trade was regulated by cartels or controlled by giant corporations. Once their private accounts were adjusted to satisfy the requirements of the official trade statistics, there was no need to record the same transactions twice, first in the bookkeeping of the syndicate and then again in the official returns made by the border posts. Why not absorb the private accounting system into the official statistics? Grävell combined Meerwarth and Platzer's atomistic conception of capitalism and the synthetic work of the German Statistical Association into a monolithic vision of social and statistical organization. As he put it: 'It is surely one of the greatest disadvantages of the current organization of statistics, that there is too much duplication of effort. The aim of

[103] C. Berliner, 'Die Reform der deutschen Außenhandelsstatistik', *Weltwirtschaftliches Archiv*, 29 (1929), pp. 320–333.

organizational reform must be, to connect all agencies involved in statistics, private and public, into a single unitary chain, producing a single set of statistics, satisfying everyone's needs.'[104] The pursuit of administrative efficiency thus led Walter Grävell to a remarkably radical vision of statistical organization. A 'single unitary chain' would replace the imperfect censuses and the cumbersome and inaccurate system of trade statistics. Over the course of his career, Grävell was to push this fantasy of administrative rationalization to quite remarkable practical conclusions.

VII

The creation of the Weimar Republic marked a fundamental break in the history of German official statistics. It may be true that conservatism and reactionary tradition prevailed in many arms of the German state. However, in the fields of social and economic administration the creation of the Republic unleashed a genuine process of innovation. It established for the first time a national system of economic administration. There was no possibility of continuity here, simply because no such institutions had existed before 1916. Most of the key staff in these new agencies of the state entered government either during the war or in its immediate aftermath. They showed scant respect for the Wilhelmine past and set a new agenda for national economic government, to which the statisticians struggled to respond. The early 1920s saw a major effort by the Reich to reorganize the statistical system inherited from the Wilhelmine period. In the decades before 1914 the official statisticians had held the development of modern capitalism at arm's length, both conceptually and in organizational terms. Now corporate capitalism took centre stage. For men like Platzer and Meerwarth this meant the chance to realize long-held professional dreams and rapid promotion. For others, like Zahn, it spelled professional disaster. The aggressive new programme of official statistics also met resistance from outside the state. The guerrilla tactics of German business came close to paralysing official enquiries. But despite the retrenchment that accompanied the end of inflation in 1924, innovation at the Reich's Statistical Office continued and began to gather momentum.

[104] W. Grävell, 'Statistische Abgabe und Anmeldung zur Handelsstatistik', *ASA*, 22 (1932/1933), pp. 69–80, p. 80.

3 Weimar's macroeconomic statistics, 1924–1929

On a summer's day in 1925 a crowd assembled in the conference hall of the Reich's Statistical Office in Berlin to inaugurate a new centre for economic research, the Institut für Konjunkturforschung (Institute for Business-Cycle Research, IfK). The attendance list was even more comprehensive than that assembled in August 1920 for the relaunch of the Statistical Office.[1] Leading the proceedings was Professor Dr Ernst Wagemann, the recently appointed President of the Reich's Statistical Office. The German state was represented by the Ministry for Economic Affairs (RWM), delegates from Prussia and Bavaria, the Reichsbank, the National Railway and the Council of Municipalities. What was more remarkable was the wide range of private interests. The Institute was an exercise in full-blown corporatism. The peak associations of German agriculture and industry – the German Agricultural Council, the National Council of Chambers of Commerce and the Reich's Association of German Industry – were each to claim two votes on the Institute's governing body (Kuratorium). Commerce and finance were represented by the Central Association of German Wholesalers, the Peak Association of German Retailing, the Central Association of German Banks and Bankers, and the Central Association of German Consumer Co-operatives, each with one vote. Finally, to complete the tripartite construction, the General Federation of German Trade Unions (ADGB), the General Association of Christian Trade Unions and the Council of Salaried Workers' and Civil Servants' Associations were all included in the Kuratorium. In fact, Wagemann boasted that the only group to have declined his invitation to join the Institute were the shipyards, and even they had promised their cooperation.

The aim of the new Institute was to combine intensive statistical monitoring of the fluctuations of the economy (Konjunkturbeobachtung) with scientific analysis of the business-cycle (Konjunkturforschung). As the early 1920s had taught, economic data were now

[1] GStA I Rep. 120 C VIII 2a Nr. 33 Bd. 1 Bl. 2, Protokoll über die am 16.7.1925 stattgehabte Sitzung zwecks Gründung eines Instituts für Konjunkturforschung.

required in an entirely new volume and speed. The Institute and the Statistical Office together would produce quarterly, monthly and even weekly reports. At the same time the new research centre would organize the data using 'socio-economic methods', uncovering 'the larger regularities in the process of economic circulation'.[2] The Institute would make a study of statistical time-series with a view to separating regular seasonal variations from the underlying trends and cycles. It would explore the relationship between monetary variables and physical production over the course of the cycle as well as the relationship to the balance of trade. It would also seek to analyse the impact of the business-cycle at the level of the individual firm. For raw material the Institute would draw on the Reich's Statistical Office, as well as the cooperation of its Kuratorium. This would keep its budget to a minimum. At the same time, its independent status would allow it to engage in a far more adventurous exploration of the data than was possible for the Statistical Office. In particular, it would venture into speculative areas of statistical estimation that were off-limits to official statisticians.

The formation of the Institute for Business-Cycle Research was to be a defining moment in the history of German official statistics. Over the following decades the Reich's Statistical Office and the Institute became the vehicles for an extraordinarily ambitious programme of economic investigation. There was an outpouring of new data, different not only in quantity but also in kind from anything that came before. Whereas the reforms of the early 1920s can be traced back to the discussions of the Wilhelmine period, the innovations of the years after 1925 marked a fundamental break with the past. Economic expertise entered into a new relationship with political power. What is more, Wagemann and his staff claimed to have the power of prediction, providing policy-makers with a definite outlook on which to base long-term decisions. At the same time, Wagemann's establishment rewrote the history of the German economy. To this day, it is to the output of the Institute and Weimar's Statistical Office that historians turn for information.[3] This longevity is owed largely to the intellectual precocity of Wagemann's research establishment. As this chapter will argue, the programme of Konjunkturforschung sponsored by the Weimar Republic was a pioneering effort in

---

[2] GStA I Rep. 120 C VIII 2a Nr. 33 Bd. 1 Bl. 2, Protokoll, p. 7.
[3] See for example the articles in C. Buchheim, M. Hutter and H. James (eds.), *Zerrissene Zwischenkriegszeit. Wirtschaftshistorische Beiträge* (Baden-Baden, 1994) and A. Ritschl and M. Spoerer, 'Das Bruttosozialprodukt in Deutschland nach den amtlichen Volkseinkommens- und Sozialproduktsstatistiken, 1901–1995', *Jahrbuch für Wirtschaftsgeschichte* (1997), pp. 27–54.

empirical macroeconomics. The Institute and the Statistical Office helped to shape the intellectual universe that we still inhabit today.

I

How to account for this extraordinary development? The literature to date offers no answers. The few authors who have concerned themselves with the history of empirical economics in Weimar Germany have failed to recognize the significance of the statistical initiatives launched after 1925.[4] In part this no doubt stems from the habit of undervaluing empirical knowledge by comparison with the history of ideas and economic theory. But this begs the question. Why has the conceptual originality of Weimar's new macroeconomic statistics not been recognized? The answer lies in the title of the Institute for Business-Cycle Research. Perhaps not surprisingly, the work of Weimar's statistical economists has tended to be viewed as a local variant of the contemporary fashion for cyclical analysis.[5] In the 1920s this was an international phenomenon. Research centres sprang up in the United States, the Soviet Union, Britain, France, the Netherlands, Sweden and Italy. However, as this chapter will argue, Konjunkturforschung as practised by the Berlin Institute and the Reich's Statistical Office differed in fundamental respects from conventional business-cycle research of the 1920s. The identification of the two has tended to obscure the intellectual originality of the work of Wagemann and his staff. It has also minimized their practical significance. Business-cycle research as practised in the 1920s went out of fashion in the 1930s. It was discredited by the failure of its practitioners to predict the biggest cyclical downswing of them all – the Great Depression of 1929–32. In intellectual terms it was displaced by the 'Keynesian revolution' and the advent of mathematical econometrics. This has reinforced the tendency to end histories of German business-cycle research in 1933. In fact, Konjunkturforschung lived on after the Nazi seizure of power. As this book will show, the Institute, still under the control of its founder Ernst Wagemann, was to provide the intellectual foundations for the organization of the Nazi war economy.

All of this is obscured by the identification of the Institute with business-cycle research. And it was Ernst Wagemann himself who was

---

[4] B. Kulla, *Die Anfänge der empirischen Konjunkturforschung in Deutschland 1925–1933* (Berlin, 1996) and E. Coenen, *La 'Konjunkturforschung' en Allemagne et Autriche 1925–1933* (Paris, 1964).

[5] The best survey is provided by M.S. Morgan, *The History of Econometric Ideas* (Cambridge, 1990).

initially responsible for the confusion. Wagemann quite self-consciously placed the work of his establishment in the intellectual tradition of business-cycle economics.[6] This dated back to the 1860s with the simultaneous publication of works by the British economist William Stanley Jevons and the French economist Clément Juglar. They founded the academic study of the business-cycle by identifying the high drama of commercial crises as just one stage in the continuous process of economic fluctuation, in which a crisis initiated a phase of liquidation, which in turn created the conditions for a phase of prosperity, boom and another crisis. It was not until the turn of the century that the academic study of business-cycles achieved critical mass. The first in a flurry of major publications was the study of British cycles by Tugan Baranowski, published in Russian in 1894 and in a German translation in 1901. This was followed in the United States by Irving Fisher's *The Purchasing Power of Money* (1911) and Wesley Mitchell's *The Business-Cycle* (1913). In Britain one could point to A.C. Pigou's *Wealth and Welfare* (1912), R.G. Hawtrey's *Good and Bad Trade* (1913) and Dennis Robertson's *A Study in Industrial Fluctuation* (1915). In the German-speaking world, interest was similarly intense. Schmoller conferred the ultimate stamp of respectability by incorporating a discussion of cycles into his *Grundriss* (1904). The Verein für Sozialpolitik weighed in with annual studies beginning in 1903. These set the stage for the younger generation: Werner Sombart, Arthur Spiethoff and Joseph Schumpeter were all to take up the question of crises and cycles in the decade before the war.

However, what really attracted Wagemann was not this academic literature, which tended to be historical and theoretical in character, but the early efforts to make business-cycle economics into a practical science. It was in the United States that business-cycle economics was for the first time put to work. Around the turn of the century a number of commercial organizations began to produce regular analyses of the economic situation along with prognoses of the future. Babson's Statistical Organization and Brookmire's Economic Service made economic statistics and research into a commercial enterprise.[7] Drawing on the model of meteorology, they attempted to construct indicator systems with which to interpret the flow of current data collected from markets and business reports.[8] Stable patterns, which were believed to have

---

[6] This historical sketch is taken from E. Wagemann, *Konjunkturlehre* (Berlin, 1928), pp. 3–9.

[7] R.W. Babson, *Actions and Reactions. An Autobiography of Roger W. Babson* (New York, 1935).

[8] On the contemporaneous development of meteorology, see R.M. Friedman, *Appropriating the Weather. Vihelm Bjerknes and the Construction of a Modern Meteorology* (Ithaca, 1989).

predictive power, were captured in so-called 'business barometers'. The most widely disseminated barometer was that produced by the Harvard Committee for Economic Research (see figure 1). The Committee based its analysis on three curves showing price movements in the market for capital (Group A), commodities (Group B) and money (Group C). Tracing their development back to the late nineteenth century the Committee believed it had established a regular sequence with the capital market, leading commodity prices and interest rates.

The truly innovative aspect of the Committee's work was the sophistication of its statistical techniques. The Committee pioneered the basic approach to statistical time-series with which we are still familiar today. Each series was decomposed into three components: the underlying trend, the element of seasonal variations and the true 'business-cycle'. The cyclical movements of different series were 'normalized' by setting their standard deviation at one. The Committee then aimed to find indicators that moved in systematic patterns, either in parallel or in opposition. This comparison was done largely by visual means. Calculating the correlation coefficients for each pair of series was simply too laborious. Once a clear pattern of 'leads' and 'lags' had emerged, the series were grouped together to form so-called 'barometers'. While the Harvard Committee's statistical techniques were innovative, its work was barren in theoretical terms. The Committee's proud claim was to operate entirely without the aid of economic theory. Time-series were sifted mechanically and chosen simply according to the degree of correlation. Nevertheless, the American example spawned numerous imitators across Europe in the early 1920s. In England, the LSE and the economics department of the University of Cambridge were joined together in the so-called London and Cambridge Economic Service. In the Soviet Union Kondratieff began his famous experiments.[9] And in Germany, as well, the work of the Harvard Committee was followed with enthusiasm.

It is no surprise therefore that Wagemann identified his project with the fashion for business-cycle research. It allowed him to locate his Institute as the German arm of an international movement, taking in all the major nations of the industrialized world. More importantly business-cycle research offered an attractive vision of practical empiricism. To Wagemann it seemed to promise an escape from the methodological impasse which he believed had crippled German economics since the late nineteenth century. And it is undeniable that the techniques of the Harvard Committee had a powerful influence on the first experiments in

[9] V. Barnett, *Kondratiev and the Dynamics of Economic Development: Long Cycles and Industrial Growth in Historical Context* (London, 1998).

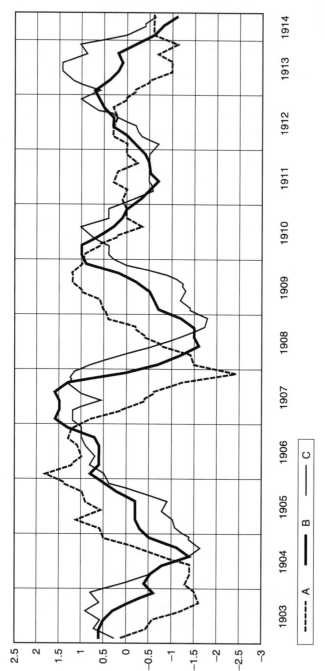

Group A: Yields of 10 railroad bonds; price of industrial stocks; price of 20 railroad stocks; NY clearings
Group B: Pig-iron production; outside clearings; Bradstreet's prices; Bureau of Labor prices; Reserve of NY banks
Group C: rate on 4–6-month paper; rate of 69-day paper; loans of NY banks; deposits of NY banks

Figure 1 Harvard Barometer for the US economy, 1903–1914
Source: *Review of Economic Statistics* (April 1919)

official business-cycle research in Weimar Germany. At the RWM it was Wagemann who oversaw the production of the monthly economic report for the Reich's President. From their modest beginnings these grew into increasingly elaborate memoranda in which general economic analysis was combined with specific sectoral reports. In 1923, while Wagemann was still at the RWM, this development reached its end-point with the publication of *Deutsche Wirtschaftszahlen*, a set of Harvard-style indicators for use by the Reich's bureaucracy.[10]

However, Wagemann's enthusiasm for American empiricism came at a heavy price. His initial aim in founding the IfK was to create an Academy of economic research. This was prompted by the acute sense of the intellectual and institutional incoherence of German academic economics, which he shared with contemporaries such as Schumpeter.[11] The Institute, Wagemann hoped, would help to give coherence to economic research in Germany by providing a focal point for empirical economics. German economics was to be remodelled along American lines.[12] But Wagemann was to be frustrated. The Americanization of the Weimar Republic produced a number of contradictory responses and nowhere more so than in the Universities.[13] Given the state of the economics discipline in Germany one cannot speak of anything resem-bling an academic consensus opposed to Wagemann and his establish-ment. However, Wagemann did manage to collect a number of vocal enemies. And their chief objection was to the 'American empiricism' of the Institute's work. Arthur Spiethoff, the leading exponent of historical business-cycle analysis, refused his cooperation from the outset.[14] He subsequently sponsored a PhD devoted to rubbishing the work of Wagemann's Institute as nothing more than an inadequate imitation of the Harvard Committee.[15] Professor Karl Diehl, a leading figure in the still-influential Verein für Sozialpolitik, weighed in against the Institute with two edited collections in the prestigious Verein series.[16] Among the

---

[10] BAP 07.01 film 19065N/2110 no. 3, Präs. SRA to Reichskanzlei 3.10.1924. The Reichschancellory was sufficiently interested to order three copies, BAP 07.01 film 19065N/2110 no. 8, Reichskanzlei to SRA 8.10.1924.
[11] J.A. Schumpeter, 'Die Wirtschaftstheorie der Gegenwart in Deutschland', in *Dogmen-historische und Biographische Aufsätze* (Tübingen, 1954), pp. 255–284.
[12] Wagemann, *Konjunkturlehre*, pp. iii–v, 1–20.
[13] M. Nolan, *Visions of Modernity. American Business and the Modernization of Germany* (Oxford, 1994).
[14] E. Coenen, *La Konjunkturforschung* (Paris, 1964), pp. 45–52.
[15] H. Kuschmann, *Die Untersuchungen des Berliner Instituts für Konjunkturforschung. Darstellung und Kritik* (Jena, 1933).
[16] K. Diehl (ed.), *Beiträge zur Wirtschaftstheorie. Erster Teil: Volkseinkommen und Volksvermögen. Begriffskritische Untersuchungen. Schriften des Vereins für Sozialpolitik* (SVS) 173 I (Munich, 1926) and *Zweiter Teil: Konjunkturforschung und Konjunkturthe-orie* 173 II (Munich, 1928).

younger generation, Adolph Löwe, himself a former member of Wagemann's staff, was the leading critic of the Institute. Having himself engaged in a brief flirtation with the methods of the Harvard Committee, Löwe espoused a methodological purism that insisted on the unbridgeable gap between inductive empiricism and rigorous *a priori* theorizing.[17] Again, the tar brush of Harvard was applied. Wagemann defended himself against these accusations. But his protestations were in vain. In academic circles the credibility of the IfK was to remain fundamentally in doubt. Subsequent historians have echoed the judgements of scornful contemporaries. They have taken the protestations of Diehl, Löwe and Spiethoff at face value rather than reading them as interventions in a long-forgotten 'culture war'.

II

The aim of this chapter is to provide a reassessment of the IfK. And the starting point for this must be a reassessment of its founder – Ernst Wagemann. Historians have not given him his due. The few who have commented on his remarkable career have tended to be misled by contemporary assessments of a man who trailed controversy in his wake. The creator of Weimar's innovative economic statistics is by no means an easy character to pin down. Unfortunately, he left no accessible cache of personal papers. We can reconstruct the bare bones of his early career from his c.v.[18] He was born in Chile in 1884, the son of German emigrants. After studies at Göttingen and Berlin he completed his PhD at Heidelberg University in 1907. He then began a teaching career at the new Institute of Colonial Economics in Hamburg. It was the war which launched his precipitous career in the civil service. From 1916, Wagemann headed the statistical department of the War Food Office. In the postwar years his wartime contacts were to serve him well. In 1919 Wagemann began lecturing at the prestigious University of Berlin. Then, in the same year, his former boss at the Food Office, Julius Hirsch, recruited him back into government service. Wagemann's task at the RWM was to oversee general economic analysis and to manage relations with the Statistical Office. In Friedrich Zahn there was at least one rival for the Presidency of the Statistical Office. But Zahn did not match the modernizing ambitions of the Ministry (see chapter 2). In December 1923 Wagemann took effective control of the Office and in March 1924 he was formally inaugurated as Delbrück's successor. In

---

[17] A. Löwe, 'Wie ist Konjunkturtheorie überhaupt möglich?', *Weltwirtschaftliches Archiv*, 24 (1926), pp. 165–196.

[18] For Wagemann's c.v., see Archiv der Humboldt Uni. U.K.W.9 no. 1.

personal terms, the break with the Wilhelmine past was less radical. In December 1927 Wagemann married Ernst Delbrück's daughter Hertha.

Over the following years Wagemann was to earn a near-legendary reputation as a networker and political operator. He is said to have ruled his establishment like an enlightened despot. One Festschrift, playing on his Latin American origins, dubbed him a Conquistador.[19] Certainly he was a man of bureaucratic action. From the outset he stamped his authority on German statistics. Immediately after his appointment, the Reich's Statistical Office was reorganized.[20] Three Departments were expanded into four. A reorganized Department I under Wagemann's direct control, provided a home for a new section for general economic observation, business-cycle statistics and reparation statistics. Financial statistics were allocated to a new Department IV. Most significantly, social and economic statistics, which had been inseparably welded together in the nineteenth century, were split apart. Social statistics were lumped together with demography and medicinal statistics. This reorganization was not to be the last in the 1920s. However, it established the pattern for all that followed. In the summer of 1925 Wagemann established the Institute for Business-Cycle Research. By the following spring it had produced the first of its famous quarterly reviews. We shall have much more to say about the expansion of the Statistical Office. However, the crude figures are extraordinary. During Wagemann's reign staff levels tripled (see table 2). In 1933, even Wagemann's arch-rival Friedrich Zahn was forced to acknowledge him as one of Germany's greatest 'scientific entrepreneurs'.[21]

But, there is something ambiguous in the accounts of Wagemann's personality. In acknowledging his dynamism, they also hint at something transgressive. His energy exceeded the conventional boundaries defined by his double role as a civil servant and 'man of science'. From an establishment figure such as Zahn, 'scientific entrepreneur' was a double-edged compliment. Wagemann's personal style was flamboyant. He wore white suits. He lived well. And in both the Weimar Republic and the Third Reich he faced charges of high-handedness and corruption. He was accused of mismanaging the Statistical Office and showing undue favour towards a small coterie of trusted staff. There were ugly rumours about the 'laxity of his personal morals', allegedly substantiated

[19] A. Wissler, *Ernst Wagemann: Begründer der empirischen Konjunkturforschung in Deutschland* (Berlin 1954), pp. 10–15.

[20] U. Roeske, 'Die amtliche Statistik des Deutschen Reichs 1872 bis 1939. Historische Entwicklung, Organisationsstruktur, Veröffentlichungen', *Jahrbuch für Wirtschaftsgeschichte* (1978), pp. 85–107.

[21] 'Das große Schlagwort', *Der Deutsche* 67, 19.3.1933.

Table 2. *Staff levels at the Reich's Statistical Office, 1923–1932*

Date	Numbers
1923 October	1,300
1924 June	1,000
1924 October	1,030
1925 April	1,299
1926 April	1,538
1927 April	2,093
1928 July	2,566
1929 July	3,016
1932 July	1,784

Notes: Figures include civil servants, clerical and temporary personnel.

Sources: 1923: GStA 1. HA Rep. 77 3884 no. 188, 'Konferenz', p. 15. 1924-7: Verhandlungen des Reichstags III. Wahlperiode 1924 Anlagen vol. 398 Nr. 343, vol. 403 Nr. 1147, vol. 409 Nr. 2562, vol. 416 Nr. 3503. 1928 and 1929: Verhandlungen des Reichstags IV. Wahlperiode 1928 Anlagen vol. 433 Nr. 724, vol. 439 Nr. 1568.

by his chauffeur.[22] And there were persistent questions about money. How did Wagemann pay for his high living? How did he account for the considerable income he derived from the many quasi-official publications of the Institute? Was he taking bribes from publishers in return for putting official work their way? Wagemann's bureaucratic empire siphoned money from a bewildering variety of sources. The highly irregular accounting procedures were designed to give him wide latitude in fixing the salaries of his staff: the material foundation of his large and loyal research team. However, the lack of transparency aroused jealousies within the ranks and excited the suspicion of accountants at the Ministry. More fundamentally, the undercurrent of bureaucratic unease reflected the tensions generated by Wagemann's restless drive to expand the role of the Statistical Office. He sought to redefine both the boundaries of economic science and economic policy and to recombine the two in new ways. Not surprisingly, he provoked a reaction. On the one hand, he was accused of diverting resources away from the proper administrative functions of 'traditional' official statistics towards dubious 'scientific' research. More dangerous was the suspicion that he was seeking to sideline the traditional administrative guardians of government, inserting new-fangled expertise in place of the tried and trusted civil servants.

In a world in which energetic action and passive contemplation are

[22] BAK R 43 II/1157e no. 14, Staatssek. Reichsmin. Innern to Reichskanzlei 10.3.1933, p. 7.

often viewed as polar opposites, Wagemann's reputation as a fixer has not been good for his standing as a thinker. He has generally been dismissed as an intellectual lightweight.[23] And this has reinforced the tendency to see the IfK as little more than a local variant of the Harvard Committee's simplistic empiricism. In fact, establishing a productive dialogue between economic theory and statistical measurement was at the heart of Wagemann's project. Like other contemporaries such as Sombart and Schumpeter, Wagemann's fundamental ambition was to repair the damage done by two generations of methodological disputes in German economics. Economics, he believed, could become a practical science if the new methods of empirical enquiry were harnessed to the right theoretical framework. What, then, were the analytical underpinnings of Wagemann's project? Joseph Schumpeter, a long-standing admirer of the Institute's work, provided a vital clue in his *History of Economic Analysis* (1954). According to Schumpeter, Wagemann regarded the output of the Statistical Office and the IfK as a substitute for the uncompleted second volume of his *Treatise on Monetary Economics*.[24] The first and only published volume of the *Treatise* was completed in May 1923, during the final descent into hyperinflation, less than a year before Wagemann took control of the Statistical Office.[25] This book, which has been completely ignored by historians of German economics, in fact provides the key to a proper understanding of German economic statistics after 1924.[26]

Along with a number of other theorists in this period, Wagemann used classical monetary theory as a springboard from which to develop a radical new vision of the macroeconomy. In the manner of much German academic economics, Wagemann's *Treatise* offered both a history of money and a history of monetary thought. He thus sought to provide his own position with a double justification. He not only offered a synthesis of the most influential strands of monetary theorizing in the German- and English-speaking worlds. He also set out to show that his conceptual framework was the historically necessary accompaniment to the latest stage of capitalism. Like many of his contemporaries discussed in chapter 1, Wagemann was convinced that the world was entering a new stage of so-called 'high capitalism'. This demanded a new conception of money. The detail of Wagemann's account need not detain us

[23] Kulla, *Die Anfänge*, pp. 43–48. Another study dismisses him as a 'pure empiricist', R. Vilk, *Von der Konjunkturtheorie zur Theorie der Konjunkturpolitik. Ein historischer Abriß 1930–1945* (Wiesbaden, 1992), p. 186.

[24] J. Schumpeter, *History of Economic Analysis* (New York, 1954b), p. 1166.

[25] E. Wagemann, *Allgemeine Geldlehre* (Berlin, 1923).

[26] For an extensive and laudatory review, see H.S. Ellis, *German Monetary Theory 1905–1933* (Cambridge, 1937).

here. Suffice to say that he distinguished three historical epochs. The first era in the modern history of money was that of mercantilism, which stretched according to Wagemann from the sixteenth to the mid-eighteenth century. In this period, the royal hoard of gold was seen as identical to the stock of national wealth. It was followed in the aftermath of the French revolution and the triumph of liberal political economy by the era of metallism. Theorists such as Adam Smith treated money just like any other commodity. Its value was determined by the relationship between its utility as a means of exchange and the cost of producing the money substance, gold or silver. The late nineteenth century saw metallism enthroned as official dogma in the form of the international gold standard. But in a dialectical fashion this arrangement was hollowed out from within by the innovations in banking and finance that accompanied the emergence of high capitalism. By the turn of the twentieth century, gold or cash money backed by gold, played a diminishing role in business transactions. Cash, whether in the form of metal coins or paper notes, was the money of petty consumption. The foundation of capitalist business was not the gold-backed currency but the system of cashless, giro transfers enabled by the banking system. This unprecedented privatization of money demanded a new theory and for Wagemann this theory was nominalism.

Nominalism is normally associated with the Strasburg professor of economics, Georg Friedrich Knapp.[27] Money, according to Knapp, was able to perform its symbolic functions as a means of exchange and a symbol of value, not because of gold backing, but because it was endorsed by the symbolic authority of the state. According to Knapp, the validity of money was not a natural, but a legal fact. Therefore, any physical object might be money, a gold coin, a bank note, but also a ledger entry in a banker's account books so long as it was sanctioned by the authority of the state. For Wagemann, Knapp's nominalism served as a launching pad for a critique of metallism. However, in the age of high capitalism, Knapp's fixation on the state was an unnecessary encumbrance. Far from representing the universal truth about money, the imposition of money by official fiat was merely a particular stage in political and economic development. The validity of money was ultimately founded neither in the laws of the state nor in the laws of nature. It was, rather, a complex, in some sense, paradoxical socio-psychological phenomenon. The validity of money for one individual depended on its validity for other individuals. It was founded ultimately on the common and repeated experience of social exchange. Under conditions of high

[27] N. Dodd, *The Sociology of Money: Economics, Reason and Contemporary Society* (Cambridge, 1994), pp. 26–30.

capitalism the validity of money was founded on the global network of capitalist production and exchange. This was what Wagemann called the 'accounting-constitution of money' (Bilanzverfassung des Geldes). Money had validity because it formed the basis for the entire ramified system of modern business accounting and rational calculation. Not coincidentally it was precisely these mechanisms of calculation that the younger generation of non-Marxist economists, notably Weber and Sombart, had identified as the true essence of capitalism.

A nominalism shorn of its fixation with the state would provide the basis for a conception of money appropriate to the era of high capitalism. However, what it provided was a socio-psychological account of money rather than an economic theory. Wagemann set himself the task of linking nominalism with economics. To do so, he constructed a bridge to the classical quantity theory. To put it simply, the quantity theory claimed that the value of money was determined principally by the relationship between the stock of money tokens in circulation and the number of transactions to be accomplished with them. This ancient theory of money was undergoing a major revival in Anglo-American economics in the late nineteenth century at the same time as nominalism emerged in Germany.[28] For Wagemann this was no coincidence. Nominalism and the quantity theory were both based on the same fundamental insight: money was a symbol not a good like any other. The starting point for both theories was to counterpose money to all other commodities.[29] The quantity theory was thus the appropriate monetary theory for the high capitalist age.

The revival of the quantity theory in the late nineteenth century was led above all by Irving Fisher, who was to have a profound impact on Wagemann's macroeconomics. One of Fisher's key contributions was to restate the intuition of the quantity theory in algebraic terms:[30]

$$MV = PT$$

According to this so-called 'equation of exchange', the stock of money (M) multiplied by the 'velocity' (V) of its circulation was equal to the total number of transaction (T) times the average price level (P). 'The value of money' was simply the inverse of this price index. To arrive at the strict quantity theory, one imposed specific causal connections on this tautologous equation. In particular it was claimed that the principal

---

[28] D. Laidler, *The Golden Age of the Quantity Theory* (Princeton, 1991).

[29] Wagemann noted with satisfaction that Irving Fisher himself recognized this parallel, see I. Fisher, *The Purchasing Power of Money* (Boston, 1911), p. 32.

[30] Fisher's equation actually ran as follows: $M'V'+MV=PT$. M' stood for the volume of bank deposits and V' was their rate of circulation.

cause of changes in the value of money, or prices, was variation in the size of the money stock.

The so-called equation of exchange was a very powerful and highly aggregated statement about the economy. In fact it can claim to be the root of modern macroeconomics. However, despite its tautological logic it defied empirical verification until the late nineteenth century. The crucial problem was the measurement of the key variables in the equation. Debate continues to this day over the appropriate definition of the money stock. By the late nineteenth century it was clearly inappropriate to restrict the definition of money merely to notes and coins in circulation. Irving Fisher demonstrated that by extending the definition of money to cover bank deposits as well as cash, it was possible to validate the equation in empirical terms. Unlike many German contemporaries, Wagemann was an admirer of Irving Fisher's work. For Wagemann, Fisher had demonstrated the capacity of a holistic theory of the economy to serve as the foundation for empirical enquiry. Unlike contemporary marginalists who struggled to make sense of abstract entities such as subjective utility, Fisher was able to produce an empirical image of the entire economy. Wagemann, however, was not content with the conventional formulation of the equation of exchange. The variables contained in the standard equation, in particular the money stock and the velocity of circulation, were problematic. While they could be defined at any particular moment in time, they were not stable entities. They were historically contingent on the development of the banking system. In his *Treatise*, Wagemann set out to demonstrate how a new equation of exchange could be built on 'categories, which have a more comprehensive economic content'.[31]

The result was Wagemann's national economic account:[32]

(1) price * net output =
(2) production costs including profit =
(3) income =
(4) consumption + saving =
(5) (consumed and capitalized output) * price

These five lines will be familiar to any reader of a modern textbook in macroeconomics. They are as tautologous as the equation of exchange of the quantity theory, but by spelling out the same identities in five different forms Wagemann provided an algebraic description of the so-called 'circular flow' (Kreislauf) of economic activity. Starting at the top, line (1) registered the value of production. Line (2) recorded the

[31] Wagemann, *Allgemeine Geldlehre*, p. 146.
[32] See appendix (p. 292) for a more precise discussion of these equations.

way in which this revenue flowed back to the 'factors of production' as wages and profits. On line (3) the flows of income were summarized as total national income, which as line (4) states, was either consumed or saved. Finally, in line (5) this was equated to the value of all goods produced either for consumption or new investment. There was no line recording total expenditure, the sum of consumption and investment. But, Wagemann did not fail to draw the conclusion from lines (4) and (5) that 'under normal conditions' there should be a 'parallel' between saving and investment (Neubildung von Produktivgütern).

How did Wagemann arrive at this radical restatement of the quantity theory? In his effort to expand the equation of exchange, Wagemann followed a small band of German and Austrian economists, who in the decade before World War I moved towards an aggregative understanding of the economy through their efforts to extend the quantity theory.[33] The most direct influence on Wagemann was Joseph Schumpeter. Schumpeter is now remembered largely for his 'discovery' of creative entrepreneurship as a driving force in economic development. But to contemporaries his work was more remarkable for its insistence on the need for aggregative economic analysis. The starting point for Schumpeter's *Theory of Economic Development* was an account of the circular flow of economic activity in which total production generated the flow of national income which in turn financed national expenditure.[34] As Schumpeter himself acknowledged, this conception of the economy harked back to the eighteenth-century foundations of economic theory.[35] Most immediately he derived his inspiration from the second volume of Marx's *Das Kapital*. But Marx was a conduit for an even deeper influence. Marx was responsible for 'rediscovering' the eighteenth-century writings of the French physiocrat Quesnay, whose *Tableaux économiques* presented for the first time in tabular form the ramified interconnections of the economy. Around the turn of the century, Quesnay was very much *en vogue*. In the 1890s very early editions of Quesnay's tableau, dating to 1758–9 were discovered in the French National Archives and the private collection of the Du Pont family.[36] A flurry of monographs and articles in French, English and German brought Quesnay to academic attention. In the aftermath of the war, at the time that Wagemann was composing his *Treatise*, Quesnay's

[33] H. Janssen, *Nationalökonomie und Nationalsozialismus. Die deutsche Volkswirtschaftslehre in den dreißiger Jahren* (Marburg, 1998), pp. 274–306.

[34] J. Schumpeter, *Theorie der wirtschaftlichen Entwicklung* (Munich, 1931, 3rd edn.), pp. 1–87.

[35] J. Schumpeter, *The Great Economists from Marx to Keynes* (London, 1952).

[36] M. Kuczynski and R.L. Meek (eds.), *Quesnay's Tableau Economique* (London, 1972), pp. ix–xxxiv.

tableaux were, for the first time, being popularized in German textbooks.[37] In the early 1920s Emil Lederer could write that the concept of Kreislauf, or circular flow, was the common denominator of all contemporary theorizing.[38] The link to the quantity theory was provided in 1918 by an article published by Schumpeter on 'The social product and the units of account', in which he sought to apply his method of aggregative analysis to the central problem of monetary theory.[39] Here he outlined a 'basic equation of monetary theory' which related the aggregate price level – the inverse of the value of money – not to the money stock but to the generation and expenditure of national income. Schumpeter's attempt was marred by his adoption of some peculiarly restrictive assumptions. However, the basic import of his analysis was clear. The aggregate price level could be expressed not simply as a function of technical banking variables. It could also be regarded as a function of aggregate income and expenditure. The crucial significance of Wagemann's *Treatise* was that it developed this rather slippery idea into a comprehensive accounting framework.

Wagemann's equations of exchange related the price level to flows of production, income and expenditure. How did this representation in terms of flows relate to the quantity theory in which the price level was expressed as a function of the stock of money? To clarify this question Wagemann returned to the accounting metaphor. Following the principles of double entry bookkeeping, he argued that the monetary flow of national income in any given period should be treated as a claim on the real flow of production. Money incomes would therefore appear on the liability side of the national account (Passivkonto) whereas the new goods and services produced would be booked on the asset side (Aktivkonto). This accounting framework could then be extended to embrace not only current flows, but also the stock of national wealth. Here he again drew on Irving Fisher, who had introduced in 1911 the fundamental distinction between income as a flow and wealth as a stock variable.[40] If national income was a liability set against the asset of production, then national wealth could be thought of as a monetary claim matched by a stock of physical assets. The entirety of shares, debt, mortgages, property titles and idle hoards of money were matched for

---

[37] J. Plenge, 'Zum "Tableau Economique"', *Weltwirtschaftliches Archiv*, 24 (1926), pp. 109–129.

[38] E. Lederer, 'Der Zirkulationsprozess als zentrales Problem der ökonomischen Theorie', *Archiv für Sozialwissenschaft und Sozialpolitik* 56 (1926), pp. 1–25. Given the incoherent state of the discipline, such claims should be read as performative.

[39] J. Schumpeter, 'Das Sozialprodukt und die Rechenpfennige', *Archiv für Sozialwissenschaft und Sozialpolitik* 44 (1918), pp. 627–715.

[40] I. Fisher, *The Nature of Capital and Income* (Boston, 1906), pp. 51–118.

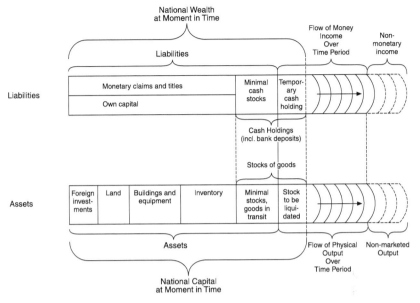

Figure 2 The national balance sheet, 1923: income and wealth
Source: E. Wagemann, *Allgemeine Geldlehre*, I (Berlin, 1923), p. 155

the economy as a whole by the diverse stock of 'real' assets – houses, land, productive equipment, household goods, stocks of raw materials and finished goods. Putting together the current and capital accounts resulted in a comprehensive image of the national economy. This would start with a balance sheet of national capital at a particular moment in time and then move on to capture the flow of income deriving from that capital over a discrete period in which a full cycle of production income and expenditure was accounted for (see figure 2).

The *Treatise* of 1923 did not include a graphical presentation of the national economic accounts. This was supplied in Wagemann's textbook of business-cycle analysis, the *Konjunkturlehre*, published in 1928.[41] Following the logic of the accounting scheme the flow of goods and money was treated separately. The circular flow of goods was represented by a diagram showing the utilization of net national production. Goods were tracked to their threefold destinations: first, additions to the 'circulating capital of the economy' (stocks of raw materials and intermediary goods destined to re-enter production), second, exports and

[41] Wagemann, *Konjunkturlehre*, pp. 26–43.

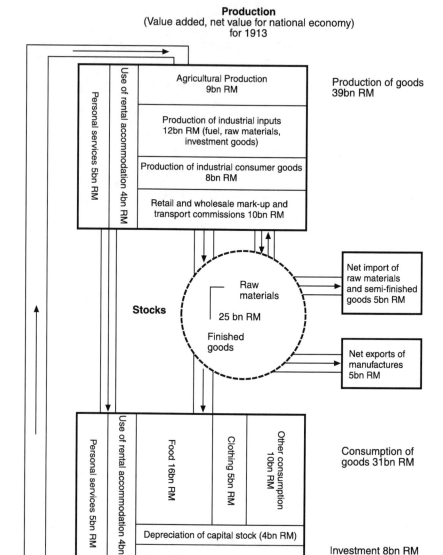

Figure 3 The circular flow of goods: schematic representation for 1913
Source: E. Wagemann, *Konjunkturlehre* (Berlin, 1928), p. 27.

third, final utilization. Final utilization itself could be distinguished into consumption and investment in plant and buildings. The circular flow of goods thus captured the physical process of economic production and reproduction. Money entered into this analysis only in its function as a unit of account. In principle one could enumerate the process of production in some physical unit, such as calories. Money was far simpler (see figure 3).

A second set of diagrams represented the flows of money corresponding to this real productive activity. The money-cycle was subdivided into two basic circuits. The first involved the flow of income and expenditure to factors of production. In this circuit money was repeatedly exchanged for goods and services, which were then in turn sold for money. This first circuit interconnected with the second circuit involving the circulation of money capital between the wholesale market for goods, the market for shares and long-term debt, and the short-term money market. Savings flowed from the incomes of workers and capitalists into the capital markets. Conversely, money capital flowed onto the market for goods in the form of overdrafts or commercial bills to finance stock-building or in the form of loans or shares to finance long-term investment (see figure 4).

Henceforth, the image of the circular flow was to become a trademark for the work of Wagemann's establishment and its graphical department. To the modern reader, acquainted with the conventions of macroeconomics, Wagemann's efforts in national accounting will seem commonplace. The distinction Wagemann laboriously introduced between the stock of wealth and the flow of income seems barely worthy of note. Similarly his elaboration of the identity of income, expenditure and production appears rudimentary. However, it is precisely this extreme familiarity that constitutes their significance. The point here is not to emphasize Wagemann's personal originality. He did not 'invent' macroeconomics. The elements of his synthesis were borrowed from American, Austrian, British and German sources. Originality is not the issue here. The important thing is to locate the *Treatise* within the emerging field of twentieth-century macroeconomics and thereby to properly contextualize the statistical programme of the Weimar Republic. Though not outstandingly original in its own right, the *Treatise* clearly stands very close to the origin of macroeconomics as we know it today. It marks a point at which the rudimentary concepts of aggregative economics were sufficiently widely understood to be combined in a synthetic approach, but were still sufficiently unfamiliar to require considerable exposition. Contemporaries who trivialized the work of the Institute and the Statistical Office as 'mere' empiricism failed to

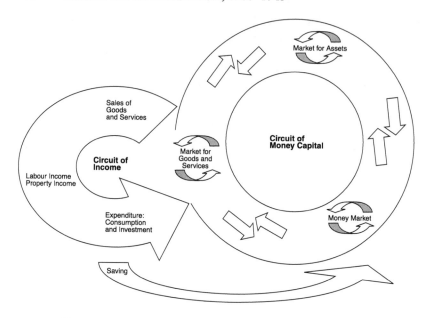

Figure 4 The circuit of payments
Source: E. Wagemann, *Konjunktlehre* (Berlin, 1928), p.

appreciate the conceptual apparatus that gave coherence to its extensive data-gathering. It was early macroeconomics not business-cycle research à la Harvard Committee that fired Weimar's statistical economics.

III

Wagemann intended to explore his macroeconomic equations in detail in volume II of the *Treatise*, but it was never to appear. From the spring of 1924, Wagemann's time was taken up with the running of the Statistical Office and the IfK. As Schumpeter suggested, the work of Weimar's statistical establishment should be taken as a substitute for Wagemann's missing synthesis. The business-cycle barometers that cluttered the Institute's publications were not the most characteristic products of Wagemann's statistical establishment; what really lay at the heart of its work was a precocious system of national accounts, the first regular series to be produced by any major capitalist state. The centre-piece of this system were the estimates of national income which first began to appear under the auspices of the Institute in 1926. They culminated in a volume published by the Reich's Statistical Office in

1932, which provided the first macroeconomic assessment of the development of the German economy over the long run.

The national income estimates of the 1920s followed in an intellectual tradition that can be traced back to the seventeenth and eighteenth centuries. The first efforts to estimate a nation's income were made by the servants of absolutist princes. But until the twentieth century national income estimation remained a cottage industry. As was discussed in the introduction, more systematic efforts began to be undertaken in the late nineteenth century, stimulated by the dual pressures of class tension and imperialism. But it was World War I that made the level of German national income into a key political issue. Karl Helfferich, the author of the most authoritative prewar estimate and a leading figure amongst the nationalist opponents of reparations, claimed that German national income had collapsed to no more than 20–22 billion RM in 1923, a disastrous collapse when compared to his estimate of 43 billion RM ten years earlier.[42] Foreign observers and German advocates of fulfilment were less pessimistic. But the statistical battle over German national income really began with the end of inflation. In the ensuing shakeout, employers and trade unions produced widely divergent figures. For 1924 estimates varied between 26 billion RM and 44 billion RM. And there was little convergence in the following years. The left believed that German capitalists had done well out of the inflation. Business, for its part, complained of the depreciation of assets, inflated wages and crushing taxes. In 1926, the Reichsverband der deutschen Industrie (RdI) estimated national income in the preceding year to have been between 43 billion and 48 billion RM. By contrast, the socialist trade unions suggested a figure between 52 billion and 60 billion RM.

At the same time, of course, the German economy was under intense international scrutiny. By the early 1920s the debate over reparations had come to hinge on Germany's capacity to pay. Here again, national income, together with the balance of payments, was the crucial variable. The British economist John Maynard Keynes in his famous commentaries on the reparations question relied on crude extrapolation from Karl Helfferich's prewar estimate.[43] The Dawes Committee, which provided a temporary settlement of the reparations issue in 1924, was forced to improvise. From 1929 onwards, the Dawes Plan envisioned that German payments would be made conditional on a rough and ready index of national prosperity.[44] Given the lack of reliable statistics

[42] BAP R 401 628 no. 504 ff and *VzK* 1 (1926), Heft 1 Mid May 1926, pp. 39–48.
[43] J.M. Keynes, *A Revision of the Treaty. Vol. III, The Collected Writings of J.M. Keynes* (London, 1971), pp. 55–59.
[44] J.A. Tooze, 'Imagining National Economies: National and International Economic

from German sources, this was made up of a truly bizarre combination of data. *Per capita* production figures from heavy industry were combined with customs and excise returns in a simple arithmetic average. The index embodied the aspiration to make payments conditional on economic capacity. But what it really demonstrated was the desperate need for more adequate measures of German economic activity. A rationalist approach to reparations demanded the estimation of national income.

Wagemann demonstrated his skill as a scientific entrepreneur in harnessing the theoretical project outlined in the *Treatise* to the practical needs of the Weimar Republic. Work on Germany's official estimate of national income began in the summer of 1925, immediately after the creation of the IfK. And the first edition of the Institute's quarterly review, published in May 1926, staked out a quasi-official position in the debate over German national income. On the basis of income tax figures, the IfK put German national income in 1925 at between 50 and 55 billion RM. It thus came close to endorsing the trade union's relatively optimistic assessment.[45] Significantly, the IfK took the Reichsverband to task for failing to distinguish between the logic of private and national accounting. The industrialists' low estimate was arrived at by subtracting a debit item to reflect the falling value of shares. As the Institute pointed out, this involved double-counting since the decline in share values was a reflection – on the capital account – of falling levels of corporate profits and incomes. One could count either symptom of economic problems, but not both. Once the extra adjustment was removed, all three estimates converged.

In the autumn, after a comprehensive review of methods used by economists abroad, the Statistical Office embarked on a major revision of the figures for both the prewar and postwar periods.[46] Under the overall leadership of Platzer, Dr Gerhard Colm headed the research team. Initially, the statisticians concentrated their efforts on revising Helfferich's much-cited estimate for the prewar period. Their suspicions focused above all on his underestimate of tax evasion. The introduction of a compulsory income tax by the Weimar Republic had revealed large swathes of uncounted income. Working from Prussian, Saxon and Bavarian tax records, Colm's staff arrived at a figure for prewar income as high as 50 billion RM, substantially greater than Helfferich's estimate. Work then progressed on the postwar accounts, new data being

Statistics, 1900–1950', in G. Cubitt, *Imagining Nations* (Manchester, 1998), pp. 212–228.
[45] *VzK* 1 (1926) Heft 1 Mid May 1926, pp. 39–48.
[46] BAP R 401 628 no. 490 ff.

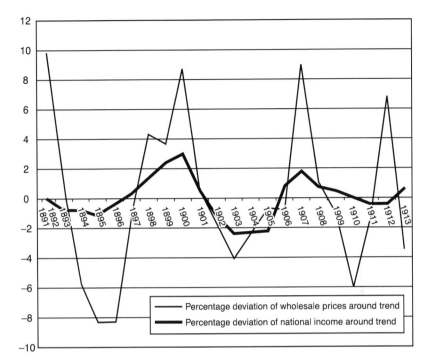

Figure 5 The cyclical fluctuation of German national income, 1891–1913
Source: SRA, *Das Deutsche Volkseinkommen vor und nach dem Kriege. Einzel-schriften zur Statistik des Deutschen Reichs*, Nr. 24 (Berlin, 1932), figure 6, p. 69

sporadically released to the public through the organs of the Statistical Office and the Institute.[47] The culmination of these efforts came in 1932 with the publication of a study which traced the development of the German economy since 1890 in strictly macroeconomic terms (see figure 5).[48]

The contrast between this image of the business-cycle and that developed by the Harvard Committee could hardly have been more stark. The Americans drew their conclusions from the relative movements of an arbitrary collection of symptomatic indicators. By contrast, Wagemann's Institute provided an absolute measurement of national

[47] *Wochenbericht des Instituts für Konjunkturforschung* 2 (1929), 23.12.1929 and *VzK* 4 (1930), pp. 44–49.
[48] SRA, *Das deutsche Volkseinkommen vor und nach dem Kriege. Einzelschriften zur Statistik des Deutschen Reichs*, Nr. 24 (Berlin, 1932).

income, the key macroeconomic variable.[49] For the first time the cycle could be analysed not by reference to the fluctuations of sensitive but unrepresentative industries, but through the actual movement of the economy as a whole. This approach provided an entirely new sense of the proportions of economic cycles. And it was applied first to the depression of 1925–6. In 1925, the Institute estimated, German national income had stood at 50 billion RM. During the following year 5 billion marks was wiped off the value of production. This revealed the gigantic scale of macroeconomic fluctuations, but it also put the cycle in an entirely new perspective. The Institute estimated that over the course of a serious depression national income had fallen by at most 10 per cent. Fluctuations in total output were proportionally far smaller than the swings suffered by sensitive industries such as steel, which had hitherto hogged the limelight. Acute fluctuations were concentrated in markets driven by discretionary expenditure. Industries producing consumer durables and investment goods were worst hit. Extending the data series back to 1890 confirmed this initial intuition. The economy developed in a wave-like motion. Billions of marks ebbed and flowed through the circuits of production, income and expenditure while, at the same time, an even larger process of production and reproduction developed according to its own rhythm, largely untroubled by the turmoil of the cycle (see figure 6).

From the mid-1920s onwards the entire repertoire of the Statistical Office and the Institute was built around this innovative national accounting framework. New surveys were established to fill holes in the accounting scheme.[50] Existing data series were reorganized and reinterpreted. Let us focus on the three variables that, together with national income, were highlighted in the introduction as constitutive of the modern conception of the economy.

After 1926 the IfK and the SRA dedicated themselves systematically to piecing together the complex picture of the balance of payments.[51] The reporting of visible trade resumed normally in 1924 after the chaos of the hyperinflation. But this was only part of the picture. The balance

---

[49] This important distinction between different approaches to the business-cycle is highlighted in K. Borchardt, 'Wandlungen des Konjunkturphänomens in den letzten hundert Jahren', in *Wachstum, Krisen, Handlungsspielräume der Wirtschaftspolitik. Studien zur Wirtschaftsgeschichte des 19. und 20. Jahrhunderts* (Göttingen, 1982b), pp. 73–99. However, Borchardt dates the macroeconomic perspective to the postwar period and does not consider the interwar work of the Institute.

[50] The first estimates of national investment for interwar Germany were published by the Institute as G. Keiser and B. Benning, *Kapitalbildung und Investitionen in der deutschen Volkswirtschaft 1924 bis 1928*, VzK Sonderheft 22 (Berlin, 1931).

[51] 'Introduction' in VzK 1 (1926) Ergänzungsheft 2 (Berlin, 1926).

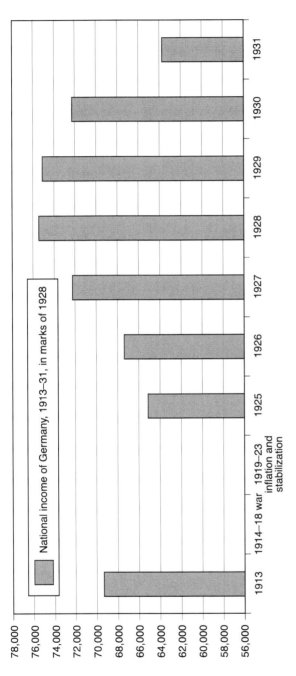

Figure 6 The postwar business-cycle, national income of Germany, 1925–1931 (Reichsmarks of 1928)
Source: *Das Deutsche Volkseinkommen vor und nach dem Kriege. Einzelschriften zur Statistik des Deutschen Reichs*, Nr. 24
(Berlin, 1932), figure 7, p. 70

of trade in services was estimated for the first time in 1926, as was the balance of interest payments.[52] Taken together, Germany sustained a significant deficit on current account in the 1920s. As Wagemann's national balance sheet made clear, this was matched by a corresponding inflow of both short-term and long-term borrowing on the capital account. Information on long-term foreign borrowing was systematically collated from the press. Short-term capital movements were estimated as a residual. By the late 1920s the new concept of the balance of payments acquired formal legitimacy with its inclusion in the annual handbook of German official statistics.

Estimates of national income, closely tied to figures for public expenditure and the balance of payments, provided a fundamentally new framework for the analysis of the German economy. However, the Institute and the Statistical Office did not confine themselves to such annual and quarterly data. The bulletins of the Institute were swollen with a mass of short-term indicators.[53] Price data and data on unemployment were key variables in the Institute's monitoring of the economy. Price data were of course the staple of traditional business-cycle analysis. And the Institute filled the pages of its publications with barometers done up in the style of the Harvard Committee. However, the stylistic similarities should not obscure the fundamental differences in their construction. The wholesale price index may serve as an example. When it was first introduced in 1921 it was designed as a typical cyclical indicator, registering the prices of a small group of highly volatile raw materials.[54] Wagemann's macroeconomics required something far more ambitious. In terms of the circular flow diagram, the purpose of the wholesale index was to measure fluctuations in the value of the nation's working-capital. The index represented the prices that producers paid for their raw materials and the prices paid by retailers for their stocks. It was of strategic importance because the Institute believed fluctuations in stock levels to be one of the motors of the cycle. In December 1926, the coverage of the index was therefore expanded to include the prices of no less than 170 raw materials and 230 finished and semi-finished products carefully weighted to reflect their economic significance.[55] Each type of price movement could now

[52] *VzK* 1 (1926), Supplement 2. Estimates of the balance of payments appeared annually in *Wirtschaft und Statistik*.

[53] By the early 1930s at least 84 different sets of economic data were being analysed in the quarterly bulletins, see Kuschmann, *Die Untersuchungen*, pp. 8–11.

[54] A. Jacobs, 'Die neue amtliche Großhandelsindexziffer', *ASA*, 16 (1926/1927), pp. 619–623.

[55] *WuS* 6 (1926), pp. 875–879.

be assessed in terms of its quantitative significance and its relation to the behaviour of all other prices.[56]

However, unlike earlier analysts of the business-cycle, the Institute did not accord prices pride of place. The key variable in its short-run analysis was employment. To our eyes today, this may seem an obvious choice. However, early business-cycle economists tended to steer clear of the labour market. For one thing, unemployment was much harder to measure than prices or the output of key industries such as steel. Furthermore, the strait-jacket of equilibrium theory made unemployment a variable with dubious theoretical connotations. The very idea of involuntary unemployment opened the door to subversive theories of underconsumption. The jobless were a problem for social policy. Not until the 1920s did unemployment begin to enter the mainstream as an object of legitimate economic theory. By then, the labour market had become a central preoccupation of the governing class. The creation of a national system of official labour exchanges produced a regular stream of statistical information. What the IfK provided was a theoretical scheme capable of making sense of unemployment in macroeconomic terms. Rather than viewing unemployment chiefly as the result of dysfunction in the market for labour, the Institute viewed it as the consequence of inadequate levels of overall economic activity. And according to the logic of the circular flow, this was self-reinforcing as lower levels of wage income meant lower consumption and lower aggregate demand.

After 1925 the existing repertoire of German statistics was reorganized around a novel conception of macroeconomics. One could cite many more examples. The statistics of German public finance were reconceived as part of the circular flow of income and expenditure.[57] The Institute also prepared new figures for private investment. But perhaps most indicative of the systematic vision behind the statistical expansion was a plan that did not actually to come to fruition in the Weimar Republic: the census of industrial production. The most vital piece of information missing from Wagemann's scheme was comprehensive data on production. Both the United States and Britain regularly conducted comprehensive industrial censuses. And, most significantly from Wagemann's point of view, they had been able to confirm the first three lines of his macroeconomic equations. Independent estimates of the value of production and the national income did indeed agree to within a remarkably small margin of error. Germany, by contrast, for

---

[56] *VzK* 1 (1926), 4, pp. 139–145.
[57] G. Colm, *Volkswirtschaftliche Theorie der Staatsausgaben. Ein Beitrag zur Finanztheorie* (Tübingen, 1927).

reasons discussed in earlier chapters, had never carried out a census of industrial production. The war had put paid to the stunted system of Wilhelmine production statistics. And for the first nine years of its existence the Weimar Republic was forced to do almost entirely without official production data. By 1925, even the Reichstag was becoming restless. Germany had regained the freedom to set tariffs but parliament had no statistical basis on which to debate the issue. Practical political interest converged with Wagemann's macroeconomic project. In the first instance the Reich's Statistical Office resumed the partial industrial surveys carried out on an annual basis before 1914.[58] However, Wagemann had more ambitious plans. In 1927 he ordered his staff to begin preparing Germany's first census of industrial production.[59] This would provide the corner-stone of the emerging system of national accounts. The target year was 1930. The first priority was to obtain a figure for industrial value added, the counterpart to national income. But following the US example, Wagemann's staff also planned to explore the connections between industries by requiring a full enumeration of the type, quantity and value of raw materials used in each case. In the *Konjunkturlehre* Wagemann had suggested the possibility of deciphering the business-cycle as a series of fluctuations transmitted from one sector to another. The census would provide a comprehensive overview of these input–output relationships. In the event, the Great Depression intervened and the census was put on hold. Nevertheless, the preparations provide further confirmation for our basic hypothesis: after 1925 the statistical apparatus of the Weimar Republic was being systematically reorganized around Wagemann's macroeconomic accounting scheme.

IV

This programme of macroeconomic research constitutes a remarkable innovation. It should be considered alongside the Weimar Republic's many other experiments in government as a classic modernist project: an attempt to create a practical economic science that would direct the state in its efforts to tame the fluctuations of the capitalist economy. Wagemann himself certainly set his activities against a grand historical backdrop centred on the crisis of liberalism. In the speech inaugurating the Institute for Business-Cycle Research, Wagemann contrasted the economy of 1925 to that 150 years earlier, at the time when Adam Smith

---

[58] E. von Roeder, 'Die industrielle Produktionsstatistik', in *Die Statistik in Deutschland nach ihrem heutigen Stand* (Berlin, 1940), pp. 1012–1024.

[59] BAP 31.02 6181, 'Die industrielle Produktionsstatistik im In- und Ausland' (ORR Leisse, Ref. Dorth) (1927/8).

published *The Wealth of Nations*.[60] Smith had written about a world of small producers, whose individual economic actions were marvellously coordinated by the powerful, 'invisible hand' of the market. This comforting metaphor no longer applied. Since the late nineteenth century capitalism had moved to a higher level of organization centred on the interaction of giant corporations, mediated through the private system of finance Wagemann had analysed in his *Treatise*. Meanwhile, states struggled to satisfy the demands of their populations through policies of intervention, which Wagemann dubbed 'protectionism'.

Wagemann viewed the Bolshevik experiment as one particularly radical response to the crisis of liberalism. In the era of NEP Wagemann and his Institute saw direct parallels between the efforts of Soviet economists to create a coherent framework for national economic planning and their own projects in Germany.[61] Western Europe had avoided revolution, but only by embarking on an experiment of its own. Capitalist 'protectionism' had expanded in an ad hoc fashion, intruding new spheres of regulation and organization between the remaining fragments of the liberal market economy. Wagemann estimated that no less than 50 per cent of all transactions in Weimar Germany were at prices that were fixed by private cartels or by government regulation. Germany could no longer claim to be a liberal, free-market economy.

In the interwar years the idea that the world had entered a new phase of capitalist development was commonplace.[62] Wagemann's approach is remarkable above all for its realistic scepticism. Though he rejected prophecies of doom, Wagemann warned of the dangers inherent in the new, adulterated form of capitalism. Whereas the polar opposites of free-market liberalism and central planning could both claim to offer inbuilt guarantees of stability, the dynamics of a 'protectionist' mixture of organization and free markets were unknown. In Wagemann's view, partial and uncoordinated efforts at stabilization were likely to lead to generalized disorientation and instability. The invisible hand was enfeebled. The system of prices no longer offered a reliable guide to business decisions. Similarly, it was no longer safe for the state to treat the economy as an independent variable and to conduct its finances without regard to their wider economic impact. As the state committed itself to a widening array of welfare expenditure, the public budget became inseparably intertwined with the economy. A government that failed to realize this could easily provoke an economic crisis. Through higher social expenditure and reduced tax income, this would rebound

[60] GStA I Rep. 120 C VIII 2a Nr. 33 Bd. 1 Bl. 2 Protokoll.
[61] *Russische Arbeiten zur Wirtschaftsforschung, VzK Sonderheft 12* (Berlin, 1929).
[62] Vilk, *Von der Konjunkturtheorie zur Theorie der Konjunkturpolitik*, pp. 69–196.

on the state's finances, necessitating further involuntary adjustments. Economic innocence was irretrievably lost. What was required was deliberate and collaborative management involving both the state and the major actors of the private economy. And this, in turn, provided Wagemann's new brand of economic research with its *raison d'être*.

Wagemann found willing backers for his vision of economic stabilization in his parent Ministry, the RWM. At the Ministry the technocratic enthusiasm of the postwar era survived the austerity of the stabilization period. The budget cuts that stopped German inflation hit the RWM hard. However, in key positions there was a continuity of personnel that connected the experiments of the 1920s to the experience of the war and its aftermath. Most important was Hans Schäffer. He belonged to the first cohort of officials recruited to the Ministry by Moellendorff. By 1924 he had risen to second in command, with responsibility for Department I and formulation of general economic policy.[63] Though Schäffer had a conventional civil servant's training in law, he was an intellectual who developed a substantial interest in economic research. His understanding of politics was technocratic, driven by a belief in the power of expertise. In practice, he made a habit of in-depth consultation on all matters of general economic policy.[64] His diaries record regular conferences with his own impressive collection of junior officials and with outside economists, but above all with Ernst Wagemann and his staff.[65] Schäffer would compile agendas of both general and technical questions. He would then collect lists of particularly important statistics, including the Institute's more adventurous estimates of national income. On Sundays he devoted his reading time to the Institute's early ventures in elementary econometrics. Between 1924 and 1929, when Schäffer departed to take the top job at the Ministry of Finance, Wagemann could hardly have hoped for a more congenial interlocutor. At the top, Wagemann and his establishment enjoyed the backing of State Secretary Ernst Trendelenburg, another Moellendorff recruit, and Dr Julius

---

[63] E. Wandel, *Hans Schäffer. Steuermann in wirtschaftlichen und politischen Krisen 1886–1967* (Stuttgart, 1974). Within Schäffer's Department, a further element of continuity was provided by Fritz Soltau who had worked under Wagemann in the War Food Office and was to be responsible for statistical affairs at the RWM from the early 1920s until 1940, see K. Szameitat, 'Fritz Soltau im Ruhestand', *ASA*, 36 (1952), pp. 374–376.

[64] Both F. Blaich, *Die Wirtschaftskrise 1925/26* (Kallmünz, 1977) and D. Hertz-Eichenrode, *Wirtschaftskrise und Arbeitsbeschaffung. Konjunkturpolitik 1925/26 und die Grundlagen der Krisenpolitik Brünings* (Frankfurt, 1982), p. 248 acknowledge the influence of the Institute's economic research on the RWM. See also H. Staudinger, *Wirtschaftspolitik im Weimarer Staat. Lebenserinnerungen eines politischen Beamten im Reich und in Preußen 1889 bis 1934* (Bonn, 1982) and J. Curtius, *Sechs Jahre Minister der Deutschen Republik* (Heidelberg, 1948).

[65] Schäffer's diary is preserved in IZG MA 1559.

Curtius who served as Minister for Economic Affairs in a series of coalitions between 1926 and 1930. Curtius had a training in historical economics. And one of his central ambitions was to turn the RWM into a national centre for economic observation.[66] He shared the common hope of the 1920s that the official promotion of 'economic self-know-ledge' would moderate the need for coercive state intervention.[67] In speeches to the Reichstag he described the activities of his Ministry in new-fangled language taken straight out of Wagemann's textbooks. He divided the RWM's functions into 'structural' and 'cyclical'.[68] Trade policy and infrastructural development created favourable structural conditions, whereas a judicious deployment of public expenditure would help to stabilize the cycle.

Curtius and Schäffer were enthusiasts. But, in backing Wagemann, they were doing more than merely spreading the technocratic faith. The Ministry of Economic Affairs was staking a double claim to political authority. As we have seen, the crisis of the Wilhelmine state unleashed a dramatic process of state-formation. The new ministries struggled in the aftermath of the war to assert themselves against the awesome power of the interest groups. Even after the period of revolu-tionary turmoil came to an end in 1924, the German state never remotely resembled the 'Weberian' image of a rationalized bureaucracy with well-established administrative systems working within clearly defined spheres. The state resembled far more a chaotic building-site in which different bureaucratic apparatuses struggled to assert their par-ticular self-interest while at the same time pursuing more general visions of how the state should be organized and what its purposes should be. The RWM faced two challenges from within the state apparatus. On the one hand it had to defend itself against the other Reich's ministries. Unlike the ministries for Finance, Agriculture and Food, Labour and Transport, the Reich's Ministry for Economic Affairs lacked a clearly demarcated constituency.[69] During the economy drive of 1924–5 there were even suggestions that the RWM

[66] J. Curtius, *Bismarcks Plan eines Deutschen Volkswirtschaftsrats* (Heidelberg, 1919). Curtius made a point of making a personal tour of the SRA, see J. Curtius, *Sechs Jahre*, pp. 24–25.

[67] Curtius' budget speech in March 1927 in *Verhandlungen des Reichstags III. Wahlperiode 1924. Stenographische Berichte* (Berlin, 1927), vol. 392, pp. 9439–9440, see also J. Curtius, *Sechs Jahre*, pp. 58–59.

[68] On the new language of economic 'structure' see H. Wolff, 'Struktur und Konjunktur', *ASA*, 17 (1927/1928), pp. 205–235.

[69] G. Schulz, *Zwischen Demokratie und Diktatur. Verfassungspolitik und Reichsform in der Weimarer Republik. Vol. I, Die Periode der Konsolidierung und der Revision des Bismarckschen Reichsaufbaus 1919–1930* (Berlin, 1987, 2nd edn.), p. 525.

should be disbanded.[70] In this battle, national economic statistics were a powerful weapon. Whereas the other ministries stood for the interests of particular sections, the RWM claimed to stand for the interests of the entire national economy. This now took on concrete reality in the national income figures published by the Institute and the Statistical Office. At the same time, the Reich's Ministry also had to assert itself against the entrenched interests of the Länder. Despite their straitened circumstances, the Länder retained their independent ministries of Trade and Commerce. Unlike the Reich's Labour Administration, the Reich's Finance Ministry and the Reichsbank, the RWM lacked routine administrative responsibilities and was therefore unable to justify the creation of its own regional infrastructure. The RWM remained cut off from the day-to-day activities of business.[71] In the early 1920s an attempt was made to require the chambers of commerce to report directly to the RWM; however, this was vetoed by the Länder Ministries.[72] The expansion of the Statistical Office and the Institute was a way for the RWM to escape the vacuum that surrounded it in Berlin.[73]

The RWM thus had a clear interest in the pursuit of economic statistics and economic research. However, as a spending department it had to argue its case against the competing claims of other agencies. Why was so much money forthcoming? The Reich's Finance Ministry was certainly not predisposed to grant the Statistical Office its every wish. Indeed, a traditional animosity opposed the revenue departments of the state to the apparatus of official statistics. Since the early nineteenth century official statisticians had defined themselves against the tax authorities. During the fiscal crackdown of the mid-1920s, statisticians found themselves having to ward off intrusive enquiries by the new national tax administration. Furthermore, the new Reich's Finance Ministry harboured statistical ambitions of its own. The Finance Ministry planned an independent system of fiscal statistics to govern the new, all-embracing, national system of income tax and to regulate the balance of fiscal competencies between the Reich and local government.[74] This posed a threat to the monopoly of data-gathering tradition-

---

[70] F. Facius, *Wirtschaft und Staat die Entwicklung der staatlichen Wirtschaftsverwaltung in Deutschland vom 17. Jahrhundert bis 1945* (Boppard, 1959), p. 113.

[71] W.A. Boelcke *Die deutsche Wirtschaft 1930–1945 Interna des Reichswirtschaftsministeriums* (Düsseldorf, 1983), p. 43.

[72] BAP RAM 39.01 film 33203/896.

[73] This led to protests from the Bavarian Statistical Office, see the correspondence in BHStA MA 103895 and BHStA MWi 3092 SLa to Staatsmin. für Handel 16.3.1928.

[74] GStA 1. HA Rep. 77 3884 no. 188, Konferenz der Reich- und Landesstatistiker, Baden-Baden 4.-6.6.1924, pp. 5–6, 56–58.

ally claimed by German official statisticians. More worryingly, it posed a threat to Wagemann's bold plans for macroeconomic statistics. Tax records were the basic source for national income estimation.

The key to the prosperity of Wagemann's empire in the 1920s was an alliance struck with the Office of the Reich's Sparkommissar (Reich's Savings Commissioner). The office of the Sparkommissar was established in the aftermath of inflation, to exert consistent pressure for fiscal retrenchment. It soon became clear, however, that rationalization of the public administration was a highly political matter. The demand for efficiency posed a direct challenge to the lop-sided federalism inherited from the Wilhelmine era.[75] In the name of rationalization, the Sparkommissar was to become one of the leading advocates of administrative centralization and 'constitutional reform'. And in the case of the Statistical Office, this political ambition overrode the Sparkommissar's more specific duty to contain costs. The basis for the deal between Wagemann and the Sparkommissar was the concentration of all statistical functions on the Reich's Statistical Office. The Sparkommissar envisioned the Reich's Office as a high-tech data-processing centre around which to build a streamlined, national information system. For Wagemann this brought obvious advantages. Far from seeking to rein in Wagemann's empire-building the Sparkommissar encouraged him.

The boldest proposal was for the incorporation of the Prussian statistical office into the Reich's Office.[76] However, this was blocked by Prussian resistance. The alliance between the Sparkommissar and the Statistical Office had more practical success within the Reich's bureaucracy itself. The ambitions of the Labour Administration were sharply curtailed. With the exception of unemployment data, all major surveys were returned to the Statistical Office by 1927.[77] Similarly, the Reich's Finance Ministry was forced to agree to the concentration of the nation's financial statistics on the Statistical Office. With a decree issued in February 1926, the Statistical Office was empowered to carry out a compulsory survey of the finances of the Reich, Länder and Communes.[78] For the first time the activities of the entire ramified apparatus of the German state were encompassed within a single set of figures, starting at the level of local government and proceeding upwards to the Reich.[79] In 1928 the annual surveys were extended to include a complete survey of government indebtedness.[80] In fact, the Reich's

[75] Schulz, *Zwischen Demokratie und Diktatur*, pp. 527–542.
[76] GStA 1. HA Rep. 77 3884 no. 178–244.
[77] BAK R 43 I/965 no. 13, Verordnung 21.8.1927.
[78] *WuS* 7 (1927), pp. 446–457.
[79] *WuS* 9 (1929), pp. 106–111.
[80] SRA, *Öffentlicher Kredit und Wirtschaftskrise. Ergebnisse der Reichsschuldenstatistik 1929*

financial statistics became the largest single item in the Statistical Office's workload, accounting for half the new staff taken on in the period between 1924 and 1929. By the end of the 1920s there were three Departments, employing a total of almost 1,000 staff, devoted exclusively to tax statistics, budget statistics and general finance statistics.[81] With the backing of both the Ministry and the Sparkommissar it was not hard to muster support in the Reichstag for statistical spending. Discussions of the Reichstag's Budgetary Committee and the Plenary Sessions reveal cross-party support for the expansion of statistics and economic research during the 1920s.[82] Even the communists welcomed the formation of the Institute in 1925.[83]

The *quid pro quo* for the Sparkommissar's political backing was a rigorous programme of administrative rationalization. In the 1920s the Statistical Office not only grew in size, it changed shape; it became a factory for data-processing. Under the influence of the Sparkommissar, the production of official statistics was transformed from a proto-industrial putting-out system, to a centralized, mechanical operation. Rationalization included the introduction, in 1924, of a battery of psychometric tests, to establish the aptitude of new staff for the rigours of number-crunching work.[84] A central administrative office was set up to maintain a continuous overview of all departmental activities. Cost accounts were used to track the allocation of the Statistical Office's resources.[85] Employment in each Department was related to the volume of 'declarations' processed and the number of pages contributed to official publications (see table 3).

Large-scale mechanization was the technical rationale behind the Sparkommissar's drive towards centralization. Labour accounted for 75 per cent of the costs of producing statistics. 'Scientific' labour accounted for only a very small proportion. The vast bulk of statistical work consisted of the routine activities of sorting and counting millions of questionnaires and reports. This was a task ripe for mechanization. And it was a task in which there were substantial economies of scale. The

bis 1932 und Zusammenstellung von Rechstvorschriften über das öffentliche Schuldenwesen, Nr. 27 Einzelschriften zur Statistik des Deutschen Reichs (Berlin, 1933).

[81] BAP 31.02 SRA 4169, Das SRA, Dezember 1929.

[82] See responses by von Raumer (German People's Party) and Schlack (Centre) to Curtius' budget speech in *Verhandlungen des Reichstags III. Wahlperiode 1924. Stenographische Berichte* (Berlin, 1927), vol. 392, pp. 9448–9449, 9466.

[83] See the comments by Koenen (Communist) in *Verhandlungen des Reichstags III. Wahlperiode 1924. Stenographische Berichte* (Berlin, 1926), vol. 389, p. 6428.

[84] GStA 1. HA Rep. 77 3884 no. 188, Konferenz der Reich- und Landesstatistiker Baden-Baden am 4.-6.6.1924, p. 15.

[85] BAP 23.01 2234 no. 4, Bericht über die Untersuchungsergebnisse der Kommission zur Nachprüfung des statistischen Dienstes, p. 19b.

Table 3. *Staff allocation, data-processing load and published output of the Statistical Office, December 1929*

Department	Total staff	Items of data processed, p.a. (million)	Pages of statistics published
I General administration	479	16.8	330
II Trade and transport	515	531.6	5,050
III Social statistics	189	57.2	2,053
IV Census and industrial production statistics	231	183.6	17,275
V Finance and administrative statistics of Reich	71	0.6	1,427
VI Tax statistics	847	690.0	2,472
VII Finance statistics	369	40.8	6,300
VIII General economic statistics	116	4.5	1,343

Source: BAP 31.02 4169, 'Das SRA und seine Arbeiten. Stand Dezember 1929', p. 1.

larger the batches of data, the more efficiently the punch-card machines operated. Hence the need to concentrate all data-processing. After 1924 the Statistical Office acquired a substantial park of machines, principally from the German subsidiary of the Hollerith Corporation, the ancestor of IBM.[86] The first statistics to be mechanized were the trade data, for which more than 2 million import and export returns had to be processed every month.[87] This was followed by the mechanization of the Reich's tax statistics, involving the processing of 20–30 million items of data, as well as the statistics of bankruptcy and goods traffic.[88] By 1929, the 260 staff of the Statistical Office's Hollerith section processed 40 million punched cards annually, resulting in a net saving of 800 jobs at the Statistical Office, more than 25 per cent of its total staff.[89]

V

Wagemann's project of Konjunkturforschung thus stands in a direct line of descent from the state-building of the early Weimar years. However,

[86] K. Koch, 'Die Verwendung von Speziallochkartenmaschinen bei der Volkszählung 1930 unter Berücksichtigung ihrer technischen Entwicklung', *ASA*, 19 (1929), pp. 560–568.
[87] BAP 31.01 RWM 2436 no. 103, Präs. SRA to RWM 6.12.1924 and P. Schwartz, 'Zur Frage der Anwendbarkeit der mechanischen Auszählung bei statistischen Erhebungen', *ASA*, 20 (1930), pp. 266–270.
[88] *Festschrift zur 25. Jahresfeier der Deutschen Hollerith Maschinen Gesellschaft* (Berlin, 1935), pp. 72–73 and BAP 23.01 2234 no. 4, 'Bericht über die Untersuchungsergebnisse der Kommission zur Nachprüfung des statistischen Dienstes' May 1932, p. 11.
[89] BAP 39.01 RAM 10683 no. 28, Bericht, p. 4.

this begs a crucial question. How was Wagemann's project situated in relation to the forces of civil society? As we have already seen, relations between official statisticians and the business community eased after 1924. The enquiries that had met such dogged resistance in the early years of the Republic were largely accepted. But Wagemann's programme of enquiry was far more expansive than anything that had been proposed to date. How did he gain the support of key groups in civil society? The macroeconomic approach itself provides part of the answer. Many of the key data could be obtained from the internal administrative records of the state, such as tax returns. However, such data provided, at best, a slow-moving retrospective record of economic activity. For more specific and more immediate information on the business-cycle, the statisticians needed access to business records of employment, production and turnover. In any case, the tacit support of business opinion was crucial if the pronouncements of Wagemann's establishment were to carry weight with the public. Systematic criticism by Germany's business leaders could easily have destroyed the entire project. Konjunkturforschung had to be sold to the business community.

The Reichsverband der deutschen Industrie (Reich's Association of German Industry, RdI) was the key to Wagemann's success. The Reichsverband was by far the most important organization of German business. Gaining its support and cementing it in place as a consistent backer of the Institute ensured the legitimacy of the entire programme. The crucial turning point came in 1924 when the leadership of the RdI changed hands. Under its new chairman, Duisberg, the RdI made its peace with the Republic.[90] Rather than resisting the new state, the RdI now sought to shape the democratic political agenda to its advantage. Its first attempts, however, were crude and the results disappointing. In the winter of 1925, after months of preparatory work by a committee of tame academics, the RdI presented a memorandum pretentiously entitled, *German Economic Policy*.[91] This blunt statement of business principles made little impact. Civil servants regarded it with suspicion and the details were rendered obsolete by the onset of a severe economic crisis.[92] This experience convinced forward-thinking groups in the RdI to adopt a more subtle approach to shaping public opinion. The Reichsverband would sponsor the creation of an 'independent' centre

[90] Duisberg replaced the Krupp Director Kurt Sorge in the winter of 1924–5. The precise significance of Duisberg's accession is disputed in the literature. See the review in P. Hayes, 'History in an Off Key: David Abraham's Second Collapse', *Business History Review*, 61 (Autumn 1987), pp. 452–472.

[91] B. Weisbrod, *Schwerindustrie in der Weimarer Republik* (Wuppertal, 1978), p. 217.

[92] Blaich, *Die Wirtschaftskrise 1925/26*, p. 96.

for economic research that would provide an authoritative running commentary on the state of the German economy. It would produce 'reliable' statistics and would thereby serve the wider aim of asserting 'unpolitical' economic and technical criteria in policy debate. The RdI had sent a delegation to the opening meeting of the Institute, but initially they were far from enthusiastic. Only an 'independent', 'scientific' research centre dominated by business and excluding the trade unions would do.[93] In the course of 1926, however, it became clear that there was no hope of raising sufficient funds from business resources.[94] By the end of the year the RdI was forced to arrive at an agreement with Wagemann.[95] The association would make a substantial annual contribution to the Institute in exchange for a 'permanent observer'. This relationship with the RdI proved robust.

In part it was founded on genuine technocratic enthusiasm, in part on a cynical give-and-take in which the moderate leaders of the RdI played a key role. Conservative industrialists such as Paul Reusch continued to regard the Institute with suspicion. He regularly took offence at its publications and demanded that Wagemann should not be allowed to forget who was paying the bills.[96] Faced with such attitudes the leadership of the RdI played a vital mediating role. The moderate executive secretary of the RdI, Ludwig Kastl, patiently explained the need for compromise. And Kastl could count on the backing of liberals such as the brown-coal baron Paul Silverberg, who took an active role in the Institute's affairs as well as being one of the leading advocates of a conciliatory stance towards the trade unions.[97] Though the trade unions made only a small contribution to the Institute's budget their presence on the Kuratorium was vital in providing a counter-weight to the overweening influence of business. If Reusch had his way and industry pulled out, the Institute would be left to the sole control of labour. Or, at least, this was the reasoning of Wagemann and the moderates on the RdI board. The trade unions themselves needed little encouragement to join. Since the turn of the century the socialist unions had come to regard statistics as both an effective tool of labour market management

[93] BAK Nl 13 Silverberg 225 and 330.
[94] BBA 15 523, RDI to Hölling 9.2.1926 and BBA 15 523, Fg Bergbau to RDI 16.2.1926.
[95] BAK Nl 13 Silverberg 259 no. 154, agenda for RDI Presidium meeting 8.10.1926 and BAK Nl 13 Silverberg 226 no. 161, Presidium meeting 10.12.1926.
[96] RWWA 20 Niederrheinische IHK Duisburg-Wesel 996/3, Reusch to Kastl 30.12.1927 and Kastl to Reusch 2.1.1928.
[97] R. Neebe, *Großindustrie, Staat und NSDAP 1930–1933. Paul Silverberg und der Reichsverband der deutschen Industrie in der Krise der Weimarer Republik* (Göttingen, 1981), pp. 35–49.

Table 4. *Budgeted Income of the Institute, 1925–1932 (RM 000 p.a.)*

Item	1925	1926	1927	1928	1929	1930	1931	1932
Budgeted income (RM 000)	201	254.1	374.9	376.8	401.4	302.9	396.9	249.9
Shares (%) Public sector	45	58	60	61	56	56	56	51
Business	47	33	31	32	37	36	34	38
Agriculture	n.a.	4	3	1	1	0.5	2	2
Labour	8	5	6	6	6	7.5	8	9

Notes: All years run from 1 April to 31 March.
Public sector: RWM, Reich's Labour Ministry, Reichsbank, Reichsbahn, Reichspost, Bank fuer Industrieobligationen, Prussian government, Staedtetag.
Business: RdI, DIHT, Bergbaulicher Verein, Zentralverband des deutschen Grosshandels, Hauptgemeinschaft des deutschen Einzelhandels, Zentralverband der deutschen Konsumgenossenschaften, Centralverband des deutschen Bank und Bankiergewerbes, Sparkassen und Giroverband, Reichsverband des deutschen Handwerks.
Agriculture: Deutscher Landwirtschaftsrat.
Labour: ADGB, Christlichen Gewerkschaften Deutschlands, Gewerkschaftsring deutscher Arbeiter-, Angestellten-, und Beamtenverbaende.
Sources: BHStA Mwi 3092; Geheimes Staatsarchiv I Rep. 120 C VIII 2a nr. 33 Bd. 1.

and as a propaganda weapon. The Christian trade unions were no less enthusiastic in their support. The support of organized industry and labour enabled Wagemann to pull in other interest groups. The range of backers and their relative importance was reflected in the opening meeting in July 1925 and more importantly in the Institute's annual budget statements (see table 4).

But money and political protection were not the only issues. The collaboration of the key interest groups was to provide the Institute with unprecedented access to information. Every one of the major statistical initiatives after 1924 was carefully negotiated with German business. Each one of the Institute's barometers was built on an alliance with a particular segment of business or labour. The Institute's monthly index of industrial production, the first such index to be published for Germany, depended entirely on such cooperative arrangements. When the index first appeared in August 1927 it consisted of 19 individual components from both the primary industries (coal, iron and steel) and manufacturing (textiles and paper industries).[98] By February 1930 the index had been expanded to 31 components with the addition of information from the non-ferrous metal industries, the construction materials industry, mechanical engineering, the motor vehicles industry, the shoe industry, the porcelain industry, the watch and clock industry

[98] *VzK* 2 (1927), 2, pp. 26–27.

and the association of piano manufacturers.[99] Each of these data series represented a new alliance between the Institute and an industrial association. And the traffic was not one way. The Institute became a clearing house for economic information, taking in raw data and supplying friendly business associations with processed indicator systems.[100]

The most important collaborative venture between the statisticians and the RdI was the so-called Industrial Reporting System. The Labour Statistics Department of the Imperial Statistical Office had first introduced the Reports in 1903. They provided a rough guide to the state of the labour market by asking firms to rate the level of employment and sales on a scale of one to five. After the war the system had been lost to the Labour Ministry, but was regained by the Reich's Statistical Office in 1927 as part of a deal brokered by the Sparkommissar.[101] At the time, the Statistical Office was beginning preparations for the census of production. The Industrial Reports promised to provide the ideal short-run complement. Dr Paul Bramstedt, Wagemann's right-hand man, envisioned a 'total statistics of the business-cycle', with firms supplying monthly reports on the number of employees, the number of hours worked, the value of incoming orders from home and abroad, stock levels and goods shipped, as well as the level of outstanding orders.[102] This bold proposal clearly required the consent of the RdI. A meeting was duly arranged in January 1928. This revealed the limits of the new cooperation between the Reich's statisticians and the German business community. The RdI insisted that there should be no compulsion.[103] As it was well aware, the wartime provisions of Auskunftspflicht were still on the statute books. Only a voluntary system was acceptable. The industrialists also rejected the idea of making reports within five days of the end of each month. Furthermore, the iron and steel industries, the chemical industries and the metal goods industries were unwilling and unable to supply data on sales, orders and stocks. And the collection of data on the numbers of hours worked was opposed on political grounds. Dividing hours worked by the number of workers one could arrive at a number for hours per worker, a critical figure in the struggle over the eight-hour day. Bramstedt and Wagemann were forced to abandon their

---

[99] *VzK* 4 (1930), 4, pp. 37–43. By 1930 the index was estimated to cover a quarter of total industrial value added.

[100] The arrangements with the motor vehicle industry are described by Hilsman in BBA 15 1092, 'Sitzung betr. Industrieberichte 11.1.1928 im RDI'.

[101] Frölich's speech in BBA 15 1092, 'Sitzung betr. Industrieberichte 11.1.1928 im RDI'.

[102] BAK 11/51 Fol. 1 no. 150, Paul Bramstedt speech to the Committee for economic statistics of the RgI, 'Dezentralisierung der Industrieberichte', 6.8.1938, p. 1 and BBA 15 1092, RDI to Hölling 31.12.1927.

[103] BBA 15 1092, 'Sitzung betr. Industrieberichte 11.1.1928 im RDI'.

dream of 'total statistics of the business-cycle'. The Industrial Reports would be limited to employment and hours worked. Furthermore, the Institute would encode the results. Total hours and the number of workers would appear in the form of index numbers, based on notional levels of full-capacity working and full-capacity employment. The definition of the baselines would be left deliberately vague. Despite these concessions, business attitudes towards the new questionnaire were grudging. Important industries such as chemicals refused to participate at all. In total, 3,500 firms with a workforce of 2.8 million took part. The first encrypted results were not released until 1930.[104]

Despite the difficulties over the Industrial Reporting system there can be little doubt of the wide range of influential support enjoyed by Wagemann's establishment. In the autumn of 1927, when the Institute's funding was up for renewal, Paul Reusch commissioned his representative in Berlin to conduct a straw poll of attitudes amongst key figures in the capital. Dr Blank's report strikingly confirms the breadth of Wagemann's coalition. Representatives of the three peak associations of German business all expressed their enthusiasm for the Institute's work. If there were flaws in its analyses, these were blamed on the shortage of adequate statistics. Interestingly, both Lemmer of the Employers' Association and Kastl of the RdI advised Reusch's representative to ignore criticism from academic economists. Such dissent merely reflected the incoherent state of the economics discipline in German universities. The techniques of the Institute were the methods of the future. Even those hostile to Konjunkturforschung credited its influence. Buchmann of the Association of German Iron and Steel Industrialists opined: 'There is a danger that our entire way of viewing the economy will be contaminated by the "theoretical" methods of the Institute.'[105] Herle of the RdI even asked that his sceptical comments be treated confidentially, since his boss, Kastl, was such a strong advocate of the Institute. In enlightened business circles in the 1920s it was not the done thing to be critical of Wagemann's Institute.

VI

The apotheosis of Weimar's technocratic vision of economic policy-making came in 1927.[106] The occasion was a motion put through the Economic Policy Committee of the Reichswirtschaftsrat, the consulta-

---

[104] BBA 15 1092, IfK to Fg Bergbau 19.10.1929 and *VzK*, 5, 1, A, pp. 44–46.

[105] RWWA 20 Niederrheinische IHK Duisburg-Wesel 996/3, Blank to Reusch 30.11.1927, pp. 2–3.

[106] R. Meister, *Die große Depression. Zwangslagen und Handlungsspielräume der Wirtschafts- und Finanzpolitik in Deutschland 1929–1932* (Regensburg, 1991), pp. 162–170.

tive corporatist assembly, in July. The Christian Trade Unionist Baltrusch appealed for the procurement of the Reichsbahn and the Reich to be strategically deployed so as to achieve the most beneficial impact.[107] Such demands were not new. Calls for public works dated back to the turn of the century.[108] And Baltrusch's motion certainly had the flavour of nineteenth-century 'Sozialpolitik' about it. His main concern was that the bunching of public contracts, particularly for building materials, led to overtime working in the quarries, night-shifts, the employment of old and unsafe equipment and an increase in the number of industrial accidents. What is remarkable is the way in which Baltrusch's old-fashioned appeal was instrumentalized by the RWM and Wagemann's establishment as the occasion to air a quite different policy agenda. It was not social policy, but macroeconomics, that was to dictate the course of fiscal policy.

A memorandum prepared jointly by Schäffer of the RWM and representatives of the Reich's Labour Ministry set the tone. This ignored the social policy issues altogether. Instead, it focused on the possibility of deploying public expenditure in such a way as to stabilize the business-cycle. The aim was 'to maintain the scale of public contracts in inverse proportion to the scale of private contracts',[109] in other words, to stabilize aggregate demand. There can be no doubting the influence of the Institute here. The scale of the stabilization problem envisioned by the memorandum was clearly based on the Institute's calculations.[110] On the basis of experience in 1923–4 and early 1926, Wagemann reckoned with registered unemployment of 10 per cent at the depth of a depression. According to the Institute's calculations, unemployment at this level during a depression resulted in an immediate shortfall in discretionary consumption of 3 billion RM per annum. Given total public procurement of 6–7 billion RM, Wagemann estimated that no more than 10 per cent would have to be set aside during the good years of the cycle to create a substantial stabilization·fund. The influence of the Institute can also be inferred from the strong advocacy of public works. Most of the more prominent business-cycle theorists both in Germany and abroad preferred monetary policy as a tool of stabilization. Lowering interest rates in the wake of a depression was supposed to stimulate investment, raise demand and restore full employment. The Berlin Institute was sceptical about this 'transmission mech-

---

[107] BAP R 401 781 no. 3, 'Antrag to Wipo Cttee. Vorlf. Reichswirtschaftsrat 15.7.1927 Baltrusch und Genossen'.

[108] A. Faust, *Arbeitsmarktpolitik im Deutschen Kaiserreich. Arbeitsvermittlung, Arbeitsbeschaffung und Arbeitslosenunterstützung 1890–1918* (Stuttgart, 1986).

[109] BAP R 401 781 no. 55, RWM report for Reichswirtschaftsrat 16.12.1927, p. 3.

[110] See the article by Wagemann filed in BAP R 401 781 no. 198.

anism'. Investment depended as much on final demand as it did on the interest rate. Without the prospect of profit, business men would not invest, whatever the cost of funds. Wagemann and his economists therefore regarded government expenditure as a far more powerful tool of economic stabilization. It acted directly on the circulatory system of the economy, pumping in purchasing power. This in turn would stimulate private consumption and investment. Of course, the upholders of orthodoxy had always argued that government expenditure financed by loans would merely 'crowd' private investment out of the capital market. The Institute acknowledged that this was a valid deduction from the static comparison of equilibria. But it doubted the relevance of such models to the analysis of the cycle. At the trough of a recession the credit system was awash with funds. What held the economy back was not a shortage of finance, but the depressed expectations of investors. Government expenditure would break the deadlock, providing a powerful stimulus to recovery, putting unused funds to work.

This argument depended crucially on timing.[111] The Institute had to be able to identify precisely the moment at which the economy moved from crisis to liquidation. To stress this point, Baltrusch was supplied with a helpful chart illustrating how accurately the Institute had forecast economic development over the preceding years.[112] On what were these forecasts based? Essentially the Institute derived its predictions by extrapolation from past business-cycle patterns. In the prewar period it identified a 7- to 10-year cycle. Since the war, this pattern had become compressed. Counting forward from the depression of 1925–6, the Institute expected a downturn for the German economy in the latter half of 1928. There was cause for concern, but not for panic. The Institute had convinced itself that the German economy was swinging out of step with the other major industrialized countries. This meant that any German recession would be cushioned by the so-called 'export-valve', which permitted German heavy industry and light manufacturers to liquidate their excess stocks on foreign markets. Furthermore, Germany could hope to benefit from a continued flow of foreign investment. If necessary, the funds for the stabilization package could be borrowed from abroad.

In the early 1930s Hans Schäffer was to be one of the most passionate advocates of fiscal retrenchment. So why was he willing to underwrite this adventurous proposal? Schäffer had at least two motives for wanting

[111] For a sceptical contemporary view see F. Köhler, 'Die Aufträge der öffentlichen Hand', Die Bank (1928), pp. 340–345.
[112] BAP R 401 781 no. 196, 'Die Diagnosen des Instituts für Konjunkturforschung und die tatsächliche Wirtschaftsbewegung' (Februar 1928).

to ensure that German budgetary policy was conducted with a view to its macroeconomic impact. First and most immediately Schäffer was one of the leading advocates of reparations fulfilment. It was this which dictated a determined policy of fiscal restraint both to raise the funds and to create the conditions for a trade surplus. This was a tough line to take during periods of economic crisis such as 1925–6. But in 1927 Germany was enjoying a period of prosperity. And yet, precisely at this moment of peak activity, the public sector was indulging in a spending spree. This was fuelling a trade deficit and an unsustainable level of foreign borrowing. The Institute's model of stabilization provided Schäffer with a domestic rationale for his foreign policy line. Irresponsible state spending during prosperity not only made it impossible to service reparations, it also destabilized the business-cycle and narrowed the government's room for manoeuvre in the ensuing recession. Fiscal prudence was called for on both counts.

And who better to impose this discipline than the RWM? With the help of Wagemann's establishment, Schäffer's Ministry would exercise macroeconomic supervision over total spending, ensuring that it was compatible both with domestic stability and Germany's foreign obligations. To feed into the Baltrusch discussions, the Statistical Office compiled figures for the purchasing of the Reich, the Länder and the Reichsbahn in the budget years 1926 and 1927.[113] These tables enumerated the total value of orders placed by the main procurement agencies with each major branch of German industry. In future it would be possible to monitor the impact of particular public procurement policies on the turnover and employment of specific industries (see table 5).[114]

After protracted deliberations, the main recommendation of the Baltrusch Committee was that public procurement should be coordinated through a regular statistical survey.[115] All major contracts placed by the Reich and the Länder were to be reported to a committee chaired by the Reich's Ministry of Economic Affairs. This would allow Schäffer and the RWM to exercise oversight, if not control, over the scale and timing of public procurement. The statistics, at least, were collected on a regular basis thereafter.[116]

---

[113] BAP R 401 781 no. 66, RWM to Reichswirtschaftsrat 22.12.1927, see also H. Arons, 'Behördliche Konjunkturpolitik', *Die Arbeit* 5 (1928), pp. 527–529.

[114] See the Reichsbank study BAP 25.01 6707 no. 202, 'Welchen Einfluß hatten die Aufträge der öffentlichen Hand auf die Konjunkturentwicklung der deutschen Wirtschaft in den letzten Jahren?', pp. 6–7.

[115] BAP R 401 781 no. 363, 'Gutachten des Arbeitsausschusses zur Beratung des Antrags Baltrusch u.a.' (March 1928).

[116] *WuS* 10 (1930), pp. 856–860.

Table 5. *Procurement of the German public sector, 1929 and 1930, by industry*

Industrial sectors	Monthly average July–December 1930 (1,000 RM)	(%)	Monthly average in the budget year 1929 (1,000 RM)	(%)
Mining	21,711	28.8	26,236	27.4
Quarrying	1,646	2.2	4,080	4.3
Iron and metal production	10,912	14.5	10,590	11.1
Iron, steel and metal goods	1,535	2	4,720	4.9
Mechanical engineering and vehicles	17,387	23.1	17,314	18.1
Electrical engineering, fine-mechanical and optical industries	9,529	12.7	13,481	14.1
Chemical industry	2,675	3.6	2,362	2.5
Textile industry	1,223	1.6	2,037	2.1
Paper industry and printing	247	0.3	525	0.5
Leather industry	290	0.4	480	0.5
Rubber and asbestos industry	146	0.2	463	0.5
Woodworking industry	1,614	2.1	2,419	2.5
Meat, fruit and vegetable canning	22		23	
Clothing industry	238	0.3	256	0.3
Construction	6,138	8.2	10,726	11.2
Totals	75,313	100	95,712	100

Source: Wirtschaft und Statistik, 11 (1931), p. 186.

VII

In the space of a generation between 1900 and the 1920s, the official image of the German economy had been transformed. The statistical picture presented by the Imperial Statistical Office at the turn of the century was barely recognizable to modern eyes. By contrast, the publications of the Reich's Statistical Office and the Institute for Business-Cycle Research are eerily familiar. Here is a truly modern conception of the economy. The centrepiece, as we would expect today, was not the census of workplaces and occupations, even in the revised form of 1925, but the new national accounts. These in turn derived directly from the macroeconomic balance sheet of the economy sketched in Ernst Wagemann's early writing on monetary theory. And this new vision of the economy implied a new conception of economic policy as well. Historians of welfare policy and medical policy have long stressed the radical, technocratic forces at work in the Weimar Republic. By contrast, the literature has tended to treat economic policy as a reflex of interest group action, or outdated dogma. Outside the years of the depression, little attention has been paid to the intellectual context in which policy was formulated. Some have even gone so far as to claim that economic knowledge and the practice of economic government moved in opposite directions in this period.[117] This is surely a mischaracterization. The Reich's Ministry of Economic Affairs was attempting quite systematically to map out a new field of economic policy. Most radically, it was attempting to impose a new view of the government budget not as a cameralist account but as an integral element in the circular flow of economic activity. More generally the national economic statistics being produced by the Institute and the Statistical Office carried a strong productivist message. Policy in the first instance should clearly be directed towards maximizing and stabilizing the flow of national income.

The novelty of this conception of policy should not be underestimated. It was not finally accepted as the common sense of short-run macroeconomic policy until the 1950s. Here the emergence of this new concept of economic policy has been examined in technical terms. But it must surely be related to wider intellectual and political currents in interwar Germany. The economics of Wagemann's establishment partook of the spirit of Neue Sachlichkeit (New Sobriety), in more than its graphical presentations and sans serif typefaces. It was mundane and functional in its ambitions. It was popular in its desire to tame the instability of capitalism and to minimize the risks of unemployment. But it was also intolerant of social conflict, deliberately seeking to repress any debate about issues of distribution. And in the 1920s, it must of course be stressed, it failed to establish itself as the common sense of economic policy. As has been pointed out in relation to welfare policy, we should not get lost in the abstract logics of policy.[118] We must always remain aware of the mundane pressures and obstacles that conditioned the formulation and frustrated policy implementation. The technocratic vision that was emerging from the Reich's Ministry for Economic Affairs remained on paper. As we shall see, the elaborate plans for countercyclical stabilization were overwhelmed by the intensity of the Great Depression. The statistics produced by Wagemann's establishment told the tale. But to comprehend the true dimensions of that disaster we must look beyond the facts. We need to understand the rationalist dreams that were shattered by the economic crisis. For it was those

---

[117] H. James, 'What is Keynesian about Deficit Financing? The Case of Interwar Germany', in D.A. Hall (ed.), *The Political Power of Economic Ideas: Keynesianism across Nations* (Princeton, 1989), pp. 233–262.

[118] Y.-S. Hong, *Welfare, Modernity and the Weimar State 1919–1933* (Princeton, 1998).

dreams that gave birth to the statistics on which we still rely today. And Wagemann's research establishment was to survive the crisis of the Depression. The project of Konjunkturforschung had developed a momentum of its own. Launched in 1925, it was to have a sustained impact on German government for the next two decades and beyond.

4   The crisis of Weimar's statistical establishment, 1930–1933

In February 1930 the Institute announced that the economy was finally settling into a period of depression. Since early 1929 Wagemann and his team had been in a pessimistic mood. But, at first, the key indicators stubbornly refused to conform to their predictions. For the Institute, this was potentially dangerous. Its dark vision contrasted with the rosier outlook offered by other observers, in particular bank economists. The Institute needed signs of a downturn to confirm its basic cyclical scheme. In early 1930 the evidence began to pour in. Germany had not suffered a dramatic crisis like the calamity that had struck Wall Street, but the phase of high activity, which had lasted since 1927, was definitely over. The German economy was in recession. This was the moment for which Wagemann's statistical apparatus had been created. The Institute had foreseen the end of the boom. It now proclaimed the state of depression. According to the scenario laid down in the 1920s it was now time for the Reich's economic administration to swing into action. Otherwise, the recession would be sharp and prolonged. On the basis of postwar experience it would take at least a year for investment and household consumption to begin to revive. Meanwhile, the impact on the government budget would be dire. As unemployment rose, so would social expenditure. At the same time, tax revenues would tail off. A well-timed injection of government expenditure would hasten the rapid turnaround. If the right moment was chosen, there would be no shortage of funds. And government borrowing would not need to be sustained, since private investors would soon be encouraged by the better prospect of finding a market. The stabilization of the labour market would unleash a wave of consumer spending on clothes and household equipment. General prosperity would be restored. At the same time the imbalance in public finances would be righted. Both the state and its economic advisors would emerge from the crisis with their authority enhanced.

This optimistic vision did not survive the first half of 1930. Rather than collaborating in a successful effort to manage the crisis, Wage-

mann's statistical establishment and Brüning's government found themselves in conflict. Tensions mounted during 1930 and had reached such
a pitch by the end of the year that the Chancellor effectively broke off
relations with the Institute. There began a determined attack on
Weimar's statistical apparatus. The Statistical Office suffered deep cuts
and the entire project of Konjunkturforschung came in for heavy
criticism. The link between the Statistical Office and the Institute for
Business-Cycle Research was challenged. The technocratic programme
of the 1920s was in danger. In 1932, relations between Brüning's
government and the statistical establishment broke down altogether.
Wagemann became famous as one of the most prominent critics of
Brüning's continued policy of deflation. At the moment of Weimar's
deepest crisis, the economist who had aspired to advise government
found himself in opposition. And, in 1932, this meant an alliance with
Hitler's National Socialists. What led to this disastrous breakdown?
Why did the technocrats of the 1920s turn against the state, which had
been their ally?

I

Some tensions between Brüning's government and the statistical establishment were, probably, inescapable. Since 1926 the Statistical Office
and the Institute had documented a happy story of economic stabilization and recovery. This had obscured the political risks involved in the
expansion of official economic information. It was unfortunate both for
Brüning and for German democracy that the Great Depression was not
only the worst economic crisis in history, but also by far the best
reported. For the first time in its history the German state was publishing a running commentary on the national economy. In liberal
democracies today we take this for granted. However, in Germany in the
1920s it constituted a dramatic innovation. The fortnightly bulletin
Wirtschaft und Statistik first appeared in 1920. Its pages were filled with
the new prices indices, reports from the labour market administration
and whatever other data were to hand. But the new era really began in
1926 with the appearance of the Institute's first quarterly bulletin
(*Vierteljahrshefte zur Konjunkturforschung*). Between them, *Wirtschaft und
Statistik* and the *Vierteljahrshefte* provided an unprecedented overview of
the state of the German economy. And Wagemann was not satisfied. In
1927 he proposed a weekly bulletin to inform the public of the Institute's very latest results. At first, the RWM was sceptical. Was it possible
to produce authoritative, 'scientific' analysis at such short intervals? But
Wagemann was undeterred. In the spring of 1928 Hans Schäffer of the

Ministry finally gave the go-ahead.[1] Quasi-official reporting on the economy was now more or less continuous.

Even Wagemann was surprised by the readiness with which this information found an audience. *Wirtschaft und Statistik* flourished from the start. But the real surprise were the quarterly bulletins of the Institute. The initial expectation was that these dense publications would circulate only amongst the sponsoring organizations. In fact, the first issue sold almost 1,000 copies in bookshops and news-stands. A year later circulation had risen close to 4,000.[2] And the stream of data pumped out by the official statistical establishment was multiplied through the channels of the private media. In the 1920s, the business pages of Germany's newspapers underwent a dramatic transformation. No longer were they limited to reporting the affairs of local companies or the state of the markets. Increasingly they commented on the general state of 'the economy', as described by the new national indicators.[3] There was a substantial market for guides to the new business pages. One such volume, produced by the Social Democrats Ernst Kahn and Fritz Naphtali, sold more than 110,000 copies over the decade.[4] As never before, the economy was discussed in numerical terms. The language of Konjunkturforschung became the common stock of 'business-speak'. The audience was introduced to new concepts and techniques: trend and cycle; structure and process; seasonal adjustments; leading and lagging indicators. The Institute's technical style of presentation was the standard imitated by all other business publications in Weimar Germany. This was particularly marked in the reviews issued by the Berlin banks, many of which began to experiment with their own forms of business-cycle analysis.[5] The editor of the influential *Berliner Börsen Zeitung*, Walter Funk, considered the Institute's publications 'in many respects, the only available material . . . with which a newspaper man can work'.[6] The Institute's dominance of contemporary economic

[1] GStA I Rep. 120 C VIII 2a Nr. 33 Bd. 1 Bl. 124, 'Bericht über Sitzung des Kuratoriums des IfK 24.11.1927', pp. 6–9 and GStA I Rep. 120 C VIII 2a Nr. 33 Bd. 1 Bl. 142, *Industrie und Handelszeitung*, 56, 6.3.1928, p. 1.

[2] BHStA MWi 3092, Jahresbericht des IfK 1926/7 and GStA I Rep. 120 C VIII 2a Nr. 33 Bd. 1 Bl. 246, 'Bericht über die Sitzung des Kuratoriums des IfK am 6.11.1929', pp. 3–4.

[3] F. Wirth, *Die Wirtschaftsteile Deutscher Zeitungen* (Leipzig, 1927).

[4] E. Kahn and F. Naphtali, *Wie liest man den Handelsteil einer Tageszeitung?* (Frankfurt, 1930, 2nd edn.).

[5] *Magazin der Wirtschaft*, 4 (1928), II. Hj., pp. 1289, 1358–1359 and 5 (1929), I. Hj., pp. 571–572, 894–589. See also M. Pohl, 'Gedanken zur Entstehung und Bedeutung der Grossen Bankarchive', *Bankhistorisches Archiv, Zeitschrift zur Bankgeschichte*, 2 (1976), pp. 46–52.

[6] RWWA 20 Niederrheinische IHK Duisburg-Wesel 996/3, Blank to Reusch 30.11.1927, p. 3.

reporting was such that rival information agencies were driven out of business. The Statistical Service operated by Richard Calwer since before the war was a notable casualty.[7] By the late 1920s, the Institute's output was being plagiarized so flagrantly that Wagemann considered charging a fee for reprints.[8]

What can we say about the readership of these publications? Certainly, the Institute's reports were read in the Head Offices of German business. As we have seen, the Institute had many followers in the charmed circle of Berlin insiders. But its influence also extended well beyond the capital. In August 1929, the joint statistical agency of the Ruhr Chambers of Commerce conducted a poll among local businessmen to assess the value of the Institute. This revealed that the bank managers of the Ruhr region were all avid followers of the Institute's weekly reports. The comments of a large, anonymous heavy industrial firm summed up the general tenor of opinion. The Institute's reports were essential reading because they provided an unrivalled overview of the state of the national economy. And the anonymous industrial giant went on, 'The importance of the [Institute's weekly] reports for us as an individual corporation is hard to define, since the daily newspapers we read not only reprint the Institute's reports, but are also influenced in their opinions, one way or another, by these reports. Thus, when one reads the daily newspapers, one is unconsciously drawing on the work of the Institute for Business-Cycle Research.'[9]

The constraints that this new media machine might impose on government were initially disguised by the favourable state of the economy. It took the onset of a major crisis to reveal the public relations problem facing Brüning's government. By the autumn of 1930 the flood of bad news generated by the statistical apparatus was overwhelming. Of course, working people did not need statistics to inform them of the reality of the recession. The role of the new statistics was to act as a multiplier, confirming millions of individual experiences and aggregating them into an image of a national catastrophe. And there was no shortage of spokesmen in Weimar Germany, ready to accomplish this translation of individual misfortune into political issue. The constant stream of bad numbers supplied Brüning's opponents with all the material they needed. Adolf Hitler's movement proved particularly adept at using official statistics to demonstrate the bankruptcy of the

---

[7] On the circumstances surrounding the suicide of Richard Calwer and his wife, see 'Der Fall Calwer', *Die Bank* (1927), pp. 414–416.

[8] GStA I Rep. 120 C VIII 2a Nr. 33 Bd. 1 Bl. 246, 'Bericht über die Sitzung des Kuratoriums des IfK am 6.11.1929', p. 4.

[9] SWWA K 1 571, Gemeinsame Stat. Stelle to IHK Dortmund 3.8.1929 and attached Report 3.8.1929, p. 4.

Weimar 'system'. In Hitler's rhetoric the 3 million unemployed registered in October 1930 became an expression of the Republic's 'lack of political character' and the failure of its fawning, 'so-called statesmen'.[10] In February 1931, Hitler pounced on the official declaration that there were a total of 4.89 million unemployed.[11] For the rest of the spring the figure of 5 million jobless Germans echoed through his speeches. He liked to dramatize the situation by claiming that a total of 20 million men, women and children had been thrown on public relief, more than the entire population of Czechoslovakia. And in Hitler's rhetoric, the message was clear. Only National Socialist leadership, by ending the drain of reparations, could restore the health of the German economy.

It is hardly surprising, therefore, that Brüning's frustration should have vented itself in an intemperate attack on the Statistical Office. Any one of a number of indicators might have caught his attention. But it was the Reichsindex of the cost of living that he singled out. The restoration of German competitiveness by means of deflation – a general reduction in prices and wages – was central to Brüning's policy. The Reichsindex thus assumed a strategic significance.[12] Without a significant fall in the cost of living, it was politically dangerous to push through major cuts in wages. From the outset, however, Brüning's policy was undermined by a contradiction. The bulk of working-class expenditure was devoted to foodstuffs. It was the price of agricultural products that had to fall if the cost of living was to be appreciably reduced. But, Brüning's policy of deflation was lop-sided. While the government advocated wage and price cuts for industry and services, it simultaneously committed itself to stabilizing the incomes of German farmers. And this became an even more urgent priority after the elections of September 1930 in which northern peasants defected en masse to National Socialism. Agricultural prices were kept up by means of protection and price support. Not surprisingly, therefore, the Reichsindex of the cost of living remained stuck at pre-depression levels whilst industry and commerce were put under enormous pressure to cut wages. Given the weighting scheme of the Reichsindex, even a halving in industrial prices would have reduced the cost of living by no more than

---

[10] C. Goschler (ed.), *Hitler. Reden Schriften Anordnungen*, part IV *Von der Reichstagswahl bis zur Reichspräsidentenwahl Oktober 1930–März 1932* (Munich, 1994), 1, Doc. 17 *Illustrierter Beobachter*, 1.11.1930, 'Der Metallarbeiterstreik', p. 43.

[11] *Hitler Reden Schriften Anordnungen*, part IV, 1, doc. Nr. 57, 'Rede auf NSDAP-Versammlung in Weimar 8.2.1931', doc. Nr. 63, 'Rede auf NSDAP-Gauparteitag in Braunschweig 22.2.1931' and doc. Nr. 96, 'Rede auf NSDAP Versammlung in Kaiserslauten 16.4.1931'.

[12] T. Koops (ed.), *Akten der Reichskanzlei, Weimarer Republik, Die Kabinette Brüning I u. II* (Boppard, 1982), 1, doc. Nr. 66, Ministerial meeting 8.7.1930, p. 267 and doc. Nr. 114, Ministerial meeting 16.9.1930, p. 429.

10 per cent. Brüning refused to accept this logic. By December 1930 he had convinced himself that it was the statistics that were at fault. In a cabinet meeting Brüning declared: 'In carrying out individual statistical surveys the civil servants are refusing to record the actual prices. They are attempting to keep the cost of living index at an artificially high level. He [Brüning] will insist that checks be carried out on a sample of individual local authorities . . . As long as this was not sorted out there would be no peace in the economy, particularly not in agriculture. Currently, the index numbers were nowhere near the real price level.'[13]

In the early 1920s the Reichsindex had been vulnerable to such charges, on both political and technical grounds. But, by 1930 the SRA and its parent Ministry, the RWM, were more confident. Director Platzer, representing the Statistical Office, subjected Brüning and the rest of the cabinet to a lengthy lecture on the methodology of price statistics.[14] The allegation of exaggerated price reports, Platzer refuted outright. The reporting system of the Statistical Office was politically neutral. If anything, the local reports tended to exaggerate the extent of the deflation. The Reichsindex was not perfect, but what worried the statisticians was the weighting scheme.[15] A new survey of working-class budgets suggested the need for substantial reweighting. However, the impact of these changes was unpredictable. They certainly did not translate into the straightforward reduction that Brüning was looking for. When the technical reform was finally implemented in 1934, the level calculated for 1930 was higher than that originally released, the opposite of what Brüning intended.[16] By the early 1930s, the Statistical Office had sufficient authority to resist crude political pressure. The government was forced to 'face the facts'.

II

By contrast, the Institute for Business-Cycle research was to prove vulnerable. Ernst Wagemann's empire was built on two optimistic assumptions, both of which were to prove unfounded. The first assumption was that experts could provide an authoritative and accurate diagnosis of the economic situation and that they could provide at least a short-term prognosis. This was essential if the Institute aspired to

[13] *Die Kabinette Brüning*, 1, doc. Nr. 194, Cabinet meeting 9.12.1930, p. 712.
[14] BAP 07.01 film 19065N/2108 no. 174, 'Sitzung des Reichsministeriums – Ministerbesprechung 28.2.1931 Besprechung des Lebenshaltungsindex', p. 1.
[15] BAP 07.01 film 19065N/2110 no. 148 SRA, 'Nachprüfung der Grundlagen der Reichsindexziffer für die Lebenshaltungskosten' (1931).
[16] Statistisches Reichsamt, 'Neuberechnung der Reichsindexziffer für die Lebenshaltungskosten', *Vierteljahrshefte zur Statistik des Deutschen Reichs*, 43 (1934), pp. 102–113.

advise and direct government policy. The Great Depression stretched the analytical capacities of the Institute to breaking point. Ironically, the Institute was betrayed by its own 'realism'. In forming its immediate forecasts it relied on extrapolation from past cycles. But the short period since World War I offered little material to work with. A more general survey of economic development over the last half century gave grounds for cautious optimism. Gustav Cassel's standard textbook of the 1920s was one of the first to put a figure to the long-run trend of economic growth: 'For the countries of Western Europe we may assume that in pre-war days an increase of about 3 per cent was normal.'[17] This implied rates of industrial growth of 4–5 per cent per annum. Wagemann was more cautious.[18] Industrialization in Europe had reached a level of maturity. Nevertheless, modest growth was to be expected for the future. The Institute certainly predicted a recession in the late 1920s, but it did not foresee an unprecedented economic disaster. In this respect, its failure was neither unique, nor inexcusable. Nor would it have mattered much if the Institute had not been relied upon so heavily both by the German government and the wider public.

However, the Institute was not alone in failing to live up to the optimistic, interventionist scenario of the late 1920s. The second assumption on which Wagemann's project was based was the willingness and capacity of the German state to respond proactively to economic events. Between 1930 and 1932 this hope was cruelly dashed. Ever since the 1930s, argument has raged about the options open to Chancellor Brüning and Reichsbank President Luther. Few would now argue that the German state was in any position to respond positively to the recession before the autumn of 1931.[19] The Institute's interventionist plans of the 1920s had been premised on the optimistic assumption that the cyclical downturn would be confined mainly to domestic industry, that agriculture would be largely immune and that industry would be cushioned by exports and foreign credits. This was very far from the realities of the early 1930s. The depression was not confined to industry. The bottom fell out of the international commodity market, imposing

[17] G. Cassel, *The Theory of Social Economy* (London, 1932, trans. of 5th German edn.), I, pp. 62–63.

[18] E. Wagemann, *Konjunkturlehre* (Berlin, 1928), p. 71.

[19] For the most important statement of the constraints on Brüning's government see K. Borchardt, 'Zwangslagen und Handlungsspielräume in der großen Weltwirtschaftskrise der frühen dreißiger Jahre', in *Wachstum, Krisen, Handlungsspielräume der Wirtschaftspolitik. Studien zur Wirtschaftsgeschichte des 19. und 20. Jahrhunderts* (Göttingen, 1982), pp. 165–182. For an overview of the subsequent debate see J. von Krüdener (ed.), *Economic Crisis and Political Collapse: The Weimar Republic 1924–1933* (Oxford, 1990) and C. Buchheim, M. Hutter and H. James (eds.), *Zerrissene Zwischenkriegszeit. Wirtschafthistorische Beiträge* (Baden-Baden, 1994).

drastic strain on German agriculture. This triggered a turn to protectionism, which penalized domestic consumers and jeopardized Germany's exports. Meanwhile, the collapse of the US economic boom and the perversity of French policy drained the world economy of credit. The balance of payments constraint suddenly became binding. No longer could the German economy borrow abroad to fund its current account deficit. And the German state could not borrow at all, at home or abroad. Chancellor Brüning and Reichsbank President Luther had no option but to adopt a brutal policy of deflation. Far from acting as a stabilizing force, economic policy accelerated the downturn, provoking a major crisis in the German banking system by the summer of 1931. Brüning and Luther were forced to impose exchange controls and suspend all payments on Germany's foreign obligations. This drastic decision was followed in September by Britain's departure from the gold standard.

Taken together, the banking crisis and the disintegration of the international monetary system marked a turning point. With the system of private credit in tatters it seemed increasingly hopeless to count on a spontaneous recovery. State intervention was required simply to keep the banking system afloat. Britain's devaluation then cast into doubt the policy of deflation. In a world of flexible exchange rates Germany could not hope to gain sustained competitive advantage from further wage and price cuts. An intense debate began about the appropriate policy response, a debate that continues to this day. Why in the autumn of 1931 did Brüning and Luther not engage in a more sustained effort to restart the German economy using both fiscal and monetary policy? The continuing economic crisis, after all, drove voters away from the mainstream parties towards the extremes of both left and right.[20] Some historians have answered that an attempt was in fact made to relax monetary policy,[21] but this is disputed. Others argue that funding for an expansive fiscal policy was not available and that a small-scale programme could not have made an appreciable difference. Some even contend that the policy of fiscal retrenchment and wage and price cuts continued to be the correct solution to Germany's deep-seated economic problems. For our purposes it is not essential to take a stand in this debate. The point to make here is simply that Ernst Wagemann viewed the continued policy of retrenchment as both a serious threat to

[20] For a summary of critical views see I. Kershaw (ed.), *Weimar: Why Did German Democracy Fail?* (London, 1990).

[21] H. James, *The Reichsbank and Public Finance in Germany 1924–1933. A Study of the Politics of Economics during the Great Depression* (Frankfurt, 1985), pp. 292–305. For a critical view see T. Balderston, *The Origins and Course of the German Economic Crisis 1923–1932. November 1923 to May 1932* (Berlin, 1993), pp. 179–180.

his statistical establishment and more generally as a betrayal of the interventionist promise of the 1920s. It was this which led him into opposition and into the arms of the Nazis.

However, if we return to 1930, there can be no doubt that it was the business-cycle economists who were the first to break the bargain of the 1920s. In its early days, the Brüning administration stuck closely to the script laid down in the discussions of counter-cyclical policy in 1927–8. Wagemann was initially on good terms with Brüning.[22] Friends of the Institute occupied key positions in his government. Hans Schäffer was State Secretary at the Finance Ministry and Curtius was now serving as Foreign Minister. Whenever economic issues were discussed in cabinet, it was the work of the Institute that was referred to.[23] The Statistical Office and the Institute, for their part, played their appointed role in setting in motion a policy of economic stabilization. In the spring of 1929, the Institute for Business-Cycle Research diagnosed an imminent economic crisis and in the winter of 1929–30 it announced that Germany was settling into a period of depression.[24] There was no certainty about the length of such a depression. However, there was no sense of an impending disaster.[25] By the spring of 1930, the first phase of the crisis was assumed to have passed and, according to the Institute's model, this was the moment in which it was safe for the government to take measures to reduce unemployment and hasten the recovery. This diagnosis was shared by most of Brüning's cabinet. Accordingly, in the late spring and summer of 1930, the ministries began to make preparations for a work-creation programme of the kind discussed in the late 1920s.[26] The SRA compiled information on the procurement programmes of the Reich, the Länder, the Reichsbahn and the Reichspost with a view to putting together a generous programme of public spending. The issue of finance was, of course, unresolved. However, the

---

[22] Following a hint from one of Brüning's underlings, Wagemann commissioned a dozen articles explaining the German recession as an effect of the worldwide slump, see BAK R 43 I/1150 no. 2, IfK to Staatssekretär Püender, Reichskanzlei 26.5.1930. See also BAK R 43 I/965 no. 77, Wagemann to Brüning 20.8.1931.

[23] Koops, *Die Kabinette Brüning I u. II*, 1 doc. Nr. 11 Cabinet meeting, 7.4.1930, p. 24, 1, doc. Nr. 21, Ministerial meeting 30.4.1930, 1 doc. Nr. 66, Ministerial meeting 8.7.1930 and 1 doc. Nr. 118, Cabinet meeting 25.9.1930.

[24] The 'crisis' was announced in *VzK* 4 (1929), 1, 25.5.1929, A and *VzK* 4 (1929), 2, 24.8.1929, A. The depression phase was announced in November, see *VzK* 4 (1929), 3, 23.11.1929, A and more firmly in *VzK* 4 (1929), 4, 24.2.1930, A and *VzK* 5 (1930), 1, 23.5.1930, A.

[25] G. Plumpe, 'Wirtschaftspolitik in der Weltwirtschaftskrise. Realität und Alternativen', *GuG* 11 (1985), pp. 326–357.

[26] R. Meister, *Die große Depression. Zwangslagen und Handlungsspielräume der Wirtschafts- und Finanzpolitik in Deutschland 1929–1932* (Regensburg, 1991), pp. 190–208.

optimistic assumption seems to have been that funds would be provided by an international loan.

What undermined Wagemann's attempts to consolidate his position at the heart of government was the failure of the Institute's analytical scheme. The Institute's essential problem was to determine how far the process of deflation was going to go. In February 1930 the Institute was convinced that the German economy had passed out of the phase of crisis into a period of depression.[27] For the future it expected to see counteracting forces gathering strength, which would lead the economy into recovery. In light of this optimistic outlook, the Brüning government decided to accept the budget drafted by its predecessor as the basis for its financial planning.[28] This degree of influence flattered the Institute. However, as the year of 1930 was to show, it exposed both the Institute and Brüning's government to considerable risks. As the Institute revised its quarterly forecast in line with the increasingly bad news, it ran the risk of contradicting the forecast implicit in government budgetary policy. Given that the Brüning government was committed to maintaining at least the appearance of a balanced budget, and given that both the estimates of expenditure and revenue for the coming year depended sensitively on the economic outlook, the risks involved in unstable quarterly forecasts were great. Conflict between the Institute and the government was not inevitable. If the politicians had been more cautious in using the Institute's optimistic quarterly predictions as a basis for their annual budgetary plans, disappointment might have been avoided. If the Institute had been more modest in its claims and restricted its forecasts strictly to a quarterly period, then it might have escaped the accusation of inconsistency.[29] But both the budget-makers and the Institute succumbed to the temptation of an alliance. The politicians and civil servants were seduced by the Institute's optimism, which eased the problem of finding a compromise on spending cuts and tax increases. The Institute, for its part, was constantly tempted to increase the range of its forecasts, making them more attractive for political decision-makers.

The first unpleasant surprise came in April 1930, when the Institute revised its outlook in a pessimistic direction. The Institute now expected only a slight recovery in the labour market during 1930. The Reich's Labour Ministry had to inform the cabinet that, on the basis of the

[27] *VzK* 5 (1930), 1, 23.5.1930, p. 5.
[28] Meister, *Die große Depression*, p. 172.
[29] In 1931 the Institute was to suppress a particularly gloomy forecast GStA I Rep. 120 C VIII 2a Nr. 33 Bd. 1 Bl. 363, 'Sitzung des Kuratoriums des IfK 27.2.1931', p. 15. And in August 1931 it abandoned the effort to forecast altogether, see BAK Nl 13 Silverberg Nr 231 Fol. 1, RDI circular to members of Präsidium 29.8.1931.

Institute's new forecast, the unemployment fund would face a substantial deficit by the end of the year.[30] To balance the budget as it had promised, the government was forced into painful cuts, which in turn led to the fateful dissolution of the Reichstag. By August 1930, having curtailed spending and raised tax rates and insurance contributions, the Finance Ministry viewed the Reich's position with cautious optimism. Certainly, in the run-up to the elections Schäffer put a brave face on the financial situation, only for this optimism to be punctured in the first weeks of September by the monthly returns for tax and customs revenues. It appeared that there had been a further serious decline in national income. To avoid political damage, the Reich's Finance Ministry delayed publication of the returns until after the elections.[31] The Institute was not bound by similar considerations. Over the summer of 1930 it had come to a decidedly more pessimistic view of the medium-term outlook.[32] Indeed, it had fundamentally revised its model of the cycle. Speaking in confidence to the Institute's Kuratorium on 18 June 1930, Wagemann explained that the Institute's economists now believed that Germany was undergoing a 'change in the period of the cycle'.[33] In the immediate postwar years the economic cycle had been unusually short. In the summer of 1930 the German economy appeared to be returning to its longer, prewar pattern and to be falling more closely into line with international cyclical developments. The duration of the full cycle might, therefore, be as long as eight years. Rather than expecting an imminent upswing, the Institute now predicted a prolonged period of depression perhaps lasting as long as two years.

At the end of August 1930, heedless of the delicately balanced political situation, the Institute published its new, more pessimistic analysis.[34] This clashed with the optimistic outlook being fostered by the Finance Ministry in the weeks prior to the general election. And this conflict did not go unnoticed. On 6 September 1930 a report in the *Kölnische Zeitung*, a West German daily closely connected to heavy industry, highlighted the contrast between the economic forecasts of the Ministry and the Institute. The newspaper demanded a clarification of

---

[30] *Die Kabinette Brüning*, 1, doc. Nr. 21, Ministerial meeting 30.4.1930, p. 66.
[31] *Die Kabinette Brüning*, 1, doc. Nr. 114, Ministerial meeting 16.9.1930, p. 429.
[32] The first hint of this reassessment came in a letter from Wagemann to Brüning on 16 June 1930, see G. Schulz, *Von Brüning zu Hitler. Der Wandel des politischen Systems in Deutschland 1930–1933*, vol. III of *Zwischen Demokratie und Diktatur. Verfassungspolitik und Reichsreform in der Weimarer Republik* (Berlin, 1992), pp. 99–100.
[33] GStA I Rep. 120 C VIII 2a Nr. 33 Bd. 1 Bl. 291, 'Sitzung des Kuratoriums des IfK 18.6.1930', p. 3 and the slightly different version of the meeting in GStA I Rep. 120 C VIII 2a Nr. 33 Bd. 1 Bl. 287, Prussian Min. für Handel und Gewerbe note 19.6.1930, p. 2.
[34] *VzK* 5 (1930), 2, 30.8.1930.

the Institute's ambiguous status.[35] Wagemann's position as Director of the Institute and President of the Reich's Statistical Office conferred on the Institute's predictions a semi-official status. Official credibility was thus at stake in any clash between the outlook of the Institute and the government. The newspaper insisted that the Institute's position was untenable and that it should be detached as soon as possible from the Statistical Office. This would allow the Institute to pursue its research unfettered by political constraints – and, more importantly, it would save the government from being embarrassed by its own economists. Despite this unprecedented attack, the Institute was unabashed. The last quarterly report for 1930 published in early December, was even more pessimistic than its predecessors.[36] The Institute described the situation of the German economy as unprecedentedly severe and offered no prospect of a recovery in the coming year. Again, the Institute's outlook conflicted with the comparatively optimistic assumptions built into government policy. This time, the Institute's analysis contradicted the projections made in the Financial Plan announced on 30 September 1930.[37]

For Brüning this was the last straw. At a cabinet meeting in early December the irate Chancellor declared: 'Whenever the Reich's government issues statements, the Institute for Business-Cycle Research makes claims that contradict it. He [Brüning] was, therefore, considering whether to make a public statement against the Institute.'[38] The Institute's lack of tact is certainly remarkable, but Brüning's indignation was disingenuous. It is hardly likely that the Institute would have been more popular in political circles if, in the spring of 1930, it had published a bleak forecast of future levels of unemployment. Such a prediction would certainly have come closer to the actual course of events, but if it had been believed it would have had drastic implications for the budget. Brüning would have been forced into unpopular measures at an earlier date. He would have found it even more difficult to form a viable coalition and the outcome of the September election might have been even worse. The repeated downward revision of the Institute's forecasts over the course of 1930 may have embarrassed the government and resulted in disorderly budgets, but given the dire economic outlook, unrealistic expectations were necessary for Weimar's political process to function at all. Brüning, needless to say, did not see it this way.[39] In his

[35] R. Krengel, *Das Deutsche Institut für Wirtschaftsforschung (IfK) 1925 bis 1979* (Berlin, 1985), pp. 27–28.
[36] *VzK* 5 (1930), 3, 1.12.1930.
[37] *The Economist* 11.10.1930, pp. 663–664.
[38] *Die Kabinette Brüning*, 1, doc. Nr. 194, Cabinet Meeting 9.12.1930, p. 711.
[39] On Brüning's style of government see H. Mommsen, 'Heinrich Brüning as Chancellor:

eyes, the Institute's behaviour smacked either of betrayal or incompetence. As he recorded in his memoirs, he was henceforth to exclude Wagemann from policy discussions.[40] Furthermore, Brüning demanded that the Institute be muzzled. He ordered the RWM to compile a report 'on the changing opinions of the Institute for Business-Cycle Research in relation to public statements of the Reich's government',[41] and suggested that the Institute's finances should be subject to critical scrutiny. The Chancellor recalled that a few years earlier, Wagemann's contacts in the Reichstag had allowed him to secure a larger grant for the Institute than had been proposed by the Reich's government. Brüning clearly intended that the Institute should be less fortunate in future.

III

The break with Brüning came at a particularly inopportune moment for Wagemann as it coincided with a concerted attack on the funding of the statistical establishment. As we have seen there had been a staggering increase in statistical spending since the early 1920s. In 1928–9 total spending by the Reich, Länder and Communes was estimated at no less than 29.5 million RM.[42] The statistical service was thus an obvious target for deflationary cost-cutting. The first critical questions were asked in the Reichstag Budget Committee in 1928 and by the end of the year the Sparkommissar was calling for a general review of statistical spending.[43] But the RWM stalled any such enquiry.[44] The financial attack on Wagemann's empire did not begin in earnest until 1930. The Reich's budget for that year proposed the first cuts to statistical spending since 1923. Outstanding work was wound up ahead of time and all new projects were cancelled, the major casualty being the ambitious industrial census planned for 1930. With a view to making more far-reaching incisions in future, Dr Bernhard Dernburg was appointed to head a Commission of Enquiry into the Statistical Service.[45] Dernburg's Com-

The Failure of a Politically Isolated Strategy', in H. Mommsen, *From Weimar to Auschwitz. Essays in German History* (Cambridge, 1991), pp. 119–140.

[40] H. Brüning, *Memoiren 1918–1934* (Stuttgart, 1970), pp. 503–504.

[41] *Die Kabinette Brüning*, 1, doc. Nr. 194, Cabinet meeting 9.12.1930, p. 714.

[42] BAP 39.01 10683 no. 28 Dernburg Kommission, 'Bericht', p. 3.

[43] BAP 01.01 Reichstag film 31648 file 2588 no. 432, 'Reichstag III. Wahlperiode 1924/28. Ausschuß für den Reichshaushalt 309. Sitzung 31.1.1928'. See BAP 23.01 2234 no. 113 Der Reichssparkommissar, 'Gutachten über den statistischen Dienst in Deutschland' (1933), p. 73.

[44] BAP 01.01 film 31648 file 2589 no. 84, '16. Sitzung des Haushaltsausschusses 21.1.1929'.

[45] BAK R 43 I/965 no. 35, RWM to Reichskanzlei 3.6.1930.

mission was to go beyond the technical rationalization imposed by the Sparkommissar in the 1920s. He was to investigate the entire repertoire of statistics built up since the 1920s and to devise a strategic plan with which to guide but also to limit the development of the Reich's Office.[46] The intention was clearly to put an end to Wagemann's freedom of action and to curtail his expansive project of Konjunkturforschung.

Dernburg placed the relationship between the Institute for Business-Cycle Research and the Statistical Office at the heart of his report. In earlier periods the combination of statistical work with scientific research had been a functional arrangement. In 1920s, however, the apparatus of official statistics had been highjacked by the business-cycle economists. The Institute had diverted the statistical system away from the administrative needs of the state towards research for its own sake. Entire new branches of statistics had been created that had no immediate administrative purpose. More ominously, the statisticians and economic experts were seeking to usurp the prerogative of framing political decision-making, traditionally exercised by the civil servants. To reassert administrative and political control over this unwieldy complex, the key was to separate the Institute from the statistical apparatus. The Dernburg Commission thus joined the growing band of critics demanding that Wagemann's empire be broken up.

The report of the Dernburg Commission makes fascinating reading for a historian of statistics, but it did not deliver the point-by-point recommendations expected by the Sparkommissar. Instead, Dernburg advocated across-the-board reductions in statistical funding. As the Sparkommissar's officials pointed out, this left it up to the statisticians to decide where to make the cuts. There was nothing to stop them from deliberately diverting funds away from vital statistical work, thereby creating an artificial crisis and generating irresistible political pressure for the cuts to be reversed. The final report of the Dernburg Commission was an embarrassment. Despite repeated demands from the Reichstag, it was never published.[47] In 1932, the Sparkommissar established an enquiry team of his own to finish the job, which Dernburg had left half done.[48] This, too, ran into problems. The RWM refused even to provide a full transcript of the Dernburg hearings. But the

---

[46] BAP 39.01 10683 no. 28 Dernburg Kommission, 'Bericht über die Untersuchungsergebnisse der Kommission zur Nachprüfung des statistischen Dienstes 7.1.1932', p. 1.

[47] See BAP 01.01 film 31649 file 2590 no. 453, 'Drucksache des Reichstages Nr. 1428. Reichstag V. Wahlperiode 1930. Übersicht über Antworten der Reichsregierung auf Beschlüsse des Reichstages'.

[48] BAP 23.01 2234 no. 4 Reichssparkommissar, 'Bericht über die Untersuchungsergebnisse der Kommission zur Nachprüfung des statistischen Dienstes', May 1932, p. 33 and BAP 23.01 2234 no. 91, 'Nachprüfung des statistischen Dienstes 5.12.1932'.

reason for Dernburg's failure soon became clear: he had been out-numbered. Dernburg had faced Wagemann's staff of 3,000 with a single assistant and two temporary secretaries. The Statistical Office, with the full backing of the RWM, had deliberately set about swamping him with enormous memoranda, full of specious reasons for retaining each and every survey. In early 1931, the position became altogether hopeless when Wagemann's friends in the Reichstag cut Dernburg's budget in half.[49] As a result, the final report was restricted to generalities. And in light of the Sparkommissar's own experience, this was entirely justified. The core of the problem was Wagemann and his Institute. Unless the influence of the economists could be removed, there was little hope of exerting systematic external discipline over the machinery of statistics.

Having foiled the attempt to carry out a detailed review of the statistical service, Wagemann administered the *coup de grâce* with a rationalization memorandum of his own. Even the staff of the Sparkommissar, veterans of countless bureaucratic battles, were struck by the aggressive tone of his reply.[50] Having warded off Dernburg's initial assault, Wagemann was free to avoid all discussion of details. He also ignored the proposal to separate the Institute for Business-Cycle Research from the Statistical Office. Answering the advocates of rationalization in their own terms, Wagemann demanded that the Prussian Statistical Office should be incorporated into the Reich's Office and that the Offices of the other Länder be reduced to mere subsidiaries of the Reich's Office. As we have seen the Sparkommissar had for a long time been advocating precisely such an amalgamation. But, it was now apparent that in backing Wagemann, the Sparkommissar had created a bureaucratic monster. Fusing the Statistical Offices of Prussia and the Reich might lead to some administrative economies, but by enlarging Wagemann's domain it would only exacerbate the overall problem of financial control.[51] For the moment at least, Wagemann's counter-attack put a halt to all further discussion of statistical reorganization.

Wagemann's success in derailing the Dernburg Commission prevented a comprehensive rollback of the Statistical Office. However, he was not able to insulate the statistical establishment from the general retrenchment of the Weimar state. The 1930 budget brought the first reduction in spending since the early 1920s. There were no cuts to the

---

[49] BAP 01.01 film 31649 file 2590 no. 441, 'Reichstag V. Wahlperiode 1930. 5. Ausschuß für den Reichshaushalt 27. Sitzung 21.1.1931', p. 337.

[50] BAP 23.01 2234 no. 113 Reichssparkommissar, 'Gutachten über den Statistischen Dienst in Deutschland' (1933), p. 18.

[51] BAP 23.01 2234 no. 34 Reichssparkommissar, note 23.9.1932.

Office's permanent establishment, but plans for new surveys were cancelled and work was halted on a backlog of data-processing from the 1920s.[52] This led to an immediate fall in employment. Much deeper cuts followed in 1931. The Reich's Finance Ministry agreed to reduce the national financial statistics of the Länder and local authorities from an annual to a triennial rhythm. Along with further administrative economies this allowed cuts of 3.5 million RM, almost a quarter of the 1930 budget.[53] In 1932 the Office's staff stabilized around a core of 586 permanent civil servants, 35 civil servants temporarily employed by the Office and 1,265 clerical and manual employees. Compared to July 1929 when the total white-collar staff of the office stood at 3,005 only 1,784 remained in July 1932.[54] This was a dramatic reduction, but the vast bulk of the cuts were concentrated in Department VI, responsible for the revenue statistics of the Reich, the Länder and the Communes. Its staff fell from 847 in December 1929 to 121 by July 1932. Economic statistics, the heart of Wagemann's project, survived unscathed.[55]

Like the Statistical Office, the Institute for Business-Cycle Research was, at first, protected from the worst effects of the Depression. The interest-group coalition which Wagemann had carefully assembled remained intact. In 1930 the Institute was able to budget for an increase in reserves.[56] The actual flow of income from the Institute's backers was, in fact, substantially lower than had been promised, but none of the major contributors formally withdrew. As the Institute repeatedly pointed out to donors, this continuity of support was essential to its survival. Any major withdrawal risked provoking a chain-reaction.[57] The continued loyalty of the trade unions was particularly important. As the Reichsverband der deutschen Industrie (RdI) pointed out to its more recalcitrant members, if they did not come up with subscriptions, the labour movement would be left in sole control of the Institute. Business could ill-afford to lose its grip on what was undoubtedly the most influential centre of economic research in Germany.[58] At least until 1931, this was sufficient to keep business in place. The Institute also retained powerful support in the political system. In 1931, presumably to punish the Institute for its indiscretions in the preceding year,

[52] BAP 01.01 film 31649 file 2590 no. 1 and no. 218.
[53] Reichstag Budget Committee, BAP 01.01 film 31649 file 2590 no. 302–441.
[54] BAP 31.02 4169, 'Das SRA, sein Aufbau und seine Arbeiten Stand Dezember 1929' and BAP 23.01 2234 no. 44e, Summary table of personnel of the SRA 1.7.1932.
[55] BAP 31.01 8654 no. 124, 'Haushalt des RWM für das Rechnungsjahr 1932', Preface, p. 2 and p. 27.
[56] GStA I Rep. 120 C VIII 2a Nr. 33 Bd. 1 Bl. 282, 'Haushaltsplan des IfK 1930/31'.
[57] GStA I Rep. 120 C VIII 2a Nr. 33 Bd. 1 Bl. 340, Prussian Min. für Handel und Gewerbe Abt II to Staatssekretär 17.2.1931.
[58] BBA 15 523, RDI to Fachgruppe Bergbau 9.4.1930.

Brüning attempted to cancel the Reich's contribution. However, this was opposed both by the Prussian government and by Wagemann's friends in the Reichstag, who restored the Reich's contribution to its normal level of 100,000 RM.[59] The statistical project of the 1920s remained firmly entrenched within the German state.

IV

The statistical establishment thus survived the initial breakdown in relations with Brüning's government. And Wagemann was not to remain on the defensive for long. In the second half of 1931 Brüning's policy of deflation was cast seriously into doubt and Wagemann was to play a prominent role in the search for an alternative. In the summer of 1931 Germany's banking system was paralysed by a collapse in confidence.[60] This was triggered by a withdrawal of foreign deposits. Mass bankruptcies, as a result of the deflation, had upset the balance sheets of the banks. An ominous gap opened between the bank's unrealizable assets and billions of marks outstanding in short-term liabilities, domestic and foreign. In July, confidence failed and the major Berlin banks were forced to close their doors. With the banking system in tatters, hopes of a spontaneous, private sector recovery seemed increasingly illusory. Germany was dealt a further blow by Britain's decision to abandon the gold standard and to allow its currency to devalue by 30 per cent. In a matter of days Germany's hard-won competitive position was wiped out. For the foreseeable future, at least, there was no prospect of a return to the prewar world of the gold standard and liberal free trade. This had been the long-term prospect that motivated Brüning's drastic cure for the ills of the German economy. Now he was left stranded. In a world of competitive devaluations the costs of painful wage and price cuts far outweighed the fleeting benefits. The business lobby that had been so powerful in Brüning's defence was enfeebled and divided. It remained loyal to his political vision and adamantly opposed to any return to parliamentary government. However, the dire state of the economy called for desperate measures. Brüning and Luther's policy of continued deflation provoked mounting opposition. Prominent busi-

---

[59] On the Prussian intervention see GStA I Rep. 120 C VIII 2a Nr. 33 Bd. 1 Bl. 313–5. On the Reichstag: BAP 01.01 film 31649 file 2590 no. 430. *Verhandlungen des Reichstags V. Wahlperiode 1930. Anlagen* (Berlin, 1932), 449, Nr. 678; *Verhandlungen des Reichstags V. Wahlperiode 1930. Stenographische Berichte* (Berlin, 1932), 445, p. 1914.

[60] G.D. Feldman, 'The Deutsche Bank from World War to World Economic Crisis 1914–1933', in *The Deutsche Bank 1870–1945* (London, 1995), pp. 130–276 and K.E. Born, *Die deutsche Bankenkrise 1931. Finanzen und Politik* (Munich, 1967).

nessmen of all stripes began to call for a revival of the domestic economy. With the collapse of the gold standard the prime obstacle to national economic action had, after all, been removed.

Not that the Reich was entirely inactive. As an emergency measure, exchange controls were imposed in July 1931 to halt the flight of capital. Though the parity remained fixed, Germany had effectively left the gold standard. An attempt was made to reconstruct the banking system. The DANAT was closed. The Dresdner was taken into state ownership. Other institutions were propped up by state loans. In September, Schäffer of the Finance Ministry and Luther of the Reichsbank held secret meetings with a number of prominent advocates of reflation, notably Lautenbach of the RWM.[61] The possibility of an emergency work-creation programme was discussed. However, it was generally agreed that the stability of the currency had to have priority. No risks could be taken with international confidence. In the autumn of 1931, Brüning sought to relieve the pressure for action by reshuffling the cabinet.[62] The liberal Dietrich was replaced as Minister for Economic Affairs by Professor Warmbold, a specialist in agricultural economics, who also happened to be Wagemann's brother-in-law. More importantly, Warmbold was a member of the IG Farben Supervisory Board (Aufsichtsrat).[63] He thus represented the growing body of industrial opinion that was calling for positive government action to alleviate the catastrophic state of the national economy. Warmbold joined the cabinet only on the condition that Brüning would seriously consider a programme of credit-financed relief for German industry. The stage was set for a re-entry by Wagemann and his interventionist economists.

Under Warmbold's direction, Wagemann's Institute was entrusted with a central role in formulating a response to the crisis. Working in cooperation with associates of IG Farben, Wagemann was encouraged to develop plans for a structural reform of the banks:[64] Only a reconstruction of the financial system would enable a general economic recovery. In the long term Wagemann hoped to create a robust new transmission belt for a powerful monetary policy. A first draft of the Plan was presented to the Reichsbank in October 1931, but no action

[61] K. Borchardt and H.O. Schötz (eds.), *Wirtschaftspolitik in der Krise. Die (Geheim-) Konferenz der Friedrich-List-Gesellschaft im September 1931 über Möglichkeiten und Folgen einer Kreditausweitung* (Baden-Baden, 1991).

[62] R. Neebe, *Großindustrie, Staat und NSDAP 1930–1933. Paul Silverberg und der Reichsverband der Deutschen Industrie in der Krise der Weimarer Republik* (Göttingen, 1981), pp. 103–106.

[63] P. Hayes, *Industry and Ideology. IG Farben in the Nazi Era* (Cambridge, 1987), pp. 48, 59.

[64] H. Tammen, *Die IG Farben-Industrie AG (1925–1933). Ein Chemiekonzern in der Weimarer Republik* (Berlin, 1978), pp. 207–211.

followed. The winter of 1931 brought frustration for those who hoped for an end to deflation. Warmbold was unable to dissuade Brüning and Reichsbank President Luther from continuing with their course. He tendered his resignation and remained in government only to preserve a facade of unity during the most delicate phase of the reparations negotiations. Wagemann did not feel bound by the same discretion. At the end of January 1932, he publicly unveiled his plan in a pamphlet entitled 'Monetary and Credit Reform'.[65] It was the first open breach in the facade of orthodoxy that Brüning and Luther were desperately struggling to preserve, and it unleashed a scandal of international proportions. The Wagemann affair was to become a *cause célèbre* of depression politics.[66]

Despite its prominence, the literature to date has given few insights into the background and motivations to the Wagemann Plan.[67] This book provides the necessary context. *Money and Credit Reform* did not come out of the blue. The diagnoses offered by the Plan followed directly from Wagemann's discussion of monetary economics in the *Treatise* of 1923.[68] According to Wagemann, the crisis of 1931 resulted from the failure of Germany's bankers to understand the nature of money in high capitalism. As Wagemann had argued in the *Treatise*, a gold-backed currency was of diminishing significance for the workings of the economy. It was the modern banking system and the private pyramid of credit that was the essential medium for capitalist business. The foundation for this pyramid of private credit was public confidence in the private financial system. The deflation was the root cause of the bank failures of 1931. However, the crisis might have been averted if banking regulation had kept abreast of the development of the modern financial system. Not surprisingly, however, the system of monetary regulation put in place in Germany in 1924 was shaped primarily by the experience of inflation. Its central purpose was to prevent official misuse of the printing press. To forestall excessive monetary creation, the

[65] E. Wagemann, *Geld- und Kreditreform* (Berlin, 1932).

[66] The story of the Wagemann Plan has been told in many places: C.-D. Krohn, *Wirtschaftstheorien als politische Interessen. Die akademische Nationalökonomie in Deutschland 1918–1933* (Frankfurt, 1981), pp. 157–166; Krengel, *Das Deutsche Institut für Wirtschaftsforschung*, pp. 33–39; G. Kroll, *Von der Weltwirtschaftskrise zur Staatskonjunktur* (Berlin, 1958), pp. 396–399; R. Regul, 'Der Wagemann-Plan', in G. Bombach, K.-B. Netzband, H.-J. Ramser and M. Timmermann (eds.), *Der Keynesianismus III. Die geld und beschäftigungstheoretische Diskussion in Deutschland zur Zeit von Keynes* (Berlin, 1981), pp. 421–447; James, *The Reichsbank and Public Finance*, pp. 302–304.

[67] K. Borchardt, 'Zur Aufarbeitung der Vor- und Frühgeschichte des Keynesianismus in Deutschland. Zugleich ein Beitrag zur Position von W. Lautenbach', *Jahrbücher für Nationalökonomie und Statistik*, 197 (1982), p. 360.

[68] See chapter 3.

Reichsbank was required to hold gold and foreign currency reserves to cover at least 40 per cent of the value of notes in circulation. These requirements were stringent. But, as Wagemann argued, they applied to the wrong kind of money.[69] The Reichsbank's rules provided protection against the kind of flight out of cash that could occur during an extreme inflation. But in the deflationary conditions prevailing since 1929 no one needed an extra inducement to hold money. As prices fell, cash became an attractive asset. By contrast, the regulations of 1924 provided no protection whatsoever for the private credit system. And yet it was the pyramid of cashless transactions on which business, under conditions of high capitalism, was vitally dependent. German banks were not subject to the minimum reserves requirements conventional in Britain and required by law in the United States. They were free to transform short-term liabilities into illiquid, long-term assets at will.

Until the spring of 1931, it was the risks posed by short-term foreign credits that preoccupied Wagemann and his staff. In the 1920s, the balance sheets of German banks had become dangerously dependent on short-term foreign funds. Long-term loans had been extended on the basis of short-term foreign deposits. The entire pyramid of credit was vulnerable to sudden withdrawals of this money. In May 1931, this was a central theme in Wagemann's study of the world economy, *Struktur und Rhythmus der Weltwirtschaft*.[70] Two months later, the run on the banks exposed a more general imbalance in the German financial system. There was a fundamental mismatch between the long-term loans extended by German banks and their short-term deposits not only from foreign but from domestic sources as well. The deflation bankrupted the banks' debtors, leaving the banks with no way of meeting their obligations. Given the precariousness of the situation a run on the banks was almost inevitable. Far from needing to limit the supply of currency, the Reichsbank needed to pump cash back into the banks. Though this action forestalled complete disaster, the credit system was paralysed. As a result, the economy lost its spontaneous capacity to recover from the depression. Unless something was done, there was a risk of a downward spiral into ever greater unemployment and bankruptcy.

In this catastrophic situation conventional tools of Reichsbank policy were ineffective. The Reichsbank and the government might seek to inject new funds into the stricken banking system. But the mountain of

---

[69] Wagemann, *Geld- und Kreditreform*, p. 21.

[70] E. Wagemann, *Struktur und Rhythmus der Weltwirtschaft. Grundlagen einer Weltwirtschaftlichen Konjunkturlehre* (Berlin, 1931), pp. 136, 352, see also the papers in BAP 31.02 2591.

bad debts prevented any loans being made. The Wagemann Plan combined a structural reform of the banking system with a modest cash injection. Its goal was to establish a rationalized monetary system capable of providing a flexible supply of cash, a secure and efficient means for conducting cashless business transactions and a steady flow of investment funds. The essential room for manoeuvre would be gained by suspending the requirement for the Reichsbank to back the currency issue with gold and foreign currency reserves. Protecting against a flight from the currency was unnecessary when the public had an insatiable appetite for cash. Having loosened the restrictions on the cash economy, Wagemann proposed the introduction of a much firmer system of banking regulation. It was the cashless transactions of business that needed protection. All banks would be required to separate their current account and chequing facilities from their investment business. In future, the practice of using short-term current accounts to fund long-term investments would be banned. The new rules would require the banks' short-term liabilities, current accounts and chequing accounts to be covered by first-class assets of similar maturity plus substantial minimum reserve deposits to be held with the central bank. The Reichsbank's reserves of gold and foreign currency would be used to underpin these reserve deposits. Savings and current accounts would be clearly distinguished. Small savers would be diverted into secure public debt. Other investors would be encouraged to place their funds not with banks, but directly into bonds or shares.

The sharp political edge to Wagemann's Plan was its indictment of the Reichsbank. The German central bank had failed to establish effective control over the modern monetary system. With its regulatory powers restricted to the cash money supply, the Reichsbank had the power to throttle a boom, but not to regulate the cycle. Only at the very peak of the upswing did the upsurge in activity impose a serious strain on the cash money supply. Only then did the Reichsbank's restrictions have any real bite. In normal circumstances the Reichsbank could regulate economic activity only by restricting the influx of foreign credits or by using its political influence to limit public borrowing. Even if it had wanted to, the Reichsbank of the 1920s had no effective means of conducting a counter-cyclical monetary policy. By contrast, Wagemann's Plan offered a vision of a reconstructed financial system that would provide monetary policy with an in-built 'transmission mechanism'. The Reichsbank would be in a position to regulate the availability of business credit in all phases of the cycle. And here Wagemann's ambition shone through. The Reichsbank had always been a generous donor to the Institute, but hitherto it had regarded the work of Konjunkturforschung with scepticism.[71] If the bank were to use its new powers wisely, it would have to follow the example of the US Federal Reserve in making much greater use of business-cycle economics. A modern banking system required a proactive central bank and a proactive central bank could not afford to ignore the benefits of modern economic science. In future, the reformed Reichsbank would need to work closely with Wagemann's Institute.

Given its highly technical content, the political impact of the Wagemann Plan was truly extraordinary. Since the autumn of 1931 Germany had been abuzz with schemes for reflation and Wagemann's was far from being the most radical.[72] The basic structure of banking regulation that Wagemann proposed was sound. The Reich's Banking Law of 1934 adopted many of his proposals.[73] Work-creation was no more than a side-effect of Wagemann's proposal. The difference lay not in the substance of the proposals. What set Wagemann apart from the other economists who criticized Brüning's policies was that Wagemann had the capacity to do the government real political damage. The most obvious comparison is with Wilhelm Lautenbach, a middle-ranking official in the RWM, who authored a radical plan for credit-financed government spending.[74] Lautenbach offered a far more thoroughgoing 'Keynesian' analysis of the German depression and in the autumn of 1931 it was his scheme that was the subject of the secret conference hosted by Luther and Schäffer. But none of the participants at that meeting dared to break the vows of silence imposed upon them. The facade of orthodoxy remained unbroken. The public remained ignorant of the radical policy options being given such serious consideration. Even if Lautenbach had had the personal courage to publicize his proposals, he would first have had to find a platform. By contrast, Wagemann was a public figure in his own right. As Director of the Institute for Business-Cycle Research and President of the Statistical Office he had built up an unrivalled network of contacts in politics and business as well as privileged access to the media. His research empire had an authoritative reputation both at home and abroad. This put him in a unique position. He released his proposal for credit reform without prior consultation with the cabinet. And Wagemann was quite capable of generating his own publicity. In advance of his speech he scheduled a full-scale press conference at the Statistical Office. He was even able to

[71] See for instance BAP 25.01 6472 no. 311, Stat Abteilung der Reichsbank 'Soll die Reichsbank Konjunkturpolitik treiben?' 9.6.1928.

[72] For a review of the alternatives see Meister, *Die große Depression*, pp. 280–393.

[73] C. Kopper, *Zwischen Marktwirtschaft und Dirigismus. Bankenpolitik im 'Dritten Reich' 1933–1939* (Bonn, 1995), p. 49.

[74] W. Lautenbach, *Zins, Kredit und Produktion*, ed. W. Stützel (Tübingen, 1952).

have copies of his Plan produced by the Reich's printers.[75] What explains the extraordinary public reaction to Wagemann's highly technical proposals is the position he had carved out for himself in the 1920s. The deflationists might easily have ignored a similar proposal from a lesser authority. In the case of Ernst Wagemann this was simply not an option. Instead, the deflationists and their supporters were forced into extraordinary and ultimately unsuccessful efforts to discredit the chief economic expert of the German state.

The battle over the Wagemann Plan proved to be a decisive defeat for the conservative forces fighting to defend the 'deflationary consensus'.[76] The Reichsbank got wind of Wagemann's intentions at the last moment. With the Chancellor's full support, Luther initiated a hasty exercise in damage control.[77] Brüning ordered Wagemann's press conference to be cancelled and insisted on a disclaimer, distancing the government from his Plan. Reichsbank President Luther sought to stage a public debate in which he would triumphantly reassert the line that all forms of credit reflation amounted to irresponsible inflation. The popular fear of a second hyperinflation was cynically invoked, as a weapon with which to bludgeon unorthodox proposals of all kinds.[78] Behind closed doors the views of the cabinet were quite different. In principle, Warmbold, the Finance Ministry and even Brüning agreed that some form of credit-financed work-creation might be both feasible and desirable. However, in the short run there were other priorities. Brüning was determined to obtain the cancellation of reparations. At home he was dedicated to continuing the attack on the labour movement and the welfare state.[79] A public commitment to economic orthodoxy was the necessary ideological accompaniment. Anxious international observers were assured that the Wagemann Plan did not enjoy the backing of the cabinet. Luther even managed to enlist the chief economists of Chase National Bank, the spokesman for Germany's foreign creditors, who was persuaded to give an interview denouncing Wagemann's scheme.[80]

This official response rallied the deflationist front. Relations with the

---

[75] Schulz, *Von Brüning zu Hitler*, pp. 737–740.

[76] G.D. Feldman, 'From Crisis to Work Creation. Government Policies and Economic Actors in the Great Depression', in J. Kocka, H.-J. Puhle and K. Tenfelde (eds.), *Von der Arbeiterbewegung zum modernen Sozialstaat. Festschrift für Gerhard A. Ritter zum 65. Geburtstag* (Munich, 1994), pp. 703–718.

[77] *Die Kabinette Brüning*, 3, doc. Nr. 651 and G. Schulz, I. Maurer and U. Wengst (eds.), *Politik und Wirtschaft in der Krise 1930–1932. Quellen zur Ära Brüning* (Düsseldorf, 1980), 2, doc. Nr. 412 and 2, doc. Nr. 414.

[78] Meister, *Die große Depression*, pp. 343–351.

[79] H. Mommsen, 'State and Bureaucracy in the Brüning Era', in H. Mommsen, *From Weimar to Auschwitz. Essays in German History* (Cambridge, 1991), pp. 108–109.

[80] Kroll, *Von der Weltwirtschaftskrise*, p. 402.

Institute's industrial backers had been strained since early 1931, following the publication of a controversial study of capital formation in interwar Germany.[81] The industrialists feared that the report would provide ammunition for those who argued that German business had largely recovered from the ravages of war and hyperinflation.[82] Complaints were made to the Chancellor.[83] To reassure the RdI Wagemann was forced to set up a Supervisory Committee to oversee the Institute's publications.[84] Business reaction to the Wagemann Plan was mixed.[85] The majority of industrialists appear to have been quietly in favour of reflation. Many of them favoured the proposed financial reconstruction. But, the RdI leadership was adamant in its support for Brüning and reactionaries such as Paul Reusch hogged the limelight. For him, the Plan was final confirmation of Wagemann's unreliability and disloyalty. Reactionary elements in the Ruhr led an unprecedented campaign of vilification against Wagemann, demanding his immediate resignation. Heavy industrial contributions to the Institute's funds were slashed.[86] The academic opponents of Konjunkturforschung joined in the fray.[87] The Dernburg Commission had noted in 1930 the rising tide of academic resentment against the Institute. Wagemann was accused of monopolizing government funding for business-cycle research and attracting undue public attention.[88] In 1932, he faced a carefully stage-managed outcry of academic opinion. The high point came in May, when a newspaper well known for its links to heavy industry published a 'Declaration by 32 Economists'. In this extraordinary display of unity, the Plan was denounced as folly and as an act of disloyalty that was incompatible with Wagemann's continued employment as a civil servant. The names of the signatories were kept secret and were made available only to government ministries. The campaign against

---

[81] G. Keiser and B. Benning, *Kapitalbildung und Investitionen in der deutschen Volks-wirtschaft 1924 bis 1928. VzK Sonderheft 22* (Berlin, 1931).

[82] These fears were not unjustified. See the intervention by Tarnow in the debate of the Reichstag's Budget Committee BAP 01.01 film 31649 file 2590 no. 418, '25. Sitzung des Haushaltsausschusses 19.1.1931. Drucksache Nr. 311', p. 300.

[83] BAP 07.01 film 19065N/2110 no. 132, Dr Reichert to Reichskanzlei 19.8.1931 and BAP 07.01 film 19065N/2110 no. 183–207, J.N. Reichert, 'Kapitalbildung und Industrielle Investitionen'.

[84] See the divergent accounts of the meeting given in GStA I Rep. 120 C VIII 2a Nr. 33 Bd. 1 Bl. 408, Prussian Min. of Handel und Gewerbe Vermerk 13.5.1931 and the 'official minutes' in GStA I Rep. 120 C VIII 2a Nr. 33 Bd. 1 Bl. 519, 'Sitzung des Kuratoriums des IfK 28.4.1931'.

[85] H. Kim, 'Die Großindustrie und die Konjunkturpolitik unter der Kanzlerschaft Brünings', *Jahrbuch für Wirtschaftsgeschichte* (1998), pp. 181–200.

[86] GStA I Rep. 120 C VIII 2a Nr. 33 Bd. 2 Bl. 16, 'Haushaltsplan des IfK 1932/3'.

[87] Krohn, *Wirtschaftstheorien*, pp. 157–166.

[88] BAP 39.01 RAM 10683 no. 28 Dernburg Kommission, 'Bericht', p. 27.

Wagemann continued even after the replacement of Brüning as Chancellor by Franz von Papen and the adoption of the first work-creation programmes.[89] Luther remained as President of the Reichsbank and saw to it that the Institute received dramatically reduced contributions in 1932–3.[90] In November 1932, the RWM was forced to call a series of meetings to put an end to the attacks on Wagemann by industry.[91] Though no agreement was reached, this put a lid on the embarrassing public argument.

V

Whatever the technical merits of Wagemann's Plan, the accusations of disloyalty were to the point.[92] By 1932, after two years of frustration at the hands of Brüning, Wagemann was willing to risk confrontation. As we have seen, he was struggling to defend his establishment against attacks by the Chancellor and the financial pressure of the Dernburg Commission. Retreat would most likely spell the end of his ambitions. Within the Statistical Office, the pressure was beginning to take its toll. The Office represented in microcosm the tensions that were tearing the Weimar Republic apart. Labour relations were deteriorating seriously. Wagemann increasingly divided the senior staff by surrounding himself with a clique of trusted colleagues. To make matters worse the expansion of the 1920s had been accomplished on the cheap. The new civil service posts were filled with juniors, leaving the overworked departmental Directors increasingly out of touch. The clerical grades, for their part, were stretched by continuous overtime and by the burden of extra responsibilities for which they were not properly rewarded. Meanwhile, the Sparkommissar's rolling review spread insecurity through the ranks.[93] Discipline began to break down as early as 1927. Special orders had to be issued reminding the Office's workers that statistical questionnaires should not be damaged or removed from the premises. The walls of the Office washrooms were scrawled with abusive graffiti. In one

[89] BAP 62 DAF 3 17502 no. 26, *Vorwärts* 425, 9.9.1932 'Kesseltreiben. Unternehmerverbände gegen Wagemann'. BAP 62 DAF 3 17502 no. 71, 'Zentral-Archiv des D.H.V., Pressebericht 25.10.1932'.

[90] GStA I Rep. 120 C VIII 2a Nr. 33 Bd. 2 Bl. 16, 'Haushaltsplan des IfK 1932/3'.

[91] BAP 62 DAF 3 17502 no. 69, *Kölnische Zeitung*, 640, 22.11.1932 'Wagemann und die Wirtschaft'. BAP 62 DAF 3 17502 no. 35, *Deutsche Allgemeine Zeitung* 549, 23.11.1932 'Auseinandersetzung mit Wagemann'. BAP 62 DAF 3 17502 no. 36, *Tägliche Rundschau* 276, 23.11.1932 'Vorstoß gegen Wagemann'.

[92] K. Borchardt, 'Noch Einmal: Alternativen zu Brünings Wirtschaftspolitik?', *Historische Zeitschrift* 237 (1983), p. 78.

[93] BAP 31.02 5665 no. 1, *Mitteilungsblatt für Beamte und Angestellte beim SRA* 1 (1927), 2, p. 4.

extraordinary incident the toilets themselves were stuffed with the export returns of the mechanical engineering industry.[94] The elected representatives of the statistical staff were hard pressed to keep control of increasingly undisciplined protests. The monthly magazine of the clerical and civil service grades appealed in vain for the staff to vent their frustrations through the appropriate channels.[95] A low point was reached in 1930, when the overworked Director of tax statistics committed suicide.[96] The funeral degenerated into a nationalist demonstration. As early as May 1930, Social Democratic members of the Reichstag Budget Committee reported that the Statistical Office was a hotbed of Nazi agitation.[97] The Social Democratic chair of the elected Staff Council (Beamtenrat) faced constant harassment from Nazi activists. The dramatic redundancies of 1931 can hardly have calmed nerves. By 1933 a substantial Nazi factory cell (NSBO) was at work within the Reich's Statistical Office.[98]

Wagemann did nothing to counter the rightward drift amongst his staff. On the contrary, faced with ostracism, he himself was driven into an ever-closer embrace of National Socialism. Brüning's single-minded pursuit of deflation had the disastrous effect of making Hitler's movement into a credible oppositional force.[99] The Social Democrats in their desperation to preserve at least the remnants of Republican legality sided with Brüning. Only in the spring of 1932, after the publication of Wagemann's Plan, did the labour movement begin to develop constructive economic policy plans of its own. The Nazis, by contrast, appeared dynamic, forward-looking, youthful and popular. And they had no qualms about economic liberalism or extensive state intervention. In 1932 Wagemann was one of a number of so-called reformers – unorthodox opponents of deflation – who drifted into the orbit around the Nazi party.[100] Wagemann's contacts with Hitler's movement were numerous. The plan for credit creation established a link to Gregor Straßer

[94] BAP 01.01 film 31648 file 2589 no. 84, '16. Sitzung des Haushaltsausschusses vom 21.1.1929. 1. Lesung des Nachtrags zum RWM für 1928. Nr. 697 Drucksache', p. 8.
[95] BAP 31.02 SRA 5665 no. 20, *Mitteilungsblatt für Beamte und Angestellte beim SRA* 2 (1928) Nr. 2 (February), p. 4.
[96] BAP 01.01 film 31649 file 2590 no. 218, 'Reichstag IV. Wahlperiode 1928. 5. Ausschuß (Reichshaushalt). 150. Sitzung (Reichshaushalt 1930: RWM) 9.5.1930', p. 15.
[97] BAP 01.01 film 31649 file 2590 no. 218, 'Reichstag IV. Wahlperiode 1928. 5. Ausschuß für den Reichshaushalt. 150. Sitzung 9.5.1930', p. 15.
[98] BAK R 43 II/1157e no. 3, NSBO SRA to Goering 28.2.1933.
[99] W. Jochmann, 'Brünings Deflationspolitik und der Untergang der Weimarer Republik', in D. Stegmann, B.-J. Wendt and P.-C. Witt (eds.), *Industrielle Gesellschaft und politisches System. Beiträge zur politischen Sozialgeschichte* (Bonn, 1978), pp. 97–112.
[100] A. Barkai, *Das Wirtschaftssystem des Nationalsozialismus. Ideologie, Theorie, Politik 1933–1945* (Frankfurt, 1988, 2nd edn.), p. 49 and U. Kissenkoetter, *Gregor Straßer und die NSDAP* (Stuttgart, 1978), pp. 104–108.

on the left wing of the party, the most vocal advocate of work creation.[101] Wagemann was also connected to Gottfried Feder the senior economic ideologue of Hitler's movement.[102] And, on the conservative wing, he was closely linked to Walter Funk, the economic journalist who served as one of the Party's more respectable economic advisors[103] From later correspondence it seems that Wagemann also had personal dealings with Hitler on at least one occasion prior to 1933. Later press reports claimed that Wagemann had threatened to resign from his post as director of the National Electoral Commission in protest at the efforts of the Interior Ministry to exclude Hitler from the presidential election of March 1932.[104]

And Wagemann further underlined his affinity with the far right in a series of publications that marked a turn towards economic nationalism. In 1931, in his study of the world economy, *Struktur und Rhythmus der Weltwirtschaft*, this was not yet fully apparent. Wagemann elaborated the basic themes of his earlier work. The world economy was racked by multiple tensions that resulted from the superimposition of different modes of economic organization. The free flow of goods, capital and labour was interfered with everywhere. Each intervention had its own logic, but together they produced a highly unstable system. As the single most important source of instability he highlighted America's protectionism.[105] However, in the spring of 1931, Wagemann still clung to his fundamental optimism about the future of international trade. The world might be passing through the down-phase of one of Kondratieff's 50-year waves, but in the long run the growth prospects of the international economy were good. It was events between July and September 1931 – the banking crisis and the British abandonment of gold – that propelled Wagemann into the nationalist camp.[106] The tensions both

---

[101] A.R. Herrmann, the monetary economist who prepared the groundwork for Wagemann's Plan, was later to work for Strasser. See A.R. Hermann, *Verstaatlichung des Giralgeldes* (Munich, 1932) in the NS-Bibliothek. Kissenkoetter, *Gregor Straßer und die NSDAP*, pp. 105–107. Krengel, *Das Deutsche Institut*, p. 54 suggests that Wagemann was involved in secret talks with Schleicher and Straßer in 1932/3 with the aim of keeping Hitler out of power. Krengel dates the last meeting with Straßer as 16 January 1933. For a sceptical analysis of the real import of Straßer's 'connections' see Schulz, *Von Brüning zu Hitler*, pp. 975–978.

[102] BAK R 43 II/1157e no. 3, NSBO/SRA to Goering 28.2.1933.

[103] BAK R 43 II/7 1157e no. 23, Wagemann to Reichskanzler Hitler 23.3.1933.

[104] BAP 62 DAF 3 17502 no. 53, *Tägliche Rundschau* 80, 4.4.1933 'Wirrwarr um Wagemann'.

[105] E. Wagemann, *Struktur und Rhythmus*, pp. 353–356.

[106] E. Teichert, *Autarkie und Großraumwirtschaft in Deutschland 1930–1939. Außenwirtschaftliche Konzeptionen zwischen Wirtschaftskrise und Zweitem Weltkrieg* (Munich, 1984), p. 93 and BAP 62 DAF 3 17502 no. 75 *Kölnische Zeitung* 175, 31.3.1932 'Propaganda der Autarkie'.

within and between national economies were too great. A period of relative isolation was essential for national governments to resolve the triple crisis of finance, industry and agriculture. Only then could the world economy be rebuilt. As in previous long waves, after a period of prolonged depression, a creative impulse would carry the world forward into a new epoch of growth. In the past this impulse had come from entrepreneurs and technologists. Now it was the nation-state which had to take 'vigorous, creative' action. And there can be little doubt where Wagemann saw the source of such energy in German politics.

VI

The scandal surrounding Wagemann's Plan in 1932 is a staple of the literature. It generally serves to illustrate the deep hostility facing the advocates of reflation. This chapter places this famous incident in a wider historical context. The intense public response to Wagemann's Plan is puzzling unless one appreciates the prominent position that the Institute, the Statistical Office and their Director had come to occupy in the public life of the Weimar Republic. Konjunkturforschung had established itself at the centre of economic policy discussion. And this point is strengthened if we look behind the scenes. The struggle over statistical spending revealed how deeply entrenched was Wagemann's project. His influential friends in the RWM and in the Reichstag effectively protected the statistical establishment against the worst effects of the fiscal crisis. The content of the Plan itself also takes on a new meaning. Wagemann's proposals were directed towards the German banking system. But the Plan can also be seen as part of the on-going effort to invent new tools of economic policy. It aimed to provide the Reichsbank with powerful new levers of monetary policy, allowing it to regulate not just the cash money supply but the entire system of credit. And this in turn gave added prominence to the role of business-cycle research. The Plan can thus be read as an aggressive attempt to redefine the role of the Reichsbank, thereby restoring the influence of Wagemann's establishment. Finally, the Plan's intellectual origins can clearly be traced to the analysis of money under conditions of high capitalism, which Wagemann had been elaborating since the early 1920s. The attack on the Reichsbank's misguided reserve requirements followed directly from the critique of metallism and Knapp's state-theory of money that Wagemann had developed in the *Treatise*. The tragedy of the Weimar Republic was that Wagemann, like so many other reformers and technocrats, came to see Hitler's movement as the best hope of realizing his ambitions.

5   Statistics and the 'Strong State', 1933–1936

On 30 January 1933, Hitler was appointed Chancellor of the German Republic. Over the following months the Nazi movement staged a brutal seizure of power. The institutions of a free society were systematically destroyed. It had long been fashionable to speak of the end of liberalism: this was the bloody reality. But what came after liberalism? What kind of regime were the Nazis creating? The 'National Revolution' was an open-ended process. Its protagonists ranged from the thugs of the SA to highbrow revolutionaries such as Martin Heidegger. The result was a situation of flux, which historians puzzle over to this day.[1] What kind of system took shape after 1933? Was the influence of Nazi ideology dominant from the start? Or are the early years of Hitler's dictatorship best described as a form of authoritarian conservatism? This chapter argues that at least as far as the Reich's economic administration was concerned, the early years of the Nazi regime can be understood as an authoritarian extension of earlier trends. There was a dramatic expansion of the statistical instruments of Konjunkturforschung with the aim of imposing state control on an increasingly militarized economy. The full force of Nazi radicalism was not to impact on the Reich's statistical system until the late 1930s, with the second seizure of power.

I

The role played by Konjunkturforschung in the Nazi regime has been obscured by the personal fate of its creator. In the spring of 1933, it seemed that the future belonged to Ernst Wagemann. After all, he could count himself amongst the prophets of the National Revolution. He was even rumoured to be in line to succeed his arch-enemy, Hans Luther, as head of the Reichsbank.[2] This, of course, was idle gossip. Hjalmar

---

[1] For a useful survey see G. Jasper, *Die gescheiterte Zähmung. Wege zur Machtergreifung Hitlers 1930–1934* (Frankfurt, 1986).
[2] BAP 62 DAF 3 17502 no. 32, *DAZ* 131, 18.3.1933 'Unsere Meinung' and BAP 62

Schacht was destined for that strategic post. Nevertheless, Wagemann certainly seemed well placed to take advantage of the Nazi seizure of power. It therefore came as a shock when in March 1933 he was suspended from all his offices. Wagemann fell victim not to the Nazis but to their coalition partners, the nationalist right. In the early months of the new regime, Hitler's grip on power was not yet complete. The popular nationalist backlash, which the Nazis had unleashed, was not fully under central control. And in cabinet, Hitler and Goering were still struggling to assert themselves against the nationalist conservatives led by Hugenberg. In the course of this tactical manoeuvring, responsibility for the RWM was assigned to the nationalists. This left Wagemann exposed. Hugenberg was amongst the most bitter opponents of Wagemann's Plan.[3] All Hugenberg needed was an excuse to act. This was provided by the upsurge of nationalist resentment within the Reich's Statistical Office itself.

In the spring of 1933, the staff of the Office were in an ugly mood and they found a spokesman in the form of Dr Wilhelm Leisse.[4] Leisse was the proud scion of a nationalist family. He completed a PhD on the steel industry in 1912 and then served with distinction as an artillery officer during the war.[5] In the early 1920s, he joined the Statistical Office, occupying a post in Wagemann's personal office. But this was not to last. Leisse was accused of plagiarism and removed;[6] to redeem himself, he was given the task of preparing the industrial census planned for 1930. However, the census fell victim to Brüning's cuts, and Leisse's route to rehabilitation was blocked. His resentment found expression in politics. He had been active in 'national' circles since the 1920s and in March 1932 he formally joined the Nazi Party. In 1933 his moment had come. Together with other leading party members in the Statistical Office and with the backing of the NSBO cell, Leisse drafted a denunciatory memorandum entitled 'Corruption in the Statistical Office'. This portrayed Wagemann as an example of the Weimar 'system' at its worst: an economist corrupted by his venal dealings with publishers; a political civil servant who maintained disreputable contacts with the parties of the left; a promoter of Catholics and Jews; a failed leader out of touch

DAF 3 17502 no. 22, *Frankfurter Zeitung* 19.3.1933 'Warum wurde Wagemann beurlaubt?'.

[3] C.D. Krohn, *Wirtschaftstheorien als politische Interessen. Die akademische Nationalökonomie in Deutschland 1918–1933* (Frankfurt, 1981), p. 166.

[4] Barch Lichterfelde ehm BDC PK, Dr Wilhelm Leisse and the material in Barch Lichterfelde ehm. BDC OPG, Leisse, Dr Wilhelm.

[5] W. Leisse, *Wandlungen in der Organisation der Eisenindustrie und des Eisenhandels seit dem Gründungsjahr des Stahlwerksverbandes* (Munich, 1912).

[6] BAK R 43 II/1157e no. 88, Wagemann to Lammers Reichskanzlei 19.5.1933, p. 2.

with his 'German' staff; a crypto-Marxist whose 'scientific' writings heaped praise on the achievements of Stalinist planning. Wagemann was even accused of speaking disrespectfully of the house of Hohenzollern. In early March Leisse personally submitted this document to the Chancellery, demanding a personal audience with the Führer. When he was refused, he stormed out declaring 'If not with Hitler then with Hugenberg.'[7] On 17 March 1933, Hugenberg duly obliged, suspending Wagemann from all his offices.

Press speculation over Wagemann's dismissal was furious. Wagemann was a prominent advocate of activist economic policy with well-known connections in the Nazi movement. What did his suspension imply for the future of economic policy? In the conservative papers his removal was heralded as a clear indication that Hitler's government rejected economic planning.[8] Elsewhere, Hugenberg was criticized for a high-handed decision that ran contrary to the intentions of the Führer.[9] Wagemann himself fought back. After all, he had every reason to expect a sympathetic hearing from the people who were emerging as the real holders of power. Under pressure from Wagemann's attorney, Hugenberg was forced to retract the slanderous charges of personal corruption. At the same time Wagemann appealed personally to Hitler for a decision based on his record as an early advocate of National Socialism.[10] Wagemann's dismissal was attracting international attention and German commentators feared that the removal of such a prominent economist would be read as a bad omen for the future of social sciences under Nazi rule. Given the heavy dependence of German research institutions on American money, this was a matter of serious concern. The Rockefeller Foundation was known to be reviewing its position in Germany.[11] In April 1933, Bullock, Chairman of the Harvard Committee for Economic Research, issued a public statement in support of Wagemann. Bullock even obtained a promise from the Rockefeller Foundation that it would support the Institut für Konjunkturforschung, if no alternative source of funds could be found.[12]

The response of Hitler's office to Wagemann's petitions was remarkable. Wagemann did not get the audience he wanted but, from the

---

[7] BAK R 43 II/1157e no. 14, Reichsmin. des Innern to Reichskanzlei 10.3.1933 and the attached report 'Korruption im statistischen Dienst'.

[8] BAP 62 DAF 3 17502 no. 32, *DAZ* 131 18.3.1933 'Unsere Meinung'.

[9] BAP 62 DAF 3 17502 no. 53, *Tägliche Rundschau* 80 4.4.1933 'Wirrwarr um Wagemann'.

[10] BAK R 43 II/1157e no. 26, Wagemann to Reichskanzler 28.3.1933.

[11] C.-D. Krohn, *Wissenschaft im Exil: Deutsche Sozial- und Wirtschaftswissenschaftler in den USA und die New School of Social Research* (Frankfurt, 1987), pp. 40–46.

[12] BAP 62 DAF 3 17502 no. 51, *Tägliche Rundschau* 99 28.4.1933 'Harvard-Institut ehrt Wagemann'.

wording of the Chancellery's minutes, there can be no doubt that Hitler took a personal interest in the affair. Hugenberg was forced to provide a detailed report justifying his decision.[13] But this was not enough. Hitler wished to see evidence from the Directors of the Reich's Statistical Office. Wagemann was to be given a right of reply.[14] There cannot have been many civil servants dismissed in 1933 who received this kind of attention. At the very least, the affair provided a useful means to embarrass Hugenberg. The RWM duly convoked the Departmental Directors of the Reich's Statistical Office and each gave evidence. The depositions read like a rerun of the Dernburg Commission with the gloves off. The hard questions about the organization of Wagemann's statistical empire could no longer be avoided. This time there was no shortage of witnesses for the prosecution. The impenetrable front which the apparatus of official statistics had presented to Dernburg's enquiry dissolved into a mass of disgruntled and disillusioned individuals.[15] Apart from Leisse's denunciation, the most damaging testimony was provided by Dr Walter Grävell, who was by now installed as Director for trade statistics. He highlighted Wagemann's systematic neglect and mismanagement of the Statistical Office. The real problems were the inflated size of the Office and the distraction provided by the Institute. On 3 May 1933, the RWM restated its position insisting that Wagemann was guilty of having neglected his official duties.[16] In any case, the relationship of trust between Wagemann and his senior staff had been comprehensively undermined. Wagemann's departure from the Statistical Office had thus become inevitable. On 24 May 1933 the Reichschancellory intervened for the last time to inform Hugenberg that Hitler did not wish to see Wagemann pensioned off, or insulted by the offer of an inferior job in the Statistical Office. But Hitler's secretary concluded his letter with the cryptic comment that the 'Reich's Chancellor must [in future] remain at a distance from this affair'.[17]

If the Nazis did not save the Statistical Office for Wagemann, they did ensure that he retained control of the Institute. Over the spring, Wagemann tightened his links with the Party. Along with his other offices, Wagemann was suspended from his role as Chairman of the Electoral Commission; this meant that he was free to hold a party card.

[13] BAK R 43 II/1157e no. 39, Staatssekretär in der Reichskanzlei to Hugenberg 31.3.1933. Letter is marked 'Eilt sehr!' and opens 'Im persönlichen Auftrage des Herrn Reichskanzlers'. BAK R 43 II/1157e no. 41, RWM to Reichskanzlei 13.4.1933.
[14] BAK R 43 II/1157e no. 48, Reichskanzlei to RWM 25.4.1933.
[15] BAK R 43 II/ 1157e, Neue Reichskanzlei no. 59 Statements by Directors 26.4.1933.
[16] BAK R 43 II/1157e no. 49, RWM to Reichskanzlei 3.5.1933.
[17] '. . . der Reichskanzler sich . . . von der Angelegenheit fernhalten müsse'. BAK R 43 II/1157e no. 103 Reichskanzlei Note 24.5.1933.

And in May 1933 he joined the rush for membership of the NSDAP.[18] The same month, he obtained an audience with the Führer's deputy Rudolf Hess, which according to Wagemann 'went very well'.[19] In the end, it was the German Labour Front (Deutsche Arbeitsfront, DAF) that supplied Wagemann with the backing he needed. In June 1933, exploiting the contacts of a member of the Institute, Wagemann obtained an audience with the ambitious leader of the Front, Robert Ley. That same evening Ley's deputy, Rudolf Schmeer, was allegedly able to extract a promise from Hitler that the Institute would be protected from further attacks by Hugenberg. At the meeting of the Institute's Kuratorium on 17 June 1933 Wagemann was reinstated as Director. Hugenberg was outvoted by representatives of the National Socialist ministries, the DAF and business.[20]

The Institute, the intellectual centre of empirical economic research in Weimar Germany, thus survived 1933. Its weekly and quarterly reports remained the principal source of information on the progress of the German economy. The Institute expanded dramatically as an independent centre for economic research feeding off contracts supplied by Darré agricultural organizations and the Reich's Post Office.[21] Wagemann was able to expand the staff of the Institute from 50 in the late 1920s to more than 150 by 1939, not including a number of regional off-shoots. Wagemann himself continued to publish prolifically. In a series of books and pamphlets he provided an extensive rationalization for the new role of the state in economic policy.[22] The need for state intervention was clear from developments not only in Germany, but also in the United States, the Soviet Union and even in Britain, the bastion of liberalism. Countries that clung to the gold standard and deflation, such as France, were destined to suffer prolonged depression. Wagemann was an invited speaker at numerous party events and was despatched abroad on propaganda trips by the Goebbels ministry.[23] In 1936, he was chosen to advise Goering on the formation of the Four-Year Plan.[24] Wagemann was far from being *persona non grata* in the Third Reich.

[18] Archiv der Humboldt Uni., U.K.W. 9 no. 1 His number was 3078159.
[19] BAK Nl Moellendorff 158/66, Wagemann to Moellendorff 29.5.1933.
[20] BHStA MWi 3092, Bayerische stellv. Bevollmächtigte to Staatsmin. für Wirtschaft 17.6.1933 and BBA 15 523 RDI, 'Aktennotiz Betr: Sitzung des Kuratoriums des IfK 17.6.1933'.
[21] DIW, *Das Deutsche Institut für Wirtschaftsforschung (IfK) 1925–1945 in der Erinnerung füherer Mitarbeiter* (Berlin, 1966).
[22] E. Wagemann, *Zwischenbilanz der Krisenpolitik* (Berlin, 1935) and *Wirtschaftspolitische Strategie* (Hamburg, 1937).
[23] BAK RAM R 41/23a no. 1, 'Protokoll über die Arbeitstagung der Reichsarbeitskammer 28.11.1935'.
[24] Zentralen Staatsarchiv der Sowjetunion, Sonderarchiv MA 700 1/2.

Did this imply an ideological Gleichschaltung of the Institute? On the whole, it seems, it did not. Certainly in the early years of the Third Reich there was remarkably little pressure to conform to any particular line on the economy. In 1933 and 1934 Wagemann continued occasionally to be attacked by conservative voices in the press who mistrusted his proposed reforms of the banking system. However, other newspapers leapt to his defence, heralding him as a prophet of the new economic policy and accusing his opponents of intellectual sabotage.[25] Only in the second half of 1935 did the Institute run into real trouble. In the autumn of that year, the Institute published a pessimistic prediction of the likely course of German economic development. Government borrowing was crowding-out private investment.[26] The recovery would soon relapse into recession. The following year the Institute came under attack from Bernhard Köhler, the head of the Nazi Party's economic policy commission.[27] The Institute stood accused of clinging to a liberal dogma when the triumph of the regime was to have imposed political will on the business-cycle. However the Institute was never muzzled, it retained its name and Goering himself continued to employ the language of Konjunktur in his speeches.[28] Far more difficult was the increasing restriction of economic information. The RWM continued to hold the Institute at arm's length, policing a strict separation from the Statistical Office.[29] Wagemann's researchers found it increasingly difficult even to obtain routine data from their former colleagues.[30] This in turn rendered the Institute even more dependent on research contracts. It was not censorship but threats of a more mundane kind that kept the Institute in line: funding and access to information.

The Statistical Office also came through the turmoil of 1933 largely unscathed. The Nazis did not extend their grip to the Reich's economic administration in a determined fashion. Schmitt, a conservative insurance executive, succeeded Hugenberg as Minister for Economic Affairs in the summer of 1933. The following year Schmitt himself was replaced by Hjalmar Schacht, who was to remain in place until the autumn of 1937. Schacht was closely allied with Hitler's movement and played an essential role in organizing rearmament. However, he was scornful of

---

[25] Pro-Wagemann: *DSZ* 49 v. 14. April 1934 und Nr. 51 v. 17. April 1934; *Berliner Tageblatt* 180 v. 17.4.1934; *Wirtschaftlicher Teil der Deutschen Zeitung* 882 v. 15. April 1934. Anti-Wagemann: *DAZ* 175 v. 16.4.1934 und Nr. 187 v. 19.4.1934.

[26] *Neue Freie Presse* 25593 M v. 10.12.1935.

[27] *Braune Wirtschaftspost* 29 (1936) 16.1.1936; *National-Zeitung* 271 v. 2.10.1936; 5 1.8.1936; *Die Deutsche Volkswirtschaft* 22 1.8.1936.

[28] *Die Deutsche Volkswirtschaft* 1 1.1.1939.

[29] BAK R41/799 no. 21, RAM note 17.1.1934.

[30] BAK R 7/1287 Fol. 1 – no. 153–177.

the Party's own economic experts and tried to ensure that the initiative in economic policy remained with the Reichsbank and the RWM rather than with the Nazis. The Reich's economic administration and the Statistical Office were largely undisturbed by the seizure of power. There were surprisingly few dismissals from the Statistical Office in the first months of the Nazi regime;[31] many staff who in the 1920s had been closely involved with the Institute, notably Paul Bramstedt, now devoted themselves to the Office. A move by the Party cell in the Office to replace Wagemann with a candidate with impeccable Nazi credentials was stifled.[32] The choice instead fell on Ministerial Director Wolfgang Reichardt, formerly of the RWM.[33] In a secret report to Hugenberg, Reichardt was classified as a former supporter of the German People's Party (DVP), right-wing but liberal in economic policy.[34] Reichardt was certainly no enemy of Konjunkturforschung. Until 1933, he had served as the Ministry's most regular representative on the Kuratorium. Under Ministerial orders, he was forced to resign in 1934. Nevertheless, his appointment as President of the Statistical Office signalled a degree of continuity with the past.

As in the case of the Institute, there is no evidence in the records of the Statistical Office of any attempt to impose a coherent programme of Nazi ideology. The chief function of propaganda was to attribute to Nazi policy what was, at least initially, a largely 'spontaneous' rebound of the German economy.[35] A special section was established in the Office to monitor the triumphs of Nazi work-creation.[36] Otherwise, however, there are no signs that existing statistical series were deliberately manipulated for propagandistic purposes. What measures the Nazis would have taken towards the Reich's statistics if the economic news had been less favourable can only be imagined. There seems no reason to doubt that if the regime had faced a struggle for survival, the Statistical Office would soon have been reduced to a crude instrument of propaganda. In the event, no such measures were required – the economic news was mainly good. Though there was no fraud, the Statistical Office did become involved, after 1933, in the regime's very

---

[31] For a list of those dismissed from the Statistical Office see BAP 23.01 2233 SRA note 29.4.1933.

[32] BAK R 43 II/1157e no. 106, note for Staatssek. Reichskanzlei 9.6.1933.

[33] BAP 62 DAF 3 17502 no. 17, *Vossische Zeitung* 368 31.7.1933 'Reichardt Präsident des Statistischen Reichsamts'.

[34] BAK Nl 231 Hugenberg 85 Fol. 1– no. 116 and the biographical sketch in BAP 62 DAF 3 8788 *Deutsche Allgemeine Zeitung* 323 31.7.1933 'Neuer Leiter des SRAs'.

[35] For instance, *NS-Presseanweisungen der Vorkriegszeit*, 1, p. 98, Instructions of the Propaganda Ministry 11.8.1933.

[36] BAP 31.02 3586 no. 110, Kurze Aufzeichnung über den Aufgabenkreis des Referats Statistik der Wirtschaftstätigkeit 29.3.1935.

deliberate attempt to curtail public discussion of economic issues. After a decade of increased publicity, the trend after 1933 was towards restriction. The Propaganda Ministry attempted to ban the discussion of general economic policy issues in the press, but this was a hard habit to break.[37] A more effective weapon was the progressive tightening of restrictions on the publication of economic statistics. As the rearmament drive gathered pace, ever-greater areas of economic activity were placed off-limits.[38] The data published by the Statistical Office, the reports of Germany's business organizations and even company annual reports, were carefully edited to prevent details of the rearmament programme from becoming public knowledge.

II

At least as far as the Statistical Office and the Reich's economic administration were concerned one cannot speak of ideological Gleichschaltung in the early years of Hitler's regime. Far from it: the first four years of the Nazi regime were a period of largely unobstructed bureaucratic initiative. According to contemporary accounts, the civil servants of the RWM experienced the early years of National Socialism as an era of liberation from the fetters of parliamentary politics and class conflict. The idealized image of government by a strong state seemed within reach.[39] Such claims of a return to tradition should not be taken at face value.[40] As we have seen, there was in fact no 'German tradition' of national economic policy. In the sphere of economic government, the idea of the strong German state was a myth, an invented tradition. Harold James has characterized this period as one of conservative continuity, as a period in which fiscal policy was restrained and administrative controls developed incrementally in an improvised fashion.[41] He is certainly right to stress continuity. However, to couple continuity with conservatism is to mischaracterize the actions of the Reich's economic administration. As we have seen, the RWM before 1933 had been innovative in its approach to economic government. After 1933,

---

[37] *NS-Presseanweisungen der Vorkriegszeit* 1, pp. 99, 122–123, 268–269, and 2, pp. 197–198.

[38] BAK R 7/1287 Fol. 1 – no. 171 RWM, 'Vorlage für Hagen RWM III/Stat' 28.8.1936 and BAK R 7/1287 – Fol. 1 no. 172 RWM note 16.9.1936.

[39] W.A. Boelcke, *Die deutsche Wirtschaft 1930–1945. Interna des Reichswirtschaftsministeriums* (Düsseldorf, 1983), p. 89.

[40] As for instance in A. Barkai, *Das Wirtschaftssystem des Nationalsozialismus. Ideologie, Theorie, Politik 1933–1945* (Frankfurt, 1988, rev. edn.).

[41] H. James, 'Innovation and Conservatism in Economic Recovery: The Alleged "Nazi Recovery" of the 1930s', in T. Childers and J. Caplan (eds.), *Reevaluating the Third Reich* (New York, 1993), pp. 114–138.

far from pursuing orthodox fiscal prescriptions, Schacht embarked on a course of state-directed recovery. Central government spending was raised.[42] The flow of capital was redirected. Wages were frozen and consumer industries were throttled. Imports were tightly controlled. The economy was increasingly propelled by the political priorities of national reconstruction, rearmament and autarchy. To impose this new policy regime, the Reichsbank, the RWM, the Labour Ministry and the Agricultural Ministry all dramatically extended their reach. The Länder were finally subordinated to the Reich. For the first time, the German economy was subject to a powerful and consistent system of national controls. And this was more than administrative empire-building. It was a direct extension of the effort to build a national apparatus of economic government which we have traced back to the final stages of World War I. Shielded from the party, unfettered by parliament, released from the need to find tripartite agreement with both industry and labour, the Reich's economic administration experienced a period of unwonted freedom. And the Statistical Office was an enthusiastic participant in this new era.

State-building in the early years of the Third Reich proceeded with ruthless disregard for tradition. This was symbolized most dramatically by the fate of the Länder. After 1933, the RWM tore control of Germany's economic infrastructure away from the enfeebled regional ministries.[43] For the first time, the RWM acquired the powers necessary to intervene directly in industry and commerce at a local level. As we have seen, a merger between the Statistical Office and its Prussian counterpart had been on the cards since the 1920s. Now, with Prussian autonomy abolished, the Statistical Office, like the rest of the state administration, was fused with its Reich counterpart.[44] The oldest tradition in German official statistics thus came to an abrupt end. The Office acquired 58 new civil servants and 15 other staff.[45] More importantly, the repertoire of the national statistical office was extended into areas that had previously been the preserve of Länder statistics.

---

[42] James fails to realize that in a period of economic recovery and surging tax revenues a balanced budget implies a lax fiscal policy. A truly restrictive fiscal policy requires a budget surplus. See R. Cohn, 'Fiscal Policy during the Depression', *Explorations in Economic History*, 29 (1992), pp. 318–342.

[43] G. Mollin, *Montankonzerne und 'Drittes Reich'. Der Gegensatz zwischen Monopolindustrie und Befehlswirtschaft in der deutschen Rüstung und Expansion 1936–1944* (Göttingen, 1988), pp. 42–56.

[44] BAP SRA 31.02 3585 no. 1, Präs. SRA Decree 3.10.1934.

[45] GStA 1. HA Rep. 77 3884 no. 410, 'Verzeichnis der Beamten des Preußischen SLa' (for transfer to the SRA) 1.10.1934 and GStA 1. HA Rep. 77 3884 no. 412, 'Verzeichnis der Hilfsreferenten und wissenschaftliche Hilfsarbeiter des Preußischen SLa' (for transfer to the SRA) 1.10.1934.

Table 6. *The expansion of the Statistical Office, 1932–1935*

Staff	Year			
	1932	1933	1934	1935
Permanent civil servants	584	582	570	674
Temporary civil servants	35	22	22	29
Permanent staff	1,257	1,257	1,253	1,647
Temporary staff		101	473	467
Total personnel	1,876	1,962	2,318	2,817

Note: Data for 1936 are not available.

Source: 1932: BAP 31.01 8654 no. 124.
1933: BAP 31.01 8657.
1934: BAP 31.01 8659 no. 160.
1935: BAP 31.01 8662 no. 337.

Control over Prussian agricultural statistics and the monthly statistics of the largest group of savings banks was transferred to the Statistical Office (see table 6).[46]

Not only within the state were relations of power transformed. In 1934, Schacht moved decisively to buttress the expansive apparatus of the Reich's economic administration by harnessing the capacities of private capital. The position of German business was weakened by the Depression. Most dramatically, of course, the crisis of 1931 left Berlin's once-great banks dependent on public funds. The situation of industry was less dire, but the collapse of the international economy deprived German firms of their export markets and foreign sources of capital. A revival of the domestic market by means of national economic policy was their best hope. The violent destruction of the labour movement in 1933 certainly strengthened the employers' hand. However, the Nazis were not the puppets of German capital. Hitler headed a genuinely popular movement, which harboured many elements which were profoundly hostile to capitalism. Even after the seizure of power, German business could not feel secure. At local level employers were harassed by the SA and ambitious Nazi Gauleiter. Robert Ley's Labour Front was no more welcome to industrialists than the socialist trade unions it replaced. In this context, a strengthened system of Reich's economic administration under Schacht was much the lesser of two evils. In the summer of 1934 Schacht replaced the ineffectual Schmitt at the RWM and moved quickly to establish a system of so-called Reich's Groups

[46] For a list see GStA 1. HA Rep. 77 3884 no. 453, 'Nachweisung der einzelnen Statistiken'.

incorporating industry, banking, insurance and transport. The Reich's Groups themselves were subdivided into so-called Business Groups, each responsible for a particular industry or line of business. Membership was compulsory for all firms, whether large or small. The precise balance of powers in these organizations is unclear. However, Schacht seems to have envisioned them as a means of disciplining industry and imposing a comprehensive system of state control.[47]

Certainly for the Reich's statisticians the pay-off was immediate. Industrial statistics, the branch of economic statistics that had lagged most notably in the 1920s, was now to move to the forefront of attention. Even before Schacht had finalized the outline of the new organization, the RWM and business representatives tabled bold new plans. The moment had come to realize Paul Bramstedt's dream of 'total business-cycle statistics'. Bramstedt was one of the survivors of the seizure of power. With the separation of the Institute he concentrated all his attention on the Department for Economic Statistics (VIII) in the Statistical Office. In the course of the Depression responsibility for the Industrial Reporting System had been transferred to this Department. By 1933 Bramstedt had enrolled no less than 5,000 respondent firms. In May 1934, with the cooperation of the new Business Groups, Bramstedt achieved a breakthrough: 6,000 industrial firms were signed up to answer not only the usual questions about the number of workers and hours worked, but also to supply information on their wage bills, their monthly turnover and their export sales.[48] Never before had German industry consented to such comprehensive and regular disclosure. And Schacht's new business organizations did not shrink from coercion. The Decree on Auskunftspflicht, renewed in 1923, was invoked quite uninhibitedly by the staff of the new Business Groups, who revelled in their new powers to impose standardized statistical reports on their membership. The regional and sectoral sub-organizations, which in the 1920s had often displayed an infuriating degree of independence, could now be brought into line.[49] By 1935 Bramstedt and the Business Groups had increased the number of firms enrolled in the monthly industrial reporting system to 7,400.[50] In 1936 Bramstedt's department was

---

[47] I. Esenwein-Rothe, *Die Wirtschaftsverbände von 1933 bis 1945* (Berlin, 1965), pp. 68–83.

[48] BAP 31.02 SRA 2476 no. 292, SRA/VI/Statistik der Wirtschaftszweige to SRA/VI 30.4.1934.

[49] J.S. Geer, 'Die Statistik der Wirtschaftsgruppe Maschinenbau', in F. Burgdörfer (ed.), *Die Statistik in Deutschland nach ihrem heutigen Stand, Ehrengabe für F. Zahn* (Berlin, 1940), II, pp. 1039–1048.

[50] E. Gierth, 'Aufbau und Methode der Industrieberichterstattung', *ASA*, 30 (1941/ 1942), pp. 393–401, p. 294 and BAP 31.02 SRA 2476 no. 289, SRA/VI to Präs. SRA 10.8.1934, p. 2.

forced to apply for a brace of new Hollerith machines to cope with the enormous volume of data pouring into the Office.[51] The development of the Industrial Reports is emblematic of wider changes. The Labour Statistics Department of the Wilhelmine Bureau had initiated them on a strictly voluntary basis. Under the Weimar Republic they had been transformed into an instrument of Konjunkturforschung, founded on a corporatist deal between Wagemann's Institute and the Reichsverband der deutschen Industrie (RdI). Now, the Reports changed character again. Backed up by coercive wartime decrees they were to serve as a system for monitoring the membership of the compulsory Business Groups.

Within the framework set by fiscal and monetary policy, the main means of controlling the economic recovery in the early years of the Nazi regime was the balance of trade. As industry revived, the trade account slipped into deficit.[52] The situation became critical in July 1934 when shortages of foreign exchange threatened the supply of imported materials for the armaments programme.[53] It was this crisis which gave Schacht the opportunity to establish unchallenged control over economic policy. Combining his powers at the Reichsbank with the authority of the RWM, he quickly formalized a system of controls, which became known as the 'New Plan'. The importation of raw materials such as cotton and wool, vital to consumer sectors, was throttled. The priority of rearmament was asserted, regardless of the consequences for important industries such as textiles. The New Plan was implemented by so-called Supervisory Agencies (Überwachungs-stellen). These organizations, staffed by civil servants from the RWM and experts from the relevant Business Groups, were charged with monitoring Germany's demand for raw materials. Following the com-modity-classification scheme of Germany's trade statistics, 28 Super-visory Agencies were established.[54] Questionnaires were issued to cover import requirements, current consumption and stock holdings of raw materials, thus allowing the Agencies to anticipate future patterns of demand. The Auskunftspflicht Decree of 1923 was again pressed into service to empower the new Agencies to demand reports from all German industrial firms. The result was a set of statistics that comple-

---

[51] For budget requests, see BAP 31.02 2476 no. 289, SRA/VI to Präs. SRA 10.8.1934 and BAP 31.02 2475 no. 376, SRA/VI bid for 1937 budget, November 1936.

[52] H. James, *The German Slump*, pp. 343–418. *VzK*, 9 (1934) 1 23.4.1934, pp. 27–32.

[53] D. Döring, 'Deutsche Aussenwirtschaftspolitik 1933–35. Die Gleichschaltung der Aussenwirtschaft in der Frühphase des nationalsozialistischen Regimes', PhD thesis, FU Berlin (1969), pp. 79–84.

[54] W. Gäehtgens, 'Die rechtlichen Grundlagen der Warenbewirtschaftung', in *Probleme der gelenkten Wirtschaft* (Berlin, 1942), pp. 28–61.

mented both the regular trade statistics and Bramstedt's Industrial Reports. The first results began to flow to the Statistical Office in the autumn of 1935, and by the following spring the statisticians were receiving comprehensive reports.[55]

III

Under the protection of the RWM the Statistical Office thus found a place for itself in the Third Reich. It was at the centre of an increasingly dense system of economic controls that enabled Schacht to direct the course of the German recovery. But was there any role in this administrative system for the macroeconomics of the 1920s? Or, did this aspect of Konjunkturforschung fall victim to the separation of the Institute and the Statistical Office?

Certainly, the removal of Wagemann and his economists was in the long term to result in a loss of intellectual direction at the Statistical Office. However, this did not make itself felt until the late 1930s. The immediate consequence of the Nazi seizure of power and the creation of a more interventionist system of national economic government was to further stimulate the programme of macroeconomic research. The Statistical Office continued its innovative national accounting. The demand on the relevant section in Bramstedt's Department for economic statistics was such that applications had to be made for additional staff and counting equipment.[56] There was a particularly acute need for detailed estimates of bilateral balance of payments. However, the Statistical Office also continued its series of national income estimates. And the macroeconomic understanding of fiscal policy that had first been elaborated in the 1920s continued to resonate through the Reich's bureaucracy. The Reichsbank routinely used national income estimates to compute the volume of funds that would be available for government borrowing. By the 1930s sufficient data were available for the scale of the German economic recovery to be compared directly to the experience of Britain, France and the United States. The figures made good propaganda![57] However, the SRA's system for estimating national income had an Achilles' heel: its fastidious treatment of the public sector. Unlike the estimates prepared in the United States and Great Britain, the Statistical Office distinguished carefully between different forms of public spending. Those that corresponded to the delivery of services to final consumers were counted as part of national income.

---

[55] BAP 31.02 3468 no. 1–20 and MA 1458 Fb 35/1 129, 130, 131.
[56] BAP 31.02 SRA 3578 no. 19, Abteilung VI to Abteilung I 27.1.1937.
[57] P. Jostock, *Die Berechnung des Volkseinkommens und ihr Erkenntniswert* (Berlin, 1941).

Those that from the point of view of the economy as a whole were more properly treated as costs of production were excluded. Operationalizing these fine distinctions depended on access to detailed budgetary data. The Reich's budget was declared an official secret and in 1938 the Statistical Office was forced to terminate publication of its series.[58] However, the restriction of information flow did not become a fatal impediment until the late 1930s. In the early years of the regime, Bramstedt's staff had more pressing problems. Brüning's government had removed Germany's farmers from the net of income tax. Rather than inferring the income of the agriculture sector from its tax bill the statisticians were therefore forced to make a direct estimate of the value of agricultural production. A similar shift with more dramatic potential was heralded in 1933 by the relaunch of the plans for a census of industrial production. Rather than having to rely on figures gleaned from the income tax returns the Statistical Office would be able, for the first time, to put a precise figure on the total value of industrial production.

As we have seen, production statistics were the missing link in the Institute's account of the circular flow of income, expenditure and production. According to Wagemann's national economic account, net value of production in industry was identical to the value of incomes earned in that sector. This had been confirmed in the early 1920s by experiments conducted in the United States.[59] The crucial problem for the industrial statisticians was to avoid double-counting. The division of labour in industry meant that the value of manufactured goods at every stage in the process of production was attributable in large part to inputs provided by other producers. Simply adding up the sales of each industrial firm would thus yield a grossly inflated figure for the total value of production. The value of raw wool would appear in the value of the yarn, in the value of the raw cloth, in the value of the dyed cloth and finally in the garments sold to consumers. One could attempt to limit the count to the final link in the chain, the firms which sold 'final output'. However, identifying these firms was practically impossible. The censuses of production pioneered by the United States and Britain adopted a different methodology. They counted the value added by each firm – the difference between the value of inputs and the value of outputs. The minimalist solution to this problem was the one adopted

---

[58] Ferdinand Grünig, 'Die Anfänge der "Volkswirtschaftlichen Gesamtrechnung" in Deutschland', in *Beiträge zur empirischen Konjunkturforschung. Festschrift zum 25jährigen Bestehen des DIW (IFK)* (Berlin, 1950), pp. 71–103.

[59] G. Alchon, *The Invisible Hand of Planning. Capitalism, Social Science and the State in the 1920s* (Princeton, 1985), pp. 59–63.

after 1907 in the British censuses of production.[60] Firms were asked to declare the value of their output and the total value of all materials and work bought in. This yielded an estimate of net industrial production, but nothing more. In the United States, by contrast, firms were required to itemize the raw materials they used. Furthermore, they were required to declare not only the value but also the physical quantities of output. The result was a comprehensive anatomy of the industrial division of labour. Not surprisingly, this was the model that Dr Wilhelm Leisse had adopted in his design for the German census in the late 1920s. It would allow the Institute's economists to trace the interconnections between different branches of the industrial economy.

Having been cancelled in 1930, the industrial census reappeared in the official papers for the first time in 1932.[61] What motivated the resumption of planning remains obscure. The cancellation in 1930 was never intended to be permanent. The decision to carry out the census in 1933 may therefore simply reflect a softening of fiscal discipline. Whatever the motivation, the census was in no sense an initiative of Hitler's government. The final draft of the Census Law was circulated by the RWM, in late January, days prior to the Nazi take-over.[62] The census of production was not a Nazi initiative. Nevertheless Wilhelm Leisse was determined to make the best of the National Revolution and he was not slow to realize the potential uses of the statistical instrument he had created. Soon after the questionnaires had been dispatched in 1934, Leisse drafted a memorandum sketching the future for industrial statistics. The paper, which was ostentatiously classified 'secret', presented the industrial censuses as the solution to the conundrums of rearmament planning.

Leisse began by playing on a deep vein of anxiety:

During the course of the World War [I], the available statistical material proved inadequate for the purpose of ensuring that the immediate needs of the army and the home market were met. This experience clearly demonstrates the value of a timely, comprehensive and technically thorough statistical examination of the German industrial economy, which also takes into consideration those issues vital to national defence.[63]

By this time, it was no longer a secret in government circles that rearmament was the chief objective of Hitler's coalition.[64] The author-

---

[60] *Final Report on the First Census of Production of the United Kingdom* (1907) (London, 1912).
[61] BAP 23.01 2230 no. 15 Reichsstädtebund to RWM 1.11.1932.
[62] BAP 23.01 2230 no. 16 RWM circular 26.1.1933.
[63] BAP 31.02 2992 SRA, 'Geheimer Arbeitsplan für die Weiterführung der Industriestatistik' (1934), pp. 3–4.
[64] I. Kershaw, *Hitler 1889–1936: Hubris* (London, 1998), pp. 431–446.

itarian governments of Brüning, Papen and Schleicher had prepared the way, but it was Hitler's national socialists who made the military build-up their overriding priority. Within days of taking power the new Chancellor instructed army planners to radically revise their original rearmament programme, in an upward direction. In the light of experience in World War I, rearmament was conceived in all-embracing terms. It meant the reconstruction of the home front as well as the armed forces. Restoring national fighting strength depended on moral, social, political and material reconstruction.

For the professional soldier the comprehensive mobilization required by modern warfare posed a fundamental dilemma. How were the military to remain in control of a process that required the redirection of practically every aspect of economic and social life? For many officers in the Reichswehr of the 1920s the answer lay not in a greater modesty of military leadership, but in an aggressive extension of the sphere of military command. The problem and its solution was stated bluntly in a memo of 1924: 'The conduct of war is dependent on the possibility of economic armament . . . The leading military agencies need to master this question.'[65] 'We cannot and should not allow ourselves to become dependent on the judgement of "expert opinion"' [Fachkreise], who will always present matters to us in a light favourable to their interests.[66] As a result the Reichswehr in the 1920s began to take a serious interest in issues of economic planning and economic statistics.[67]

In 1924 a military–economic staff was set up with the aim of surveying Germany's strategic position from an economic point of view. And the military's drive for the acquisition of expertise did not stop at general enquiries. The officers responsible for weapons development in the Army indulged themselves in extraordinary fantasies of omniscience. Rather than mapping the general contours of the German economy, they planned to create a one-to-one map of German industry.[68] A card index would register every single industrial plant in Germany, listing its capacities down to the individual machine tool, its production record in World War I, its labour requirements and raw material needs. The mechanized capacity of punch card machines would allow military control of production to be extended to the workbench itself. Many of

[65] BAMA RH 8/v.1515 Waffenamt no. 62, Andreas Nr. 212, Denkschrift über die Notwendigkeit eines wirtschaftlichen Generalstabes 23.4.1925, p. 2.

[66] BAMA RH 8/v. 918, Waffenamt Heer 25.3.1925 Gedanken über die Notwendigkeit eines wirtschaftlichen Generalstabes, p. 4.

[67] E.W. Hansen, *Reichswehr und Industrie. Rüstungswirtschaftliche Zusammenarbeit und wirtschaftliche Mobilmachungsvorbereitungen 1923–1932* (Boppard, 1978).

[68] BAMA RH 8/v.1515 and 918.

the more modest information needs of the Reichswehr might have been satisfied by the civilian programmes of economic investigation underway in the 1920s. The military–economic staff was established at precisely the moment in which Wagemann was launching his project of Konjunkturforschung.[69] But sharing information with the civilian agencies of the state would have defeated the whole purpose of Reichswehr planning: to restore military control over the business of war. The energies of the Reichswehr planners therefore went into constructing a statistical network of their own. Operating under conditions of secrecy and without adequate funding this was a complete failure. Unlike Wagemann, the military were unable to mobilize a wide coalition behind their investigations. The RdI was never willing to give its full support to the military. A limited group of industrialists participated in a 'deniable' organization, euphemistically entitled Statistical Society, or Stega.[70] However, by contrast with Wagemann's Institute, this never produced more than a trickle of statistical reports. The military did acquire a Powers punched card machine. However, the reality fell ludicrously short of their vision of total economic oversight. To maintain their mechanized filing system the military could afford to employ only one, severely impaired veteran. This unfortunate was unable to keep pace even with the slow dribble of reports generated by the inadequate Stega network.[71] The Powers punched card machine gathered dust.

The Nazi seizure of power opened new vistas. The government was now firmly committed to rearmament.[72] Over the summer, Schacht concluded a framework agreement with the military which set aside a sum of no less than 35 billion RM for the next eight years.[73] Over the following months 2,800 plants with 750,000 workers were designated as armaments plants (Rüstungsbetriebe, or Rü-Betriebe), accounting for an estimated 15 per cent of the total value of German industrial production.[74] Under direct military control, these plants were to form the industrial core of the rearmament drive. To select the right capacity,

[69] For meetings between the official statisticians and the military see BAMA RH 8/v. 1887, Waffenamt Heer and BAMA RH 8/v.917, Waffenamt.

[70] On the Stega and its problems see BAMA RH 8/v.917 and RH 8/v.1516.

[71] BAMA RH 8/v. 898.

[72] BAMA RW 19/923 Reichswehrministerium, draft decree with handwritten comment dated 26.4.1933.

[73] M. Geyer, *Aufrüstung oder Sicherheit. Die Reichswehr in der Krise der Machtpolitik 1924–1936* (Wiesbaden, 1980), pp. 348–349.

[74] H.-E. Volkmann, 'Die NS-Wirtschaft in Vorbereitung des Krieges', in W. Deist, M. Messerschmidt, H.-E. Volkmann and W. Wette, *Ursachen und Voraussetzungen des Zweiten Weltkrieges* (Frankfurt, 1989, 2nd edn.), p. 286. For collaboration with industry see BAMA RW 19/923 Wa Wi I, 'Aktennotiz über die Besprechung mit RWM', 19.8.1933.

the RWM collaborated with the Reichswehr in a series of secret joint committees, the aim being to satisfy, but also to contain, the demands of the military.[75] The boundary between military and civilian industry was to emerge as a major fault-line in the political economy of the Third Reich.[76] At stake was the whole direction of the regime. For Schacht the expenditure plan agreed in 1933 was the upper limit of what was compatible with general economic stability. But the army, the Luftwaffe and the navy were not satisfied. Ever greater claims were made on the nation's resources, which Hitler and Goering did nothing to contain.[77] This struggle, which was fought out ever more openly after 1936, was to decide the future of the Third Reich. But, in the actual process of planning, these grand political issues were superimposed on problems of technical detail. What was lacking was any comprehensive map of German industry on which to draw the boundary between civilian and military capacity. A comprehensive inventory of German industry had become a technical necessity.

It was this urgent and highly political requirement to which Leisse addressed himself. After 1934 he sought to systematically promote the census of industrial production as the ideal tool of military–economic planning. In the process, he redefined its purpose. Rather than using the census to estimate net production and value added, Leisse focused on the detailed information it would produce about the physical process of production. In particular, he proposed to use the census as a tool of raw material planning. This was the central obsession which Nazi Germany's military planners had inherited from World War I. Other crucial questions – such as the organization of efficient production processes, the training of skilled labour, the provision of energy supplies, research and development – were all neglected in favour of the issue of raw materials supply. The census design of the 1920s certainly contained all the necessary information for raw material planning. It covered all the significant industrial plants in the German economy, 150,000 in total. Firms reported both the value and quantities of output produced and the raw materials, semi-finished goods, fuel and lubricants consumed. Furthermore, the census of industrial production imposed a rigorous technical definition of the units of production. The groundwork for the census of production was laid by a general census of workplaces and

[75] B.A. Carroll, *Design for Total War. Arms and Economics in the Third Reich* (The Hague, 1968), pp. 72, 78–79 and BAMA RW 19/923.

[76] G. Thomas, *Geschichte der deutschen Wehr- und Rüstungswirtschaft (1918–1943/45)*, ed. W. Birkenfeld (Boppard, 1966).

[77] K.J. Müller, *The Army, Politics and Society in Germany, 1933–1945* (Manchester, 1987) and W. Deist, *The Wehrmacht and German Rearmament* (London, 1981).

occupations.[78] This followed the compromise formula of 1925 in counting as a discrete workplace every physical unit of economic activity. On the basis of this comprehensive enumeration the Statistical Office established a card index recording all workplaces with more than five employees. It was on this clearly defined group of large industrial plants that Leisse's highly detailed census of production concentrated its attention. The physical units recorded by the census were broken down into discrete 'technical plant units' (technische Betriebseinheiten).[79] An engineering plant, for instance, which manufactured both machine-tools and textile machinery in a single factory, was required to return a separate form for each line of production. A textile mill in which raw cotton was spun into thread, woven into cloth and dyed was counted as three separate units of production. The entire range of questions had to be answered for each operation. The entire superstructure of corporate bureaucracy and even factory organization was thus stripped away. The flow of raw materials was revealed down to the level of the individual workshop.

This was, of course, precisely the terrain over which Germany's statisticians had struggled in the first decades of the century. The Wilhelmine censuses had attempted to impose a technical definition of the unit of production across the entirety of industry and trade. Meerwarth and the other reformers of the early 1920s had denounced this procedure as obsolete. In Meerwarth's view, the economic unit of the firm should be made the basic unit of all statistical enquiries. The idea of creating a detailed anatomy of production was simply inappropriate to a complex, capitalist economy. It harked back to the days of artisanal craft production.[80] The production census of 1933 revealed that Meerwarth had radically underestimated the possibilities of modern industrial statistics. Leisse's census, of course, started by excluding precisely the artisanal firms which had so preoccupied the Wilhelmine statisticians. Its aim was to produce an image of the physical process of production at the heart of German industry. The difficulties were certainly enormous. Leisse's statisticians found themselves struggling with a tangled mass of technical and administrative complexity. Many of the smaller firms did not keep cost accounts that would have allowed them to answer the statisticians' questions. Larger firms that did have cost accounting departments had great difficulty in dividing up their

---

[78] F. Burgdörfer, 'Die Volks-, Berufs- und Betriebszählung 1933', *ASA*, 23 (1933), pp. 145–171.

[79] E. von Roeder, 'Die industrielle Produktionsstatistik', in F. Burgdörfer (ed.), *Die Statistik in Deutschland nach ihrem heutigen Stand. Ehrengabe für Friedrich Zahn* (Berlin, 1940), 2, pp. 1018–1019.

[80] See chapters 1 and 2.

overheads between the technical units identified by the census. Allocating labour costs was particularly problematic. Leisse's staff, for their part, faced the problem of imposing consistency on literally thousands of arbitrary accounting decisions. Meerwarth was proved right, at least in one sense. It was impossible to encompass the necessary level of detail in a single questionnaire. The solution was to produce an interlocking system of hundreds of specialized forms, each of which detailed the rules to be followed by a particular industry in recording units of production, materials and labour. In this sense, the census was no longer a single survey. It was pieced together from hundreds of separate enquiries. The census thus demanded a new level of knowledge on the part of the statisticians. It was no longer enough simply to specify the general objective of the survey and to frame a clear set of questions. The censuses of production started from a detailed map of the technical organization of German industry. This was then progressively modified as the statisticians gained experience in operating the system and interpreting the inevitably ambiguous returns.[81] As Leisse was later to stress, the expertise demanded by the industrial censuses was in a sense more technical than statistical. Rather than an understanding of the general rules of statistical methodology, what was paramount was in-depth knowledge of specific industries. Assembling these detailed images of industry into a general picture was a monumental task over which Leisse's staff laboured for three years.

To make their results available to the military and other potential 'clients', Leisse and his team had to devise new techniques of presentation. The first was graphical. So-called 'family trees' recorded the stages through which a particular raw material entered into the production of a variety of intermediate and final goods.[82] Family trees could be linked together by means of diagrams showing how particular manufacturing industries combined different raw materials to produce an output of finished goods. Each node in the diagrams showed the quantity of materials received, the stocks consumed over the period and the output produced and passed on to the next level in the diagram (see figure 7).

Other crucial insights from the census could be summarized in the form of numerical ratios. It was possible, for instance, to compare the import-dependency of industries, with often surprising results. For planners of autarchy, margarine appeared to be an obvious replacement for butter. Germany appeared to be largely self-sufficient in the production of margarine, whereas it imported large volumes of butter. Leisse's census revealed that margarine was, in fact, a Trojan horse: 30 Pfennig

[81] See the correspondence in BAP 31.02 6274.
[82] For examples see MA 1458 35/276.

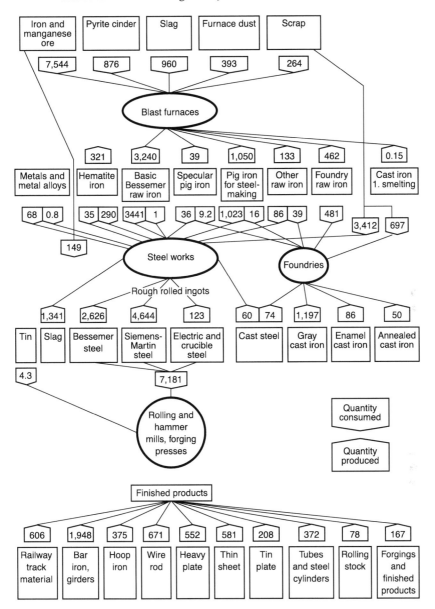

Figure 7 'Family tree' of iron and steel, 1933, quantities, 1,000 tons
Source: BAP 31.02

in every mark of margarine was paid to foreign suppliers of imported ingredients. By contrast, a naïve trade policy would be tempted to regard the German rubber industry as a dangerous drain on the country's foreign exchange. After all, the industry depended entirely on imported raw materials. Leisse's statistics demonstrated that the industry was in reality a substantial earner of foreign exchange. The value added by Germany's exporters of rubber goods more than covered the cost of their imports.[83]

Information on the regional structure of German industry was another highlight of the census. The statisticians were able to put a figure on Germany's economic vulnerability to enemy attack. In the early stages of rearmament the German military were much concerned about the prospect of fighting a defensive battle on German territory.[84] In terms of exposure to enemy invasion the country was divided into two zones, a zone of evacuation, zone A – including most of the industrial heartland west of the Rhine as well as the Eastern territories – and zone B – the central zone which would form the industrial base of Germany's defences. The census revealed the full extent of German vulnerability. When the Third Reich began its rearmament drive, 87 per cent of its rolling-mill capacity was located in the exposed west, 50 per cent of the capacity which distilled glycerine into explosives lay in the west, 64 per cent of the production of cellulose, a basic input both in the manufacture of nitro-cellulose and sandbags, was concentrated in regions designated for evacuation. To make matters worse, two-thirds of truck production was located in vulnerable areas. The only comforting news was that Germany's meagre oil stocks were almost entirely in safe areas.[85]

Finally, Leisse promised to make real the military fantasy of omniscience. The production census was organized around a database of the largest plants in German industry. The vital statistics of all 150,000 plants had been registered. In the course of an ordinary census, the individual returns would have been discarded after the aggregate results had been calculated. Indeed, explicit guarantees would have been given to the respondents assuring them of anonymity and confidentiality. Statistical returns were reserved for exclusively statistical purposes. No such security was provided in 1933. Leisse placed the 'Factory Card File' (Fabrikkartei) at the military's disposal.[86] This database consisted of cards recording each plant's employment, the age structure of its work force, type and scale of production, total capacity, consumption of

[83] BAP 31.02 2999 Leisse, 'Wehrwirtschaftliche Ergebnisse' (Februar 1936), pp. 28–30.
[84] Geyer, *Aufrüstung oder Sicherheit*, pp. 363–385.
[85] BAP 31.02 2999 Leisse, 'Wehrwirtschaftliche Ergebnisse' (Februar 1936), pp. 12–17.
[86] BAP 31.01 8659 no. 160, RWM Budget 1934, E5, tit. 6.

raw materials and raw material stocks in 1933. The Factory Card File was classified by industry and within each industry by Military–Economic District (Wehrwirtschaftsbezirk). It was therefore possible, in principle at least, to trace exactly how much industrial capacity would be lost in the evacuation of any particular area. The card index also revealed how badly individual firms would be affected by the draft.

The industrial census of 1933 clearly provided a planning tool of immense potential. However, in its original version it was cumbersome. The processing of tens of thousands of complex questionnaires was done mainly by hand and took more than a year. The first results from the production census of 1933 were not available until 1935. In the interval, the accelerating recovery and the early stages of rearmament had transformed crucial elements of German industry. The data from 1933 were of no more than historical interest. To stay up to date the surveys needed to be repeated regularly. The leisurely decennial rhythm of the nineteenth century was inadequate for the purposes of Nazi economic planning. Leisse envisioned a triennial series.[87] Preparations for the second census were completed in February 1936.[88] Hollerith machinery would solve the problem of speed. The 1936 survey was specifically designed for machine-processing. The questionnaires were rewritten and the process of coding the returns was streamlined to hasten the count. Basic results were to be produced in a matter of months.[89] Furthermore, the triennial census was to be complemented by a standardized system of annual surveys in particular key industries. These surveys would not explore all the backward and forward linkages of each industry, but they would permit the most important results of the census to be extrapolated for the intervening years.

IV

Leisse's reorientation of the census towards the issue of raw material planning did not of course preclude other uses. Alongside their work on raw material balances, Leisse's industrial statisticians were also to publish, on the basis of the 1936 census, a comprehensive set of figures for industrial value added, sector by sector.[90] However, it was Paul

---

[87] BAP 31.02 2992 SRA, 'Geheimer Arbeitsplan für die Weiterführung der Industriestatistik' (1934).

[88] BAP 31.02 2993, Präs. SRA to RWM 6.2.1936, forwarding 'Grundzüge des Gesamtplans der kommenden Generalerhebung für 1936'.

[89] BAP 31.02 3037 SRA, 'Gutachten über die Eignung des Lochkartenverfahrens für die Aufbereitung der Industriellen Produktionsstatistik', p. 36.

[90] Reichsamt für wehrwirtschaftliche Planung, *Die Deutsche Industrie. Gesamtergebnisse der Amtlichen Produktionsstatistik* (Berlin, 1939).

Bramstedt's Department of the Statistical Office which realized the truly radical potential of the census.[91] As we have seen, the German census followed the American example in requiring firms to divide their raw materials bill into different sources of supply. Leisse's industrial statisticians used this information to derive an image of the physical process of production. However, it could also be used to trace the economic interrelationships between the sectors of industry and the relations between industry and the rest of the economy. One could then study movements in industrial output as the product of impulses originating in particular sectors of the economy, propagating outwards as the result of backward and forward linkages. As we have seen, this approach to business-cycle analysis was sketched in rough form in the analysis of sectoral interconnections offered by Wagemann's *Konjunkturlehre*.[92] And there can be no doubt that the industrial census carried out in 1933 was designed very much with this possibility in mind.

To an Anglo-American audience this may come as something of a surprise. In the postwar world this disaggregated approach to economic analysis has come to be associated with the name of Wassily Leontief, who won a Nobel prize for his celebrated work in 'input–output analysis'.[93] The first results of Leontief's research were published in a seminal article on 'Quantitative Input and Output Relations in the Economic System of the United States', which appeared in *The Review of Economic Statistics*, the journal of the Harvard Committee of Economic Research, in August 1936.[94] In this essay Leontief used the results of the US industrial census of 1919 to generate a matrix showing the interconnections between 40 sectors of the US economy. Each row showed the purchases of a particular industry from all other industries. Each column showed the destination of a particular industry's output. In the Anglo-American literature it is common to present Leontief's work as a direct descendant of the first analysis of economic interrelations offered by the eighteenth-century French economist François Quesnay. Quesnay was the first to show in tabular form the flow of payments between different sectors of the economy. In the 1950s in a reverse process of translation it was demonstrated that Quesnay's physiocratic tableaux could, indeed, be transformed into a modern-day

---

[91] BAP 31.02 2476 no. 259, SRA/VI/Referat Volkseinkommen to Bramstedt 27.8.1934.

[92] 'Der wirtschaftliche Kreislauf (Statik)', in E. Wagemann, *Konjunkturlehre. Eine Grundlegung zur Lehre vom Rhythmus der Wirtschaft* (Berlin, 1928), pp. 25–43.

[93] 'Input–Output' and 'Leontief', in J. Eatwell, M. Milgate and P. Newman (eds.), *The New Palgrave Dictionary of Economics*, 2 and 3 (London, 1987).

[94] W. Leontief, 'Quantitative Input and Output Relations in the Economic System of the United States', *The Review of Economic Statistics* 18 (1936), pp. 105–125.

input–output matrix.[95] However, this narrative, which links Leontief directly to the Enlightenment origins of economics, obscures his more immediate intellectual context. Leontief's revolutionary input-output (I–O) table can in fact be seen as a direct outgrowth of the statistical economics of the 1920s. Of course, this does not involve erasing the link to Quesnay. As we have seen, the first decades of the twentieth century witnessed a Quesnay revival.

In his article in the *Review*, Leontief began with Quesnay. But he then went on to situate input-output analysis in the context of contemporary efforts in national accounting. The concept of net production was useful as an index of national prosperity. However, the process of reducing each stage of production to 'value added' obscured much of what was of interest to economists. The division of labour, which was vital to an understanding of the business-cycle, was hidden from view. What was also hidden from view in the 1930s was the immediate intellectual inspiration for Leontief's experiments in input–output analysis. In fact, his interest in the possibility of constructing disaggregated national accounts dated back to the mid-1920s. Before he left Russia, Leontief published a brief critical review of the national economic balances being prepared by the Central Statistical Administration of the Soviet Union.[96] These were crude input–output schemes in embryo, the theoretical inspiration for which came from Marx's schemes of reproduction, which were themselves derived from Quesnay.[97] These links were made very explicit in the Soviet literature of the 1920s. Leontief continued this interest during his sojourn in the Weimar Republic; en route to the United States he spent time both in Berlin and Kiel. Leontief's German publications include a number of reviews of contemporary Soviet experiments with sectoral economic balances.[98] In 1928, in an article in the *Archiv für Sozialwissenschaft und Sozialpolitik*, he outlined a simple algebraic model of production as an interconnected division of labour.[99] Significantly, Leontief was at pains to present this not as a startlingly original breakthrough, but as a contribution to the common preoccupation of economists in Weimar Germany: the analysis of the economy as a circular process (Kreislauf) of production and

[95] R.L. Meek, *The Economics of Physiocracy* (London, 1962), pp. 265–296.

[96] N. Spulber (ed.), *Foundations of Soviet Strategy for Economic Growth. Selected Soviet Essays, 1924–1930* (Bloomington, 1964), pp. 88–94.

[97] See the article by P.I. Popov in Spulber, *Foundations*, pp. 5–19.

[98] W. Leontief, 'Vom Staatsbudget zum einheitlichen Finanzplan. Sowjetrussische Finanzprobleme', *Weltwirtschaftliches Archiv*, 33 (1931), pp. 231–260.

[99] W. Leontief, 'Die Wirtschaft als Kreislauf', *Archiv für Sozialwissenschaft und Sozialpolitik* 60 (1928), pp. 577–623.

reproduction. This concept was at least as old as Quesnay's tableau, but in interwar Germany it had moved to the heart of economic theory.

In light of this genealogy it is less surprising to discover the close attention that was paid to Leontief's work in Nazi Germany. In Bramstedt's department of the Statistical Office, Leontief's Harvard article was read with great interest. Indeed, a bibliographical note was put on file, citing his piece as a standard reference, a model for the Statistical Office's own work.[100] The first practical experiments with multi-sectoral macroeconomic analysis had, in fact, already been undertaken in Germany. Working on the basis of data supplied by Wagemann's Institute, the idiosyncratic, engineer–economist Ferdinand Grünig had developed a simple empirical model of the German economy, with which he analysed the multiplier process driving the Great Depression.[101] In 1933 Grünig found employment first in the staff of Rudolf Hess, the Führer's deputy, and then in the Reich's Economic Chamber under the wing of Ferdinand Pietzsch.[102] Here he developed a multi-sectoral balance sheet of the German economy which was widely circulated in official and party circles. Grünig's reports were obligatory reading in the Statistical Office.[103] By the early autumn of 1935 the Reich's official statisticians had begun their own experiments in a similar vein. Economists under Bramstedt's direction began disaggregating their estimates of national income.[104] By September 1935, the outline of the project was sufficiently far advanced for Bramstedt to announce it to the annual meeting of the German Statistical Society in Königsberg.[105] At the same time, Bramstedt's Department approached the industrial statisticians with an offer of collaboration.[106] They would use the discarded questionnaires of Leisse's industrial census to calculate an input–output matrix. A sectoral account for the vehicle industry was prepared as an illustration (figure 8).

The sales of the vehicle industry together with its payments to, and receipts from, all other sectors of the economy were charted in a two-

[100] BAP 31.02 SRA 2705 no. 56 SRA/VI, working note, 1935/6.

[101] Grünig, Der Wirtschaftskreislauf (Munich, 1933).

[102] A. Pietzsch and F. Grünig, 'Grundlagen der Wirtschaftslenkung', in Grundlagen, Aufbau und Wirtschaftsordnung des nationalsozialistischen Staates, 3 (Berlin, 1936), Beitrag 45.

[103] For Grünig's influence on statistical thinking in France in the 1930s and 1940s, see F. Fourquet, Les comptes de la puissance. Histoire de la comptabilité nationale et du plan (Paris, 1980), pp. 392–394.

[104] BAP 31.02 2705 no. 29–32, Draft report 'Die volkswirtschaftliche Umsatzrechnung'.

[105] P. Bramstedt, 'Gefüge und Entwicklung der Volkswirtschaft', ASA, 25 (1936/1937), pp. 377–404.

[106] For the following see BAP 31.02 2705 no. 29–32 SRA, 'Die volkswirtschaftliche Umsatzrechnung' (draft report).

dimensional matrix. Information from the 1933 census was combined with data obtained from an analysis of corporate balance sheets compiled by the Statistical Office. The result was a statistical image that went beyond the family trees of the industrial statisticians to embrace the entire economy. In this respect the planning in the Statistical Office exceeded the detail proposed by Leontief in his 1936 article. Whereas he grouped together the entire non-industrial and non-agricultural economy into a single residual category, the Reich's statisticians proposed a complete breakdown of payments to government, banking, insurance, the Nazi Party and other agencies. Furthermore, the Statistical Office distinguished different types of payments. Rather optimistically, the Department hoped that it might be able to complete these preliminaries by the end of 1936, before moving on to data for more recent years.[107]

Bramstedt's Department provided a double rationale for this project. On the one hand the input–output table was presented as the intellectual extension of Konjunkturforschung. It allowed the flow of transactions to be traced throughout the economy. The table for 1933 would of course provide no more than a static picture but, if extended year by year, it would develop into a truly dynamic analysis of economic development and change. Bramstedt's team were somewhat less clear about the policy rationale for their work. Whereas Leisse had quickly identified the military as potential customers, the input–output analysts conceived their work as having a more general utility. As the Reich's economic administration extended its grip over the national economy an input–output table would be an invaluable tool. Given the peculiar nature of the Nazi economic recovery, driven by public spending on construction and rearmament, policy-makers were increasingly confronted with questions of structural change. They needed to know how expansion in one sector, brought about by major investment projects, would ripple through the economy, following the flow of payments for wages, materials, investment goods, interest and dividends. How would changes in taxes and public spending affect different sectors of the economy? How would restrictions on the supply of foreign exchange and new bilateral trade policies impact on key industries? How did rationalization affect the flow of income to different groups?[108] No doubt, the case study of the vehicles industry was chosen precisely because it was likely to appeal to the motor-mad Nazi leadership. Certainly, the scheme might have

[107] BAP 31.02 SRA 2705 no. 38–48, SRA/VI to Direktor Dr Leisse SRA/VII 6.2.1936.
[108] BAP 31.02 2705 no. 33–37, SRA/Abt VI to SRA Präs. September 1935 (draft, not sent).

Reich's Statistical Office, Department VI, 1936
Account (Umsatzrechnung) for Motor vehicle industry, Germany 1933 (million RM)

Types of receipt and payment	1.	2.	3.	4.	5.	6.	7.	8.	9.	10.	11.	12.	13.	14.	15.	16.	17.
I. Payments																	
1. Wages and salaries																	
Workers																	
Management																	
Other salaried																	
2. Raw materials and other process materials																	
To producers				14	3	121	83	25	5	16	9			5	14	19	
Commercial mark-up																	
Freight																	
Duties																	
Own-consumption							9										
3. Other current expenditures																	
Turnover tax																	
Other taxes																	
Social insurance																	
Voluntary contributions																	
Winter aid																	
Political subscriptions																	
Organizational subscriptions																	
Insurance premiums																	
Postal and transport																	
Rents for sales rooms																	
Advertising													4				
Legal fees																	
Other public fees																	
Licenses																	
Net interest payments																	
Bank fees																	
4. Investment						3	8	1									
5. Distributed earnings																	
Dividends																	
Supervised board compensation																	
Receipts of independent entrepreneurs																	
6. New credit and debt repayment																	
Repayment of Obligationen																	
Repayment of mortgages																	
Repayment of long-term loans																	
Purchase of shares																	
Short-term credit/repayment																	
Total payments				14	3	124	100	26	5	16	9		4	5	14	19	
II. Receipts																	
Turnover at factory	26	10	4	12	11	9	63	4	0	6	4	2	5	2	0	5	0
Own-consumption							9										
Revenue for licenses																	
Sale of tax credits																	
Capital increases																	
Sale of assets																	
Total receipts	26	10	4	12	11	9	72	4	0	6	4	2	5	2	0	5	0
III. Net receipts/payments	26	10	4	−2	8	−115	−28	−22	−5	−10	−5	2	1	−3	−14	−14	0

1. = Agriculture	8. = Electrical eng.	15. = Rubber and asbestos
2. = Forestry	9. = Fine mech. and optical industry	16. = Woodworking
3. = Fishing	10. = Chemical industry	17. = Musical instruments and toys
4. = Mining, iron and steel	11. = Textiles	18. = Food
5. = Quarrying	12. = Paper	19. = Clothing
6. = Metal Goods	13. = Printing and publishing	20. = Construction
7. = Mech. Eng. incl. Vehicles	14. = Leather and linoleum	21. = Water, electricity and gas

18.	19.	20.	21.	22.	23.	24.	25.	26.	27.	28.	29.	30.	31.	32.	33.	34.	35.	36.	37.	38.	39.
																					0
																					0
															147						147
															19						19
															58						58
																					0
			3																	6	323
				18																	18
							32														32
										1											1
										9											9
																					0
										14											14
										21											21
											18										18
													2	1	1						4
										1											1
										2											2
												2									2
						8															8
							8														8
									2												2
				8										1							13
										1											2
										1			1								1
																				1	1
																4					4
						2															2
	8																				20
																					0
																4					4
															1						1
															8						8
																					0
																		2			2
																		1			1
																		3			3
																		2			2
																			34		34
0	8	3	26		10	40		2	41	18	2	3	2	234	8		8	34	7	785	
																					0
31	7	28	1	32	75	4	127	9	0	78	1	6	4	0			112			85	763
																					9
																					0
										8											8
																		3			3
																		2			2
31	7	28	1	32	75	4	127	9	0	86	1	6	4	0			112	5		85	785
31	7	20	−2	6	75	−8	87	9	−2	45	−17	4	1	−2	−234	−8	112	−3	−34	78	−2

22. = Wholesale
23. = Retail
24. = Banking
25. = Transport
26. = Restaurants and hotels
27. = Rental housing
28. = Politics and public admin.

29. = Social insurance
30. = Business orgs.
31. = Health and legal sector
32. = Cultural sector
33. = Labour
34. = Capital ownership
35. = Household consumption

36. = Capital market
37. = Money market
38. = Foreign
39. = Total

Figure 8 Input-Output relationships of the motor vehicle industry, 1933
Source: Bundesarchiv R 3102 2580

been expected to appeal to the RWM and the Reichsbank. But the papers of Bramstedt's Department identified no specific audience.

The drafting of an input–output table had potentially dramatic implications. The Reich's statisticians were sketching out the intellectual foundations for a rudimentary system of central planning. Of course, the input–output table did not solve the problem of choice. It was up to the political leadership to identify objectives and their relative priority. However, once these were specified, the input–output table provided the means to construct so-called 'balanced plans', plans in which the production programmes of different sectors were coordinated and consistent.[109] In mathematical terms the input–output table represented the economy as a matrix. To calculate the set of productions required to guarantee a specified set of final outputs one had to calculate what is known as the 'inverse' of the matrix. In principle, this was simply a matter of routine number-crunching. In practice, inverting even a small – 38 by 38 – matrix, before the advent of electronic computers, was a Herculean task. Fortunately, for the would-be planners the complete mathematical solution could be approximated by less costly procedures. A process of iteration produced a good approximation to the exact solution.[110] This process started with a set of targets specified by the political leadership. Using the input–output table, the planners would calculate the inputs required to produce these target levels of final output. In a second iteration they would then calculate the inputs required to produce these inputs and so on, until the additional increments became insignificantly small. The result after a manageable number of iterations would be a consistent set of production plans. In the 1930s, this procedure was untried. Despite the endless academic and political discussions about the pros and cons of central planning no economy had ever been subject to such a systematic set of controls. But in Nazi Germany in 1935, this ultimate technocratic objective seemed within reach. To push forward, Bramstedt's Department applied for an additional allocation of funds with which to pay for fresh economists, clerical staff and calculating machines.[111] But, more importantly, Bramstedt's economists demanded that they be given access to any statistics they required for their calculations. They complained of having been held up in their work by the proliferation of official secrecy restrictions and the unwillingness of other agencies to supply data to the Statistical

---

[109] For a technical economic discussion see J. Bennett, *The Economic Theory of Central Planning* (Oxford, 1989), pp. 38–65.

[110] Various practical experiments are discussed in J.M. Montias, 'Planning with Material Balances in Soviet-Type Economies', in A. Nove and D.M. Nuti (eds.), *Socialist Economics* (Harmondsworth, 1972), pp. 223–251.

[111] BAP 31.02 SRA 2475 no. 376, SRA/VI bid for 1937 budget (November 1936).

Office. In particular, they had had difficulty obtaining reliable information on state expenditure. The Reich's budget was now a well-guarded secret and there was reason to believe that even the figures produced for internal consumption were not complete. With this complaint they addressed a problem of organization which by the mid-1930s was beginning to preoccupy the Statistical Office leadership.

V

Of course, the problem of statistical organization was not new. As we have seen, the appropriate organization of statistics in the German nation state had been an open question ever since the turn of the century. Before World War I debate had centred on the rights of the Länder *vis à vis* the Reich. In the 1920s the enormous expansion of the Reich's Office had relegated the Länder offices to a subordinate role. And the Gleichschaltung of Prussia completed this process. Centralization, however, raised its own questions. Who should define the limits of the Reich's drive for economic information? Should there be a formal limit set to the right to intrude into the affairs of private citizens? Or should this simply be decided in the struggle between business and the official statisticians? Should it be left to the statisticians to decide the information needs of the state? The Dernburg Commission had expressed anxiety that the ambitions of economic science rather than the needs of state were now driving the system. The removal of Wagemann and the separation of his Institute from the Statistical Office seemed to promise a return to greater administrative control and restraint. Certainly, in 1933 and 1934 there was little growth in expenditure at the Statistical Office. However, after that brief interlude, expansion resumed. Expenditure on staff rose in line with the expanding reach of the Office's surveys. And the renewed growth of the Statistical Office was only part of the problem. After 1933, German business was flooded by demands for information from official and unofficial, party and non-party agencies, all eager for a role in economic policy. Among the major data-gatherers were the military–economic authorities, the DAF, the economic offices of the Nazi Party's regional (Gau) organizations, the Mining Authorities, Hitler's special delegate for raw materials Keppler, the Reich's Food Estate (the Reichsnährstand) – whose remit extended across both agriculture and the food industry, the obligatory cartels into which much of the consumer goods industries were forced and the office of the Price Commissioner. The enquiries of these national agencies were multiplied by their regional and sectoral sub-offices. In the 1920s the process of centralization had created a bureaucratic monster. Now

the statistical system seemed in danger of degenerating into decentralized chaos.

This disorganization of data-gathering was frustrating for the Reich's
statisticians. But, more importantly, it created an intolerable situation
for German business. Managers were overwhelmed with questionnaires.
The burden fell particularly heavily on smaller businesses. Owner-
managers complained of unrelenting bureaucratic harassment. Statistics
again faced a groundswell of business resentment. In the Weimar
Republic German businessmen had not hesitated to defend themselves
against intrusive government enquiries. In the more intimidating political environment of the Third Reich, their opposition to government
surveys was no longer couched in terms of a right to 'privacy'. Instead,
business men made rhetorical use of Nazi ideology. They complained
about the excesses of bureaucracy. Statistical paperwork was hampering
them in their vital duty as entrepreneurial Führer of the German
economy.[112] The fussy and irrelevant routines of civil servants were
counterposed to the national socialist virtue of decisive leadership. This
rhetorical opposition did not bode well for the future of statistics in the
Third Reich. The mounting tide of resentment provoked serious
concern within the Statistical Office. Official statistics was being unfairly
blamed for the unregulated activity of semi-official or unofficial organizations; the mass of 'wild' surveys was threatening to provoke resistance
to the Office's own, legitimate enquiries. Most threatening of all were
demands from the military that armaments producers should be protected from statistical harassment.[113] Something had to be done! The
legitimacy of the entire apparatus of statistics was in question.

For the leadership of the Statistical Office the solution was obvious:
give control of all statistical enquiries to the official statisticians. This
would restore the authority of the state, reassert the traditional prerogative of German official statisticians, and ensure competent, professional
control of a technical branch of government. The Office would eliminate
duplication, tighten up sloppily worded questionnaires and see to it that
only those surveys were carried out that were absolutely necessary. Out
of the mess of incompatible enquiries, the Office would fashion a
rational information system. In the process, the Office would acquire
control over a vast amount of information, feeding the fantasies of
omniscience now flourishing amongst the Reich's statisticians. A draft
Statistical Law, embodying this ambitious design, was drawn up by

[112] MA 1458 RWM Fb 35/82 no. 6, IHK Stettin to DIHT 12.12.1934 and MA 1458
RWM Fb 35/82 no. 8, DIHT to SRA 17.12.1934.
[113] BAMA RW 19/923, 'Geheime Abschrift des W Wi, Wa Aktenvermerk betr. stat.
Veröffentlichungen, Vorbesprechung beim RWM' 1.11.1934.

Reichardt's Office and the RWM in April 1935.[114] All agencies wishing to carry out statistical enquiries were required to seek permission from the Statistical Office. For the purposes of the law, 'statistics' were defined in an all-encompassing fashion.[115] The Office would be entitled to reject a survey if: 'the proposed statistical survey threatens the vital interests of those questioned, or if the survey impeded the official statistics of the Reich, or if its timing, or manner of execution were deemed inappropriate'. The draft law would also, at last, provide a legal foundation for statistical enquiries, replacing the controversial Auskunftspflicht of 1923. Any statistical survey authorized by the Statistical Office was to have the force of law. This would resolve a problem that had been debated at least since the turn of the century. On essential principles, however, the draft law was traditional in outlook. The new powers of compulsion were balanced by provisions restricting the use to which statistical questionnaires might be put. The draft law of 1935 echoed the restrictions which had framed the major official surveys since the late nineteenth century:[116]

The individual returns . . . may be used only for statistical or general economic, social or cultural policy purposes, not for any other purpose. It is forbidden to use this material as the basis for individual measures directed against the persons making the returns. In particular, it is forbidden for statistical material to be used for the purpose of tax assessment.[117]

The law further specified that all questionnaires were to carry a clear statement of the purpose of the survey, its legal basis as well as an assurance of confidentiality.[118] The emphatic prohibition of the use of statistics for tax purposes underlined a traditional precept of statistical practice. It also reflected specific anxieties about the intentions of the Reich's Ministry of Finance.[119] Since 1933, the Reich's fiscal administration had been making renewed demands for access to statistical questionnaires in an attempt to crack down on tax evasion.[120] The Statistical Office and the RWM stubbornly resisted. In their view, the

---

[114] BAP 07.01 FC 19853/591 no. 12, RWM to Reichsminister 23.4.1935 'Entwurf eines Gesetzes über statistische Erhebungen' (1935).

[115] BAP 07.01 FC 19853/591 no. 12, para. 1(2). Statistics were defined as any survey or other type of investigation conducted as a generalized enquiry into facts, objects or processes pertaining to the Volk, the economy, society, cultural or political life.

[116] See J. Schubert, 'Die Amtsverschwiegenheit der Statistik. Eine statistisch-juristische Betrachtung', *ASA*, 23 (1934), pp. 610–618.

[117] BAP 07.01 FC 19853/591 no. 12, RWM to Reichsminister 23.4.1935 'Entwurf eines Gesetzes', para. (1).

[118] BAP 07.01 FC 19853/591 no. 12, RWM to Reichsminister 23.4.1935 'Entwurf eines Gesetzes', para. (2).

[119] BAP 07.01 FC 19853/591 no. 18, Reichskanzlei note 14.5.1935.

[120] BAP 23.01 2230 no. 36–37.

Ministry of Finance posed a potentially fatal threat to the reliability of statistical returns.[121] Anonymity and confidentiality were the bedrock of statistics. These proscriptions had defined the business of official statistics in relation both to the population at large and other branches of government at least since the nineteenth century. However, they were fundamentally at odds with the new uses to which statistics were being put in Nazi Germany. The compulsory Industrial Reports and the accounts collected by the Supervisory Agencies satisfied general statistical interests, but they also provided the database necessary for the control of individual firms. Even the census of 1933, a classic set piece of official statistics, was being transformed into a card-file of information on individual firms. The draft Statistical Law provided for such practices only in exceptional cases. An exemption clause authorized the use of statistical returns for measures against individuals, if this was 'necessary, in the opinion of a Reich's Ministry, due to an urgent need of state which could not be satisfied by any other means'.[122] In such cases, the permission of the RWM was required. The constitution proposed for German statistics in 1935 was thus fundamentally out of touch with the new realities. It treated as exceptions precisely those projects with which the official statisticians were carving out a place for themselves in the Third Reich.

Moreover, the draft proposal was out of touch with political reality. When it began to circulate among the ministries in April 1935 the Statistical Law encountered an accumulation of bureaucratic resistance.[123] While statistics were produced in an ad hoc fashion they could be regarded as a mundane administrative issue. As soon as they were identified as a governmental problem in their own right, it became clear that the dispersion and incoherence of economic information was part of a more general, unsolved problem: the unresolved distribution of power in the Third Reich. Statistical disorder was not merely a passive reflection of underlying power structures. Statistics were an important weapon in the political struggles going on beneath the monolithic veneer of the regime. Each ministry and quasi-governmental agency was desperate to preserve control of its own data. The draft Statistical Law that proposed to confer a statistical monopoly on the Statistical Office was bound to stir up powerful resistance. More specifically, what was at stake was the power of Hjalmar Schacht, Minister for Economic Affairs and President of the Reichsbank. The Statistical Office fell within

---

[121] BAP 07.01 FC 19853/591 no. 18, Reichskanzlei note 14.5.1935, p. 1.
[122] BAP 07.01 FC 19853/591 no. 12, 'Entwurf eines Gesetzes über statistische Erhebungen' (1935), para. (3).
[123] BAP 07.01 FC 19853/591 no. 19–21.

Schacht's empire. In the autumn of 1934 or even early in 1935, his authority might have been sufficient to force through the Statistical Law. However, by the autumn of 1935 his dominant position was already under threat. It was too late for the Statistical Office to secure a monopoly of governmental knowledge in the Third Reich.

One should not jump to the conclusion, that the failure of the Statistical Law demonstrates the peculiarly polycratic nature of political power in the Third Reich. Like so many other governmental problems which the Nazis failed to resolve, the lack of statistical law was a long-standing problem in German government. It was certainly not a specific failing of the Nazis. The Weimar Republic had avoided the problem precisely because it raised such troublesome political and legal issues. And the deadlock over the Statistical Law in 1935 did not end the search for a more coherent information system in Nazi Germany. The Statistical Office negotiated a series of bilateral agreements with major data-gatherers. The list of these deals gives some indication of the scale of the problem. The Reich's Ministry for Food and Agriculture was persuaded to coordinate its enquiries with the Statistical Office in December 1934.[124] In May 1935, a deal was struck with the Reich's Economic Chamber (Reichswirtschaftskammer) and its subordinate agencies, which covered all non-agricultural businesses.[125] In November 1935, the statistical activities of the Supervisory Agencies were formally placed under the control of Leisse's Department of Production Statistics in the Statistical Office.[126] In December 1935 the RWM ordered the local Chambers of Industry and Commerce to make a standard monthly economic report to the Gauwirtschaftsberater (the economic Advisors to the local Nazi bosses), so as to cut down on their independent statistical enquiries.[127] In January 1936 the Reich's Ministry of the Interior issued a decree requiring ministerial permission before any further statistical offices were set up at communal level.[128] In the summer of 1936, both the DAF and the Nazi Party took measures to restrict their statistical activities.[129] In October 1936, the Office agreed to provide information to the Reich's Regional Planning Agency (Reichsstelle für Raumordnung) to prevent that Agency from initiating its own surveys. Finally, in December 1936 the Office concluded a

[124] BAP 31.02 3568 no. 7, Präs. SRA to RWM 16.5.1937.
[125] BAP 31.02 3468 no. 5, SRA note 19.10.1935.
[126] MA 1458 RWM Fb 35/12 no. 49, RWM/IIR to Supervisory Agencies VI–XXV 5.1.1935 and BAP 31.02 3468 no. 1, RWM to SRA 14.10.1935.
[127] BBA 15 428 RgI Circular 10.12.1935.
[128] BAP 07.01 FC 19653/591 no. 22, Reichs- und Preu. Innenministerium, 'Verordnung über Neugründung von Statistischen Ämtern' 3.1.1936 .
[129] For the following see BAP 31.02 3623 no. 4–65.

'treaty' with Reich's Group Industry and its sub-units to limit industrial enquiries. The network of bilateral agreements became so dense that it emerged as a source of confusion in its own right. Agencies which had received permission from one Department of the Statistical Office could find themselves at odds with another, which claimed overlapping rights of supervision. To avoid embarrassment, Reichardt's Head Office was forced to appoint an official to coordinate the coordination arrangements. Nevertheless, the system of 'treaties' devised by the Office provided a flexible form of regulation well suited to the fluid organizational structure of the Third Reich. Certainly, they provided the Statistical Office with access to more economic information than ever before in its history.

VI

Historians still argue about the correct characterization of the political economy of Nazism. Unfortunately, however, the literature on economic policy has tended to operate within a rather restrictive framework. Nazi ideology is counterposed to bureaucratic pragmatism. At least as far as the statistical apparatus is concerned, neither of these categories is particularly helpful. In the early years of the regime, the influence of Nazi ideology was limited. But this does not mean that the National Revolution left the state apparatus untouched. We need to ask more specifically what the Nazi seizure of power actually meant to the participants. What did they hope to make of it? As far as the Statistical Office was concerned, there can be no doubt that it meant the opportunity to continue elaborating the new system of national economic administration that had begun to develop in the 1920s. There was continuity of innovation, not conservatism. The official statisticians foresaw an important role for themselves in the Third Reich at the centre of a comprehensive system of state oversight and control. And given Schacht's authority in the first three years of the regime, the Reich's bureaucracy was able to go a long way towards realizing this fantasy of authoritarian statism. Power and knowledge were centralized in an unprecedented fashion. Given the speed with which the new national organization was created, there was bound to be a fair measure of administrative confusion. However, by 1936 a new system of national economic controls did seem to be emerging.

There was far more to this than mere bureaucratic improvisation. For one thing, developments in Nazi Germany should not be seen in isolation. It was the disintegration of the gold standard and the failure of collective security that provided the wider setting for the expansion of nation-state power. The collapse of international structures freed national governments everywhere to pursue independent economic policies and to embark on increasingly confrontational power politics. In this sense, the German story of the early 1930s is far from unique. What distinguished the German case is the vigour with which the state seized the opportunity for national action. By 1936, Hitler could boast of a simultaneous recovery of economic and military strength. In part, Nazism itself provided the explanation. The popularity and dynamism of the movement gave impetus to the programme of national reconstruction. The new regime rode roughshod over legal obstacles that had seemed insurmountable in the past. In large part, however, the Third Reich owed its effectiveness to the enthusiastic collaboration of powerful elite groups. Most importantly, the German military were easily mobilized around a programme of rearmament. But it is now well established that professionals of all sorts rallied to the regime. Engineers, architects, social workers, doctors, psychologists, management specialists, philosophers and poets, all projected their fantasies of power onto Hitler's new state. The Statistical Office and, more broadly speaking, the civil servants of the Reich's economic administration, should be added to this list. In each case, the Nazi seizure of power offered the chance for individual self-promotion. However, there was more to this than mere opportunism. The reconstruction of the German state was seen as a historic opportunity to realize long-held plans and ambitions. Men like Bramstedt and Leisse set about making a reality of the grandiose plans of the 1920s. The successful expansion of the Industrial Reporting System and the industrial census of 1933 justified the boldest hopes of Konjunkturforschung. The projected input–output system was its crowning glory.

In an important sense, therefore, the early years of Hitler's regime can be seen as part of a process of state-building that stretches back to World War I. This is not to say that the priorities of the statisticians were left unchanged by the crisis of the early 1930s. In broad political terms, there is a clear shift. Konjunkturforschung had originally assigned to the state the facilitative role of ensuring the smooth development of the national economy. Now the aim was to subordinate the economy to the priorities of the regime. What those priorities were was unclear. They were to be resolved only in a process of struggle between Schacht, the military and the Nazi leadership. There was also a degree of uncertainty at the technical level. The industrial census was an ambiguous tool. It was conceived as a component of Wagemann's national accounts. The input–output scheme was a logical development in that direction. By tracking the connections between industries, it revealed the complex division of labour out of which flowed the stream of final output. True to the Konjunkturforschung of the 1920s, it measured the streams of income and expenditure in monetary terms. By contrast, Leisse's development of the census pointed in another direction. His proposals for the military drew aside the 'veil of money'. The work of his industrial statisticians focused on the flow of scarce raw materials. Rather than indirect macroeconomic control, this pointed towards a future of physical planning. But, whatever the future held in store, the Reich's Statistical Office seemed well positioned to take advantage.

6   The radicalization of the Nazi regime and the death of official statistics, 1936–1939

Up to 1936, we can extend the narrative that began in the mid-1920s. Both in intellectual and political terms, there was continuity. Konjunkturforschung survived and it remained identified with the ambitions of the Reich's economic administration. The embodiment of this continuity was the projected input–output table. The table promised to give the Reich's Ministry of Economic Affairs an unprecedented ability to calculate the ramified impact of economic policy. In administrative terms, it was to be the cornerstone of a vast network of economic information centralized in the Reich's Statistical Office. After 1933, Wagemann and his Institute may have been excluded from the centre of power and knowledge, but their aspirations lived on in the Statistical Office, until 1936. In that year, a powerful challenge emerged to Hjalmar Schacht's grip on economic policy. The state-building of the early years of the Third Reich was thrown into question. Symbolic of much bigger changes was the cancellation of further work on the input–output table. The 1937 budget gave inadequate funding to Bramstedt's Department and the team of economists associated with the project was allowed to disperse. Over the following years the Office fell apart. In 1939, the third census of production, the backbone of the entire system of planning statistics, was cancelled. What had happened? Why was the development of Konjunkturforschung as a technology of state control not continued?

I

It would be simple to give an answer in terms of the increasing radicalism of Hitler's regime. 'External forces', beyond the control of the statisticians, would thus be blamed for the termination of the macroeconomic project of statistics begun in the Weimar Republic. As the Third Reich accelerated its drive towards war, its political system became increasingly disorganized. After 1936, Hjalmar Schacht lost his grip on economic policy. The ramshackle apparatus of Hermann Goering's Four-Year Plan displaced the administrative apparatus of the state. The Third Reich embarked on a reckless, unbalanced drive towards rearmament and economic self-sufficiency. Planning tools such as the input–output table were no longer in demand. They presupposed an interest in economic balance, or at least calculated imbalance, that no longer existed in the Nazi leadership. In 1937–8 the Statistical Office, like the rest of the German state, was swept up in a 'second seizure of power', which subordinated Germany's 'traditional' elites including the army and the civilian civil service to the irrational goals of the Nazi leadership.

Such an 'externalist' account would find a complement in historical narratives produced by the statisticians themselves. The Leitmotif of the official history of the Statistical Office is the claim that a gulf existed between the proper practice of statistics and the radical ideology of the Nazi regime.[1] Scientific statistical enquiries and Nazism were fundamentally incompatible. The Urtext for this version of events was produced by none other than Wolfgang Reichardt, Wagemann's successor as President of the Statistical Office. In 1940, he contributed an introductory article to the lavish two-volume Festschrift for Friedrich Zahn, the retiring head of the Bavarian statistical office.[2] Reichardt's introduction struck a remarkably gloomy note. He portrayed the Statistical Office as an institution endangered by the short-sighted logic of unfettered power. The administrative weeds of rationing were suffocating the healthy plant of official statistics. The early efforts by the Office to contain the proliferation of statistical paperwork had failed. Since the initiation of Goering's Four-Year Plan, in 1936, the statistics of rationing and economic control had run riot. Reichardt drew an absolute distinction between the proper activity of official statisticians – disinterested, objective, scientific enquiry – and the administrative prying of 'rationing statistics'. And he did not mince his words:

At all times in the *civilized world*, the reliability of official statistics has been founded on the conviction amongst the population being questioned that their returns are protected by so-called 'statistical confidentiality', i.e. that their individual returns are made only to the statistical authority and only for statistical purposes, and may never be used for administrative measures against the individual respondent.[3]

---

[1] G. Fürst, 'Wandlungen im Programm und in den Aufgaben der amtlichen Statistik in den letzten 100 Jahren', in Statistisches Bundesamt, *Bevölkerung und Wirtschaft 1872–1972* (Stuttgart, 1972).

[2] W. Reichardt, 'Die Reichsstatistik', in F. Burgdörfer (ed.), *Die Statistik in Deutschland nach ihrem heutigen Stand. Ehrengabe für Friedrich Zahn* (Berlin, 1940), 1, pp. 77–90.

[3] Reichardt, 'Die Reichsstatistik', p. 83, emphasis added.

In the Third Reich 'statistical confidentiality' had been fundamentally compromised. And, Reichardt continued: 'I consider the threat to the reliability of statistics resulting from the use of individual returns for economic policy measures against the individual to be very serious and look forward to the day when this procedure is no longer necessary.' An 'almost complete net of surveillance, controls and regulations'[4] had become the only guarantee of statistical reliability. Statistics were mutating into a technology of coercion, a development which threatened the integrity, indeed the existence, of official statistics as a respected institution of government. In the long run Reichardt could envision official statistics surviving only if the 'normal' relationship between 'the state' and 'civil society' was restored. Published in 1940, Reichardt's piece deserves to be read as a brave defence of liberal principles. In the aftermath of the war, however, Reichardt's intervention was subject to an ironic process of reinterpretation. His plea that Germany's official statisticians *ought* to remain at a distance from the dirty business of economic control was translated into the claim that such distance *was* in fact maintained. The centenary history of German official statistics, published by the West German Statistical Office in 1972, does all it can to minimize the entanglement of official statistics in the practice of Nazi government.[5] As its evidence, it cites Reichardt's embattled appeal.

This is clearly a misreading, but it was prefigured by Reichardt's own, oversharp distinction between the practice of economic surveillance and proper, scientific statistics. Identifying the source of disorder and degeneration as coming from outside the Statistical Office, in the form of Nazi politics, allows one to describe the civil servants as innocent victims. What sustains these interlocking explanations is the simple dichotomy between irrational Nazism and the rationality of the civil service. The aim of this chapter is to blur this line, to subvert the distinction between Nazi ideology and 'science', between high politics and technical administration, between official statistics and systems of surveillance, between the 'clean' interior of the statistical office and the 'dirty' external world of the Third Reich. The Statistical Office was undermined from within as much as from without. There was no clean line separating the chaotic Party from the orderly civil servants. Official statisticians were not merely victims; they were active participants in the factional politics that tore the German state apart. And this process of disintegration was multi-dimensional. It was not simply a political process. In the late 1930s, the Statistical Office suffered a profound loss of intellectual direction. The project of Konjunkturforschung was no longer capable of

---

[4] Reichardt, 'Die Reichsstatistik', p. 86.
[5] Fürst, 'Wandlungen im Programm', p. 43.

giving unity to the work of the Reich's economic statisticians. The intellectual agenda inherited from the 1920s began to be challenged from within the Office itself.

The history of the Statistical Office thus provides a new perspective on the violent crisis afflicting the German state in the late 1930s. Classically, this has been understood in political terms, as a 'second seizure of power'. These political battles were certainly crucial. However, they had such explosive effects because they intersected with change at other levels. As Jane Caplan has shown, the personal battles for power were part of a more general crisis of the authority of the state, a crisis in the constitution of government.[6] Nazi ideology delegitimized the state as a representative institution. In its place, it invoked the ideal image of the unmediated relationship between Volk and Führer. The struggle for power at the top thus coincided with an ideological crisis. Both these processes are clearly visible in the history of the Statistical Office. The statisticians manoeuvred to place themselves in relation to key players such as Goering, Schacht and Funk. At the same time, they also attempted to answer more general questions about their place in relation to the state, civil society and the new order of power that seemed to be emerging in the Third Reich. But none of this made any sense for the statisticians as statisticians if it was not also related to the development of their technical and scientific projects. Political choices were important because they were linked to technical decisions. As this chapter hopes to show, the political turmoil of the late 1930s had explosive effects in the sphere of official statistics because it provided the opportunity for radical technical experimentation. A personal struggle for power and a struggle to redefine the political constitution of the Third Reich, coincided, in the Statistical Office, with efforts to transform the technology of government. It was this triple disturbance that gave the Third Reich, in the late 1930s, its extraordinary radicalism.

Reichardt, as President of the Statistical Office, may have found himself increasingly at odds with the politics of Hitler's regime, but his was not the only response to the challenges facing German official statistics in the late 1930s. Responsibility for economic statistics within the Office lay with an ambitious cohort of younger officials recruited by Wagemann in the 1920s. They refused to accept the personal and professional demotion that Reichardt's liberalism implied. They did not share Reichardt's view of the planned economy as a threat to civilization. On the contrary, they accepted it as inevitable and sought to exploit the opportunities it offered, both to advance themselves personally and to

[6] J. Caplan, 'National Socialism and the Theory of the State', in T. Childers and J. Caplan (eds.), *Reevaluating the Third Reich* (New York, 1993), pp. 98–113.

secure a new role for statistics in the power structure of Nazi Germany. This meant leaving the liberal past behind.

II

Perhaps not surprisingly it was Dr Wilhelm Leisse who was the first official in the Statistical Office to realize the wider opportunities offered by the radicalization of the regime. In 1933, it was Leisse who had mobilized grassroots resentment against Wagemann. Over the following years he sought to push himself to the forefront of military–economic planning using the industrial censuses as his vehicle. In 1935, Leisse received his reward. He was promoted to the rank of Director by personal order of Adolf Hitler with control over his own, newly created Department VII for Industrial Production Statistics.[7] Even greater opportunities beckoned in 1936, when Hermann Goering mounted his challenge to Schacht's monopoly of economic policy. Between 1933 and 1935 Schacht had presided over a compromise between rearmament and economic stability. Generous but clearly defined limits had been agreed in 1933 that restricted military spending to levels compatible with available economic capacity. This had allowed government regulation of the economy to be confined to controls on the balance of payments and restriction of the consumer industries. In the autumn of 1935, with Hitler's encouragement, these spending limits were breached.[8] Propelled by the Führer's aggressive foreign policy the army, the navy and Goering's Luftwaffe launched into an arms build-up, without regard for economic stability. By the spring of 1936, the strain was beginning to show in the balance of payments. Bitter squabbles broke out over the allocation of scarce foreign exchange. Desperate to divert some of the political pressure away from the Reichsbank and the RWM, Schacht supported the appointment of Hermann Goering as Commissioner for Raw Materials and Exchange Issues. Goering was to take the unpopular decisions, whilst Schacht pulled the strings in the background. The Reichsmarschall frequently boasted of his lack of experience in economic affairs and Schacht apparently took this at face value. However, Goering's public image was deceptive. Since 1933, he had used his multiple offices as Prussian Prime Minister, Air Minister and Reich's Forester to accumulate a considerable staff of economists, lawyers, businessmen and military technicians.[9] Goering never intended

---

[7] BAP 31.01 8662 no. 337, 'Haushalt des RWM 1935, Einzelplan VI'.
[8] M. Geyer, *Aufrüstung oder Sicherheit. Die Reichswehr in der Krise der Machtpolitik 1924–1936* (Wiesbaden, 1980), pp. 445–449.
[9] A. Kube, *Pour le mérite und Hakenkreuz. Hermann Goering im Dritten Reich* (Munich,

to serve merely as Schacht's front man. Within a matter of weeks Goering had established his own organization, the Raw Materials and Foreign Exchange Staff (Rohstoff und Devisenstab), and staked his claim to an independent voice in economic policy.

Goering's new staff moved rapidly to tap into the expertise of the Statistical Office. Obtaining data on Germany's raw material supply was one of their top priorities.[10] The two main sources of information were the censuses of industrial production and the monthly returns of the Supervisory Agencies. The census figures provided a periodic overview. The returns of the Supervisory Agencies provided information on a monthly basis. Both sources were controlled by Leisse's Department VII of the Statistical Office, which was to emerge as the critical interface between the Statistical Office and Goering's staff. By the end of May 1936, the quantities of information demanded from the Office had grown to such a flood that they attracted the attention of the RWM. An official was appointed to monitor the flow.[11] Meanwhile, Leisse tightened his grip within the Office. From February 1937 all information supplied to Goering's expanding organization was channelled through his Department.[12] And Leisse was even authorized to issue instructions to other Departments of the Office on Goering's behalf. After the establishment of the Four-Year Plan in the autumn of 1936, the link became closer still. Goering's personal staff insisted on remaining in direct touch with Leisse. They received a copy of every piece of information he supplied to any office of the Four-Year Plan.[13] Leisse thus established a direct line to the Reichsmarschall. Though Goering himself was no doubt only dimly aware of this relationship, it was of prime importance to the statistician: as Goering rose, so did Leisse.

Goering's appointment to head the Four-Year Plan was a decisive blow to the authority of Schacht and ultimately to the Reich's economic administration itself. Germany faced a deteriorating balance of payments and increasingly serious shortages of steel and labour. Schacht, backed by important business interests, advocated a deceleration of military spending. By contrast, Goering pushed himself into the limelight as the advocate of breakneck rearmament. Goering staked every-

1986), p. 134; E.L. Homze, *Arming the Luftwaffe. The Reich Air Ministry and the German Aircraft Industry 1919–1939* (Lincoln, Nebraska, 1976), pp. 57–62; D. Irving, *Die Tragödie der Deutschen Luftwaffe. Aus den Akten und Erinnerungen von Feldmarschall Milch* (Frankfurt, 1970), pp. 61–74; R.J. Overy, *Goering The 'Iron Man'* (London, 1984), pp. 33–34.

[10] BAP SRA 31.02 3003 no. 1, SRA/VII Industrielle Produktionsstatistik, circular 30.6.1936.

[11] BAP SRA 31.02 3468 no. 25, RWM to Überwachungsstellen 25.5.1936.

[12] BAP 31.02 4224 no. 1, RWM to RgI 20.2.1937.

[13] BAP 31.02 3586 no. 153, Goering's Referent to SRA 27.11.1936.

thing on a programme of investment which, he promised, would make Germany independent of foreign raw materials. In August 1936 Hitler himself announced the Four-Year Plan. The Plan had no pretensions to being a comprehensive or balanced programme for the entire economy. It consisted of a package of giant investment projects in synthetic fibres, oil and rubber. In the first half of 1937, Goering increased the pressure on Schacht by adding an enormous steel project, designed to exploit the low-grade iron ores of central Germany. This project was fiercely opposed by both Schacht and the heavy industrialists of the Ruhr.[14] But, Goering was now unstoppable. In the autumn of 1937 work commenced on the giant Reichswerke Hermann Goering at Salzgitter. Schacht resigned as Minister for Economic Affairs.

To the civil service, the clash between Schacht and Goering sent a clear signal. Hitler no longer trusted the state apparatus inherited from the Weimar Republic to accomplish the vital task of making Germany ready for war. To act with the necessary ruthlessness, even against the interests of private capital, new men and a new organization were required. The creation of the Four-Year Plan was as much an intervention in the German state as it was an intervention in the private affairs of German business. The bureaucracy of the Plan was staffed by a motley crew of soldiers, engineers and corporate executives mainly from IG Farben, party men and Goering loyalists. In the wake of Schacht's resignation, Goering was placed temporarily in charge of the RWM. Over the following months, the economic administration, like the German armed forces and the Foreign Ministry, suffered a major onslaught.[15] Under Schacht, who was not himself a member of the NSDAP, the RWM had been insulated from the direct influence of the Nazi Party. The National Revolution was interpreted as a licence for bureaucratic initiative. The RWM and the Statistical Office had been able to continue the process of state-building they had begun in the 1920s. Schacht's defeat ushered in a new era. Under Goering, the civil service forfeited its freedom of action. All the heads of Department in the RWM were either retired or moved elsewhere within the state administration. To replace them, Goering brought in personnel from the Four-Year Plan. The five Departments of the Ministry were now headed by military men or party members of long standing. The change in

[14] R.J. Overy, 'Heavy Industry in the Third Reich: The Reichswerke Crisis', in *War and Economy in the Third Reich* (Oxford, 1994), pp. 93–118 and G. Mollin, *Montankonzerne und 'Drittes Reich'. Der Gegensatz zwischen Monopolindustrie und Befehlswirtschaft in der deutschen Rüstung und Expansion 1936–1944* (Göttingen, 1988).

[15] W.A. Boelcke, *Die deutsche Wirtschaft 1930–1945. Interna des Reichswirtschaftsministeriums* (Düsseldorf, 1983), pp. 178–192 and M. Broszat, *Der Staat Hitlers* (Munich, 1969, 13th edn.), pp. 363–402.

political culture was dramatic. The civil servants at the Ministry revived the language of 1918–19, referring to the new leadership jokingly as the 'Soldiers and Workers Soviet' (Arbeiter- und Soldatenrat).[16] In the event, Hitler did not grant Goering permanent control of the RWM. In February 1938, the long-serving Nazi Walther Funk was named Minister. However, Funk was firmly under Goering's personal influence and the ministerial bureaucracy now took orders from the Four-Year Plan. The independent authority of the Reich's economic administration was broken.

However, Goering's seizure of power was not bad news for all of the civil service. As Goering's influence increased in the course of 1937, so did Leisse's claims for special status within the Statistical Office. If Goering was economic dictator, Leisse claimed control of the entire field of industrial statistics. In the autumn of 1937, the struggles within the Statistical Office mirrored those on the wider political stage.[17] And Leisse soon received his reward. In the last days of 1937 Department VII was given the mission for which Leisse had been preparing since the Nazi take-over. It was henceforth to concentrate all efforts on military–economic planning.[18] The information needs of civilian economic policy were to take second place. In March 1938 Leisse achieved his ultimate ambition. Department VII was cut loose from the Statistical Office and established as a separate organization in its own right, the Reich's Office for Military–Economic Planning (Reichsamt für wehrwirtschaftliche Planung, RwP).[19] Leisse's gamble had paid off. Rising from amongst the ranks of humble Referenten, he had first achieved the rank of Director with control of his own Department. Now, with the creation of the RwP, he had attained the rank of President, putting him on an equal footing with the President of the Office itself. And the RwP was immediately allotted a place on the stage of high politics. It was to give substance to Walter Funk's office of Generalbevollmächtiger für die Wehrwirtschaft (General Plenipotentiary for the War Economy, GBW). The position of General Plenipotentiary played a strategic role in the battle for control of the German economy. The office had been established in 1935 to empower Schacht to carry out military–economic preparations in the civilian sector. In times of war, it gave him authority

---

[16] Boelcke, *Die deutsche Wirtschaft 1930–1945*, p. 183.
[17] On the argument over the control of statistics carried out by commercial organizations between Department VI and Department VII see BAP 31.02 3572.
[18] BAP 31.02 2993, RWM to SRA (z.H. Leisse) 28.12.1937.
[19] BAP 31.02 3045 no. 2, GBW to Reichsamt für wehrwirtschaftliche Statistik und Planung 24.5.1938. Its title was later changed to that of Reichsamt für Wehrwirtschaftliche Planung (RwP) used in the text, see BAP 31.02 3045 no. 3, GBW to RwP 9.7.1938.

over all firms not contracting directly for the military. Given Schacht's increasing doubts about the pace of rearmament, he had in fact used his powers to shelter the civilian economy from the excessive demands of the military. This had the effect of driving the army high command into an alliance with Goering. Now, with Schacht out of the way, the military demanded the total subordination of the entire economy. This was not a demand to which Goering and Funk, any more than Schacht, were willing to cede. The creation of Leisse's RwP was part of Funk and Goering's strategy to preserve the office of the Plenipotentiary, thereby restricting the claims of the army.[20] Only a few weeks after it was formally separated from the Statistical Office, the RwP was paraded by Funk as a panacea for all problems of mobilization planning. While the Four-Year Plan focused on the task of producing substitute products, Leisse's RwP would draw up plans showing how Germany's scarce resources would be allocated in case of war.

III

By the autumn of 1938, much was invested in the RwP. Its success depended on maintaining the political balance, but it also depended on the viability of a particular approach to planning. Far too often, problems of government in the Third Reich are treated from an exclusively political point of view. There is no doubting the irrationality of Hitler himself. And the Third Reich certainly lacked a coherent system of policy-formation. However, the peculiarly irrational quality of Nazi politics tends to be assumed, rather than demonstrated by means of systematic comparison. Furthermore, real technical constraints are often obscured by the focus on political processes. Whether or not policy-making in the Third Reich was well organized there were real obstacles to be overcome in preparing Germany for war. Many of these problems were far from unique to Germany; some of them might have been overcome had other technical choices been made. But some of them were insurmountable.

In September 1938, Leisse's statisticians were given the order to develop a comprehensive and consistent raw material plan for the German economy at war.[21] A plan was to be prepared for each raw material. For each month of the mobilization period the plans were to show: the total volume of raw materials required by each industry, the

---

[20] R.-D. Müller, 'Die Mobilisierung der Deutschen Wirtschaft für Hitlers Kriegsführung', in B.R. Kroener, R.-D. Müller and H. Umbreit, *Das Deutsche Reich und der Zweite Weltkrieg* (Stuttgart, 1988), 5, 1, p. 354.
[21] BAP 31.02 6231, GBW to RwP 24.9.1938.

production target for each raw material, the amount of new production to be expected each month as well as the level of stocks held in Germany. The censuses of 1933 and 1936 would provide Leisse with all the necessary information. The monthly returns from the Supervisory Agencies and the Business Groups were available as further sources. The centrepiece of the statistical effort were the so-called 'material balances'. These balances were a tabular representation of the family trees and industrial diagrams prepared after the 1933 census. They showed, on the one hand, the sources of supply for a material and, on the other, the industries and sectors in which it was consumed. They could also be compiled for industries rather than for materials, showing on the one hand the quantities of raw materials required to produce a given volume of goods, and on the other the available supplies. In practice, however, drawing up the balances proved far from straightforward.

The first census in 1933 had encountered a variety of technical obstacles. But Leisse and his team had been confident that these were no more than teething troubles. The second census of 1936 punctured this optimism. It became clear that there were a number of limitations inherent in the method of the census that were not amenable to any simple administrative fix. A report compiled at the end of 1938, summarizing the experience in compiling raw material balances, struck a fundamentally sceptical note.[22] In many cases, there had been few problems in compiling balances. The physical process of production and consumption was completely accounted for. However, there was a large group of materials for which this was not the case. There were dozens of materials for which the statisticians had calculated either a large positive or negative balance – i.e. production whose consumption could not be accounted for, or consumption for which there was no obvious source of supply. And unbalanced balances were not even the most serious technical problem facing the industrial planners. Far more important was their inability to analyse anything but the simplest kinds of manufacturing. As the planners themselves conceded, it was practically impossible to devise raw material balances for complex manufacturing industries. The essential problem was one of measurement. Since the industrial statisticians were interested in the physical process of production, the balances were denominated in physical terms. They showed how many tons of cellulose were required to produce a ton of paper, how much bauxite went into the production of aluminium. It was even possible to draw up a meaningful balance for simple manufactured

---

[22] BAP 31.02 3129, Bericht des Referats Rohstoffversorgung über die Bilanzen 1936.

goods, such as textiles. A certain quantity of raw wool was required to produce an identifiable quantity of cloth. However, a similar statement about cars or machine tools was virtually meaningless. Even if the quantity of 'one ton of lathe' could be given some approximate meaning, the addition of 'one ton of lathe' and 'one ton of drilling machine' was gibberish. Of course, one could proceed by enumerating the physical inputs required to produce a clearly specified machine of a particular type. For example, the volume of sheet metal needed to make the projected Volkswagen was a known quantity. To create a category of medium family car one could lump together the Volkswagen with a standard Opel saloon of similar specification. However, the statistical labour required to produce balances of this kind for thousands of different types of manufactured good was well beyond the capacities of Leisse's statisticians. Soviet experience in the 1940s and 1950s demonstrated that planning in such detail was feasible. Eastern European plans routinely included balances for many thousands of manufactured products. However, nothing of this kind was being attempted in the Soviet Union in the 1930s and their later achievements were built on an infrastructure that was unavailable to either Moscow or Berlin in the interwar period.[23] Soviet-style planning rested on an enormous administrative apparatus and a thorough standardization of the underlying processes of production. The economy itself needed to be remade to suit the technology of planning.

There was, of course, an alternative to the method of physical balances adopted by Leisse's RwP. In a complex, diversified economy, the most economical solution to the problem of aggregation was to use prices. In money terms the different qualities of complex machines could be reduced to a common denominator. Broadly similar types of product could be grouped together and their relative merits and demerits as well as their different costs of production would be reflected in their relative prices. This, of course, was the route, which had been proposed by Bramstedt's experiment with input–output planning. Their first exercise had been to estimate an input–output table for the motor vehicles industry, a task that utterly defeated Leisse's physical accounting method. Rather surprisingly, however, there was not even a suggestion from the RwP that this more promising avenue might be resumed. This brings us back to the question with which this chapter began. Why was the input–output approach allowed to die? Was the political leadership of Nazi Germany simply not interested in this tool of planning? The prominence given to Leisse's RwP in 1938 seems to

[23] G. Grossmann, *Soviet Statistics of Physical Output of Industrial Commodities: Their Compilation and Quality* (Princeton, 1960), pp. 13–19.

suggest the opposite. Visions of planning could still attract high-level political backing. However, the example of the RwP also illustrated the need for statisticians to act strategically, to attach themselves to one or other of the factions competing for power, to sell their wares, to build a supportive context for their projects. This political vision seems to have been lacking amongst the proponents of input–output planning. The internal memoranda that survive certainly do not do a good job selling the plan. The wider practical and political implications of the input–output table were barely spelled out. The statisticians did not do the work of interpolating a potential customer in the Nazi power structure. There was not even an aggressive effort to sell the proposal to the RWM itself. In 1937, the civilian budgets of the Reich began to be seriously squeezed by the enormous increase in military expenditure. The Reich's Finance Ministry applied the stringency of wartime. The Statistical Office was informed that all projects should be abandoned that were not strictly essential in times of war. Work on the input–output table was allowed to grind to a virtual standstill because it was not deemed to meet these criteria.[24] The economists responsible for laying the statistical groundwork were allowed to leave the Office for more promising employment elsewhere. By April 1938 the table for 1933 had still not been completed.[25] No copy of the final table has survived in the archives. As a practical tool of government, the input–output table remained hypothetical.

Could the project have been sold? Were there insuperable technical obstacles to its application in the late 1930s? The crucial difference between the input–output table and Leisse's physical planning was the reliance of the input–output table on prices. This made possible a high level of aggregation. However, it also meant that the system was dependent on the continued existence of a meaningful system of prices. By the late 1930s, this could no longer be taken for granted. In 1936 the so-called 'price stop' had frozen prices at their current levels.[26] Did this invalidate the entries in the matrix? This again was not a matter of fact, but a matter of argument, an argument that does not appear to have taken place. On the one hand, the flows of funds recorded by input–output matrices for the late 1930s would certainly have been distorted. They could no longer represent the 'true' market relationship between sectors. On the other hand, economic policy-makers might very well

[24] BAP 31.02 SRA 2475 no. 379, SRA Abt VI to the Sachbearbeiter des Haushalts ORR Dr Jonquieres, 9.10.1936.
[25] BAP 3102 2700, SRA to the RWM 19. April 1938, p. 3.
[26] H. Dichgans, *Zur Geschichte des Reichskommissars für die Preisbildung* (Düsseldorf, 1977).

have been interested in measuring the degree of distortion that price controls were causing. All of this must have been obvious to Bramstedt's Department. So, why did they not push the project harder? The most probable cause would seem to be the internal politics of the Statistical Office. The input–output table was a project that depended critically on bureaucratic cooperation. In summarizing the activities of the entire economy it needed to draw on a wide variety of sources. This had caused problems from the outset. Even in the early stages of planning, Bramstedt's staff had complained about the difficulty of getting access to data compiled by other ministries and planning agencies. After 1936 as the authority of the Statistical Office dwindled, these difficulties increased. Critically, the success of the project depended on access to the returns of the industrial census and Leisse had raised security objections even to early drafts of the input–output proposal.[27] Secrecy was a concomitant of high political status in the Third Reich. Furthermore, relations between Bramstedt's Department for economic statistics and Leisse's industrial statisticians worsened steadily during 1936 and 1937.[28] Leisse's increasingly open demands for a monopoly of control over industrial statistics infringed the wider prerogatives of Bramstedt's Department. And there was more at stake than merely personal pique.

Leisse challenged the very idea of 'statistics' as a unified field of knowledge, the fundamental assumption behind the administrative centralization of German statistics.[29] In his view, the idea of a generalist statistician belonged to the nineteenth century. Industrial statistics required above all a detailed knowledge of German industry. The days of the cumbersome, overcentralized Statistical Office were numbered. It was hampered by its enormous size, its gigantic overheads and lack of specialist staff. In future, smaller specialist statistical agencies modelled on the RwP would take charge of each particular area of statistics, enabling them to work in close collaboration with the relevant planning agencies. By contrast, Bramstedt fought to uphold the totalizing approach of Konjunkturforschung.[30] It was possible to understand the economy only if each specialist area, such as industrial statistics, was integrated within a wider macroeconomic overview. To achieve this integration, administrative centralization was essential. The political

---

[27] BAP 31.02 2705 no. 38, SRA Abt VI to Leisse 6.2.1936.
[28] BAP 31.02 3572.
[29] Leisse summarized his views in MA 1458 35/18 no. 1 RwP, 'Denkschrift zur Neugestaltung des Statistischen Dienstes insbesondere im gewerblichen Sektor', May 1940.
[30] See BAP 62 DAF 3 17007 no. 86, Dr P. Bramstedt, 'Statistik in Bewegung', *Die Deutsche Volkswirtschaft*, 22 1.8.1938.

Table 7. *Staff levels at the Statistical Office (SRA) and the RwP,*
1937–1939

Year	Permanent staff		Temporary staff	
	SRA	RwP	SRA	RwP
1937	2,975		1,303	
1938	3,191	518	902	322
1939	3,689	592	1,598	215

Notes: Permanent staff includes civil servants, civil servants on secondment, permanent clerical staff and permanent manual workers whose salaries were included in the establishment.
Temporary staff includes all staff financed by extraordinary budget items. Figures for temporary staff in 1937 and 1938 are actual staff levels on 1 October. For 1939, only budgeted temporary staff figures are available.

Sources: 1937 and 1938: BAP 23.01 2225, 'Haushalt des RWM, Rechnungsjahr 1938'. 1939: BAP 31.01 8754, 'Haushalt des RWM, 1939' (July 1939).

Table 8. *Staff ratios at the Statistical Office (SRA) and the RwP,*
1937–1939

Year	Senior staff		Permanent staff		Ratio of senior to other permanent staff	
	SRA	RwP	SRA	RwP	SRA	RwP
1937	68		2,975		42.8	
1938	60	14	3,191	518	52.2	36.0
1939	66	14	3,689	592	54.9	41.3

Notes: Senior staff includes officials ranked as 'Referenten' and 'Direktoren' of the Office, civil service salary grades A1a to A2c2. The vast majority of these officials had PhDs. Permanent staff, see notes to table 7.

Sources: See table 7.

success of Leisse's RwP was a defeat for the integrative ambition exemplified by the input–output diagram.

Given the abandonment of the input–output option were there other technical solutions open to Leisse? One possible solution was to limit the calculative problem by starting at its source. The aim of the RwP's plans was not to regulate the civilian economy for its own sake. The aim was to organize the economy so that it could maintain civilian life at a minimum level while satisfying the demands of the military. Rather than attempting to plan the entire manufacturing sector in detail, the RwP might therefore have focused on military equipment. Weapons systems were among the most complex products of German industry. They were made up of a wide range of exotic raw materials, masses of generic items such as bolts and screws and highly specialized sub-components, such as radios, which were themselves highly complex. Weapons systems, however, were at least relatively limited in number. Detailed planning could thus focus on the industrial suppliers to the military. The bulk of the civilian economy could be mapped out more schematically. Calculating the sum of military demands on the economy seemed at least in principle to be a simple matter. It involved adding up the inputs required to make each tank, aeroplane and piece of artillery. These coefficients could then be used to calculate an overall armaments plan. The material requirements for each weapon could, it was hoped, be obtained from the engineering blue prints modified by experience on the shopfloor of the armaments firms. In any case, this was clearly a job for the military themselves.

The military–economic organization did make an effort to calculate its requirements.[31] However, by 1938 the rearmament programme of Nazi Germany was in increasing disarray. It was fundamentally unclear what kind of war the Wehrmacht would be expected to fight. Hitler's priorities shifted back and forth between the army, the navy and the airforce. Furthermore, even if there had been an agreement on the types and quantities of equipment required, the next stage in the planning process had run into trouble. The idea that the quantities of raw materials contained in each item of equipment could simply be read off the blue prints turned out to be naïve. The blue prints themselves were astonishingly numerous and there was no standardized system for referring to the materials and components listed in the diagrams. To their horror, the military discovered that opinions differed as to the technical definition of basic materials such as stainless steel. Furthermore, each complex sub-component was a 'black box', the contents of which was unknown to the armaments manufacturers who simply bolted them into their final assemblies. The military were not able even to provide a broad-brush estimate of their raw material requirement until April 1939.[32] In the meantime Leisse's planning office was left in suspense, unable to begin the planning process for lack of basic parameters. The military were unable to state their needs precisely. Furthermore, given the uncertainty of the strategic situation, Leisse's staff did not know what assumptions to make about the availability of imports and the likely level of raw material stocks when war broke out.

Of course, the RwP might have insulated itself from these uncertainties by calculating a variety of plans, each contingent on a different set of

---

[31] An attempt was made to create a mechanized system of raw materials rationing, see BAMA RW 19/1343 and 19/1348.
[32] Müller, 'Die Mobilisierung', p. 359.

assumptions. But this would have required a tight focus on crucial bottlenecks. Instead, the RwP committed itself to planning at an extra-ordinary level of detail. The input–output schema had broken down the German economy into 38 sectors. Soviet planners in 1934 were com-piling balances for 105 commodities. During World War II, Albert Speer's staff were to discover that only a dozen raw materials, plus labour, transport capacity and energy imposed real constraints on the German economy.[33] Leisse's RwP attempted to compile material bal-ances for no less than 384 separate raw materials and to build mobiliza-tion plans on the same basis! Given the RwP's staff of only 500, this was ridiculously overambitious, and it made it impossible to calculate a variety of contingency plans.

War was increasingly imminent and the RwP was making no progress on its central task. Instead, as the weeks ticked away in the first half of 1939, the resources of Leisse's office were squandered. The RwP's monthly progress reports read like a catalogue of wasted administrative energy.[34] By January 1939, the RwP had made progress in planning the allocation of iron, which had long been subject to rationing. However, Leisse complained that general guidelines had not been provided either by the military or Goering's organization. The report for March 1939 pointed out the utter futility of preparing detailed plans for items such as candles, when neither the actual quantity required, nor the availability of raw materials such as paraffin, had been determined. A month later, Leisse was complaining about a new distraction. His staff were now occupied with the fraught process of deciding which plants would be eligible for inclusion in the mobilization plans. To Leisse, this detailed paperwork seemed pointless, given the lack of a plan. However, for German industrialists the issue was of capital importance. The business community had been unsettled by the news that plants in the German border regions would be ineligible for mobilization contracts. Unwilling to make enemies, Funk promptly ordered a general review of the classification of all German firms. He thereby plunged the RwP into long-winded negotiations over the status of literally thousands of indi-vidual plants. In each case, the business organizations, rationing agen-cies and local interests demanded to be heard. Yet again, the naïve vision of control peddled by Leisse and his industrial statisticians was exposed. Since 1934 they had promised to deliver the magic combination of both comprehensive oversight and individualized control. Registered in giant databanks, Germany's industrial plants would be subordinated at will to the technical and strategic criteria of the planners. This fantasy could be

[33] See chapter 7.
[34] BAP 31.02 6231.

sustained as long as the RwP was merely compiling statistics. But as soon as its practical consequences became clear, German business rebelled against this process of abstraction. The firms neatly recorded in the filing cards came alive, appearing in the office of the Minister represented by vociferous lobbyists. Not surprisingly, Funk handed responsibility for settling the individual cases back to the planners. The simple paper world inhabited by the RwP was torn apart. Leisse and his ilk hungered after total control. It was only through hard experience that they were to learn the virtues of aggregation and insulation from the minutiae of administrative decision-making.

Bogged down in a mass of detail the RwP made little progress before September 1939. Germany went to war without mobilization plans for essential raw materials.[35] After six years of concerted preparation, the industrial statisticians of Nazi Germany had failed. Politics undoubtedly contributed to this. Hitler's drive to war in the late 1930s was at root an irrational gamble; it was not underpinned by a coherent assessment of Germany's economic potential. A system for rational planning presupposed a clarity of purpose that the leadership of the Third Reich did not possess. In a different political situation, a machinery of economic planning might in fact have been used as a political weapon to impose hard choices on an unwilling leadership. But, Goering, to whom Leisse and the RwP owed their rise, was not the man to take on this task. Clear priorities never emerged and the embarrassment of having a planning office with nothing to plan was resolved by diverting Leisse into lesser administrative tasks. However, there is more to the failure of planning in Nazi Germany than is suggested by this conventional political narrative. The failure of planning is not reducible to a failure of politics. Even if the political system had provided Leisse with clear priorities, it is far from obvious that he had the technical equipment to do the job. Planning a complex manufacturing economy turned out to be far more difficult in detail than anyone had anticipated. Though the resources at the disposal of German official statisticians were considerable, they were inadequate to the task. And the problems were compounded by the choice of technique. The RwP's exclusive reliance on the method of physical balances prejudiced the entire effort. This choice was no doubt conditioned by the preconception, inherited from World War I, that raw materials were the key to the industrial war effort. But it was also motivated by a fantasy of complete and direct control of the economy. In practice, it proved to be unworkable. It could not be applied to

[35] A. Schröter and J. Bach, 'Zur Planung der wirtschaftlichen Mobilmachung durch den deutschen faschistischen Imperialismus vor dem Beginn des zweiten Weltkrieges', Jahrbuch für Wirtschaftsgeschichte (1978), 1, pp. 31–47.

complex manufactures; it stretched the resources of the statistical system to their limit and maximized the need for cooperation with the military. The input–output method, using monetary values to produce an aggregate overview of the economy, was far less demanding in every respect. However, the input–output model was let drop in 1937. This was a crucial decision. The input–output table was the only technology that offered a realistic prospect of truly comprehensive economic planning, but its realization depended on maintaining a high degree of intellectual and organizational coherence within the statistical apparatus itself. The conditions for this kind of comprehensive national economic accounting had been created by Wagemann in the 1920s and they were sustained into the early years of the Third Reich. However, after 1936 the statistical establishment tore itself apart. Leisse's success in hitching the industrial census to the rising star of Goering secured a place for statistics at the centre of Nazi politics. But, by breaking up the Statistical Office and by narrowing the approach to one of overdetailed, physical planning, Leisse made it impossible to actually realize the dream of comprehensive economic control. Political and technological choices were thus inseparably interwoven, and this was to become even clearer in 1939.

IV

Did the RwP provide a solution to the information needs of the Third Reich? Clearly, there was room for doubt. By the autumn of 1939, the results of Leisse's efforts were extremely modest. A third, improved census of industrial production was in the works. This promised to provide an unrivalled overview of the transformation of the German industrial economy since 1936. However, as we have seen, the practical yield from the previous censuses had been small. Meanwhile, German business continued to groan under an ever-increasing burden of paperwork. And the competition between the RwP and the Statistical Office now threatened to make things worse. In 1937 the public clamour against statistical paperwork mounted in a slow crescendo. The *Deutsche Allgemeine Zeitung* diagnosed an outbreak of 'statistical hysteria', a condition common among underemployed bureaucrats.[36] Firms complained of receiving absurd numbers of questionnaires. Others were asked to fill out the same questionnaire by different agencies or multiple copies of an identical questionnaire by a single planning agency.[37]

[36] BAP 62 DAF 3 17006 no. 1, *Deutsche Allgemeine Zeitung* 564, 3.12.1937 'Zuviel Statistik?'.
[37] For examples see BAP 31.02 3568.

Resentment at petty-fogging bureaucracy was a growing source of dissatisfaction with the regime at all levels, prompting Goering himself to step into the ring. On 13 February 1939 the Reichsmarschall issued the Decree for the Simplification of Economic Statistics.[38] To solve the problem of excess paperwork, this decree established a so-called Central Statistical Committee (Statistischer Zentralausschuss, SZa). The Committee's task was, first, to establish who was asking what of whom in the German economy. Then it was to rationalize the necessary surveys and to weed out all those that were redundant. In future, new surveys would require the authorization of the Committee. Firms were entitled to ignore questionnaires without its stamp of approval. Unauthorized statistical surveys were punishable by fines.

The Decree seemed to herald a new era of centralization. As the second man in the Reich, Goering had the clout that Schacht had lacked in 1935. He could ride roughshod over the particular interests of other agencies and impose centralized discipline. And at first, it appeared that the Statistical Office might be the chief beneficiary. The Statistical Committee was dependent on the Office for its administrative staff and it was to the President of the Statistical Office that applications for permission to carry out surveys were formally addressed. President Reichardt, writing shortly after the Decree was published, expressed the hope that the Committee would rein in the proliferating 'rationing statistics' and restore the authority of the official statistics.[39]

Reichardt, however, could hardly have been further from the mark. Beneath the innocuous administrative exterior of the Central Statistical Committee lurked a radical technical and ideological project. Far from strengthening the Statistical Office, the Committee aimed to bring about a revolution in government data-gathering, transcending the limitations of conventional official statistics. The signature on the Decree was Goering's, but the driving force behind the Committee was Dr Walter Grävell, another of the Statistical Office's restless departmental Directors.[40] As we have seen, Grävell's career in the statistical service began in the early 1920s. An ambitious and difficult individual, Grävell had been despatched in the early 1920s to the Reichschancellory and from there to a series of temporary positions until returning to the Statistical Office in 1930 as Director for trade statistics. During the Depression, Grävell had seconded Wagemann's Plan for 'credit reform' and used his position in the Office to advocate autarchic trade policies.[41]

[38] *RGBl* (1939), 1, p. 389.
[39] Reichardt, 'Die Reichsstatistik', pp. 88–90.
[40] For Grävell's biography see *ASA*, 40 (1956), p. 176.
[41] E. Teichert, *Autarkie und Großraumwirtschaft in Deutschland 1930–1939*.

Nevertheless, during the hearings of 1933, he was one of Wagemann's most outspoken critics. In matters of statistical organization, Walter Grävell had always been something of a visionary. In the aftermath of the census débâcle of the early 1920s, he had concluded that the censuses would have to be replaced by sampling and estimation. In the early 1930s, when in charge of trade statistics, he had developed the vision of an integrated public–private information system that would replace customs declarations with monthly reports from the main importing and exporting firms. National accounts were thus to be fused with private bookkeeping.[42] In the late 1930s, Grävell began to exploit his connections in the Reichschancellory to lobby for a fundamental reorganization of the statistical system.[43] His long-standing hostility to the traditional techniques of official statistics now fused with a new ideological radicalism.

According to Grävell, piecemeal reform was not enough. The litany of complaint about excessive paperwork indicated a more basic failure. The existing system of official statistics was fundamentally unsuited to the demands of the Nazi Volksgemeinschaft.[44] In effect, Grävell inverted Reichardt's liberal analysis of the problems of German official statistics. Like Reichardt, Grävell believed that the Third Reich constituted a major break with the old order.[45] Like Reichardt, he associated official statistics as they had developed in the nineteenth century with 'liberalism'. Liberal restraint circumscribed the limited repertoire of statistical enquiries. The liberal distinction between 'the state' and 'civil society' was deeply inscribed in the basic practices of official statistics. The privileged position which official statisticians claimed for their knowledge mirrored the exalted position attributed to the nineteenth-century state, standing above the mêlée of civil society. Furthermore, the

Außenwirtschaftliche Konzeptionen zwischen Wirtschaftskrise und Zweitem Weltkrieg (Munich, 1984), p. 88.

[42] W. Grävell, 'Statistische Abgabe und Anmeldung zur Handelsstatistik', *ASA*, 22 (1932/1933), pp. 69–80.

[43] BAP 07.01 FC 19853/591 no. 32, Grävell to Reichskanzlei (Reichskabinettsrat Willuhn) 17.3.1938.

[44] 'Die Stellung der Statistik im nationalsozialistischen Staat', *Braune Wirtschaftspost* 7 12.3.1938.

[45] The following summary of Grävell's thinking is based on his writings between 1938 and 1941, including: 'Die Stellung der Statistik im nationalsozialistischen Staat', *Braune Wirtschaftspost* 7 12.3.1938; BAK 11 51 Fol. 1 no. 79, 'Niederschrift über die Sitzung des Ausschusses für Wirtschaftsstatistik des RwK am 17 November 1938'; MA 1458 35/13, 'Aufzeichnung über die Massnahmen, die zur Anpassung des statistischen Dienstes . . .', Grävell to Ilgner 2.10.1941; MA 1458 Fb 35/15, 'Organisation des statistischen Dienstes' (undated, probably October 1941); BAK 11 68 Fol. 1 RwK, 'Zur Frage der Ordnung des statistischen Dienstes' (confidential memo sent by Grävell to Hickmann/RwK 18.11.1941); W. Grävell, 'Die Vereinfachung und Vereinheitlichung der Wirtschaftsstatistik', *ASA*, 30 (1941/1942) pp. 57–75.

constraining rules of anonymity and confidentiality, which governed the ways in which statistical returns might be exploited, implied the recognition by 'the state' of the legitimate self-interest of private individuals. Reichardt, of course, cherished these principles as the only basis for 'scientific' statistics in a civilized society. For Grävell, this was mere nostalgia.

In the 1930s, Nazi lawyers and political theorists developed a radical critique of conventional, 'liberal' views of the state.[46] In particular, they objected to the reified, nineteenth-century distinction between state and civil society. Inspired by Hitler's own writing, Nazi theorists criticized the false dichotomy that conferred a fetishized authority upon the state.[47] The state was not an end in itself. It was no more than a means to an end, namely the welfare of the German race. Of course, they did not mean by this the liberation of civil society as a multitude of self-interested individuals. The Nazi ideal of the Volk was that of a sternly disciplined 'racial community' (Volksgemeinschaft) united under the personal leadership of the Führer. The 'natural' hierarchy of 'Führer' and 'Volk' was the only acceptable organization of political power. The state was thus displaced as the central representative institution of national society. The civil service, the estate that in the nineteenth century had been acknowledged as leaders of the German nation, was dethroned.

Grävell applied this critique to the organization of German economic statistics. The Third Reich had overturned the ideology of the free market. The ideal of the Volksgemeinschaft was realized in the regime's control of economic activity. Individual firms and workers were directed according to the will of the Führer. The function of statisticians was to serve this new economic system. Their job was to provide a comprehensive system of day-to-day surveillance. For this purpose, slow-moving periodic surveys and cumbersome censuses were useless. The planners needed immediate information on individual economic agents and to satisfy this need what was required was a system of interlocking databases. These would cover every single firm and every worker in the economy. In effect, there would need to be only one single, seamless database, a paper replica of the economy, constantly up-dated and available for consultation by any authorized agency, at any time. To obtain an overview of the national economy, all that would be needed

---

[46] E.-W. Böckenförde (ed.), *Staatsrecht und Staatsrechtslehre im Dritten Reich* (Heidelberg, 1985); M. Stolleis, *Gemeinwohlformeln im nationalsozialistischen Recht* (Berlin, 1974); M. Stolleis, 'Gemeinschaft und Volksgemeinschaft. Zur juristischen Terminologie im Nationalsozialismus', *Vierteljahrshefte für Zeitgeschichte*, 20 (1972), pp. 16–38.

[47] R. Zitelmann, *Hitler. Selbstverständnis eines Revolutionärs* (Stuttgart, 1990, 2nd edn.), pp. 64–69.

would be to sift through the database. As the experience of the RwP had demonstrated, such gigantic registers of information could not be centrally administered in an efficient manner. To be kept up to date and immediately available they needed to be managed by decentralized agencies. Duplication of entries would be avoided by obligating each database-centre to provide information to all authorized planning agencies. And this was no mere fantasy. The power of such administrative systems had been demonstrated in practice by the Reich's labour administration with its system of 'Work Books'.[48]

The Work Books had first been issued in 1935 on the initiative of the military, who were in the process of reintroducing conscription.[49] All Germans employed under private employment contracts were required to register a Work Book with their employer. A copy of this Book was held by the Labour Administration, which thereby acquired a comprehensive database of the employed population. The books contained information on age, marital status, occupational history and training.[50] By the late 1930s, compulsory Work Books were introduced for the entire economically active population. The result was a database of awesome capacity. In the summer of 1938 a survey of more than 22 million workers was carried out simply by sifting through the card files held by the Reich's Labour Administration. Since the entire operation was internal to the labour administration, and did not involve issuing questionnaires to the public, the survey was completed with unprecedented speed. Regional and national figures classified by sex, age and 200 occupational categories were compiled in the space of only five weeks.[51]

In Reichardt's terms, Grävell's project meant the abolition of official statistics as a separate branch of the state administration, or as a branch of knowledge endowed with a particular authority. Statisticians working at the centre of the database system would retain their function as providers of numerical overviews. But, since their data would be drawn from the common databases administered by the planning agencies, the 'official statisticians' would no longer be able to claim a special authority for their results. Whilst Reichardt viewed this prospect with dismay,

[48] H. Kahrs, 'Die ordnende hand der arbeitsämter. Zur deutschen Arbeitsverwaltung 1933 bis 1939', in *Arbeitsmarkt und Sondererlass. Menschenverwertung, Rassenpolitik und Arbeitsamt* (Berlin, 1990), pp. 9–61.

[49] T.W. Mason, *Sozialpolitik im Dritten Reich. Arbeiterklasse und Volksgemeinschaft* (Opladen, 1977, 2nd edn.), p. 162.

[50] R. von Valta, 'Das Arbeitsbuch in der Statistik', *ASA*, 27 (1937/1938), pp. 263–273.

[51] R. von Valta, 'Die Statistik des Arbeitseinsatzes', in *Die Statistik in Deutschland nach ihrem heutigen stand. Ehrengabe für Friedrich Zahn*, ed. F. Burgdörfer (Berlin, 1940), 2, pp. 663–675 and R. von Valta, 'Die erste Arbeitsbucherhebung vom 25. Juni 1938', *ASA*, 28 (1939), pp. 401–421.

Grävell looked forward to the day when the distinction between centralized 'official' data and decentralized 'unofficial' data would be abolished altogether. Grävell's system also, of course, had implications for civil society. Germany's business men would be protected against arbitrary surveys. In future, they would be required only to make regular reports to the database-centres, which would serve as intermediaries between the economy and the planning agencies. Businesses would thus be relieved of much paperwork. Similarly, however, they would be exposed to comprehensive observation and control by the planning agencies acting through the database-centres. There would be an 'official statistician' in every office, the product of systematic training in a new National Academy of Statistics. Rules of anonymity and confidentiality made no sense in such a system. Firms could no longer expect their returns to the Statistical Office, the raw material control agency and the tax office to be treated separately and in isolation. Grävell acknowledged that this infringement of 'privacy' might tempt firms to falsify their reports. However, he argued, that the comprehensive system of economic regulations in the Third Reich would make fraud easy to detect. And, in any case, Grävell had convinced himself that in the 'Volksgemeinschaft' such self-interested behaviour would be the exception, not the rule. In truth, German business did not object to Grävell's scheme.[52] The overriding priority of the Reich's Group Industry was to obtain a reduction in rogue surveys. By 1939 anonymity and confidentiality counted for little. If one planning agency was denied access to information by another, it could simply demand the information for itself. There was no escaping the net of enquiries. Grävell's Committee would at least ensure that the paperwork was kept to a minimum.

It is worth pausing to consider the departure constituted by Grävell's initiative. Both Leisse and Grävell were seeking to profit from the increasing radicalization of the Nazi regime. Leisse saw the increasing incoherence of the statistical system as a signal for the division of the Statistical Office into separate, specialist statistical agencies. By contrast, Grävell saw the disintegration of the existing structure of the state as indicative of a far deeper problem in the relationship between state and civil society. He addressed directly one of the central themes of this book, the interdependence between technical ideas about the organization of governmental knowledge and assumptions about political organization. Grävell chose to phrase this in terms of Nazi ideology, but this was a problem that had preoccupied German statisticians at least since World War I. The war had profoundly destabilized the German state and

---

[52] BAK R 11/51 no. 36, note about meeting of the RwK Cttee for Economic Statistics 2.6.1939. For individual cases see MA 1458 35/64 and 35/75.

with it assumptions about the proper scope and organization of official economic knowledge. Grävell was surely right to dismiss the conception of the state that Reichardt so desperately invoked as an entity counter-posed to and superordinate to civil society. In the Wilhelmine era, this fiction had been maintained only by the limitation of official enquiries. In the 1920s, official statisticians had had to learn how to negotiate with private interests over access to information. This had been the practice of Konjunkturforschung. But it was also in this context that Grävell had first hatched his plans for an integrated system of trade statistics. In the early years of Hitler's regime it was possible to imagine that the National Revolution would usher in a phase of authoritarian statism in Germany. The Statistical Office would oversee a centralized system of information solidly based on the compulsory Business Groups. The Nazis' 'second seizure of power' undid this statist fantasy. What became clear in the late 1930s was that Nazism was not simply a variant of authoritarian conservatism. Its unfettered drive towards power, in fact, posed a profound challenge not only to the existing state apparatus but also to the ideology of the 'strong state' as such. The state was to serve the Volksgemeinschaft and it was the Führer who would command. For Reichardt, the radicalization of the regime was nothing short of disaster. For Grävell, by contrast, it offered the opportunity to release the practice of statistics from the fetters of liberalism.

Grävell was thus able to recast his long-standing plan for an integrated system of economic information. In other respects as well, Grävell harked back to the early 1920s. Grävell's entire system of surveillance rested on the firm. Like the reformers of the early 1920s, Grävell rejected the abstract 'technical production unit', as the fundamental unit of industrial statistics. The firm, not the workshop, was the basic building block of the modern economy. Grävell's aim was to build an effective system of practical surveillance and control. This had to rest on the managerial organization of the modern firm, which was capable both of providing an up-to-date supply of information and of taking orders from the centre. The economy would thus be pictured in Grävell's databases not as an abstract system of circulation but as a population of firms. Economic government conceived in these terms was an elaborate exercise in management, the aim being to regulate the inputs and outputs of the most important businesses. The necessary aggregative information, Grävell believed, could be obtained simply by adding together the facts about all the nation's firms, contained in the national system of databases. There was no room in his conception of the planning for economic categories independent of those in use in businesses themselves, no provision for specialized surveys to satisfy the needs of economists, indeed no economics as such. The statisticians' role was essentially technical. Their task was to organize a streamlined system of surveillance, maximizing the volume of available information, whilst minimizing the cost of data-gathering.

V

Not surprisingly, the impact of Grävell's Central Statistical Committee on the information system of the Third Reich was deeply ambiguous. The Central Statistical Committee went into operation in the spring of 1939 and set about making a ruthless triage of 'unnecessary' surveys. The sheer size of the problem facing the Central Statistical Committee was daunting. The Committee started by compiling statistics of statistics. From the applications received by the Committee, it appears that there were at least 1,600 regular statistical surveys in progress in the non-agricultural economy in April 1939.[53] In the first nine months of its existence between February and October 1939 Grävell's Committee received 852 applications. By April 1940, 12 months after the Committee had begun its work, this figure had risen to 1,195. This mountain of paperwork overwhelmed the Committee's small staff. By October 1939, the Committee had managed to process only 322 applications.[54] Surveys for which authorization was pending were left in limbo, awaiting a final decision from the Committee. Grävell's problems worsened at the outbreak of war, when the Committee lost half its staff to military recruitment.[55] In its first year of operation, the Committee managed to wade through 604 applications. It rejected 135, accepted 194 and gave conditional authorization to 237;[56] 32 unsanctioned surveys that came to the attention of the Committee were banned.[57] At this rate, it would have taken almost three years to review the entire statistical system. Nevertheless, there is no denying the Committee's impact on the administrative undergrowth of the Third Reich. Of the periodic surveys in operation in the spring of 1939, 450 (28 per cent) had been stopped by October 1943. The other 1,150 were authorized, in some cases only after substantial simplification.[58] The Committee thus brought signifi-

[53] Gädicke, 'Kriegswichtige Statistik', *National Zeitung* 174 10.10.1943.
[54] MA 1458 35/1 no. 114, 'Bericht über die Tätigkeit und Erfahrungen des Statistischen Zentralausschusses', undated but probably late October 1939.
[55] BAP 31.02 2945 no. 11, SZa to Präs. SRA 1.11.1939.
[56] BAP 62 DAF 3 17006 no. 48, 'Ein Jahr SZa', *Deutsche Wirtschaftszeitung* 17 25.4.1940.
[57] BAK R 7/1266 Fol. 1 no. 46 W. Grävell, 'Ordnung in der Wirtschaftstatistik. Ein Jahr SZa', *Vierjahresplan* 20.4.1940.
[58] BAP 62 DAF 3 8828 no. 36, 'Wirtschaftsstatistische Erhebungen nur mit Genehmigung des SZa', *Deutscher Handelsdienst* 8.7.1943.

cant relief to Germany's harassed businessmen and restricted the proliferation of form-filling and paperwork that normally accompanied the
outbreak of war.

But Grävell's aspirations did not stop at administrative pruning. He
foresaw the creation of an entirely new statistical system in which
cumbersome centralized censuses would be replaced by decentralized
surveys and interlocking databases. A major step in this direction was
taken in 1938–9 with the transfer of the monthly Industrial Reports to
Reich's Group Industry. As we have seen, the system of Industrial
Reports had been dramatically extended after the seizure of power. By
1938 the monthly reports covered some 60 per cent of German industrial workers. Now, Bramstedt aimed to make the Reports into the
definitive statistics of German industry, by expanding their coverage to
embrace 90 per cent of the workforce. No less than 80,000 firms were to
be enrolled in the monthly reports. This gigantic expansion implied a
new role for the Reports. They had started life as a cyclical indicator
system. After 1933, they had become a tool of control in the hands of
the compulsory Business Groups. Now, the expanded system of
monthly reports was to form a cornerstone of Grävell's new database
system. The reports were to update a decentralized system of card files
administered by the Business Groups themselves. The monthly reports
would update the files held on each firm by the Business Groups. When
handling data on this scale, decentralization was a technical necessity.
Bramstedt's Department was at full stretch coping with 16,000 monthly
reports. To deal with 80,000 reports would have required an enormous
expansion in staff. Instead, the Business Groups themselves would take
full responsibility for distributing, collecting and processing the monthly
questionnaires. Reich's Group Industry would provide Hollerith capacity to any Business Group that needed it. The Statistical Office would
coordinate the decentralized process and compile the national results.[59]

The organizations of German industry would thus be provided with a
truly comprehensive and up-to-date database. They would no longer
have to wait for the results to filter down from the Statistical Office.
Instead, the results would accumulate upwards. The official statisticians,
for their part, gained an unprecedented extension of coverage. The
Industrial Reporting System was probably the largest system of its kind
in the world. Never before had so many firms made such frequent and
detailed reports. Only the smallest firms were now beyond the statisticians' reach. However, at the same time the Statistical Office was
preparing to put its official imprimatur on a system over which it exerted

---

[59] BBA 15 433, RgI to Wg Bergbau 3.8.1938 and RgI to Wg Bergbau 28.9.1938.

only indirect control. This was the logic of Grävell's grand design. And it provoked anxieties at statistical headquarters. Bramstedt was emphatic that decentralization should not be interpreted as a licence for indiscipline. Any deviation from the standard questionnaire would cast into doubt the value of the entire survey. As Bramstedt emphasized in his final meeting with the Reich's Group, he was a 'fanatic for aggregation'. He would not shrink from coercive measures to defend the integrity of the system. The limits of liberalism had been reached. If surveillance was to be extended into the finest capillaries of the economy, the Statistical Office would not be able to preserve its neutral distance from civil society. It had to base itself directly on the resources of the compulsory business organizations, and if necessary it, too, had to resort to coercion. By the end of 1939 the target had been reached. Close to 80,000 firms, employing 93 per cent of the German industrial work force were making monthly returns to their Business Groups.[60]

Grävell's vision demanded more than decentralization. It also implied the need for cooperation across the information-gathering system. A system of decentralized databases made sense only if the organizations in charge of maintaining the databases were willing to provide access to all comers. This was one of the most radical features of Grävell's design. It broke fundamentally with the principle of confidentiality, which had traditionally debarred official statisticians from divulging information about individual respondents even to other governmental agencies.[61] By contrast with these rules of self-restraint Grävell envisioned a unified surveillance apparatus in which information about individual citizens circulated freely, maximizing the coercive power of government. In practice, however, it soon emerged that Grävell's vision ignored important political realities. The barriers of confidentiality that screened different arms of the state apparatus from one another reflected more than squeamish statistical sensibilities. The barriers demarcated the boundaries of bureaucratic empires. Planning agencies jealously guarded information about their 'client' firms and opposed any suggestion from the Central Statistical Committee that they should share access to their records.[62] Given the patchy archival record, there is no way of knowing the full extent of data-sharing achieved by the Central Statistical Committee. The records we do have suggest that it had only

[60] E. Gierth, 'Aufbau und Methode der Industrieberichterstattung', *ASA*, 30 (1941/ 1942), pp. 298–299.
[61] The issue was discussed at the meeting of the SZa in June 1939 see MA 1458 35/1 no. 96, SZa meeting 27.6.1939.
[62] BAK R 7/1266–1270 document a three-cornered struggle between the Mining Department of the RWM, the Labour Front and Grävell's Committee over access to the questionnaires of mining firms.

limited success.[63] By August 1941, after having reviewed over 1,000 statistical surveys, the Committee had imposed cooperation in only a dozen comparatively minor cases. Clearly, the feasible scope for data-sharing was much more limited than Grävell had envisioned.

Grävell's decisive intervention was in fact negative. In the summer of 1939, Leisse's RwP applied to the Central Statistical Committee for permission to carry out the next industrial census. There ensued a bureaucratic struggle that was to decide the future of economic statistics in the Third Reich. As usual, there was office politics at stake. Grävell regarded the independent RwP as incompatible with his integrated view of the statistical system. Leisse for his part objected to Grävell's peremptory claim to total authority in the field of economic statistics. Grävell might have the signature of Goering, but the RwP could invoke the authority of the General Plenipotentiary. As usual, however, in disputes between the statisticians the issues were technical as well as political. Leisse's census threatened to make a mockery of Grävell's grand design. The censuses of industrial production stood squarely in the tradition of nineteenth-century official statistics, the tradition that Grävell had declared obsolete.[64] The censuses were designed to serve the needs of central government not local agencies of control. They were rigidly centralized. They were driven by an overriding concern to impose a single conceptual scheme on the entire industrial economy. Individualized information was produced merely as a by-product and was made available only from a single, slow-moving, centralized agency. The attempt to make the RwP responsible for the mobilization planning of individual firms had proved a non-starter. For Grävell, the RwP exemplified all the failings inherent in classical official statistics. The complex questionnaires of the census imposed a major burden on Germany's industrial firms. And they overlapped with a large number of regular administrative surveys, such as those of the Supervisory Agencies, the Business Groups and the Reich's Food Estate (Reichsnährstand). At the end of this laborious process, the aggregate results emerged after a delay of months if not years. And the RwP had proved itself incapable of efficiently handling the database it had collected. Not surprisingly, the RwP's application to the Central Statistical Committee became a test case.

The conflict between the Central Statistical Committee and the RwP began as a matter of administrative details. The Statistical Committee

[63] BAK R 7/1270 Fol. 1 no. 167, 'Übersicht über die Genehmigungsbescheide des SZa' August 1941.
[64] BAP 31.02 3090 no. 65 RwP, 'Verf. Vorbereitung der Generalerhebung 1939' 20.5.1939.

refused Leisse's application for a general warrant.[65] Instead, the RwP was forced to submit separately each of the hundreds of specially tailored industrial questionnaires that made up the census.[66] By the summer of 1939, this administrative argument had developed into a full-scale battle over the future of the German statistical system, in which the Committee and the RwP figured themselves as fundamentally opposed alternatives. As literally dozens of census questionnaires passed the muster of the Central Statistical Committee, points of administrative detail were translated into matters of principle. Did the future lie in ever-more sophisticated, centralized censuses or in the creation of a network of decentralized, continuously updated databases? Grävell called into question the very existence of the RwP. In his view production statistics were no longer an independent element of economic statistics. 'They must be integrated into a total system of economic statistics.'[67] The RwP's style of large-scale centralized surveys was obsolete:

Today, at least a dozen interest groups, e.g. the Regional Economics Offices, the Business Groups with their substructures, the Technical Offices of the Labour Front, the Armaments Inspectorates, etc. require statistical material on individual firms. This must be kept up-to-date at all times and must be accessible immediately. It is impossible to meet these statistical demands through large-scale, once-off centralized surveys. Experience shows that it is impossible to supply either the aggregate results, or the individual data of such surveys to the interested parties on time.[68]

The only efficient way of supplying such information needs was through locally managed and continuously updated databases. Against the attacks of Grävell's Committee, Leisse and the RwP defended themselves by arguing that their surveys provided an essential overview of the German economy.[69] A comprehensive survey required an elaborate system of interrelated questionnaires with which one could register the complex interconnections between industries. It was not feasible to replace such a census by a hotchpotch of decentralized surveys. The agencies of planning and control were too preoccupied with particular problems and the data they collected were too unreliable to provide suitable foundations for a strategic overview of the industrial economy.

In this struggle for the future of German statistics, Leisse had the weaker hand. The RwP was at first excluded altogether from the deliberations of Grävell's Central Statistical Committee. It did not

[65] BAP 31.02 3628 no. 21, RwP to Führungsstab GBW 31.3.1939.
[66] BAP 31.01 8916, SZa meeting 21.8.1939.
[67] BAK R 7/1266 Fol. 1 no. 59, SZa to RWM 18.4.1940.
[68] BAK R 7/1266 Fol. 1 no. 59, SZa to RWM 18.4.1940, pp. 1–2.
[69] MA 1458 35/68 no. 48, note 21.8.1939 and BAP 31.01 8916, SZa meeting 21.8.1939.

finally obtain representation on the Committee until the summer of 1939, as one of the last major planning agencies.[70] Leisse was also at a political disadvantage since his Office was formally subordinate to Walter Funk, the weak Minister for Economic Affairs. By comparison, the Central Statistical Committee could claim the personal backing of Goering and the Four-Year Plan.[71] Grävell could also invoke the backing of the Business Groups, which opposed any further increase in the paperwork burden.[72] The outbreak of war in September 1939 exacerbated this problem. The draft resulted in an acute shortage of skilled clerical workers. Businesses struggled to keep their accounts and paperwork up to date and were less than willing to take on the additional work of the census questionnaire. But, what was ultimately to prove decisive was the failure of Leisse's efforts in civilian mobilization planning. Planning provided the *raison d'être* of Leisse's industrial censuses. The 1933 and 1936 censuses were extraordinary technical achievements. If Leisse had managed to realize their practical potential, the preparations for a census in 1939 would no doubt have been invulnerable to Grävell's attacks. However, the RwP had failed to come up with a practical methodology. It was all too easy for Grävell to argue that the third industrial census was a luxury that the Third Reich could not afford.[73]

VI

In the late 1930s, the statistical system of the Third Reich began to self-destruct. The chaotic high politics of the Third Reich formed the essential backdrop for this crisis. However, it is unlikely that the power-play between Goering, Schacht, Funk and the military would by itself have resulted in the complete disintegration of the Reich's apparatus of official statistics. The destructive linkages between politics and statistical technology were knotted by the statisticians themselves. It was their technical disagreements, their rivalry and their opportunism, that actually pulled the Statistical Office apart. The promise of advancement led Leisse to dismember the Statistical Office; and in his desperation to serve the needs of the regime, he discredited what remained of the macroeconomic vision of Konjunkturforschung. The RwP led German economic statistics into a technical dead-end. If the industrial census

[70] MA 1458 35/1 no. 96, SZa meeting 27.6.1939.
[71] BAK R 7/1266 Fol. 1 no. 22, RWM note 19.8.1939, p. 2.
[72] MA 1458 35/54 no. 61–67.
[73] See IWM FD 2691/45 Intelligence report on the SRA 15.5.1945 appendix 5B Langelütke, p. 3.

had been developed along the lines of the input–output table, it is at least conceivable that it might have formed the backbone of an overarching system of economic control. Instead, the census came to stand for a patently unrealistic system of highly centralized and individualized planning. This opened the door to Grävell and his toxic cocktail of technical and ideological radicalism. In the late 1930s, the German State disintegrated from within.

7   World War II and the return of macroeconomics

If this story ended in 1939, it would be an ironic tale of technocratic pretension. The extravagant bureaucratic build-up of the 1930s did not give Nazi Germany an effective information system. Instead, the rival statisticians squabbling for Wagemann's inheritance undercut each other. Konjunkturforschung bequeathed the legacy of the industrial census, but its promise emboldened Leisse to split the Statistical Office and create the Reich's Office for Military–Economic Planning (RwP), a separate bureaucratic fiefdom. Grävell, in turn, in pursuit of his own grand vision, set about dismantling not only the Statistical Office, but Leisse's RwP as well: a technocratic *reductio ad absurdum*. Each programme had its own logic, but none was able to deliver a working information system. And, in any case, it was far from clear whether there was an audience 'out there' in the jungle of Third Reich politics. The would-be technocrats laboured over their questionnaires and surveys, but to what effect?

Extending the narrative into the war years provides an answer to this sceptical question. As this chapter will show, the planning system that helped to make Albert Speer's Armaments Ministry famous was a direct descendant of the macroeconomic accounting schemes drawn up by Ernst Wagemann in 1923. A grand arch of continuity connects the modernist experiments of the 1920s to the planning of World War II. In the 1940s, Wagemann and his Institute returned to the very heart of power, restoring order, realism and intellectual vision to the statistics of the Third Reich. But if this is not a farce, it is not a story with a happy ending either. This is a tragedy. By the 1940s, the fragile structures of the German state were in tatters. Speer and his cohorts treated the Reich's economic administration like scrap in an organizational breaker's yard. Neumann memorably described the political structure of the Third Reich in the 1940s as a non-state.[1] The criteria of power were brutally simple: access to the Führer, control of one or other of the

---

[1] F. Neumann, *Behemoth. The Structure and Practice of National Socialism 1933–1944* (New York, 1944), p. xii.

246

means of violence, command of the means of production. Useful experts could seek a place for themselves among the power blocs. Wagemann and his Institute did well. By 1943, they were the main source of statistical information for the Central Planning Committee of the German war economy. But the final realization of Wagemann's technocratic fantasy came at a high price: a Faustian pact with Hans Kehrl, one of the most ruthless Nazi technocrats to come to the fore in the final years of Hitler's regime.[2] Inspired by a fierce ideological commitment Kehrl drove his staff to develop a radical new model of governance and to explore the very limits of centralized economic planning. Wagemann's Institute became complicit in a vision of coercion undreamed of in the 1920s.

I

The outbreak of war caught German statistics in flux. After years of preparation, Leisse's RwP was still struggling to finish mobilization plans for essential raw materials. In the Central Statistical Committee the battle was raging over the industrial census scheduled for 1939. What decided the issue was the political failure of Leisse's principal backer, Walther Funk. The mission of Leisse's RwP had been to prepare plans for a ruthless mobilization of the civilian economy under the leadership of the GBW. And at the outbreak of war in the autumn of 1939, the GBW's staff promptly began to implement their plans. Wages were cut, price controls enforced, taxes raised and a closure programme begun in civilian trades. But, the merest hint of these measures produced a wave of protests from the small business constituency. Funk might have hoped for support from the organizations of the Nazi Party. But, instead, they channelled local grievances back to Berlin in an amplified form. Hitler and Goebbels, whose support was crucial for any hard-hitting programme, passed the buck back to Funk. Within weeks, the closure programme and the tightening of fiscal policy were reversed. Funk was humiliated, and the ripples spread back downwards through the administrative system. Leisse found himself without political backing, while Grävell, with Goering at the peak of his power, was riding high. The outbreak of war was the perfect excuse to cut short the debate over the industrial census of 1939. The Central Statistical Committee refused to authorize the questionnaires. The RwP was left without purpose, and in June 1940, it was disbanded. Leisse, along with

---

[2] R.-D. Müller, *Der Manager der Kriegswirtschaft. Hans Kehrl: Ein Unternehmer in der Politik des Dritten Reiches* (Essen, 1999).

his remaining staff, were reintegrated into the Statistical Office in their former position as a Department of industrial statistics.[3]

The German economy lurched into the war without central direction.[4] In an ad hoc fashion the military seized ever-larger allocations of steel, metals, oil and labour. Control of the civilian sector was left largely to the decentralized activity of the Business Groups. At the outbreak of war the Supervisory Agencies, which since 1934 had been charged with the distribution of raw materials, were retitled Reich's Agencies and handed over to the relevant industrial groupings. As in World War I, German industry was placed in control of its own raw materials supply. In accordance with Grävell's vision, the Business Groups thus emerged as the commanding centres of industrial statistics, producing the Industrial Reports and overseeing the raw material data of the Reich's Agencies. The former staff of the RwP were restricted to a supervisory role. Rather than designing and carrying out their own surveys, Leisse's industrial statisticians worked at one remove from the raw data. Their task was to assemble monthly overviews from information supplied to them by the Reich's Agencies and the Business Groups.[5] Perhaps not surprisingly, these reports throw an unflattering light on Grävell's decentralized system. The returns from the Reich's Agencies were riddled with inconsistencies. As organizations intimately involved in the raw materials economy, they had difficulty in obtaining reliable reports. Firms underestimated the level of their stocks and overstated their requirements. Furthermore, the Reich's Agencies lacked statistical expertise. In fact, many Reich's Agencies appeared to follow no consistent statistical methodology whatsoever. And the cancellation of the census robbed Leisse's staff of their only means of checking the dubious returns. They were forced to rely on internal consistency, basic plausibility and the experience they had gained from the censuses of 1933 and 1936. On this basis, they questioned whether the Reich's raw material statistics should be supplied to policy-makers at all.[6]

If the data on raw material supplies were doubtful, the data on industrial employment were positively misleading. Paul Bramstedt's Industrial Reporting system appeared to have emerged a winner from

[3] BAP 31.02 3045 no. 21, SRA Präs. order 4.6.1940.
[4] R.-D. Müller, 'Die Mobilisierung der Deutschen Wirtschaft für Hitlers Kriegsführung', in B.R. Kroener, R.-D. Müller and H. Umbreit, *Das Deutsche Reich und der Zweite Weltkrieg* (Stuttgart, 1988), 5, 1, pp. 347–689. Regrettably, the second Halbband of this important volume appeared after the completion of this manuscript, and could not be fully integrated into the text.
[5] MA 1458 35/129, 35/130, 35/131.
[6] MA 1458 35/18 no. 1 RwP, 'Denkschrift' May 1940, p. 7.

the arguments of the late 1930s.[7] Every industrial firm that remained in operation during the war was now required to make a monthly return. And with Funk having delegated so much responsibility to the Business Groups, the surveys did indeed take on a new importance. However, the technical suitability of the Industrial Reports to the task of wartime planning should have been in doubt from the start. The Reports were designed to satisfy the interests of short-term business-cycle observation not detailed physical planning. Employment and sales were not recorded in a way that allowed inputs and outputs to be related in a systematic fashion.[8] Furthermore, the entire system was based on the organizational infrastructure of the Business Groups. The classification of statistical returns thus followed an organizational rather than a technical or an economic logic. Of course, under normal conditions, if a firm's line of business changed so did its membership. This was a frequent cause of organizational disputes. In July 1939 the Reich's Group Industry therefore froze the membership of the Business Groups.[9] At a time of war, there was to be no more bureaucratic squabbling. The consequences for industrial statistics were disastrous. If a firm was manufacturing pianos in the summer of 1939, it remained classified as a piano maker throughout the war, regardless of whether its output now consisted entirely of munitions boxes. As the war dragged on, the monthly figures supplied by Bramstedt's Industrial Reports became increasingly inaccurate. Germany's planners, not to mention historians of Germany's war economy, were never quite sure how far 'conversion' had in fact progressed.[10] The Industrial Reports presented a misleading image of an economy frozen in civilian patterns of production (see table 9).

Because of these problems the Reich's decentralized and fragmented system of industrial statistics added to the general confusion that prevailed in the early war years. One set of figures told an upbeat story. The disastrous fall in industrial output, widely feared at the outbreak of war, had not materialized. Unemployment barely increased. Industrial

---

[7] BAP 31.02 3586 no. 162, RWM 27.9.1939, Vermerk.

[8] For large companies with many lines of production the sales figures were broken down by industrial category. This was not feasible in the case of the monthly employment returns. All the firms' employees were allocated to its 'main' line of business. See the instructions in BBA 15 433 'Richtlinien zur Vorbereitung der Ib', p. 3 and E. Gierth, 'Aufbau und Methode der "Industrieberichterstattung"', *ASA*, 30 (1941/1942), pp. 293–301.

[9] IWM Sp film 20 3046/49 Sc. 323 Fol. 1 no. 134, Gierth, 'Die Zusammensetzung' 4.6.1943.

[10] R. Wagenführ, *Die deutsche Industrie im Kriege 1939–1945* (Berlin, 1963, 2nd edn.), pp. 40–41 and R.J. Overy, *War and Economy in the Third Reich* (Oxford, 1994), p. 28 both note this problem, but give no indication of its scale.

Table 9. *The effects of the 'organization stop' on the Industrial Reports,*
second quarter 1942

| Business Group | % of production within Business Group misallocated between: | | |
	Sub-groups of the same Business Group	Business Groups	Total misallocation
Wood-working	35.5	3.1	38.6
Leather industry	33.3	2.2	35.5
Iron, steel and tin goods	24.0	12.7	36.7
Vehicles ind.	19.8	16.8	36.6
Paper-processing	18.9	9.8	28.7
Electrical ind.	15.4	9.8	25.2
Printing	14.9	11.1	26.0
Clothing industry	8.8	0.8	9.6
Metal goods	8.4	22.8	31.2
Saw industry	8.0	5.9	13.9
Iron and steel	1.5	3.2	4.7
Metal ind.	1.1	9.4	10.5
Brewing	0.3	3.5	3.8

Source: IWM 3046/49 Sc. 323 Fol. 1 134 RgI, 'Die Zusammensetzung der Absatzwerte in der Industrie im zweiten Vierteljahr 1942' 4.6.1943.

output seemed to have remained high. However, the level of weapons output stagnated and in some particularly disappointing cases even declined. The military blamed a lack of resources. They were convinced that civilian industry was hoarding labour and raw materials and this seemed to be borne out by the monthly Industrial Reports from the Business Groups themselves. The number of workers in piano making remained stubbornly high! The representatives of civilian industry could only argue that their own statistics were at fault.[11] They were convinced that a major process of conversion was underway. And they prepared revised statistics, which showed no less than 58 per cent of all industrial workers employed on Wehrmacht work. Production was hampered not by a shortage of resources but by the gross inefficiency of the armaments industry under military supervision.

Whatever the facts of the matter, it was the critics of the military who carried the day. In the spring of 1940, the engineer Fritz Todt was appointed Minister for Munitions to resolve the acute crisis of ammunition supply. Todt applied to ammunition the lessons he had learned on the giant building sites of the Third Reich. The first step to increase

[11] IWM EDS D MI 14/463–II, RWM to OKW 26.11.1940 and IWM EDS D AL 1571, Besprechung 9.1.1941.

production was to sideline the cumbersome bureaucracies of the state, in particular the German army, leaving production management to private business. Todt's efforts were anti-bureaucratic. His focus was on technical efficiency at the plant level, rather than organizational change. And he was able to achieve substantial increases in output. However, he made no progress towards the creation of a centralized system for planning the allocation of scarce labour and raw materials, even in the sector under his control. In light of Germany's stunning military successes, this is hardly surprising. By the summer of 1940, Germany was in command of the entire resources of Western Europe. A year later, with the invasion of the Soviet Union successfully launched, the Nazi State seemed poised to seize control of the entire continent.[12] Rather than husbanding Germany's limited domestic resources, the Third Reich turned its attention to the organization of the Grossraum. The occupied territories offered welcome relief from the administrative trench warfare on the home front. The basic components of the Reich's statistical system were imposed across occupied and defeated Europe.[13] As each country adjusted to the pressure of German demands by creating a system of compulsory business organizations and planning agencies, the model of Grävell's Central Statistical Committee was applied to regulate the proliferating paperwork. Raw material statistics were compiled by agencies modelled on the German Reich's Agencies. Translated versions of the German Industrial Reporting System, warts and all, provided a basic supply of industrial information. Grävell sketched grandiose plans for a standardized system of statistics stretching across the entire Grossraum.[14]

II

It was the crisis in Russia in the winter of 1941–2 that forced the question of statistical reorganization back onto the domestic agenda. In the late autumn of 1941, Hitler's armies were finally halted deep in Soviet territory and in December the Red Army launched a desperate counter-offensive outside Moscow. Contrary to all expectation the Soviet regime had not collapsed. The Blitzkrieg had failed. Hitler was still confident that the Soviet Union could be defeated, but this would

---

[12] This moment of euphoria is well captured by R. Overy, *Why the Allies Won* (London, 1995), pp. 14–15.

[13] J.A. Tooze, 'La connaissance de l'activité économique. Reflexions sur l'histoire de la statistique économique en France et en Allemagne, 1914–1950', in B. Zimmermann, C. Didry and P. Wagner (eds.), *Le Travail et la Nation. Histoire croisée de la France et de l'Allemagne* (Paris, 1999), pp. 55–80.

[14] W. Grävell, 'Europäische Statistik', *Deutsche Wirtschafts-Zeitung* 4.12.1942.

require a huge second effort in 1942. The resources that had seemed limitless in 1941 now needed careful management. The Führer's impatience vented itself in tirades against the ineffectual institutions of the German state and in particular the civil service.[15] Mountains of useless paperwork were suffocating the heroic energies of the German people. The plague of redundant statistical questionnaires was symptomatic of everything that was wrong with the old institutions of government. Even the Nazi party was at risk of catching the bureaucratic disease. In early September 1941 the Reich's Chancellery recorded: 'The Führer would like a circular on the restriction of questionnaires from state authorities and party offices.'[16] In the records of the Party the Führer's outburst was rendered in less measured terms. According to Bormann, 'the Führer has commented very sharply against the current "questionnaire madness"'.[17] A circular ordered all party officials to desist immediately from unnecessary statistical work. A month later the Reich's Chancellery instructed the civil service to cease work on all non-essential statistics.[18] Neither order gave any indication of how redundant surveys were to be identified. It was left to Göering's staff to remind all ministries that Grävell's Central Statistical Committee was still in existence and that all statistical surveys required its authorization.[19] In the New Year, a Führerbefehl (Führer Decree) on the Simplification of Administration again emphasized the need for a reduction in unnecessary paperwork. However, the Party was still not satisfied. In March 1942, Goebbels demanded yet more measures against unnecessary statistics. At this point the Reich's Chancellery felt it necessary to remind the political leadership that appropriate instructions had already been given twice in the space of three months: 'it would not appear to be in the interests of state authority and it is not compatible with administrative simplification . . . to refer to this topic again in a circular. . .'.[20]

Hitler thus expressed his contempt for the state and the bureaucratic procedures associated with it. The task of actually designing an effective information system was left to the technocrats who finally took control of the German war economy after the winter crisis of 1941–2. To rebuild the fighting strength of German armies in the Soviet Union, Fritz Todt's remit was extended to all armaments. The army was

---

[15] J. Caplan, *Government Without Administration. State and Civil Service in Weimar and Nazi Germany* (Oxford, 1988b), p. 228.
[16] BAP 07.01 FC 19853/591 no. 53, Note of the Reichskanzlei 4.9.1941.
[17] BAP 07.01 FC 19853/591 no. 53, NSDAP Parteikanzlei 13.9.1941.
[18] BAP 07.01 FC 19853/591 no. 54, 63 and 70 ff.
[19] BAP 07.01 FC 19853/591 no. 81, Reichsmarschall circular 12.12.1941.
[20] BAP 07.01 FC 19853/591 no. 86, Reichsmin. für Volksaufklärung und Propaganda to the Reichsminister 6.3.1940.

removed from industrial management. Committees staffed by the main producers, one for each major type of weapon, were to take responsibility for production. The suppliers of the most essential sub-components were grouped together in so-called Rings. Before Todt was able to complete the reorganization, he was killed in a mysterious mid-air explosion. His successor as Armaments Minister, the architect Albert Speer, radicalized his reforming drive. A central committee, the so-called Zentrale Planung, chaired by Speer and including all the main players in the war economy, was placed in charge of allocating the key resources to the Committees and Rings. Here, finally, was the audience that power-hungry statisticians had dreamed of. The importance of economic information to the work of the Zentrale Planung was publicly underlined by a Führerbefehl of 21 March 1942. Albert Speer, the newly anointed Armaments Minister, was given the authority to carry out incisive measures for the standardization and simplification of the reporting system.[21] Even the wording of the Decree – replacing the old-fashioned language of 'statistics' with the new term 'reporting system' (Berichtswesen) – was suggestive of new priorities. The purpose of questionnaires and accounts was no longer to generate statistics, information for its own sake. The problem of economic information was too important to be left to the statisticians. In future, enquiries were to generate reports, reports that would be used by planners in Speer's Ministry, reports that would reach to the very top of the Third Reich. The Decree was accompanied by dire threats against those who dared to falsify or evade the Ministry's enquiries. Making false reports was punishable by death!

Speer's drive to re-energize the Nazi war economy provided the impetus for a final wave of statistical initiatives in the Third Reich. The last years of World War II witnessed the culmination of the statistical projects which this book has traced back to World War I. The ambitions of the technocrats who served Speer's Ministry went beyond mere administrative pruning. Ultimately, their aim was to develop a comprehensive new information system for central planning. Working for Speer's Ministry, they enjoyed unprecedented advantages. In the 1920s and 1930s the Reich's Statistical Office had broken new ground in technical terms, but its access to the highest levels of government had been insecure. The statisticians had worked in a speculative mode. They had been forced to imagine the system of planning that would make use of their data. At their boldest, they may have hoped that statistical reform would, by itself, create the will for systematic planning. By

---

[21] G. Janssen, *Das Ministerium Speer. Deutschlands Rüstung im Krieg* (Frankfurt a.M., 1968), pp. 65–66.

contrast, the statistical reorganization that began in 1942 had the explicit endorsement of Speer and through Speer of the Führer himself. The new data fed directly into a decision-making process which, if not rational, was, at least, rationalized. None of this, however, meant that the Reich's Statistical Office recovered its former authority. By the early 1940s, the disintegration of the German state was in a terminal stage. Albert Speer built his organization on an ad hoc coalition consisting of business organizations, Todt's empire of technical and engineering organizations, elements of the DAF and the Party, mixed with cannibalized components of the civil service and military organizations. It was a Ministry in name only. Given Speer's distaste for anything that smacked of the state, membership in the civil service was a liability. While the institutions of official statistics dwindled into insignificance, statistical expertise, cut loose from its attachment to the state, took on a new and greater importance. Given the disappearance of the public sphere, the universality of censorship and secrecy restrictions, statisticians could no longer hope for the kind of independent, public status enjoyed by Ernst Wagemann in the 1920s and early 1930s. However, the opportunities for direct political influence that opened up in the later stages of World War II were unprecedented. Speer was only the most important example of a new breed of men who assumed increasing importance in the wartime Nazi regime. At the RWM, the war years saw the rise of first Hans Kehrl and then the sinister Dr Otto Ohlendorf.[22] Another prominent technocrat was Herbert Backe at the Reich's Ministry for Food, who was responsible for the planned starvation of Eastern Europe.[23] Kehrl, Ohlendorf and Backe combined technical expertise with impeccable ideological credentials and a considerable portion of political skill. For the Reich's statistical establishment they were an ideal audience. Amid the ruins of the German state a new relationship flourished between expertise and politics. And this relationship bore the traces of the preceding 20 years of experimentation. How could the economy best be represented for the purposes of government? How could an efficient information system be designed to supply these information needs? In one form or another, under more or less favourable political conditions, these questions had preoccupied Germany's statisticians since the early 1920s. The Speer Ministry now faced them in deadly earnest.

---

[22] On Ohlendorf see L. Herbst, *Der Totale Krieg und die Ordnung der Wirtschaft. Die Kriegswirtschaft im Spannungsfeld von Politik, Ideologie und Propaganda 1939–1945* (Stuttgart, 1982), pp. 182–188.

[23] G. Aly and S. Heim, *Vordenker der Vernichtung. Auschwitz und die deutschen Pläne für eine neue europäische Ordnung* (Darmstadt, 1991), pp. 366–374.

III

To implement the Führer's Berichtswesen Decree Speer, not surprisingly, did not appoint an official statistician. As Beauftragte für das Berichtswesen (Commissioner for Reporting Systems), he chose the Deputy Leader of the Labour Front, Rudolf Schmeer. Schmeer had been an Under-Secretary of State in the RWM since it had been taken over by Goering at the end of 1938. He had good contacts in the party and, of course, to Robert Ley of the Labour Front. As his chief agent for industrial statistics Schmeer chose the engineer Dr Seebauer, a veteran of Weimar's rationalization movement with excellent contacts in the business community. However, when it came to choosing advisors on the technical issues of statistical organization, the choices open to Schmeer and Seebauer were more limited. Fear soon spread around the statistical community that Speer's reforming drive was being highjacked by none other than Walter Grävell.

In the spring of 1942, Grävell found a new audience. In the publicity announcing their reform agenda Schmeer and Seebauer were at pains to acknowledge the pioneering work done by the Central Statistical Committee.[24] Like Grävell, Schmeer's key concern was with the technical rationalization of statistical reporting. His watchwords were rationalization and the minimization of paperwork and he liked to frighten his audiences with horror stories of firms receiving up to 12,000 questionnaires a month.[25] His ideal was a system in which firms would return a single standardized questionnaire to a regional processing centre.[26] Somewhat surprisingly, this model of statistical organization was attributed to the Soviet Union. Each regional centre would have a monopoly of statistics in its territory. From its databases, it would satisfy the information needs of all other planning agencies.[27] The parallels to Grävell's proposed system of decentralized databases were obvious. The new ingredient added by Schmeer and Seebauer was a focus on mechanization. The regional statistical centres were to be based on the Hollerith processing capacity of the Wehrmacht's armaments inspectorates.

As was discussed in chapter 5, the German military had been fascinated with the potential uses of mechanical data-processing since the 1920s. But their early efforts had come to nothing. Hollerith

---

24 Schmeer, 'Neuordnung des Berichtswesens', *Der Deutsche Volkswirt* 47 21.8.1942.
25 IWM Sp film 18 3038/49 Sc. 182 no. 345, Reichsmin. Bewaffnung und Munition 'Niederschrift' 15.7.1942.
26 IWM Sp film 18 3038/49 Sc. 182 no. 361, DIFW Berlin 18.6.1942, Vm Betr: Pläne zur Neuordnung der Statistik (Wagenführ).
27 IWM Sp film 18 3038/49 Sc. 182 no. 353, RgI Zangen to Schmeer 3.7.1942.

processing in the military did not begin in earnest until November 1937, when the German Army set up a Punched Card Division headed by Colonel Passow.[28] The most pressing problem was the supply of steel and metals to the weapons producers. And the initial hope was that Passow's Hollerith machines would lay the foundations for a new system of rationing. The aim was to calculate the precise quantities of steel and other materials required for each item of equipment. In practice, this proved too ambitious. Instead, Passow set about mechanizing the routine data-processing of the German army. By the early 1940s, the entire paperwork of military procurement and equipment administration flowed through his Office. For the internal administrative purposes of the army Passow's Department elaborated a complex numbering system which gave a precise designation to each item of equipment, to different branches of the armed forces, to the orders they placed, and to the firms they placed them with. As the volume of military orders swelled, it came to seem increasingly irrational that this numbering system should be restricted to the internal workings of the military. Large industrial corporations all had their own internal systems of numbering, which required translation whenever they interacted with the military. In 1941 Passow proposed a standardized, national numbering system that would make the entire economy 'machine-readable'. Numbers would identify all goods whether civilian or military, all major procurement agencies, whether military or civilian and all plants in the economy. These numbers would be used in all business correspondence and paperwork, in accounts and statistics. Public and private bureaucracies would thus be welded together by a common numerical code. There was a natural affinity between this military scheme and Grävell's vision of the entire economy pictured in a system of decentralized databases. In the spring of 1941 the Central Statistical Committee therefore appointed a sub-committee on numbering chaired by a representative of Passow's Department.[29] But work on this dour project proceeded slowly. Devising a comprehensive system of numbers required the collaboration of all three service arms as well as the civil service and business, and what was the incentive at a time when the Third Reich was preparing for a peacetime bonanza?

It was the military crisis of the winter of 1941 that gave real urgency to the drive for mechanization. The rise of Todt and Speer spelled the end of any military ambition to control the economic war effort.

[28] BAK R 3/17 a/1–63 W. Lauersen, 'Organisation und Aufgaben des Maschinellen Berichtswesens des Reichsministers für Rüstung und Kriegsproduktion, report' 5.12.1945, p. 1.
[29] MA 1458 RWM FB 35/34 no. 26, Aktennotiz 7.4.1941.

Passow's Hollerith Department was subordinated to Rudolf Schmeer as Speer's Maschinelles Berichtswesen (Mechanical Reporting System, MB). But within Speer's Ministry the Hollerith technicians discovered a wide new field of activity. They were to provide the technical fix for the statistical problems of the Third Reich. The numbering drive stepped up into a high gear. Numbers were issued to all firms in June 1942.[30] To assert central control of the procurement process a standard numbering system for military orders was introduced over the summer.[31] A special set of numbers identified the orders placed by the Committees of armaments producers and Rings of components suppliers to the Speer ministry.[32] But numbering did not stop there; the most sinister activity of Passow's organization was the project to create a numbering system for the entire workforce and ultimately the entire population of the Third Reich.[33] This project, which for obvious reasons attracted the interest of the SS, was developed through local case studies carried out in 1943 and 1945. Though undoubtedly dramatic in its potential implications the administrative complications involved in the system of Personaleinzelerfassung (Individual Personal Registration) were nightmarish. It involved coordinating the registers of the personnel offices of local business, the local population register, the registers of local hospitals and the local police. Not surprisingly, no workable system was ever devised. Though these experiments have attracted the rather uncritical attention of some historians, the consensus in the Speer Ministry was that they were a waste of time. Personaleinzelerfassung owed more to Colonel Passow's personal ambition and to what might be termed the aesthetics of total control than to any real need of the Nazi regime.[34]

The real test of the new design came in the second half of 1942, when the entire Industrial Reporting system was transferred to Passow's regional processing centres. So far, Passow's machines had never handled monthly employment returns from more than 5,000 armaments firms. Now they were to take on no less than 80,000. The aim was to produce an extremely fast set of standardized reports, covering the entire industrial workforce. To achieve a smooth transfer of this enor-

---

[30] BAK R3/23 no. 173, Verfügung 15.6.1942.
[31] BAMA RW 19/1360, OKW Wi Rü Amt/leiter MB/OKW to the OKH VA and AHA Stab 12.5.1942.
[32] BAK R 3/17 a/1–63 W. Lauersen, 'Organisation und Aufgaben', p. 16.
[33] G. Aly and K.H. Roth, *Die restlose Erfassung. Volkszählen, Identifizieren, Aussondern im Nationalsozialismus* (Berlin, 1984), pp. 128–131.
[34] One senior member of the MB referred to Personaleinzelerfassung as Passow's 'personal hobby', IWM Bios Final Report 273, Symposium of Interrogations and Reports on German Methods of Statistical Reporting, Report II, Toenjes, p. 127.

mous data-processing task would have required very close cooperation between the MB and the current owners of the system, the Business Organizations. But the industrial organizations were deeply suspicious of any scheme that deprived them of control of their Industrial Reports.[35] The idea of each firm completing a single comprehensive questionnaire was attractive, but not if it meant that industry was no longer in control of its own statistics. In July 1942 Zangen of the Reich's Group Industry (RgI) wrote to Schmeer, couching his objections in technical terms: 'The result of transferring the reporting systems of industries as different as mining, engineering, textiles and food to a single mechanical processing centre, which lacks the necessary expertise would be to reduce the reporting system to a pure game with numbers.'[36] However, in the summer of 1942 even the RgI did not have the power to stop an initiative which had the full backing of Speer. What industry could ensure was that the Hollerith technicians failed.

The first set of figures from Passow's mechanical reporting system appeared in August 1942 and it was immediately apparent that the new system was not working.[37] Without adequate advice from industry, the military technicians were out of their depth. The address list supplied to Passow by the RgI was out of date and included far too many tiny firms. The date of the survey had been rescheduled to suit the MB rather than industry, resulting in masses of late returns. The new questionnaires demanded unreasonable levels of detail. And the MB failed to realize the need to maintain comparability between monthly figures by eliminating all firms that had made no return in the previous period. At a critical moment in the war, two months of employment data were lost. The MB's reputation never recovered.[38] In future, Passow and his machines were relegated to number-crunching roles.[39]

The technical fix to the statistical problem had failed. The basic organizational design on which Schmeer, Seebauer and Grävell had converged was a non-starter. A decentralized, mechanized system looked attractive on paper. But, as the experience with the MB demonstrated, mechanical efficiency did not guarantee that the results were useful. Nor did Schmeer's design answer any of the really difficult questions about the information that was actually required by Speer's

35 Aly and Roth, by contrast, following a monopoly capitalism model of the Third Reich, claim that there were no problems in the transfer of the Industrial Reports, see G. Aly and K.H. Roth, *Die restlose Erfassung*, p. 125.

36 IWM Sp film 18 3038/49 Sc. 182 no. 353, RgI Zangen to Schmeer 3.7.1942, pp. 2–3.

37 See the papers in BAK R3/23 Heft 2, R3/25 and R3/28 Heft 2.

38 See the uniformly negative comments on the MB in IWM BIOS Final Report 273, Symposium, including remarks by Albert Speer.

39 BAK R 11/65 Fol. 1 – RwK no. 70, RgI to Wg/Industrieabteilung 19.12.1942.

Zentrale Planung. From the point of view of the decision-makers, it was entirely irrelevant how the statistics were produced. What mattered was to obtain a reliable and up-to-date supply of the right kind of information. Judged against these basic criteria, Schmeer had failed. The system that actually informed the Zentrale Planung was to emerge from a second statistical initiative set in motion in the RWM in the second half of 1942.

IV

After the resignation of Schacht in 1937 the Ministry for Economic Affairs had been brought progressively under the influence of the Nazi Party. Though Funk remained nominally in charge, the most influential figure in the Ministry by the early 1940s was Hans Kehrl.[40] In the final years of the war Kehrl was to emerge as one of the most important organizers of the home front. Characteristically, Kehrl was not a civil servant. He was the owner-director of a medium-sized textiles firm and a passionate Nazi. He had entered government after the Machtergreifung through his connections with Keppler's Raw Material Office. Kehrl's first project was the development of Germany's synthetic fibres programme and in this role he had been incorporated into Goering's Four-Year Plan. Only with very great reluctance was he persuaded to join the RWM in 1938 as a free-lance trouble-shooter. Even when he became head of the largest Department in the Ministry, embracing more than half the entire staff, Kehrl refused to accept a formal rank in the civil service hierarchy. In his contempt for the slow-moving and arrogant state apparatus, Kehrl was a typical exponent of Nazism. What was less typical was his refusal to accept the simple-minded rhetoric of decisive personal leadership and improvisation that was so much favoured by Fritz Todt and Albert Speer. For them, strength of personal leadership was paramount, inspired improvisation was the secret to success. As Kehrl liked to point out, Speer had no appreciation of the backroom work that enabled him to act the part of the decisive leader.[41] By contrast, Kehrl was a product of the corporate rationalization movement of the 1920s. He had a long-standing interest in business organization, statistics and market research. And this was sharpened by his experience in the rationing of two crucial sectors: textiles and coal. At the RWM Kehrl was responsible for imposing a brutal system of controls on the textiles industry, Germany's largest consumer sector. Production

---

[40] Müller, *Der Manager der Kriegswirtschaft*.
[41] H. Kehrl, *Krisenmanager im Dritten Reich. 6 Jahre Frieden, 6 Jahre Krieg. Erinnerungen* (Düsseldorf, 1973), p. 330.

was directed by the flow of 'ration points', which was carefully monitored with the help of the mechanical clearing machinery of the German banks. Kehrl's ration points replaced money as a unit of account. In 1941, Kehrl's party-friend Paul Pleiger was placed in charge of the reorganization of the coal industry. The so-called Reichsvereinigung Kohle (Reich's Coal Union) was created to manage the growing shortage of energy supplies. Again, Kehrl's contribution was to create an effective information system for monitoring the production and distribution of coal and it was this, which finally brought him to the attention of Speer.

In the spring of 1942, steel was the most fundamental bottleneck in the German war economy. The existing steel allocation system set up in 1937 under joint control of the military and the Four-Year Plan was in a state of collapse. Speer asked Kehrl to devise a more effective system. Kehrl agreed under the condition that he be allowed to carry out a complete overhaul of planning procedures in all areas not under the control of Speer's Committees and Rings, i.e. the entire 'civilian' economy. Kehrl announced his new plan to the heads of the Reich's Agencies in a remarkable speech on 28 April 1942: 'I am going to behave like God himself at the moment of creation and will on the basis of conditions in each industry attempt to invent a new . . . rationing system.'[42] Kehrl's vision was a characteristic blend of technology and ideology. Did Nazi Germany need a tighter system of state control? Should Germany imitate the Soviet Union, its fearsome opponent? The answers had been provided by the Führer's insight into the nature of the racial struggle. Bureaucratic state planning was no doubt ideally suited to the primitive masses of the East; but to apply such methods to the advanced peoples of Western Europe, led by Germany, would be to squander their best asset, the creativity and initiative of their entrepreneurs. It was this insight, according to Kehrl, that had led Hitler to delegate responsibility to Albert Speer and his Committees of industrialists. Kehrl did not question the Führer's decision, but he was concerned that delegation should not lead to disorganization. Entrepreneurial energy needed to be systematically harnessed to the wider aims of the regime. In the armaments sector the urgent improvisations of Todt and Speer had achieved great successes, but Kehrl doubted whether these could be sustained in the long run. For his sphere of responsibility, he proposed a more systematic approach. Kehrl's system was built to last. 'Our new system is not meant just for the war time. It is a matter of course that we will require economic controls for an indefinite period

---

[42] IWM Sp film 18 3038/49 Sc. 182 no. 159, Excerpt from the speech of President Kehrl to the Reichsbeauftragten on 28.4.1942 in the RWM.

after the war. The more simple the means of control, the better it will work in peacetime. There will be changes in the degree of control, but not in the methods used.'[43] If World War I had sounded the death knell of liberalism, then World War II was its wake. The problem was how to devise a system of state control that was not grotesquely bureaucratic. Kehrl faced head-on the Nazi dilemma of conceiving of an all-powerful system of central direction that was not undermined by its own administrative realization. His solution was to impose a radical separation between decision-making and the implementation of orders. The execution of central directives would be left entirely to the organizations of business. Entrepreneurial energy had its proper freedom in this realm. But, decision-making would be reserved for the central planning agencies of the state. This, however, would not be the civil service government of old. The agencies of planning would be shorn clean of routine administrative functions. Kehrl's staff were under strict instructions to avoid involvement in any cases to do with individual firms.[44] Their job was to prepare the ground for ultimate political decision. Kehrl's rationalization drive was to bring a new level of technocratic effectiveness to the central organization of the German war economy. But this should not obscure the fact that its inspirations were highly ideological. His objective was to build a new state, structured around the Nazi concept of leadership, a state capable of prevailing in the mortal struggle of the Ostfront.

As his ally in creating this new system of wartime administration, Kehrl chose Wagemann's Institute. As we have seen, the Institute had been on the fringes of power since 1933. Characteristically, Wagemann had made the best of the opportunities presented by the war.[45] Following in the tracks of the German armies the Berlin Institute had seized control of its counterparts in Eastern and Western Europe, establishing branch offices in Vienna, Kattowitz, Prague, Paris, Amsterdam and the Sudetenland. In June 1941, the flag of Konjunkturforschung was finally abandoned in favour of the more grandiose title of Deutsches Institut für Wirtschaftsforschung (DIW), the name that the Institute still bears today. Through its relationship with Kehrl, Wagemann's Institute was to move back to the very centre of power in Germany. Kehrl for his part regarded the Institute as his secret weapon, the foundation on which he built his reputation as the 'man who knew everything'. By 1943, Kehrl

---

[43] IWM Sp film 18 3038/49 Sc. 182 no. 159, Excerpt.
[44] IWM Sp film 18 3038/49 Sc. 182 no. 220, Kehrl speech to Reichsbeauftragten 15.12.1942, p. 11.
[45] DIW, *Das Deutsche Institut für Wirtschaftsforschung (IfK) 1925–1945 in der Erinnerung früherer Mitarbeiter* (Berlin, 1966).

and the Institute had together established an unprecedented degree of control over economic information in the Third Reich. While Kehrl converted knowledge into power, the Institute used its new position of power to revive the intellectual ambitions of the 1920s. In a desperate last effort, the principles of macroeconomic Konjunkturforschung were brought to bear on the problem of central planning.

The DIW brought itself to Kehrl's personal attention in June 1942 when, on its own initiative, it presented a set of diagrams depicting the Byzantine organizational structure of the German war economy.[46] Kehrl, as a true product of the 1920s rationalization movement, set great store by vivid graphics. And he soon began to involve the Institute in the wider work of planning.[47] The lead was taken by Dr Rolf Wagenführ, who had been recruited to the Institute in the 1920s and who had since emerged as the leading expert on industrial statistics. In July, Wagenführ was given the top priority task of preparing a plan for the production and allocation of non-ferrous metals for the fourth quarter of 1942. Wagenführ was also charged with the longer-term task of investigating the structure of the existing Reich's Agencies with a view to creating a more streamlined and functional distribution of responsibilities. As the outline of Kehrl's new organization was developed over the summer, the role of Wagenführ's statisticians became increasingly prominent. In October, Wagenführ's position was formally recognized when he was appointed to head the statistical section of Kehrl's ministerial staff (GRA3). This section, though nominally part of the Ministry, was in fact made up of the DIW's Department for Industrial Statistics. It was located in the Institute's offices in the Fasenenstrasse, just off the Kurfürstendamm in West Berlin. The DIW, after having been separated from the German statistical system for almost 10 years, was back in government. The bureaucratic civil war, which had been raging within the statistical apparatus since the late 1930s, had reached a turning point.

The alliance between the DIW and Kehrl provided a powerful counter-weight to the rival project of statistical reform being pushed by Grävell and his allies. Grävell had long been antagonistic towards Wagemann and his Institute. In Grävell's vision of the statistical future, there was no room for a private research empire such as the DIW. The Institute thus had reason to fear the convergence of Schmeer and

---

[46] IWM Sp film 18 3038/49 Sc. 182 no. 214, 'Umriß der Arbeiten für Präsident Kehrl', Wagenführ undated probably late 1942, p. 1. Wagenführ emphasizes that the diagram was prepared 'ohne Auftrag'.

[47] IWM Sp film 22 3038/49 Sc. 388 no. 459, DIfW 18.6.1942 Vermerk. On Wagenführ's career, see the conclusion.

Grävell's plans in the summer of 1942. As Wagenführ recorded in a memo of June 1942:

What is particularly dangerous about the plan for regional mechanized processing [Schmeer], is that it revives Dr Grävell's old idea of establishing regional offices of the SRA with a monopoly of all statistical work. Herr Dr Seebauer has already begun to speak of a 'Reich's Commissioner for Statistics' and since Seebauer and Grävell are working very closely together it is altogether possible that Grävell may be appointed to this post.[48]

The Institute's new relationship with Kehrl provided the springboard for a counter-attack. The botched attempt to transfer the Industrial Reports to the military Hollerith apparatus in the autumn of 1942 discredited Schmeer and Grävell's grand design. The creation of Kehrl's statistical staff, GRA3 signalled Grävell's final defeat. The powers of the Central Statistical Committee were transferred to Wagenführ's office. In early 1943, when Seebauer wound up his work, it was agreed that all further statistical initiatives would require the prior approval of Wagenführ's office.

Apart from countering the threat posed by Walter Grävell, the new arrangement with Kehrl was of enormous advantage to the Institute. The benefits were set out in a memorandum which Wagenführ prepared in late 1942. This deserves to be quoted at length since it reveals the clear-sighted opportunism with which the DIW secured its position at the nexus of power and knowledge.

Apart from the financial advantages that the DIW derives from the collaboration with President Kehrl, there are the following considerations:

1. Contact with the planning agencies of the industrial economy is intensified to the greatest degree. Previously we had practically no contact to the Reich's Agencies . . . Now, through GRA3 [Wagenführ's office in the RWM] every Agency is most tightly connected to the DIW.
2. We have insight into the work of all rival research agencies, since, through GRA3, we can demand access to relevant material at any time.
3. We can compile the richest collection of material on the industrial economy, so that after a pause of many years it is possible to resume the sectoral analysis of the economy. Statistical material flowing to GRA3 flows also to the DIW. In the foreseeable future, we will have accumulated a more complete collection than any other central agency.
4. Finally, we will gain valuable experience in general questions of planning, that cannot remain without influence on other areas (labour deployment, transport, energy etc.).[49]

---

[48] IWM Sp film 18 3038/49 Sc. 182 no. 361, DIfW 18.6.1942 Pläne.
[49] IWM Sp film 18 3038/49 Sc. 182 no. 214, 'Umriß' late 1942.

For the Institute the victory was not merely institutional, it was a vindication of the entire project of Konjunkturforschung. This was spelled out by Wagemann himself in the autumn of 1942.

Once we have assembled a substantial collection of balances for raw materials and manufactures, then we will have made an important step towards a better understanding of the total circular flow [Gesamtkreislauf] of the German economy in its concrete form. The most important principle of economic research, as practised by my Institute, has always been that the economy is a total process and that it is therefore of fundamental importance to understand the interrelationship of individual phenomena. In the midst of the war, we are approaching this goal with giant strides. More than ever we are working to compile a total account of the national economy [Gesamtbilanz der Volkswirtschaft]. Only then can planning of the economy – whether it be the control of the labour force, or raw material consumption, or stock movements, investment, consumption or trade – really begin.[50]

The aggregative vision of the economy, which Wagemann had first elaborated in the early 1920s, was now to be applied to the problem of planning.

The basic principles of Kehrl's new organizational structure were worked out over the summer of 1942.[51] Wagenführ's investigations revealed that the most fundamental organizational obstacle to an effective system of planning had, in fact, been erected at the founding moment of the Nazi economy – Schacht's New Plan of 1934. The two institutional structures created in that year were incompatible and incapable of delivering comprehensive oversight of the economy. The Reich's Agencies (formerly the Supervisory Agencies), on the one hand, were organized around a list of raw materials. The Business Groups, on the other, organized firms into a rough and ready classification of industries. In fact, the Business Groups largely perpetuated the private associational structure of the 1920s. There was thus a fundamental inconsistency between the two organizational structures: raw materials on the one hand, broad industrial groupings on the other. Since the late 1930s the Reich's Agencies had been under the control of the Business Groups, but the allocation of Agencies to Groups was arbitrary and there was no provision for the systematic planning of anything other than raw materials. The new scheme devised by Kehrl's staff was a breakthrough in three respects.[52] First of all, it was organized around final products, the

[50] IWM Sp film 18 3038/49 Sc. 434 no. 61, p. 6; this undated document is contained in the Wagenführ files. From its position in the files and its content the most likely date is the second half of 1942. It may have been drafted by Wagenführ, but it was clearly intended to bear Wagemann's name.

[51] IWM Sp film 22 3038/49 Sc. 388 no. 431, Bemerkungen 23.6.1942.

[52] See the graphic representation in IWM Sp. reel 18 FD 3039/49 Sc. 346, Neuordnung der Bewirtschaftung.

actual object of the entire exercise, rather than raw materials or 'industries'. Secondly, it aimed to achieve consistency across the plans. Thirdly, plans were to take account not only of raw materials but of all other inputs necessary for production. In the language of the Institute, the plans were to extend to the entire physical 'circuit of the economy' (Kreislauf der Wirtschaft). Raw materials, labour, energy, transport and investment were all to be taken into account. Each major area of production was assigned to a so-called Lenkungsbereich (Lb) headed by an expanded Reich's Agency. Wagenführ's Department would see to it that the circuit of production was 'closed' for the entire national economy by imposing consistency across the plans of the Lenkungsbereiche.[53] Execution of the plans was to be left entirely to the Business Groups assigned to each Lenkungsbereich. Kehrl banned both his ministerial staff and the head offices of the Reich's Agencies from any involvement in individual cases. The macroeconomic perspective first elaborated in the 1920s was thus institutionalized. Planning was to abstract from the individual firm and to concentrate on the overall flow of production. Wagenführ and his staff were to be spared the obsession with detail that had swamped Leisse's ill-fated RwP.

For all the errors made in that earlier effort at planning, the production census of 1936 remained the only reliable overview of German industry. The results of the census were to serve as the basic reference for all future attempts at wartime macroeconomic planning. Leisse's census was the only source of information on industrial value added and the only way of assessing input–output relationships between industries in a systematic fashion. For those of Kehrl's staff who were not acquainted with the convoluted politics of German statistics, the cancellation of the 1939 census of industrial production was an inexplicable mystery.[54] In his postwar discussion of the problems of wartime planning Erich Welter referred to the winding-up of the RwP as 'one of the great riddles of this period . . . There is no good reason to be found.'[55] The Third Reich had inexplicably deprived itself of the basis for rational planning. By 1942, the mistakes of the early war years were irreversible. There was no hope of carrying out a full-scale industrial census. Wagenführ set about salvaging what he could from the wreckage left by Grävell's misguided effort at reorganization. The remnants of the RwP were harnessed to the programme of reorganization.[56] Leisse's staff

[53] IWM Sp film 18 3038/49 Sc. 182 no. 184, Dorn 'Bemerkungen' 23.6.1942.
[54] IWM Sp S Box 368 no. 82 Baudisch 15.9.45, p. 6.
[55] E. Welter, *Falsch und Richtig Planen* (1954), p. 112–113. Welter, a journalist, was employed by Kehrl as an economic intelligence officer. After the war he was the founding editor of the *Frankfurter Allgemeine Zeitung*.
[56] IWM Sp film 18 3039/49 Sc. 346 no. 349 and 378.

were put to work mapping the results of the 1936 census onto Kehrl's new structure of Lenkungsbereiche. The fragments of the once-integrated programme of Konjunkturforschung were thus reassembled and brought to bear on the practical problems of planning.

To provide a flow of up-to-date statistics Wagenführ had no option but to rely on the Business Groups and Reich's Agencies that were now being incorporated into the Lenkungsbereiche. However, as we have seen, there was good reason to doubt the ability of either of these organizations to produce useful data. During the autumn of 1942, representatives of the DIW and Leisse's Department were sent on tours of inspection across the bureaucratic jungle of Berlin, to establish the statistical capacities of each of the newly formed Lenkungsbereiche.[57] As Kehrl put it, the aim was to develop a common language across the entire corps of planners.[58] Each Lenkungsbereich was to be equipped with a historical review of the relevant statistics, a set of data predicting likely future developments, a means of making systematic comparisons between the plan and the actual levels of production, data on the external balance of the Lenkungsbereich, a set of up-to-date reports from the largest firms and a variety of other data with which to cope with emergencies.[59] Actually compiling the statistics and the plans was the job of the Statistical Sections to be created in each Lenkungsbereich. Kehrl was emphatic on this point. Addressing the heads of the Reich's Agencies on 22 October 1942, he stressed: 'we must break with the prejudice that less well qualified staff are suitable for statistical work. I make it the personal responsibility of each Reichsbeauftragten to find good staff to fill this department, on which his whole work is based.'[60] As the experience with the military Hollerith machines had shown, cutting costs in the production of statistics was a false economy. Once an adequate organization was in place, the Lenkungsbereiche were given formal responsibility for statistics in their area, thus ensuring that no further damage could be done by Grävell's Central Statistical Committee.

The investigations of the autumn of 1942 fully bore out the criticisms made by Leisse's industrial statisticians earlier in the war. The decentralized system of statistics founded on the Reich's Agencies was unsound. Wagenführ's staff were unable to obtain usable information on

---

[57] IWM Sp film 22 3038/49 Sc. 388 no. 413, Planungsamt, GRA 3 21.10.1942 Statistische Arbeitskreise.

[58] BAP 31.02 3589 no. 63, 'Erläuterungen zum Schema eines Bewirtschaftungsplanes' Planungsamt, GRA3.

[59] BAP 31.02 3589 no. 61, Arbeitsgrundlagen für die Planung, 19.10.1942.

[60] IWM Sp film 18 3038/49 no. 115, RWM to the Reichsstellen 22.10.1942 Betr. Aufstellung eines Geschäftsverteilungsplans für Lenkungsbereiche.

raw material allocation for any period prior to 1942. Kehrl's planning effort would have to start from scratch without an overview of past experience. Consequently, the preparation of the overview of the Lenkungsbereiche dragged into the spring of 1943. The so-called Strukturbild der Lenkungsbereiche (Structural Overview of the Lenkungsbereiche) was the most comprehensive image of the German economy to have been produced since the late 1930s.[61] It covered not only industry but also the commercial and craft establishments associated with each Lenkungsbereich. The entire economy was now to be included within the ambit of the war effort. The overview recorded the number of workers and the number of establishments as well as the value of their output in gross and net terms. For lack of any better data, the net value of production was estimated by applying the ratio of output per worker derived from the 1936 industrial census to the current workforce. The immediate conclusion was that the procedures of planning in each Lenkungsbereich would have to vary with the structure of production. In some cases, production was highly self-contained with little difference between the net and gross values of production, other industries relied heavily on raw materials, components and supplies bought in from outside. There were also enormous variations in the balance between craft and industrial production, the scale of industrial production and the labour and capital intensity of different sectors. A uniform system of planning would therefore be inappropriate.

To bring together the mass of information flowing in from the Lenkungsbereiche Kehrl's staff experimented with new forms of visual presentation. In the early years of the war, the Reich's Agency for Paper and Cellulose had experimented with so-called 'planning-altars'. These were cupboards resembling medieval triptychs which were plastered on the inside and outside with all the vital statistical information relevant to an industry. The Führer of each industry would 'stand in front of the Altar', literally facing the facts. Kehrl was much taken with this device and commissioned Wagenführ to bring together the data from all the Lenkungsbereiche in a single room.[62] Each of the 21 Lenkungsbereiche was to have its own Altar. The density of data was to be increased by hanging the charts from rails suspended in the cupboard, in the manner of contemporary railway timetables. The relevant image could be dropped down, as needed. The centrepiece was to present the basic circular flow of production in each Lenkungsbereich. The left- and right-hand wings of the Altar were to present the structural data for the

---

[61] Speer Documents Herford series Reel 18 FD 3039/49 Sc. 346 no. 45, Strukturbild der Lb 29.3.1943.
[62] IWM Sp film 22 3039/49 Sc. 342 no. 35–42, GRA 3 memos on the Altar-room.

sector. A total of 145 charts and tables were compressed in each Altar. A statistical journal provided a log of monthly information. The focus of the entire room was a so-called 'General Cupboard' (Generalschrank) which brought together data from all the Lenkungsbereiche and related it to aggregate measures of the economy. The data was to be supplied by the Institute and included an estimate of national income, Wagenführ's index of industrial production and indices for raw material stocks, imports and exports. This Altar was to be 'the real key to the comparison of developments in the individual Lenkungsbereiche'. Wagenführ took Kehrl on a tour of the new room in January 1943.

Why go to such lengths to give the dream of central planning a physical form? There were no doubt practical reasons. The Altars allowed a vast amount of information to be displayed in an accessible form. They were easier to handle than a large pile of papers. A complex image of the German economy was compressed into a single space. There may also have been security considerations. Concentrating the information in a single physical location reduced the number of reports that needed to be circulated. A subordinate official who needed to be put in the picture could be given a guided tour through the Altar-room, instead of being entrusted with copies of the documents. However, there was surely more at stake than this. The concentration of knowledge in a single location was also an expression of power. On the one hand, anyone wanting to obtain this unparalleled overview of the war economy had to visit Kehrl's observatory. On the other hand, the creation of a unique visual assembly must surely have been intended to create an aura of 'presence', that could not be generated by endless copies of statistical tables and reports. A man standing in this unique space could feel himself to be in direct command of all of German industry. The Altar-room was not merely a representation of the economy. It provided a unique vantagepoint. It actually *was* the centre of the economic war effort.

V

To some extent, however, one must suspect that the Altar-room provided a form of psychic compensation. The totality suggested by the physical array of information was illusory. The Altars suggested a complete overview. But, in fact, despite Wagenführ's efforts, coverage remained incomplete. The all-important armaments sector was beyond Kehrl's reach under the control of Speer's Committees and Rings. Furthermore, despite their visual compression, the statistics arranged in the 'Altars' remained fundamentally heterogeneous. The data series arrayed side by side on the charts and diagrams were fundamentally incomparable. What planners needed were ratios, above all the ratios expressing the relationship between inputs and outputs. How much labour, energy and steel was required for the production of each major item of military equipment and the essential commodities of civilian life? To calculate these ratios one needed comparable sets of statistics for outputs and inputs. This had been achieved with the industrial censuses of 1933 and 1936. But in 1943 there was no way back to the missed opportunities of the late 1930s. The wartime planners of Nazi Germany had to make do with an information system that followed the organizational outlines of the war economy, rather than providing a systematic dissection of the productive process. The result was an incoherent collection of data from which it was impossible to calculate the basic parameters required for planning.

The Committees which managed final weapons assembly for the Speer Ministry were able to provide information on the output of weapons. If their accounts were in order, they were also capable of answering questions about the labour and raw materials consumed in the final stage of production. In large part, however, weapons manufacture was an assembly operation. A complex weapons system such as a fighter plane was assembled out of semi-finished materials, such as aluminium sheeting, generic components, such as nuts and bolts, and specialist components, such as radios, which were themselves highly complex. How did one account for thousands of such components? The most important sub-components were administered by the so-called Ring organizations and some of these had accounts which allowed one to identify their major customers. But it was the Lenkungsbereiche in the 'civilian sector' that were responsible for raw material supplies and the production of generic inputs. After Kehrl's reforms, they collected data on output and their use of labour and other inputs. However, only in exceptional cases was it possible to trace a complete chain starting with the final assembly operations of the armaments Committees, via the sub-component Rings, back to the output of the Lenkungsbereiche which, of course, were themselves multiply interconnected. The most acute problem was labour. For the Central Planning Committee, this was the most vital issue. Yet, it was extremely difficult to be precise about the actual labour needs of armaments production. The only comprehensive employment statistics were provided by the Industrial Reports, which were based on the broad outlines of the Business Groups. And there was no meaningful relationship between these broad-brush data and the specific output figures supplied by the Rings and Committees.

In the last two years of the war, in a final spasm of organizational activity, Kehrl and his staff struggled to resolve this fundamental informational problem. Against the apocalyptic backdrop of the Eastern Front and the firebombing of Germany's cities, this preoccupation with the technical detail of planning cannot but seem like a flight from reality. In the summer of 1943, after the incineration of Hamburg, even Kehrl's faith was shaken. The orders for quicklime, with which to destroy the bodies of the dead, passed across his desk.[63] He remained at work only under orders from Speer who equated resignation with desertion. Victory might no longer be possible; but it was their duty to stave off defeat for as long as possible. Inevitably, however, thoughts turned away from the present. As one member of Kehrl's office commented to his interrogators in 1945, 'The main thing . . . was to think of the future.'[64] This took many forms. For Speer, much preoccupied with his place in history, the statistics of his Ministry would provide a glorious testimony to historians. For the statisticians themselves, work in Berlin no doubt offered a safe haven from the horrors of the Eastern Front. But the obsessive search for statistical solutions also had a wider political meaning. The effort to demonstrate the viability of central planning was part of a struggle over the future of the German economy.

In the last years of the Third Reich, public discussion of the postwar era was forbidden. Nevertheless, a subterranean debate about the future order divided the power blocs.[65] Kehrl's feverish activity was driven by his conviction that central planning was not just a necessity of war. It was Germany's destiny. It was now inevitable that the United States and the Soviet Union would emerge from World War II as economic and military superpowers. Germany's only hope of asserting itself alongside them lay in a powerful, state-controlled economy. In case of defeat, central planning would be Germany's only hope of survival. It is unclear whether or not Kehrl's staff shared his convictions. But whatever their views, in the force field of Nazi politics Wagenführ and the DIW came to be closely identified with Kehrl and a policy of central planning. By contrast, the possibilities of a so-called 'soziale Marktwirtschaft' (social market economy), were being explored by a group of liberal economists, among them Ludwig Erhard, the architect of West Germany's postwar economic policy. Erhard enjoyed the backing of business, but also the protection of the SS. In 1943, Speer and Himmler arrived at a division of labour that gave control of the war effort to Speer, whilst allocating responsibility for long-term planning to the RWM. The Ministry in turn

---

[63] Kehrl, *Krisenmanager*, pp. 299–310.
[64] IWM Speer Box 368 no. 82, Interrogation of Baudisch 15.9.1945, p. 2.
[65] Herbst, *Der Totale Krieg*, pp. 341–452.

was brought under SS control by the installation of Otto Ohlendorf as Under Secretary of State. Over the following years, an intense but silent rivalry emerged between Kehrl and Ohlendorf. In this struggle, economic expertise was an important resource and the DIW was a prime target. In 1944, Ohlendorf made a determined effort to assert control over the Institute.[66] However, in a last display of political virtuosity Wagemann escaped his grasp. Wagenführ and his staff continued their work for Kehrl until the final days of the war. They embarked on an increasingly radical exploration of the problems of physical planning.[67]

The political basis for their efforts was created in 1943 by the upheavals that followed the Stalingrad disaster. If Germany was to stay in the war, a new level of economic effort was required. In his address to the Sportpalast Goebbels proclaimed 'Total War'. Foreign workers were enslaved in ever-larger numbers. For the first time, the entire German population was to be registered for war work. In the Zentrale Planung Kehrl made himself the foremost advocate of a massive closure programme in the civilian economy. Shutting hundreds of thousands of small shops and workshops would release further resources for the war effort. This may have looked good in the 'Altar-room' but on the ground, the Zentrale Planung faced determined opposition from the Gauleiter, who bitterly opposed the 'big business conspiracy' in Berlin. By the early summer of 1943, the mounting pressures on the German war economy were threatening disorganization.[68] The first closure programme yielded far less than the Zentrale Planung had hoped. At the same time, Speer's Armaments Ministry was under enormous pressure to satisfy the demands of the Führer's Tank programme. The Wehrmacht was gathering its strength for the last great offensive on the Eastern Front – the attack on the Kursk salient. The situation was desperate. The targets for tanks and self-propelled guns were being met only through a succession of so-called 'emergency programmes' (Gewaltaktionen). The production process as a whole was becoming disorganized. The Committees and Rings were losing touch with each other and the supply of coal and steel – the basic inputs – was lagging far behind expectations. The Zentrale Planung was struggling to keep overall allocations within realistic bounds. Germany could not afford

---

[66] See the negotiations in BAK R 7/2126.
[67] Speer commented after the war that he was unaware of any national income figures and suggested that the iron allocation table be used to assess the relative balance between civilian and military production. IWM Speer Box 367 no. 5, Interrogation of Speer 5th Session 30.5.1945.
[68] D. Eichholtz, *Die Deutsche Wirtschaft. Geschichte der deutschen Kriegswirtschaft vol. 2 1941–1943* (Berlin, (Ost), 1985), p. 124.

another logjam like that which had throttled production in the early years of the war.

Speer, like Kehrl, was convinced that the answer lay in the labour reserves of the civilian economy. At a meeting with Hitler in June 1943 Speer spoke of an additional 500,000 workers. In desperation, Kehrl and Speer agreed a final reorganization of the tattered state apparatus. Kehrl's portion of the RWM – responsible for the Lenkungsbereiche – would be incorporated into Speer's Armaments Ministry. The rump of the RWM would be left to Ohlendorf and the SS. With Himmler's backing, Speer would establish a stranglehold over civilian production, overriding the local party apparachiks. The result of this 'combing-out', which began in August 1943, was an additional 400,000 workers for the armaments sector.[69] At the same time, fusing Kehrl's section of the RWM with Speer's Ministry would bring order to the increasingly ad hoc management of the armaments sector. Kehrl had always doubted the claims made for Todt and Speer's system of Committees and Rings. He suspected the armaments plants of squandering the resources painfully pressed out of the civilian sector. And he despaired of the often flippant, inconclusive and ill-informed discussions in the Zentrale Planung. Now he would have the opportunity to rationalize the unified system of central planning.

The recent historical literature on the German war economy has tended to explain the dramatic surge in production after 1942 in terms of rationalization at the plant level.[70] No doubt, this is justified. However, it should not be allowed to obscure the fact that high levels of production were only sustained into the final years of the war by the creation of a crude but effective system of central economic planning. Key macroeconomic variables were brought under control. The workforce was maintained at a high level, despite the enormous demands of the military, through the brutal exploitation of millions of slave labourers. Additional capacity for weapons production was found by halting new investment projects and by pushing into production the factories and machinery installed in the early years of the war. Perhaps most importantly of all, the Zentrale Planung engaged in a continuous juggling act to offset the impact of military disasters, carpet-bombing and bottlenecks. What is miraculous about Albert Speer's miracle is not so much the levels of output that were attained but the ability of the

---

[69] F.L. McKitrick, 'An Unexpected Path to Modernization: The Case of German Artisans during the Second World War', *Contemporary European History*, 5 (1996), pp. 401–426.

[70] R. Overy, 'Rationalization and the Production Miracle in Germany during the Second World War', in *War and Economy in the Third Reich*, pp. 343–375 and N. Gregor, *Daimler-Benz in the Third Reich* (New Haven, 1998).

German war economy to sustain production in the face of massive disruption. Here, the role of central coordination is undeniable. The scenario that haunted the Zentrale Planung was a sudden downward spiral in production resulting from the multiplication of bottlenecks – a form of industrial gridlock.[71] In such a situation, the uncoordinated efforts of individual factories to sustain their output might well amplify the bottlenecks in other more important sectors of the economy. In the autumn of 1943, an acute energy crisis threatened precisely such a collapse. Kehrl promptly commissioned his staff to devise a programme that would allow production to be adjusted to a 10 per cent reduction in energy supplies.[72] The solution was to concentrate cuts in those sectors that would have least knock-on effects for the rest of the economy. Overall output was sustained. The armaments miracle continued.

The tool for this macroeconomic crisis management was the so-called Planungsamt. It was established by Kehrl as a staff office for the Zentrale Planung, preparing the data to be discussed at its meetings, coordinating the plans of all elements of Speer's Super-Ministry. Kehrl sought to use the Planungsamt as a centre from which to impose order both on the work of the Committees and the Rings and on the deliberations of the top decision-making body. At the heart of the Planungsamt, in charge of the section for Planstatistik, was Wagenführ. His position was now unrivalled, particularly after the offices of the RWM suffered a direct hit during the bombing of Berlin in the autumn of 1943.[73] Kehrl's personal collection of economic statistics was reduced to ashes and the only duplicates were in the DIW's offices in Fasanenstrasse. In the final 18 months of the war, Wagenführ and the Institute gained complete control of the information systems of the Third Reich. Routine statistical work was delegated to the rump of the Statistical Office, reorganized as the so-called Statistical Coordination Centre (Statistische Leitstelle) for the Lenkungsbereiche and run by Leisse's industrial statisticians.[74] Apart from reassembling Kehrl's personal information system, the Coordination Centre performed the routine work of checking and collating the data produced by the Lenkungsbereiche. Passow's Maschinelles Berichtswesen (MB) provided mechanical processing power. The Planungsamt meanwhile concentrated on overarching issues of planning and in the summer of 1944 it was awarded the ultimate accolade. Speer decided to present its

---

[71] FD 3048/49 Fold. 22. 16, Besprechung der ZP 23.10.1942, p. 3 and IWM FD 3048/49 Fold. 21 17, Besprechung der ZP 28.10.1942, p. 41.
[72] Kehrl, *Krisenmanager*, pp. 467–468.
[73] Kehrl, *Krisenmanager*, p. 325.
[74] BAP 31.02 3589 no. 48, RWM note 10.9.1943.

reports directly to the Führer himself.[75] A draughtsman had to be found to redraft the reports in the larger scale of the Führertype – a typeface specially enlarged to avoid Hitler having to appear in public wearing glasses!

But merely controlling the flow of information to the political leadership did not satisfy Kehrl and the Planungsamt. Over the winter of 1943–4 they formulated a vision of a thoroughly rationalized planning system, which was to motivate their work in the final year of the war. The basic outline of this system had been sketched a year earlier by a colleague of Wagenführ's in the Breslau branch of the DIW.[76] The basic idea was to rationalize discussion by focusing all attention on the margin of resources that was actually free for disposal. The first step, therefore, was for the political authorities to specify absolute minimum levels for all essential items of civilian and military consumption. An input–output table, known as the Gesamtplan (Total Plan), would be used to calculate the necessary level of resources for this level of outputs. These would be earmarked and removed from further discussion. To decide on the allocation of the disposable resources, the political leadership would be asked to indicate its priorities. To allow a real process of choice, the leadership would be asked to specify not just one maximum target, but a variety of programmes with different combinations of final outputs, ranked in terms of preference. The statisticians would then calculate, based on their input–output coefficients, how far each of these targets could be met. The leadership would be presented with a range of alternative options, each offering a different combination of armaments outputs. The central problem for Wagenführ and his statisticians was to draw up the Gesamtplan.

The first experiments were undertaken by Wagenführ and the statistical section of the Planning Office in the autumn of 1943. Their aim was to avoid excessive detail and to concentrate on producing imperfect but usable results within a reasonable timeframe. This was of course the preferred methodology of the Institute since the 1920s. It was also an approach supported by the results of case studies commissioned by Wagenführ in late 1943 and early 1944. These revealed the enormous problems that would be encountered by any attempt to plan the input–output relations of the economy in detail. An incomplete study of the assembly operation for the VW amphibious jeep (Schwimmwagen) counted more than 1,000 suppliers and this was far from being the most

---

[75] BAP 31.02 3472 no. 46, BV/GBR to Planungsamt 1.6.1944.
[76] IWM Sp film 18 3038/49 Sc. 182 no. 265, no. 268, Grote Mismahl report to Seebauer on 'Gesamtplanung und Planrechnung' 30.1.1943.

complex weapons system of the Third Reich.[77] Furthermore, enquiries with several of VW's competitors revealed that the balance between final assembly and sub-contracting was far from uniform even within a single industry. Even in the production of a standardized truck, there were huge differences.[78] Some firms concentrated on final assembly relying on a network of sub-contractors to maintain flexibility. By contrast, other firms chose to internalize the resources and expertise necessary to control production in depth, investing in their own foundries and extensive machine shops. The idea of a single process of industrial production was no more than a useful fiction. At this level of detail, the technical and commercial organization of production was a matter of competitive strategy. Only in some cartelized and heavily rationalized industries were sub-contracting and materials purchasing organized in a standard fashion across all manufacturers. The rolling-stock manufacturers were one example. By 1944, they were mass-producing a limited range of simplified 'war-locomotives'.[79] Materials and components were purchased on behalf of all the final assemblers by a single agency, which could supply Speer's planners with all the information they needed. However, this level of information was the exception not the rule and it was dependent on an actual reorganization of the industry itself. In general, Wagenführ and his staff seem to have drawn the conclusion that plans should be kept so general that they allowed for flexibility at the level of the plant. Otherwise, the structure of industry would have to be adjusted to the plan, or the plan would have to be tailored literally to each individual firm.

From this perspective, what was needed for central planning were orders of magnitude not high-precision statistics. And it was, in fact, quite possible to estimate the scale of the component-supply problem in broad terms, without going into fantastic detail. Early in the war, the problem of component supply had been badly neglected, leading to chronic bottlenecks in arms factories run by the military and inefficient efforts to produce components in-house.[80] Since the 'self-organization' of German industry into Committees and Rings the pendulum had swung the other way. In the allocation of labour to the armaments producers, it was routinely assumed that the direct labour allocation needed to be doubled to take account of the labour needs of suppliers

[77] IWM Sp film 5 3046/49 Sc. 170 no. 209 ff 18, Wochenbericht des Planungsamts 6.5.1944.
[78] DIW, *Die deutsche Industrie im Kriege 1939–45* (Berlin, 1954), p. 64.
[79] IWM Sp film 19 3046/49 Sc. 303 File 1 no. 208, Plaa 2 July 1944, Vermerk über einen Besuch bei dem Hauptausschuss Schienenfahrzeuge.
[80] J. Fear, 'Die Rüstungsindustrie im Gau Schwaben 1939–1945', *Vierteljahrshefte für Zeitgeschichte* 35 (1987), pp. 193–216.

and sub-contractors. Wagenführ himself had made this assumption in a preliminary study prepared in the autumn of 1943. And this certainly kept the armaments production process amply supplied with labour and other resources. However, by the end of 1943 the Planungsamt had begun to suspect that there was substantial slack in the system. When it was checked against the 1936 census results, the assumption of a one-to-one ratio between the labour requirements of final assembly and component production was shown to be excessive.[81] In February 1944, Wagenführ compiled a memorandum arguing that a much tighter allocation of labour was justified. In his view, it was inconceivable that indirect labour could account for more than 60 per cent of the total employed in final production in industries such as electrical engineering or optics and precision engineering. Motor vehicles and naval construction were exceptional cases, and even there the labour requirements of suppliers fell well short of the labour employed in final assembly. The implication was that hundreds of thousands of hours were being squandered in the metalworking industries.

Though this was an important conclusion, this kind of case study approach did not satisfy the real ambition of the Planungsamt. The aim remained a Gesamtplan summarizing in a single presentation the allocation of critical resources to production. This master table would provide the basis for Kehrl's state-directed economy. The first draft was drawn up by Wagenführ at the end of May 1944, presenting a simple physical balance sheet of the war economy in the third quarter of 1943.[82] The output of the economy was presented in two columns which recorded the physical output of major weapons systems, as well as their estimated value, along with the total sales of other broadly defined sectors of the economy. The other five columns showed the net inputs required to achieve these levels of production (see figure 9).

The form of presentation was dictated by the purpose of the table. It was designed to allow decision-makers to understand how the most critical resources entered the most important lines of armaments production. This was not therefore a classic input–output table of the kind sketched out by the Statistical Office in the mid-1930s. It was not symmetrical. It did not seek to trace the destination of all outputs as inputs of other sectors. Only the inputs that were bottlenecks were featured. Furthermore, on the output side, attention was focused on weapons, which did not enter as inputs into the production of anything else. Nevertheless, Wagenführ unhesitatingly connected his wartime work on the Gesamtplan to the intellectual tradition of classical aggrega-

[81] BAP 31.02 3472 no. 476, Plaa Ha Planstatistik to Wagenführ 8.12.1942.
[82] IWM Sp film 21 3038/49 Sc. 181 no. 163–174.

Top Secret
Planungsamt/HA. Planstatistik
Spring

Line of production	Employment in 1,000	Gross production value, million RM	Volume of production	Consumption of coal, million tons. Greater Germany incl. Protectorate	Electricity billion kWh (1940/41)	Transport, million tons, Greater Germany incl. Protectorate	Iron and Steel, million tons
I. Armaments final assembly incl. Specialized components							
Tanks	179	2,000	12,111 units	0.4	0.4		0.5
Motor vehicles	87	1,080		0.1	0.15		0.2
Weapons	241	2,228		0.5	0.4		0.9
Submarine weapons	30						
Airframes							
Aircraft engines	935	10,824	25,000 units	1.4	1.3		0.2
Aircraft equipment					0.2		
Ships	170	2,076		0.1	0.3		1
Optical military equipment	145	1,308		0.3	0.4		0.1
Electrical military equipment	180	2,004		1.1	1.4		0.3
Ammunition	638	5,828			0.3		2.1
Powder and explosives	70		p: 211,000 t e: 411,000 t				0
Other Wehrmacht equipment	150					4	
II. Other Assembly							
Machines	821	7,340		1.6	0.9		3.4
Vehicles	167	2,156		0.2	0.3		0.5
Ships	3						
Iron and steel construction	166	1,640		0.3	0.1		1.4
Optical equipment	51	492		0	0.1		0
Electrical engineering	463	5,216		0.7	1.1		0.4
Iron, steel and tinware	247	2,236		0.5	0.6		1.2
Metal manufactures	105	1,004		0.1	0.3		0.1
Processed raw materials	255	2,996		0.9	0.5	8	3.7
Ceramic goods	99	560		1.1			
Glassware	92	720		1.7	0.3	2	
Wood products	219	1,744		0.3	0	3	
Paper	123	1,604		4.7			
Paper products	104	1,036		0.1			
Printed products	202	1,788		0.1	0.9	5	
Leather							
Shoes	186	2,064		0.4	0.1		
Textile products	868	7,784		3.7	1.1	1	
Clothing	314	2,128		0.2	0.1		
Food	454	10,696		3.5		11	
Beer, malt	79	2,004		1		2	
Sugar	59	1,448		3		3	
Spirits	22	524			0.7	1	0.3
III. Raw materials							
Coal	1,023		SK 278 m t BK 287 m t	32	1.9	249	
Ores	113			2.8	0	28	0.5
Iron and steel	552		19 m t rolled products	37.9	2.7	44	
Non-ferrous metals	153	2,264	247 m t Alum.	2.1		2	
Cast products	215	1,612		1.2	5.7		1.3
Fuel	132	2,680	7.5 m t	24.9	1.8	10	
Sawed wood	154	1,620		0.1	0.1	11	
Chemicals	786	9,412		18.6	6.9	23	0.3
Non-metallic minerals (not incl. Building materials)	99						
IV. Construction							
Construction materials	198			8.2	0.8	106	
Buildings	516			0.4	0.2		1.4
Total industrial economy	11,893			156	33.4	513	19.8
A. Industrial economy	11,893			156	33.4	513	19.8
B. Energy sector	226			41	2.1		0.2
C. Transport	2,581			37	2.2		0.9
D. Artisanal sector	3,768				1		0.5
E. Agriculture	13,721				0.9	56	0.1
F. Forestry	312					14	0
G. Services	3,262				0.9		0
H. Public administration	4,216				0.9		0
I. Households	1,153			61.5	4		0
Total economy	41,132			296	46	586	21.5
Export				53			2.5

Figure 9 Total plan (Gesamtplan) of the German economy (Greater Germany without Protectorate), third quarter 1943, annualized rough estimates
Source: Planungsamt/HA. Planstatistik, Spring 1944

tive analysis. In an article published after the war he named his principal intellectual influences: the work of Soviet statisticians in the 1920s, the German national accounting experiments of the 1930s and the first input–output table to be actually completed by Wassily Leontief in the United States.[83] In light of these remarks, the wartime work of the Planungsamt can properly be said to represent the culmination of the project of macroeconomic Konjunkturforschung begun by the Weimar Republic.

Nevertheless, Wagenführ's Gesamtplan was far from complete. The problem of attributing inputs to outputs remained unsolved. The rows in Wagenführ's table purported to show the labour, iron, energy and transport consumed in the production of each type of weapon. In fact, they recorded only the resources consumed in the final process of assembly. Wagenführ was able to include sub-contracted specialized components, such as the labour and steel that went into casting the hull of a tank. However, his table did not record any of the resources that went into the mass of generic components from which the tank was assembled. In the Gesamtplan these were counted in the rows showing the inputs used by mechanical engineering and other key suppliers, rather than in the row supposedly showing the inputs required by tank production. And it was this flaw which Kehrl picked upon when he was presented with Wagenführ's first draft.[84] Rough estimates were not enough. The Zentrale Planung required precise figures on the allocation of labour.

Over the summer of 1944, the Planungsamt worked feverishly on a second draft of the Gesamtplan, the aim being to finish the historical analysis of 1943 before going on to a comprehensive plan for the first half of 1945. The result was an expanded version of Wagenführ's early draft, which was much more comprehensive in its coverage of inputs.[85] The labour force was divided between industry and the craft sector. Lignite and coal consumption were specified separately. There was a column for gas inputs. Lead, zinc, copper and aluminium were all accounted for alongside steel. Wood requirements were specified. There was also a double column recording levels of investment in machinery and buildings and a complex breakdown of transport requirements. In all, 23 categories of inputs were itemized for each line of production. However, the fundamental problem remained unsolved. Labour was

[83] R. Wagenführ, 'Die "Volkswirtschaftliche Bilanz" (II): Das "Schachbrett"', *Mitteilungen des wirtschaftswissenschaftlichen Instituts der Gewerkschaften* (1952), pp. 39–45.
[84] IWM Sp film 21 3038/49 Sc. 181 no. 150, Leiter Planungsamt to Baudisch 5.6.1944.
[85] IWM Sp film 21 3039/49 Sc. 237 no. 6, Planungsamt, Gesamtaufwandsplanung 1943.

still counted only at the final assembly stage. The only components accurately accounted for were those produced in tied sub-contracting relationships. Huge volumes of labour directed towards armaments production remained unmeasured. The DIW itself sought to provide a check on the physical accounts using the method of national income statistics.[86] On a rough estimate, it seemed probable that at least 20 per cent of German national income was being spent on armaments in 1943. Yet the Gesamtplan for 1943 recorded only 4.6 per cent of the workforce as being involved in the final production of weapons and ammunition.

The exercise of drawing up the Gesamtplan led to an inescapable conclusion.[87] The existing information systems of the Reich, mauled by successive efforts at reform and reorganization, were not capable of generating a coherent set of physical accounts. Despite the increasingly desperate situation of the German war effort, the Planungsamt was not deterred. Kehrl ordered one last assault on the problem. In a final, comprehensive reform the industrial statistics would be detached from the shackles of the administrative organization, and in particular the Business Groups, undoing the effects of Grävell's intervention in the early years of the war.[88] The planners were not interested in the Groups or even the firms they represented. What mattered was the physical process of production. This demanded a statistical system that traced not the economically and politically defined boundaries of corporate organizations, but the process of production as a physical process, tying outputs to their inputs. The firm as an economic unit was an irrelevance. Indeed, as the industrial statisticians in the 1930s had realized, firms would have to be broken down analytically into technical units of production. The connections between these units would then have to be traced both within and if necessary beyond the boundaries of the firm. Of course, the information systems of the firm could not be entirely disregarded. However, the Planungsamt refused to accept that they should impose a fundamental limit on the planners. In the autumn of 1944 Kehrl gave his approval and promised to get the backing of Speer.[89] This would certainly be needed since the new system would remove control of industrial statistics from the Business Groups.

There is no evidence that this plan ever came close to realization. It is interesting because it reveals with stark clarity the logic of the

[86] IWM Sp film 27 3037/49 Sc. 11 no. 115, Bischoff Vermerk für Kehrl 11.8.1944.
[87] IWM Sp film 21 3038/45 Sc. 181 no. 67, Vermerk: Offene Statistische Fragen der Gesamtplanung 21.8.1941.
[88] IWM Sp film 21 3038/49 Sc. 131.
[89] IWM Sp film 21 3038/49 Sc. 131 no. 44, Besprechung mit Kehrl 4.9.1944.

Planungsamt's thinking.[90] The problem of sub-contracting and components supply would be at the core of the reformed system. The new statistics would record as a discrete production process anything that produced a marketable, 'independent' product. The basic procedure first developed by Leisse's industrial statisticians in the early 1930s was thus revived.[91] However, now it was to be applied to the full complexity of industrial manufactures. This was the problem that had defeated Leisse's censuses. It was the problem that had been pronounced insoluble by Meerwarth in the early 1920s.[92] Attempting to register the economy as a giant physical process of production was in his view an anachronistic hangover of the artisanal period. The solution proposed by Kehrl's Planungsamt was to make use of the military's numbering system. If numbers were allocated to all products from the most complex manufactured goods down to their most basic inputs, then it should be possible to reduce each product to its numbered inputs. Leisse's industrial statisticians had despaired of ever being able to develop and implement a system of industrial classification sufficiently complex to trace these connections. The military numbering system confronted this problem head-on. A standardized system of classification would be imposed, not once every three years for the census, but once and for all. The language of business would be permanently adjusted to match the categories of the statisticians. The questionnaires of the statisticians would no longer impose an external scheme of classification on the economy. The language of the statisticians would be of a piece with the terminology of everyday business. A three-digit product numbering system had been completed at the end of 1942 and implemented by the Speer Ministry.[93] This provided a thousand numbers with which to identify products in the statistical reports and order forms. The Planungsamt planned to base its reorganized statistical system on a four-digit code, providing a theoretical total of 10,000 separate classifications. Cascading this system of numbers from the procurement agencies down to the raw materials suppliers would result in an extraordinary anatomy of German industry.

However, in 1944 the planners of Nazi Germany could not wait to carry out a survey of the entire process of industrial production. The Planungsamt thus proposed an even more direct attack on the problem.

[90] The options were set out at a conference held in the Planungsamt BAK R 3 74 no. 48, Planungsamt, Krähe 25.9.1944 Protokoll.
[91] See chapter 5.
[92] See chapters 1 and 2.
[93] BAK R 3/51 Reichsmin für Rü- und Kriegsproduktion/MB III no. 21 Vortragsnotiz Betr. Reichswarennummerung 22.10.1942, p. 2.

What it needed to know most urgently were the raw material and labour inputs required for the production of essential weapons systems. If such calculations could be completed for 200 major weapons systems, the Planungsamt was confident that it could account for at least 60 per cent of the total volume of military orders.[94] At least theoretically it should be possible to calculate rough benchmark figures from the blue prints using the mechanical processing power of Passow's MB to cumulate the labour and raw materials contained in thousands of components and sub-components. Archival records suggest that two systems were evaluated in this way – an aircraft and a self-propelled gun – before the late autumn of 1944 when the Hollerith capacity of MB was dispersed to regional hide-outs and central control of the German war economy began to slip away from the Speer Ministry.

VI

The return to government of Wagemann's Institute in World War II thus ties together the strands of this narrative. The efforts to rationalize the planning system of the Third Reich in the final stages of World War II did not represent a radically new departure.[95] On the contrary, they were the culmination of two decades of technocratic effort. One might argue that the war represented the final vindication of the project of macroeconomic Konjunkturforschung. After a decade of trial and error, the Planungsamt returned to the model of the circular flow first outlined by Wagemann in the 1920s. However, to describe the work of Kehrl's office as a victory for rationality over ideological unreason would be a mistake on two counts. First, the many other rejected schemes did have their own technical logics. Grävell's vision of decentralized statistical organization may have been impractical but it cannot simply be dismissed as an irrational product of ideology. Secondly, to counterpose the rationality of the Planungsamt to the irrationality of previous attempts at planning would be to underestimate the ideological component in the work of Kehrl's staff. By contrast with Albert Speer, Hans Kehrl made little attempt, even after the event, to hide his political convictions. The purpose of Kehrl's system of central planning was to prosecute the racial war. And the peculiar structure of organization he seized upon was justified explicitly in racial terms. Furthermore, with the end of the war in sight, the very effort of perfecting the planning system was a political statement in its own right. The struggles over the postwar organization of Germany anticipated the ideological battle-lines

---

[94] BAK R3/74 no. 32, MB 25.9.1944 Besprechung, Rohstoffplanung.
[95] As is suggested by Herbst, *Der Totale Krieg*, pp. 433–452.

of the Cold War. And this in turn shaped the work of the Planungsamt during the war. Rather than broadening the approach of planning towards the use of monetary variables such as national income estimates, Wagenführ's team drove ever deeper into the problems of physical planning. The numbering project was the end-point of this development. It reflected the grim realities of economic life in wartime Germany and projected them into the future. If Kehrl had had his way, consumer choice would have been curtailed by a draconian system of rationing. The organizations of business were to be sidelined. As had become clear by the early 1940s an information system designed around the self-chosen structures of business organization was not capable of delivering the consistent statistical information demanded by planning. Instead, the economy would have to be reorganized around the needs of planning. Centralized and standardized production systems would become the industrial ideal. The entire range of production would be kept under constant surveillance by the national numbering agency. Every new line of production would have to apply for a new product number. The movement of the entire production process at every stage would be subject to direct central surveillance. In this sense, the work of the Planungsamt anticipated not postwar Western macroeconomics but central planning as it came to be realized under Stalinism after the war. Wagemann, the Institute and the macroeconomic idea may have triumphed after 1943, but this was no longer the Konjunkturforschung of the 1920s. This was a truly totalitarian vision of surveillance and control.

Conclusion

This book ends in 1945 and it is surely long enough. Nevertheless, the history of economic statistics in Germany does not end with the Third Reich, nor was the history of modern economic knowledge an exclusively German story. We should conclude therefore by asking about the implications of this book for the postwar history of Germany and by briefly returning to the comparative issues raised in the introduction. What are the more general implications of this study for our understanding of the making of modern economic knowledge?

One popular way of tracing the continuities in German history is to study the biographies of individuals across the divide of 1945. This approach could certainly be applied to economic statisticians. This book has not attempted a group biography. However, the careers of certain important individuals may perhaps be taken as illustrative. For the older generation the war was the end. Rudolf Meerwarth barely survived the war, dying in Berlin in March 1946.[1] Wolfgang Platzer, his colleague of the early days and the longest serving Director of the Statistical Office, retired in 1945.[2] Wagemann's career in Germany was also finished. He withdrew to Chile in broken health, returning to Germany to die in Bad Godesberg in 1956. For the younger men, retirement was not an option. After the surrender in Berlin, Walter Grävell attempted to rally the remnants of the Reich's Office, but was arrested by the NKVD in June 1945 and spent nine months in a Soviet prison camp.[3] Having escaped to the West he took charge of the census of 1950 in Rheinland-Pfalz. A year later he was appointed Director of social statistics for that Land. Though his work in the Central Statistical Committee was not forgotten, he was chiefly remembered for his outspoken writing on trade policy. He was counted among the critics of Brüning's policy of deflation and was

---

[1] 'Rudolf Meerwarth zum Gedächtnis', *ASA*, 35 (1951), pp. 157–162.
[2] 'Hans Wolfgang Platzer', *ASA*, 46 (1962), pp. 192–193.
[3] 'Walter Grävell ist 65', *ASA*, 40 (1956), p. 176.

also cited as an opponent of Schacht's system of autarky. Ironically, Grävell thus emerged as an early advocate of the postwar common sense in economic policy.[4] By contrast, Wilhelm Leisse and Paul Bramstedt dropped out of sight. They make no further appearance in the annals of the German Statistical Association. This surely reflects the fragmentation of the German statistical scene. Two key players of the interwar decades sank without trace in the postwar era. Rolf Wagenführ, on the other hand, achieved a spectacular resurrection.

Wagenführ's extraordinary career is worth rehearsing in full. It began in the late 1920s, with a PhD from Jena University on Soviet business-cycle theory under the supervision of the liberal economist Wilhelm Roepke.[5] From Jena he was hired in 1928 to join the Institute. Five years later he made his mark with a study of Germany's long-run industrial development.[6] Rather tactlessly this was studded with reference to Marx. But Wagenführ did not take long to adjust to the new political conditions. In the 1930s he published widely on issues of rearmament and military economics and rose rapidly to become the chief industrial statistician in the Institute.[7] By 1943 he had emerged as the central figure of wartime statistics, controlling the flow of information through Speer's Armaments Ministry. Irony enough for one lifetime: an infatuation with Marx and Soviet economics that led to a prominent career within the Nazi state. In 1945 Wagenführ was a wanted man in every sense of the word. He was identified as a valuable target by Allied intelligence and was suspected of hiding 'valuable documents'.[8] Like Grävell, he first fell into the hands of the Soviets. After helping them with their enquiries he moved to the British zone of occupation where he was immediately appointed to head the statistical office of the occupying forces in Minden. Then, as if to continue his political rehabilitation, Wagenführ spent a period as chief statistician to the West German trade union federation. This prepared the way for a return to his wartime interest in European statistics. In 1952 he took charge of the temporary statistical department of the European Coal and Steel Community (ECSC). And in 1958 he was the natural choice as first Director of Statistics for the European Community (EC) – later to become Eurostat: from Großraumwirtschaft to EC in less than 15 years!

---

[4] 'Walter Grävell', *ASA*, 46 (1962), pp. 81–83.
[5] R. Wagenführ, *Die Konjunkturtheorie in Rußland* (Jena, 1929).
[6] R. Wagenführ, *Die Industriewirtschaft. VzK. Sonderheft 31* (Berlin, 1933).
[7] R. Wagenführ (ed.), *Kriegswirtschaft* (Berlin, 1935).
[8] IWM CIOS Evaluation report 317 Personalities from the Reichsministerium für Kriegs- und Rüstungsproduktion, p. 1.

Wagenführ retired in 1966 to a chair in international statistics at Heidelberg.[9]

This biographical approach is certainly fascinating. And it serves an essential public purpose. Exposing the complicity of civil servants and technicians with the Nazi regime is an important task. The responsible individuals should be named and called to account. But what wider conclusions can we draw from such extraordinary stories of continuity? Götz Aly and Karl-Heinz Roth, for instance, in their study of German statistics under Nazism, indict West Germany for its failure to master the Nazi past.[10] But they also have a bigger point to make. They see the unbroken biographies of individual statisticians as evidence for the unbroken continuity of objectifying, technocratic reason. This dehumanizing and brutalizing approach to social reality was perpetuated into the postwar period under both Christian Democrats and reformist Social Democrats. And this is of course not peculiar to Germany. It is a tendency inherent in modernity itself. The result is to erase the difference between political regimes. If the most basic mechanisms of modern power such as registration and quantification are inherently oppressive, then the differences between constitutional systems, between the Weimar Republic, Nazism and the Federal Republic are, indeed, irrelevant. And it is no coincidence that this argumentative structure closely parallels the interpretation of German history propagated by the German Democratic Republic (GDR). Beneath the veneer of Western democracy runs the same current of power that propelled fascism as well: monopoly capitalism.

Aly and Roth's analysis of the continuities in German history is deeply reductionist. The obvious and fundamental differences between the Federal Republic and the Third Reich are erased by their insistence on the unrelieved evils of technocracy, and their refusal to take politics seriously. Their account, like the orthodox Marxist critique of monopoly capitalism, is fundamentally incapable of capturing the radical specificity of Nazi ideology. The Holocaust was not impelled by some generic logic of technocracy, but by a manichean vision of the eternal struggle between Aryans and Jews. Similarly, Aly and Roth's one-dimensional interpretation is unable to do justice to the history of the Federal Republic. Here the argument becomes unavoidably political. The democracy of West Germany was and is imperfect. But it is surely

[9] See the commemorative volume G. Menges and R. Zwer (eds.), *Probleme internationaler wirtschafts- und sozialstatistischer Vergleiche. Rolf Wagenführ zum Gedächtnis* (Cologne, 1981).

[10] G. Aly and K.H. Roth, *Die restlose Erfassung. Volkszählen, Identifizieren, Aussondern im Nationalsozialismus* (Berlin, 1984).

bizarre to portray it merely as a restrained continuation of the Third Reich. This involves denying the protections of individual freedom established in the Constitution of West Germany as well as the considerable scope for effective political opposition.[11] Aly and Roth's 'history' of German statistics may have provided useful ammunition to the opponents of the 1983 census, but it provided no guide to the future. In 1984 the Constitutional Court of the Federal Republic found in favour of the protestors. The census design of 1983 was ruled to be an infringement of what the court defined as individual informational autonomy.[12] This concept has subsequently been made the basis for an elaborate system of data protection.[13] Indeed, its reach has been extended beyond Germany through its incorporation into the European Commission's 1995 Directive on Data Protection.[14] This system is no doubt imperfect and will not by itself prevent the encroachment of individual privacy by the state and private corporations, but academic administrators throughout Europe will attest to its real effects on bureaucratic practice. This course of events serves to refute Aly and Roth's simplistic image of an unbroken technocratic continuity between the Third Reich and the Federal Republic. Within the structure of the Federal Republic and the state-system in which it is situated there are powerful elements channelling, directing and curtailing the energies of number-crunching technocrats. There is no manic project of mass destruction motivating government. And rights are taken seriously. We can certainly add to our understanding of modern government by examining the detailed practices of power. This is something that Michel Foucault, Philip Abrams and others have taught us. However, the broader political forces that give a regime its character simply cannot be ignored.

In fact, one could construct an account of the practice of official statistics in Germany directly counter to that of Aly and Roth. This would centre not on individual registration and surveillance but on the history of the 'Statistikgeheimnis': the confidentiality and anonymity which have been promised to respondents since the mid-nineteenth century. These principles were constitutive of the professional identity of official statistics as it emerged in the second half of the nineteenth century. In particular, the commitment to confidentiality served to

---

[11] For the opposition to the censuses of 1983 and 1987 see R. Appel and D. Hummel, *Vorsicht Volkszählung! Erfaßt, Vernetzt und Ausgezählt* (Cologne, 1987) and J. Arnold and J. Schneider, *Volkszählung – verzählt* (Frankfurt, 1988).

[12] C.J. Bennett, *Regulating Privacy. Data Protection and Public Policy in Europe and the United States* (Ithaca, 1992), pp. 41–42, 74–82.

[13] For the views of the first federal data protection officer see H.P. Bull, *Datenschutz oder die Angst vor dem Computer* (Munich, 1984).

[14] D. Bainbridge, *EC Data Protection Directive* (1996), pp. 11–32.

demarcate the realm of official statistics from other branches of the state administration. Not surprisingly, therefore, the progressive abandonment of anonymity and confidentiality in the statistical enquiries of Nazi Germany was seen, by the likes of President Reichardt, as the road to ruin. However, such an account would be only a little less anachronistic than that of Aly and Roth. One of the central problems with their work is the tendency to project back into the 1930s and 1940s the preoccupation of the 1980s. This leads them to focus on surveillance of the individual. But, as this book has shown, in the interwar period the vast bulk of statistical resources were in fact devoted not to demographic and social statistics but to economic and financial data-collection. What was primarily at stake in struggles over 'privacy' was the boundary between state and economy, not the state and the private individual. In this arena, the politics of privacy were quite different. The issues at stake were questions of political economy not individual rights. And, in the interwar period, the demand for more information about the workings of the capitalist economy came from all sides of the political spectrum.

A focus on the history of economic knowledge also leads one to a rather different position on the question of continuity. As we have seen in chapter 7, in the final stages of the war Hans Kehrl and his staff were developing a system of economic controls that was conceived quite self-consciously as an answer to that of the Soviet Union. Kehrl paid lip service to entrepreneurial freedom and initiative. But the realities of planning led inexorably to a system of centralized control that, if fully implemented, would have extinguished the autonomy of private enterprise. By 1944, the statisticians were proposing that business organizations should be removed altogether from the reporting chain and that a standardized system of numbering should be imposed on German industry. In future, the division of labour, even within the firm itself, would be subject to central direction, allowing each stage in the process of production to be monitored in detail. The work of Kehrl's Planungsamt was undeniably modern. But this was not the modernity of postwar capitalism. Far more obviously it resembled the system of centralized planning that had begun to emerge in the Stalinist Soviet Union. In the context of the 'second cold war' it was impossible for Aly and Roth to countenance this alternative line of continuity. And the uses to which the concept of totalitarianism was put during the cold war make one wary, even today, of any comparison between the Soviet Union and the Third Reich. But from our perspective, more than a decade after the collapse of the Soviet Empire, it is surely the most convincing backdrop against which to historicize the Nazi regime. This is not to revive a crude equation between the two regimes. There were fundamental differences in the goals of their leaderships. Furthermore, Nazism, unlike the Bolsheviks, never accomplished a social revolution, a wholesale reorganization of German society. What both regimes did have in common was their origin in the interwar crisis of liberalism. Both constructed their visions of political organization around a critique of the nineteenth-century distinction between an autonomous civil society and a law-bound state. This, in turn, implied a similarity in techniques of government, including statistics. The statistical systems developed in the Eastern bloc operated in an unbroken space of power and knowledge much like that envisioned in the final years of the Third Reich by the visionaries of the Volksgemeinschaft. Not surprisingly, the technical problems faced by the statisticians of the GDR were also similar. They, too, struggled to create a single seamless information system building upwards from the identification of individual products, workers and machines, to the accounts of individual firms and from there to national economic statistics.[15] Reading the postwar issues of the East German statistical journal, *Statistische Praxis*, one is constantly reminded of the debates of the 1930s and 1940s. By the late 1980s it was even possible for a historical dissertation to be submitted to Leipzig University highlighting these parallels: 'A long period of development preceded the implementation of the present, unified system of accounting and statistics in the economy of the GDR. Under the conditions of fascist dictatorship forms and methods of accounting were developed, that . . . have also found their uses in the unified system of accounting and statistics of the GDR.'[16]

This convergence of central planning techniques in National Socialism and the Stalinist Soviet Union took place under the pressures of war. It is hard to imagine that Hitler would have tolerated the kind of austerity advocated by Hans Kehrl in the aftermath of a compromise peace. However, by 1944, defeat was a far more likely outcome. Merely to survive, Germany would certainly need to husband its resources. The activities of Kehrl's Planungsamt had therefore to be taken seriously, certainly by German business men. As in 1917–18, the organizations of German business spent the last years of World War II preparing to counter any drift towards 'German socialism'. Even during the war, Hans Kehrl found himself accused of harbouring 'Bolshevik' tendencies. And Kehrl's response was hardly reassuring. One must have the 'courage', he declared, to issue such orders, 'even if people see this as

---

[15] For a description of the East German system see G. Bondi, 'Die Rolle der Statistik in einer geplanten Wirtschaft', *ASA*, 34 (1950), pp. 126–136.

[16] G. Starke and G. Supke, 'Informationssystem', PhD thesis, University of Leipzig (1988), p. 7.

Bolshevism ... If we do not understand how to combine the great merits of the radical planned economy of Bolshevism ... with the industrial capacities and forces of our economy, then we will not be able to outdo the rest of the world in economic terms, and there will be those after us who will undertake this experiment.'[17] Reich's Group Industry was not convinced. With the backing of the SS, economists friendly to business began developing a different vision of the economic future. It was out of this confrontation with the threat of planning that a coherent 'liberal' vision of postwar policy began to emerge within Nazi Germany.[18] This centred on the concepts of 'Social Market Economy' and 'attachment to the West'. The polarization of the Cold War was thus prefigured by arguments within the Third Reich itself.

The postwar triumph of the liberal model, with the active support of the American occupation authorities, had immediate consequences for the wartime statistical technocrats. Former planners were marginalized. It is significant that Rolf Wagenführ was the chief statistician in the British not the American zone of occupation. By the early 1950s, as head of research for the West German trade unions, Wagenführ was presenting the techniques of wartime planning as the instruments of Social Democracy.[19] In fact, seen in this light, Wagenführ's meteoric European career takes on a different aspect. For someone so at odds with the market liberalism of postwar West Germany, the more dirigiste European Community must have been a comfortable exile. At home, anything resembling planning was doggedly resisted on principle. Despite the production of rudimentary national accounts by the statistical office of the Federal Republic (Statistisches Bundesamt), the Adenauer government resisted their formal integration into fiscal budgeting until the 1960s. To Ludwig Erhard they smacked of wartime state control.[20] The Statistisches Bundesamt itself was hedged around with restrictions laid down in a new law regulating federal statistical activity, the Gesetz über Statistik für Bundeszwecke of 1953. This required that all statistical enquiries conducted by the Bund should have an explicit legal justification. Technocratic initiative was to be contained within the framework of the Rechtstaat.[21] Freedom from unnecessary official

---

[17] IWM Sp Reel 18 FD 3038/49 Sc. 182 no. 220, Kehrl speech to Reichsbeauftragten 15.12.1942, pp. 14–15.

[18] L. Herbst, *Der Totale Krieg und die Ordnung der Wirtschaft. Die Kriegswirtschaft im Spannungsfeld von Politik, Ideologie und Propaganda 1939–1945* (Stuttgart, 1982), pp. 348–432.

[19] R. Wagenführ, *Mensch und Wirtschaft. Eine Nationalökonomie für Jedermann* (Cologne, 1952).

[20] E. Osterwald, *Die Entstehung des Stabilitätsgesetzes. Eine Studie über Entscheidungsprozesse des politischen Systems* (Frankfurt, 1982), p. 61.

[21] Deutscher Bundestag 1. Wahlperiode 1949 Drucksachen Nr. 4168 and Nr. 4617. For

enquiries would be guaranteed by law. But it was not individual freedom that was at stake here. The primary concern in the early 1950s was to draw a clean line between the state and the private economy. Official statistics were to be subordinated to the rules of the social market economy.

It is precisely Germany's divided history that makes it such a strategic location for our understanding of modernity. Germany's history in the first half of the twentieth century exhibits not a single predetermined continuity, but a radical open-endedness. It is this which makes it such a fascinating setting for a case study of the broader development of modern economic knowledge. With respect to that broader question, this book hopes to have done three things. Along with other recent work it has sought to establish interwar Germany as a major site of conceptual and empirical innovation in the realm of modern economic knowledge.[22] On the basis of our current knowledge Germany clearly needs to be placed alongside Britain, the United States, the Soviet Union, Sweden and the Netherlands as one of the birthplaces of modern macroeconomics. This list, encompassing a substantial chunk of the industrialized world, should surely lead us to revise our understanding of the development of modern economic knowledge. The diffusion of explicitly Keynesian ideas in the decades after 1936 deserves to be studied as an important process in its own right. But it needs to be situated in a wider context: the development of a novel macroeconomic conception of the economy that began decades earlier and that was far more widely based.

As the German case shows, this development had heterogeneous intellectual origins and its political implications were, to say the least, ambiguous. This is our second general conclusion. The 'Keynesian revolution in government' was in many respects the least revolutionary of a variety of possibilities on offer in the interwar period. Even in Britain, where the spectrum of policy debate was peculiarly narrow, 'planning' was given serious consideration as an alternative to Keynesian demand management in the 1930s and 1940s.[23] The German statisticians are so fascinating because they were led by the political turmoil of the interwar years to engage in a truly open-ended exploration of new

the frustration this restrictive law engendered see B. Gleitze, 'Das Zusammenführen volkswirtschaftlicher und betriebswirtschaftlicher Aspekte in der Wirtschaftsstatistik', *ASA*, 45 (1961), pp. 313–323.

[22] R. Vilk, *Von der Konjunkturtheorie zur Theorie der Konjunkturpolitik. Ein historische Abriß 1930–1945* (Wiesbaden, 1992) and H. Janssen, *Nationalökonomie und Nationalsozialismus. Die deutsche Volkswirtschaftslehre in den dreißiger Jahren* (Marburg, 1998).

[23] J. Tomlinson, *Democratic Socialism and Economic Policy. The Attlee Years, 1945–1951* (Cambridge, 1997).

models of economic government. In the 1920s they drew intellectual inspiration from both Irving Fisher and Karl Marx. They studied both Herbert Hoover's New Era and the Soviet NEP as novel experiments in economic governance. Nazi ideology added its own drastic challenge to any residual, liberal distinction between state and civil society. When combined with the exciting possibilities of new technology this gave rise to radical visions of a new economic order. Finally, the confrontation with the Stalinist Soviet Union forced a serious experiment in central planning. Under these pressures, Konjunkturforschung, which in the 1920s had looked like 'just' another variant of early macroeconomics, began to develop towards a totalitarian vision of command economy.

Exploring this complex variety of alternatives brings us to the final conclusion of this book. We need to broaden our analysis of the forces bearing on the development of modern economic knowledge. The literature on Keynesianism has focused very tightly on the biographies of a small group of intellectuals and their interactions within Britain's extremely narrow political elite. Through cumulative effort this work has reached a very high level of sophistication. By contrast this book, in a rough and ready fashion, breaks fresh ground. It has sought to portray the construction of a modern system of economic statistics as a complex and contested process of social engineering. This certainly involved the mobilization of economists and policy-makers, but it also required the creation of a substantial technical infrastructure. The processing of data depended on the concerted mobilization of thousands of staff. In this sense the history of modern economic knowledge should be seen as an integral part of the history of the modern state apparatus and more generally of modern bureaucratic organizations. Macroeconomic knowledge of the kind studied here has co-evolved with the accounting and information systems of private business. To plug into the great pool of private knowledge, statisticians reached out beyond the boundaries of the state. A functioning statistical system had to be based on a network of more or less stable linkages connecting the centre of calculation to a reliable and capable set of respondents. It implied therefore a particular model of political order and in particular a vision of the relationship between the state and civil society. The development of new forms of economic knowledge can therefore be understood as part of the emergence of modern economic government and as a sensitive indicator of the relationship between state and civil society. Viewed in this way, the history of economic knowledge should not be consigned to a technical sub-discipline. It should be placed at the very heart of our understanding of modernity.

Appendix: Wagemann's national economic account – explanatory notes

(1) The original German refers to prices multiplied by a quantity of 'utility effects' (Nutzeffekten). From the subsequent elaboration it is clear that what is meant is net output – i.e. goods and services that are 'directed' via the market towards consumption or net investment (i.e. new stock-building or capital equipment). The awkward term 'utility effects' points to two conceptual difficulties: first, the problem of aggregating production in non-monetary terms; secondly, the need to distinguish between physical units of production and the utility which they provided.

(2) Costs are divided, on the one hand, into personal costs (Persön-liche Gestehungskosten) including wages, interest, entrepreneurial profit and rent and, on the other hand, into material costs (Sachliche Gestehungskosten), i.e. raw materials, etc. The importance of this distinction is that it introduces a division between households (personal costs) and firms with which material costs are incurred.

(3) From the text it is clear that Wagemann presumes all income ultimately to be distributed to households. The 'material costs' of one firm become the 'personal costs' of their suppliers' firms, and so on.

(4) The original text somewhat misleadingly refers to 'Ausgaben' and 'Ersparnis' – i.e. expenditure and saving. However, from the accompa-nying text it is clear that Wagemann actually considers the household sector (the ultimate recipient of all income) to be responsible for expenditure. And his explanation of the term 'expenditure' makes it clear that he is actually referring to final consumption of goods and services.

(5) Wagemann points out that saving is not identical to the output of producer goods (Produktivgüter – i.e. both capital equipment and raw materials and semi-finished goods) since capital depreciation requires repairs and replacements and these costs are included in the price of consumer goods. He also notes that the bulk of public sector consump-tion (Staatsverbrauch) is also accounted for in this indirect way. This is the only reference to the state in Wagemann's discussion. Capitalized

output thus refers to net investment (total investment in new equipment and stock, net of replacement, reduction in stocks, etc.). The purpose of line (5) is to elaborate the way in which available net output (which appears in line (1) as production) is used.

Bibliography

ARCHIVAL COLLECTIONS

Bundesarchiv Koblenz (BAK):
Reichsministerium f. Rüstungs- und Kriegsproduktion R 3
Reichswirtschaftsministerium R 7
Reichswirtschaftskammer R 11
Reichsgruppe Industrie R 12
Reichsministerium für Ernährung und Landwirtschaft R 14
Statistisches Reichsamt R 24
Reichsforschungsrat R 26 III
Reichsarbeitsministerium R 41
Reichskanzlei R 43
Nachlaß Paul Silverberg Nl 13
Nachlaß W. von Moellendorff NL 158
Nachlaß Alexander Rüstow Nl 169
Nachlaß Alfred Hugenberg Nl 231
Nachlaß H. Posse NL 303
Bundesarchiv-Militärarchiv Freiburg (BAMA)
Heereswaffenamt (OKH/Wa A) RH 8 I
OKW/Wehrwirtschafts- und Rüstungsamt RW 19
Bundesarchiv Berlin, formerly Potsdam (BAP)
Reichstag 01.01
Vorlf. Reichswirtschaftsrat 04.01
Reichskanzlei 07.01
Reichsministerium des Innern 15.01
Rechnungshof des D.R. 23.01
Deutsche Reichsbank 25.01
Reichsjustizministerium 30.01
Reichswirtschaftsministerium 31.01
Statistisches Reichsamt 31.02
Reichsministerium für Ernährung und Landwirtschaft 36.01
Reichsarbeitsministerium 39.01
Reichsministerium f. Rüstungs- und Kriegsproduktion 46.03
DAF 3/62 DAF 3
VDMA 70 Ve 1
Berlin Document Centre

Moscow Special Archive (MA)
  Vierjahresplan 700
  Reichswirtschaftsministerium (RWM) 1458
  Reichsamt für Wirtschaftsausbau 1459
Imperial War Museum (IWM)
  Speer Collection
  BIOS Final Reports
  EDS D MI 14/463–II
Bayerisches Hauptstaatsarchiv (BHStA)
  Min. des Äußeren (MA)
  Handelsministerium (MH)
  Min. des Innern (MInn)
  Min. der Justiz (MJu)
  Bayerisches Wirtschaftsmin (MWi)
Geheimes Staatsarchiv (GStA)
  Preußisches Ministerium für Handel und Gewerbe (I. HA Rep. 120)
  Preußisches Statistisches Landesamt (1.HA Rep. 77)
  III. Hauptabteilung Preußisches Ministerium des Auswärtigen (III. HA., Abt III)
Bergbauarchiv (BBA)
  Fachgruppe Wirtschaftsgruppe Bergbau 15
Haniel Archiv
Hoechst Archiv (HoeA)
  Stammwerke Hoechst
  IG Farben
Krupp Archiv
Mannesmann Archiv
Rheinisch-Westfälisches Wirtschaftsarchiv (RWWA)
  IHK Wuppertal (22 Liste 2)
  IHK zu Neuss (27)
  Niederrheinische IHK Duisberg-Wesel zu Duisburg-Ruhrort (20)
Stiftung Westfälisches Wirtschaftsarchiv (SWWA)
  Handelskammer Münster K 5
  IHK Dortmund K 1
Thyssen Archiv
Universitätsarchiv der Humboldt Universität
LSE Archive
  London and Cambridge Economic Service

DISSERTATIONS

Bajak, C.W., 'The Third Reich's Corporation Law of 1937', PhD thesis, Yale University 1986

Döring, D., 'Deutsche Aussenwirtschaftspolitik 1933–35. Die Gleichschaltung der Aussenwirtschaft in der Frühphase des nationalsozialistischen Regimes', PhD thesis, FU Berlin, 1969

Roeske, U., 'Die bürgerliche Wirtschaftsstatistik insbesondere von Großbanken, Monopolen und Wirtschaftsverbänden. Organizations- und Strukturprobleme vom Beginn des Imperialismus bis zum Beginn des II. Welt-krieges', Diplomarbeit. Sektion Geschichte. Bereich Archivwissenschaft University of Berlin 1974

Starke, G. and Supke, G., 'Informationssystem', PhD thesis, University of Leipzig (1988)

PUBLISHED MATERIAL

Adorno, D. and Horkheimer, M., *Dialektik der Aufklärung* (Frankfurt, 1980, 7th edn.)

Agar, J., 'Modern Horrors: British Identity and Identity Cards', in J. Caplan and J. Torpey (eds.), *Documenting Individual Identity* (Princeton, 2001)

Alchon, G., *The Invisible Hand of Planning. Capitalism, Social Science, and the State in the 1920s* (Princeton, 1985)

Aly, G. and K.H. Roth, *Die restlose Erfassung. Volkszählen, Identifizieren, Aussondern im Nationalsozialismus* (Berlin, 1984)

Aly, G. and S. Heim, *Vordenker der Vernichtung. Auschwitz und die deutschen Pläne für eine neue europäische Ordnung* (Hamburg, 1991)

Andvig, J.C., 'Ragnar Frisch and Business Cycle Research during the Interwar Years', *History of Political Economy*, 13 (1981), pp. 695–725

Appel, R. and Hummel, D., *Vorsicht Volkszählung! Erfaßt, Verhetzt und Ausgezählt* (Cologne, 1987)

Arendt, H., *Eichmann in Jerusalem. A Report on the Banality of Evil* (New York, 1963)

Arnold, J. and Schneider, J., *Volkzählung – verzählt* (Frankfurt, 1988)

Babson, R.W., *Actions and Reactions. An Autobiography of Roger W. Babson* (New York, 1935)

Bähr, J., *Staatliche Schlichtung in der Weimarer Republik. Tarifpolitik, Korporatismus und industrieller Konflikt zwischen Inflation und Deflation 1919–1932* (Berlin, 1989)

Bainbridge, D., *EC Data Protection Directive* (1996)

Balderston, T., *The Origins and Course of the German Economic Crisis 1923–1932. November 1923 to May 1932* (Berlin, 1993)

Barber, W.J., *From New Era to New Deal. Herbert Hoover, the Economists, and American Economic Policy, 1921–1933* (Cambridge, 1985)

Barkai, A., *Das Wirtschaftssystem des Nationalsozialismus. Ideologie, Theorie, Politik 1933–1945* (Frankfurt, 1988, rev. edn.)

Barkin, K.D., *The Controversy Over German Industrialization 1890–1902* (Chicago, 1970)

Barnett, V., *Kondratiev and the Dynamics of Economic Development: Long Cycles and Industrial Growth in Historical Context* (London, 1998)

Bauman, Z., *Modernity and the Holocaust* (Cambridge, 1991)

Bennett, C.J., *Regulating Privacy. Data Protection and Public Policy in Europe and the United States* (Ithaca, 1922)

Bennett, J., *The Economic Theory of Central Planning* (Oxford, 1989)

Berg, M. and Hudson, P. 'Rehabilitating the Industrial Revolution', *Economic History Review*, 45 (1992), pp. 24–50

Berlepsch, H.-J. von, *'Neuer Kurs' in Kaiserreich? Die Arbeiterpolitik des Freiherrn von Berlepsch 1890 bis 1896* (Bonn, 1987), pp. 200–205

Berliner, C., 'Die Reform der deutschen Außenhandelsstatistik', *Weltwirtschaftliches Archiv*, 29 (1929), pp. 320–333

Bernstein, E., *Evolutionary Socialism* (New York, 1961)

Bessel, R., *Germany After the First World War* (Oxford, 1993)

Blackbourn, D., *Fontana History of Germany 1780–1918. The Long Nineteenth Century* (London, 1997)

Blaich, F., *Die Wirtschaftskrise 1925/26* (Kallmünz, 1977)

Böckenförde, E.-W. (ed.), *Staatsrecht und Staatsrechtslehre im Dritten Reich* (Heidelberg, 1985)

Boelcke, W.A., *Die deutsche Wirtschaft 1930–1945 Interna des Reichswirtschaftsministeriums* (Düsseldorf, 1983)

Boltanski, L., *The Making of a Class. Cadres in French Society* (Cambridge, 1987)

Bombach, G., Netzband, K.-B., Ramser, H.-J. and Timmermann, M. (eds.), *Der Keynesianismus III. Die geld- und beschäftigungstheoretische Diskussion in Deutschland zur Zeit von Keynes* (Berlin, 1981)

Bondi, G., 'Die Rolle der statistik in einer geplanten Wirtschaft', *ASA*, 34 (1950), pp. 126–136.

Borchardt, K., 'Zur Aufarbeitung der Vor- und Frühgeschichte des Keynesianismus in Deutschland. Zugleich ein Beitrag zur Position von W. Lautenbach', *Jahrbücher für Nationalökonomie und Statistik*, 197 (1982), p. 360
Wachstum, Krisen, Handlungsspielräume der Wirtschaftspolitik. Studien zur Wirtschaftsgeschichte des 19. und 20. Jahrhunderts (Göttingen, 1982)

Borchardt, K. and Schötz, H.O. (eds.), *Wirtschaftspolitik in der Krise. Die (Geheim-) Konferenz der Friedrich-List-Gesellschaft im September 1931 über Möglichkeiten und Folgen einer Kreditausweitung* (Baden-Baden, 1991)
'Noch Einmal: Alternativen zu Brünings Wirtschaftspolitik?', *Historische Zeitschrift*, 237 (1983), p. 78

Born, K.E., *Die deutsche Bankenkrise 1931. Finanzen und Politik* (Munich, 1967)

Bourdieu, P., *Ce Que Parler veut Dire. L'économie des échanges linguistiques* (Paris, 1982)

Bourguet, M.-N., *Déchiffrer la France: la statistique départementale à l'époque napoléonienne* (Paris, 1988)

Bramstedt, P., 'Gefüge und Entwicklung der Volkswirtschaft', *ASA*, 25 (1936/1937), pp. 377–404

Broszat, M., *Der Staat Hitlers* (Munich, 1969, 13th edn.)

Bruch, R. vom, *Wissenschaft, Politik und öffentliche Meinung. Gelehrtenpolitik im Wilhelminischen Deutschland (1890–1914)* (Husum, 1980)

Brüning, H., *Memoiren 1918–1934* (Stuttgart, 1970)

Buchheim, C., Hutter, M. and James, H., (eds.), *Zerrissene Zwischenkriegszeit. Wirtschaftshistorische Beiträge* (Baden-Baden, 1994)

Bull, H.P., *Datenschutz oder die Angst vor dem Computer* (Munich, 1984)

Burchardt, L., 'Walther Rathenau und die Anfänge der deutschen Rohstoffbewirtschaftung im Ersten Weltkrieg', *Tradition*, 15 (1970), pp. 169–196

Burckhardt, J., 'Wirtschaft', in O. Brunner, W. Conze and R. Koselleck (eds.), *Geschichtliche Grundbegriffe. Historisches Lexicon zur politisch-sozialen Sprache in Deutschland* (Stuttgart, 1992), 7, 511–594

Burgdörfer, F., 'Die Volks-, Berufs- und Betriebszählung 1933', *ASA*, 23 (1933), pp. 145–171

Burk, K. (ed.), *War and the State. The Transformation of British Government 1914–1919* (London, 1982)

Busch, A., 'Zur Frage der Verwendung von Lochkartenmaschinen', *ASA*, 20 (1930), pp. 260–265

Cannadine, D., 'The Present and Past in the English Industrial Revolution', *Past and Present*, 103 (1984), pp. 131–172

Caplan, J., *Government Without Administration. State and Civil Service in Weimar and Nazi Germany* (Oxford, 1988)
   'National Socialism and the Theory of the State', in T. Childers and J. Caplan (eds.), *Reevaluating the Third Reich* (New York, 1993), pp. 98–113

Carroll, B.A., *Design for Total War. Arms and Economics in the Third Reich* (The Hague, 1968)

Carter, C.F. and Roy, A.D., *British Economic Statistics. A Report* (Cambridge, 1954), pp. 79–93

Cassel, G., *The Theory of Social Economy* (London, 1932 trans. of 5th German edn.)

Chevry, G., 'Un Nouvel Instrument de travail statistique: Le Fichier des établissements industriels et commerciaux?', *Journal de la Société de Statistique de Paris* (*JSSP*) 89 (1948), pp. 245–262

Clarke, P., 'The Twentieth-Century Revolution in Government: The Case of the British Treasury', in P. Clarke, *The Keynesian Revolution and its Economic Consequences* (Cheltenham, 1998), pp. 175–189

Coenen, E., *La 'Konjunkturforschung' en Allemagne et Autriche 1925–1933* (Paris, 1964)

Cohn, R., 'Fiscal Policy during the Depression', *Explorations in Economic History*, 29 (1992), pp. 318–342

Colm, G., *Volkswirtschaftliche Theorie der Staatsausgaben. Ein Beitrag zur Finanztheorie* (Tübingen, 1927)

Corrigan, P. and D. Sayer, *The Great Arch: English State Formation as Cultural Revolution* (Oxford, 1985), pp. 124–125

Crew, D.F., 'The Pathologies of Modernity: Detlev Peukert on Germany's Twentieth Century', *Social History*, 17 (1992), pp. 319–328

Cron, H., 'Die Kriegswollwirtschaft', in Reichsarchivs, *Kriegswirtschaftliche Organizationen* (Potsdam, manuscript 1932), Heft 5 Serie II

Curtis, B., 'Administrative Infrastructure and Social Enquiry: Finding the Facts about Agriculture in Quebec, 1853–4', *Journal of Social History*, 32 (1998), pp. 308–327

Curtius, J., *Bismarcks Plan eines Deutschen Volkswirtschaftsrats* (Heidelberg, 1919)
   Sechs Jahre Minister der Deutschen Republik (Heidelberg, 1948)

Davis, R., *The Industrial Revolution and British Overseas Trade* (Leicester, 1979)

Deist, W., *The Wehrmacht and German Rearmament* (London, 1981)

Desrosières, A., *La politique des grands nombres. Histoire de la raison statistique* (Paris, 1993)

Dichgans, H., *Zur Geschichte des Reichskommissars für die Preisbildung* (Düsseldorf, 1977)

Diehl, K. (ed.), *Beiträge zur Wirtschaftstheorie. Erster Teil: Volkseinkommen und Volksvermögen. Begriffskritische Untersuchungen, Schriften des Vereins für Sozialpolitik (SVS)* 173 I (Munich, 1926)

Beiträge zur Wirtschaftstheorie. Zweiter Teil: Konjunkturforschung und Konjunkturtheorie (SVS) 173 II (Munich, 1928)

DIW, *Die deutsche Industrie im Kriege 1939–45* (Berlin, 1954)

Das Deutsche Institut für Wirtschaftsforschung (IfK) 1925–1945 in der Erinnerung füherer Mitarbeiter (Berlin, 1966)

Dodd, N., *The Sociology of Money: Economics, Reason and Contemporary Society* (Cambridge, 1994)

Dupâquier, J. and Dupâquier, M., *Histoire de la Démographie* (Paris, 1985)

Eatwell, J., Milgate, M. and Newman, P., *The New Palgrave Dictionary of Economics* (London, 1987)

Ehlert, H.G., *Die Wirtschaftliche Zentralbehörde des Deutschen Reiches 1914 bis 1919. Das Problem der 'Gemeinwirtschaft' im Krieg und Frieden* (Wiesbaden, 1982)

Eichholz, D., *Geschichte der deutschen Kriegswirtschaft vol. 2 1941–1943* (Berlin (ost), 1985)

Eisfeld, C., 'Die wissenschaftliche und praktische Entwicklung der Betriebsstatistik', *ASA*, 17 (1927/1978), pp. 432–440

Ellis, H.S., *German Monetary Theory 1905–1933* (Cambridge, 1937)

Emmison, M., '"The economy": Its Emergence in Media Discourse', in H. Davis and P. Walton (eds.), *Language, Image, Media* (Oxford, 1983), pp. 139–155

Engel, E., 'Über die Organization der amtlichen Statistik mit besonderer Beziehung auf Preussen', *ZKPSB* 1 (1860) pp. 53–56

'Die Volkszählung ihre Stellung zur Wissenschaft und ihre Aufgabe in der Geschichte', *Zeitschrift des königlich preußischen statistischen Bureaus (ZKPSB)* 2 (1862), pp. 25–31

'Die Notwendigkeit einer Reform der volkswirtschaftlichen Statistik', *ZKPSB* 10 (1870), pp. 141–408

Esenwein-Rothe, I., *Die Wirtschaftsverbände von 1933 bis 1945* (Berlin, 1965)

Eysteinsson, A., *The Concept of Modernism* (Ithaca, 1990)

Facius, F., *Wirtschaft und Staat die Entwicklung der staatlichen Wirtschaftsverwaltung in Deutschland vom 17. Jahrhundert bis 1945* (Boppard, 1959)

Faust, A., *Arbeitsmarktpolitik im Deutschen Kaiserreich. Arbeitsvermittlung, Arbeitsbeschaffung und Arbeitslosenunterstützung 1890–1918* (Stuttgart, 1986)

Fear, J., 'Die Rüstungsindustrie im Gau Schwaben 1939–1945', *Vierteljahrshefte für Zeitgeschichte* 35 (1987), pp. 193–216

Feig, J., 'Deutschlands gewerbliche Entwicklung seit dem Jahre 1882.', *Zeitschrift für die gesamte Staatswissenschaft* 56 (1900)

Feldman, G.D., *Army, Industry and Labour* (Providence, 1992, reprint)

The Great Disorder. Politics, Economics, and Society in the German Inflation, 1914–1924 (Oxford, 1993)

'From Crisis to Work Creation. Government Policies and Economic Actors in the Great Depression', in J. Kocka, H.-J. Puhle and K. Tenfelde (eds.), *Von der Arbeiterbewegung zum modernen Sozialstaat. Festschrift für Gerhard A. Ritter zum 65. Geburtstag* (Munich, 1994), pp. 703–718

'The Deutsche Bank from World War to World Economic Crisis 1914–1933', in *The Deutsche Bank 1870–1945* (London, 1995), pp. 130–276

Feldman, G.D. and Steinisch, I., *Industrie und Gewerkschaften 1918–1924. Die überforderte Zentralarbeitsgemeinschaft* (Stuttgart, 1985)

Ferguson, N., 'Public Finance and National Security: The Domestic Origins of the First World War Revisited', *Past and Present*, 142 (1994), pp. 141–168

Paper and Iron. Hamburg Business and German Politics in the Era of Inflation, 1897–1927 (Cambridge, 1995)

Fisher, I., *The Nature of Capital and Income* (1906)

The Purchasing Power of Money (Boston, 1911)

The Making of Index Numbers. A Study of their Varieties, Tests and Reliability (Boston, 1927, 3rd edn.)

Flanders, M.J., *International Monetary Economics, 1870–1960. Between the Classical and the New Classical* (Cambridge, 1989)

Fourquet, F., *Les comptes de la puissance. Histoire de la comptabilité nationale et du plan* (Paris, 1980)

Friedman, R.M., *Appropriating the Weather. Vihelm Bjerknes and the Construction of a Modern Meteorology* (Ithaca, 1989)

Furner, M. and Supple, B. (eds.), *The State and Economic Knowledge. The American and British Experiences* (Cambridge, 1990)

Fürst, G., 'Wandlungen im Programm und in den Anfgaben der amtlichen Statistik in den Letzen 100 Jahren', in Statistiches Bundesamt, *Bevölkerung und Wirtschaft 1872–1972* (Stuttgart, 1972)

Gaehtgens, W., 'Die rechtlichen Grundlagen der Warenbewirtschaftung', in *Probleme der gelenkten Wirtschaft* (Berlin, 1942)

Garvy, G., 'Keynes and the Economic Activists of Pre-Hitler Germany', *Journal of Political Economy*, 83 (1975), pp. 391–405

Gay, P., *The Dilemma of Democratic Socialism. Eduard Bernstein's Challenge to Marx* (New York, 1952)

Geer, J.S., 'Die Statistik der Wirtschaftsgruppe Maschinenbau', in F. Burgdörfer (ed.), *Die Statistik in Deutschland nach ihrem heutigen Stand, Ehrengabe für F. Zahn* (Berlin, 1940), II, pp. 1039–1048

Gerß, W., *Lohnstatistik in Deutschland. Methodische, rechtliche und organisatorische Grundlagen seit der Mitte des 19. Jahrhunderts* (Berlin, 1977)

Geyer, M., *Aufrüstung oder Sicherheit. Die Reichswehr in der Krise der Machtpolitik 1924–1936* (Wiesbaden, 1980)

'Etudes in Political History: Reichswehr, NSDAP and the Seizure of Power', in P.D. Stachura (ed.), *The Nazi Machtergreifung* (London, 1983), pp. 101–123

'The State in National Socialist Germany', in C. Bright and S. Harding (eds.), *Statemaking and Social Movements: Essays in History and Theory* (Ann Arbor, 1984), pp. 193–232

Giddens, A., *The Nation-State and Violence, Vol. 2, A Contemporary Critique of Historical Materialism* (Cambridge, 1985)

Gierth, E., 'Aufbau und Methode der Industrieberichterstattung', *ASA*, 30 (1941/1942), pp. 298–299

Godfrey, J.F., *Capitalism at War. Industrial Policy and Bureaucracy in France 1914–1918* (Leamington Spa, 1987)

Goebel, O., *Deutsche Rohstoffwirtschaft im Weltkrieg. Einschließlich des Hindenburg-Programms* (Stuttgart, 1930)

Goschler, C. (ed.), *Hitler. Reden Schriften Anordnungen* (Munich, 1994)

Grävell, W., 'Die Not der Statistik und die Repräsentativ-Methode', *ASA*, 13 (1921/1922), pp. 345–353

'Statistische Abgabe und Anmeldung zur Handelsstatistik', *ASA*, 22 (1932/ 1933), pp. 69–80

'Die Vereinfachung und Vereinheitlichung der Wirtschaftsstatistik', *ASA*, 30 (1941/1942) pp. 57–75

Gregor, N., *Daimler-Benz in the Third Reich* (New Haven, 1998)

Griffen, R., *The Nature of Fascism* (London, 1991)

Grossmann, G., *Soviet Statistics of Physical Output of Industrial Commodities: Their Compilation and Quality* (Princeton, 1960)

Grünig, F., *Der Wirtschaftskreislauf* (Munich, 1933)

'Die Anfänge der "Volkswirtschaftlichen Gesamtrechnung" in Deutschland', in *Beiträge zur empirischen Konjunkturforschung. Festschrift zum 25jährigen Bestehen des DIW (IFK)* (Berlin, 1950), pp. 71–103

Hacking, I., *The Taming of Chance* (Cambridge, 1990)

Haffner, S., *Die Deutsche Revolution* (Munich, 1979)

Hagemann, H., 'The Analysis of Wages and Unemployment Revisited: Keynes and Economic "Activists" in pre-Hitler Germany', in L.C. Pasinetti and B. Schefold (eds.), *The Impact of Keynes on Economics in the 20th Century* (Cheltenham, 1999), pp. 117–130

Hall, P.A. (ed.), *The Political Power of Economic Ideas. Keynesianism across Nations* (Princeton, 1989)

'Hans Wolfgang Platzner', *ASA*, 46 (1962), pp. 192–193

Hansen, E.W., *Reichswehr und Industrie. Rüstungswirtschaftliche Zusammenarbeit und wirtschaftliche Mobilmachungsvorbereitungen 1923–1932* (Boppard, 1978)

Hansen, F.R., *The Breakdown of Capitalism. A History of the Idea in Western Marxism, 1883–1983* (London, 1985)

Harris, J., *Unemployment and Politics* (Oxford, 1972)

Haselberger, 'Erntefeststellung und Bewirtschaftung des Getreides', *ASA*, 11 (1918/1919), pp. 50–68

Hawtrey, R., *Good and Bad Trade* (London, 1913)

Hayes, P., 'History in an Off Key: David Abraham's Second Collapse', *Business History Review*, 61 (1987), pp. 452–472

Industry and Ideology. IG Farben in the Nazi Era (Cambridge, 1987)

Heimer, W., *Die Geschichte der deutschen Wirtschaftsstatistik von der Gründung des Deutschen Reichs bis zur Gegenwart* (Frankfurt, 1928)

Hentschel, V., *Wirtschaft und Wirtschaftspolitik im Wilhelminischen Deutschland. Organisierter Kapitalismus und Interventionsstaat* (Stuttgart, 1978)

Herbst, L., *Der Totale Krieg und die Ordnung der Wirtschaft. Die Kriegswirtschaft im Spannungsfeld von Politik, Ideologie und Propaganda 1939–1945* (Stuttgart, 1982)

Hermann, A.R., *Verstaatlichung des Giralgeldes* (Munich, 1932)

Herrigel, G., *Industrial Constructions. The Sources of German Industrial Power* (Cambridge, 1996)

Hertz-Eichenrode, D., *Wirtschaftskrise und Arbeitsbeschaffung. Konjunkturpolitik 1925/26 und die Grundlagen der Krisenpolitik Brünings* (Frankfurt, 1982)

Hitler Reden Schriften Anordnungen Part IV, Von der Reichstagswahl bis zur Reichspräsidentenwahl October 1930–März 1932, ed. C. Goschler (Munich, 1994)

Hölder, E., and M. Ehling, 'Zur Entwicklung der amtlichen Statistik in Deutschland', in W. Fischer and A. Kunz, (eds.), *Grundlagen der Historischen Statistik von Deutschland. Quellen, Methoden, Forschungsziele* (Opladen, 1991), pp. 15–31

Homze, E.L., *Arming the Luftwaffe. The Reich Air Ministry and the German Aircraft Industry 1919–1939* (Lincoln, Nebraska, 1976)

Hong, Y.-S. *Welfare, Modernity, and the Weimar State, 1919–1933* (Princeton, 1998)

Hubatsch, W., *Entstehung und Entwicklung des RWM 1880–1933. Ein Beitrag zur Verwaltungsgeschichte der Reichsministerien. Darstellung und Dokumentation* (Berlin, 1978)

Hughes, H.S., *Consciousness and Society. The Reorientation of European Social Thought 1890–1930* (London, 1974)

Huhle, F., *Statistik als ein Erkenntnismittel der Wirtschaftspolitik* (Jena, 1938)

IfK, *Russische Arbeiten zur Wirtschaftsforschung, VzK Sonderheft* 12 (Berlin, 1929)

Irving, D., *Die Tragödie der Deutschen Luftwaffe. Aus den Akten und Erinnerungen von Feldmarschall Milch* (Frankfurt, 1970)

Isaac, A., 'Die betriebswirtschaftliche Statistik im Dienste der Konjunkturforschung', *ASA* 18 (1928/1929), pp. 558–565

'Zusammenarbeit der volkswirtschaftlichen und privatwirtschaftlichen Statistik', *ASA*, 19 (1929/1930), pp. 347–360

Jacobs, A., 'Die neue amtliche Großhandelsindexziffer', *ASA*, 16 (1926/1927), pp. 619–623

'Der Weg bis zum Ende der Reichsstatistik', *Jahrbücher für Nationalökonomie und Statistik*, 185 (1971), pp. 289–313

Jaeckel, R., *Statistik und Verwaltung. Mit besonderer Berücksichtigung der Preussischen Verwaltungsreform* (Jena, 1913)

James, H., *The Reichsbank and Public Finance in Germany 1924–1933. A Study of the Politics of Economics during the Great Depression* (Frankfurt, 1985)

The German Slump. Politics and Economics 1924–1936 (New York, 1986)

'What is Keynesian about Deficit Financing? The Case of Interwar Germany', in P. Hall (ed.), *The Political Power of Economic Ideas. Keynesianism across Nations* (Princeton, 1989), pp. 233–262

'Innovation and Conservatism in Economic Recovery: The Alleged "Nazi Recovery" of the 1930s', in T. Childers and J. Caplan (eds.), *Reevaluating the Third Reich* (New York, 1993), pp. 114–138

Janssen, G., *Das Ministerium Speer. Deutschlands Rüstung im Krieg* (Frankfurt a.M., 1968)

Janssen, H., *Nationalökonomie und Nationalsozialismus. Die deutsche Volkswirtschaftslehre in den dreißiger Jahren* (Marburg, 1998)

Jasper, G., *Die gescheiterte Zähmung. Wege zur Machtergreifung Hitlers 1930–1934* (Frankfurt, 1986)

Jay, P. and Stewart, M., *Apocalypse 2000: Economic Breakdown and the Suicide of Democracy 1989–2000* (London, 1987)

Jochmann, W., 'Brünings Deflationspolitik und der Untergang der Weimarer Republik', in D. Stegmann, B.-J. Wendt and P.-C. Witt (eds.), *Industrielle Gesellschaft und politisches System. Beiträge zur politischen Sozialgeschichte* (Bonn, 1978), pp. 97–112

Jonung, L. (ed.), *The Stockholm School of Economics Revisited* (Cambridge, 1991)

Jostock, P., *Die Berechnung des Volkseinkommens und ihr Erkenntniswert* (Berlin, 1941)

Kahn, E. and Naphtali, F., *Wie liest man den Handelsteil einer Tageszeitung?* (Frankfurt, 1930, 2nd edn.)

Kahrs, H., 'Die ordnende hand der Arbeitsämter. Zur deutschen Arbeitsverwaltung 1933 bis 1939', in *Arbeitsmarkt und Sondererlass. Menschenverwertung, Rassenpolitik und Arbeitsamt* (Berlin, 1990), pp. 9–61

Kehrl, H., *Krisenmanager im Dritten Reich. 6 Jahre Frieden, 6 Jahre Krieg. Erinnerungen* (Düsseldorf, 1973)

Keiser, G. and Benning, B., *Kapitalbildung und Investitionen in der deutschen Volkswirtschaft 1924 bis 1928*, Sonderheft 22 *VzK* (Berlin, 1931)

Kershaw, I. (ed.), *Weimar: Why Did German Democracy Fail?* (London, 1990)
Hitler 1889–1936: Hubris (London, 1998)

Keynes, J.M., 'The British Balance of Trade, 1925–27', *Economic Journal*, 37 (1927), pp. 551–565
A Revision of the Treaty, Vol. III, *The Collected Writings of J.M. Keynes* (London, 1971)

Keyssar, A., *Out of Work. The First Century of Unemployment in Massachusetts* (Cambridge, 1986)

Kim, H., 'Die Großindustrie und die Konjunkturpolitik unter der Kanzlerschaft Brünings', *Jahrbuch für Wirtschaftsgeschichte* (1998), pp. 181–200

Kissenkoetter, U., *Gregor Straßer und die NSDAP* (Stuttgart, 1978)

Klein, J.L., *Statistical Visions in Time. A History of Time Series Analysis 1662–1938* (Cambridge, 1997)

Knortz, H., 'Der Arbeitsmarkt in der frühen Weimarer Republik. Ein Beitrag zur "Vollbeschäftigungsthese" der Inflationsforschung', *Jahrbuch für Wirtschaftsgeschichte* (1997), pp. 119–134

Koch, K., 'Die Verwendung von Speziallochkartenmaschinen bei der Volkszählung 1930 unter Berücksichtung ihrer technischen Entwicklung', *ASA*, 19 (1930), pp. 560–568

Kocka, J., *Klassengesellschaft im Krieg. Deutsche Sozialgeschichte 1914–1918* (Frankfurt, 1988, 2nd edn.)

Kolb, E., *Die Weimarer Republik* (Munich, 1984)

Koops, T. (ed.), *Akten der Reichskanzlei, Weimarer Republik, Die Kabinette Brüning I u. II* (Boppard, 1982)

Kopper, C., *Zwischen Marktwirtschaft und Dirigismus. Bankenpolitik im 'Dritten Reich' 1933–1939* (Bonn, 1995)

Krause, W., *Wirtschaftstheorie unter dem Hakenkreuz. Die bürgerliche politische Ökonomie in Deutschland während der faschistischen Herrschaft* (Berlin, 1969)

Krengel, R., *Das Deutsche Institut für Wirtschaftsforschung (IfK) 1925 bis 1979* (Berlin, 1985)

Krohn, C.-D., *Wirtschaftstheorien als politische Interessen. Die akademische Nationalökonomie in Deutschland 1918–1933* (Frankfurt, 1981)

Wissenschaft im Exil. Deutsche Sozial- und Wirtschaftswissenschaftler in den USA und die New School of Social Research (Frankfurt, 1987)

Kroll, G., *Von der Weltwirtschaftskrise zur Staatskonjunktur* (Berlin, 1958)

Krug, L., *Ideen zur einer Staatswirthschaftlichen Statistik* (Berlin, 1807)

Krüger, D., *Nationalökonomen im wilhelminischen Deutschland* (Göttingen, 1983)

Kruse, C., *Die Volkswirtschaftslehre im Nationalsozialismus* (Freiburg, 1988)

KSA, *Die Deutsche Volkswirtschaft am Schlusse des 19. Jahrhunderts. Auf Grund der Ergebnisse der Berufs- und Betriebszählung von 1895 und nach anderen Quellen, Kaiserliches Statistisches Amt* (Berlin, 1900)

'Gebiete und Methoden der amtlichen Arbeiterstatistik in den wichtigsten Industriestaaten', in *Beiträge zur Arbeiterstatistik*, 12 (Berlin, 1913)

Statistik des Deutschen Reichs. Bd. 211, Berufs und Betriebszählung vom 12. Juni 1907. Berufsstatistik Abteilung X, Die berufliche und soziale Gliederung des deutschen Volkes (Berlin, 1913)

Kube, A., *Pour le mérite und Hakenkreuz. Hermann Goering im Dritten Reich* (Munich, 1986)

Kuczynski, M. and Meek, R.L. (eds.), *Quesnay's Tableau Economique* (London, 1972)

Kulla, B., *Die Anfänge der empirischen Konjunkturforschung in Deutschland 1925–1933* (Berlin, 1996)

Kuschmann, H., *Die Untersuchungen des Berliner Instituts für Konjunkturforschung. Darstellung und Kritik* (Jena, 1933)

Laidler, D., *The Golden Age of the Quantity Theory* (Princeton, 1991)

Lautenbach, W., *Zins, Kredit und Produktion*, ed. W. Stützel (Tübingen, 1952)

Lederer, E., 'Der Zirkulationsprozess als zentrales Problem der ökonomischen Theorie', *Archiv für Sozialwissenschaft und Sozialpolitik*, 56 (1926), pp. 1–25

Leisse, W., *Wandlungen in der Organisation der Eisenindustrie und des Eisenhandels seit dem Gründungsjahr des Stahlwerksverbandes* (Munich, 1912)

Lenger, F., *Werner Sombart 1863–1941* (Munich, 1994)

Leontief, W., 'Die Wirtschaft als Kreislauf', *Archiv für Sozialwissenschaft und Sozialpolitik*, 60 (1928), pp. 577–623

'Vom Staatsbudget zum einheitlichen Finanzplan. Sowjetrussische Finanzprobleme', *Weltwirtschaftliches Archiv*, 33 (1931), pp. 231–260

'Quantitative Input and Output Relations in the Economic System of the United States', *The Review of Economic Statistics*, 18 (1936), pp. 105–125

Lindahl, E., Dahlgren, E. and Koch, K., *National Income of Sweden 1861–1930* (Stockholm, 1937)

Lindenlaub, D., *Richtungskämpfe im Verein für Sozialpolitik. Wissenschaft und Sozialpolitik im Kaiserreich* (Wiesbaden, 1967)

Lorenz, C., *Die Statistik in der Kriegswirtschaft* (Hamburg, 1936)

Löwe, A., 'Wie ist Konjunkturtheorie überhaupt möglich?', *Weltwirtschaftliches Archiv*, 24 (1926), pp. 165–196

Luhmann, N., *Die Wissenschaft der Gesellschaft* (Frankfurt, 1991)

Luxemburg, R., *Einführung in die Nationalökonomie* (Berlin, 1925)

Machlup, F., 'Three Concepts of the Balance of Payments and the So-Called Dollar Gap', *Economic Journal*, 40 (1950), pp. 46–68

Maier, C.S., 'Society as Factory', in *In Search of Stability. Explorations in Historical Political Economy* (Cambridge, 1987), pp. 19–69

In Search of Stability. Explorations in Historical Political Economy (Cambridge, 1987), pp. 19–69

Recasting Bourgeois Europe. Stabilization in France, Germany, and Italy in the Decade after World War I (Princeton, 1988, reprint)

Maizels, A., 'The Overseas Trade Statistics of the United Kingdom', *Journal of the Royal Statistical Society*, 112 (1949), II, pp. 207–223

Mason, T.W., *Sozialpolitik im Dritten Reich. Arbeiterklasse und Volksgemeinschaft* (Opladen, 1977, 2nd edn.)

McKitrick, F.L., 'An Unexpected Path to Modernisation: The Case of German Artisans during the Second World War', *Contemporary European History*, 5 (1996), pp. 401–426

Meek, R.L., *The Economics of Physiocracy* (London, 1962)

Meerwarth, R., 'Die Erfassung der Hausindustrie durch die gewerbliche Betriebsstatistik', *Jahrbücher für Nationalökonomie und Statistik*, III, 42 (1911), pp. 313–330

'Die Berufs- und Betriebszählung im Deutschen Reich vom 12. Juni 1907 und ihre Literatur', *Deutsches Statistisches Zentralblatt*, 5 (1913), pp. 97–106

Einleitung in die Wirtschaftsstatistik (Jena, 1920)

Meister, R., *Die große Depression. Zwangslagen und Handlungsspielräume der Wirtschafts- und Finanzpolitik in Deutschland 1929–1932* (Regensburg, 1991)

Melossi, D., *The State of Social Control. A Sociological Study of Concepts of State and Social Control in the Making of Democracy* (Cambridge, 1990)

Menges, G. and Zwer, R. (eds.), *Probleme internationaler wirtschafts- und sozialstatistischer Vergleiche. Rolf Wagenführ zum Gedächtnis* (Cologne, 1981)

Middleton, R., *Government versus the Market. The Growth of the Public Sector, Economic Management and British Economic Performance, c. 1890–1979* (Cheltenham, 1996)

Charlatans or Saviours? Economists and the British Economy from Marshall to Meade (Cheltenham, 1998)

Miller, P. and Rose, N., 'Governing Economic Life', *Economy and Society*, 19 (1990), pp. 1–31

Mirowski, P., *More Heat than Light. Economics as Social Physics: Physics as Nature's Economics* (Cambridge, 1989)

Mollin, G., *Montankonzerne und 'Drittes Reich'. Der Gegensatz zwischen Monopolindustrie und Befehlswirtschaft in der deutschen Rüstung und Expansion 1936–1944* (Göttingen, 1988)

Mommsen, H., *From Weimar to Auschwitz. Essays in German History* (Cambridge, 1991)

Montias, J.M., 'Planning with Material Balances in Soviet-Type Economies', in A. Nove and D.M. Nuti (eds.), *Socialist Economics* (Harmondsworth, 1972), pp. 223–251

Moretti, F., 'Conjectures on World Literature', *New Left Review*, II, 1 (2000)

Morgan, M., *The History of Economic Ideas* (Cambridge, 1990)

Müller, A., *Die Kriegsrohstoffbewirtschaftung 1914–1918 im Dienste des deutschen Monopolkapitals* (Berlin, 1955)

Müller, K.J., *The Army, Politics and Society in Germany, 1933–1945* (Manchester, 1987)

Müller, R.-D., 'Die Mobilisierung der Deutschen Wirtschaft für Hitlers Kriegs-
führung', in B.R. Kroener, R.-D. Müller and H. Umbreit, *Das Deutsche
Reich und der Zweite Weltkrieg* (Stuttgart, 1988), 5, 1, pp. 347–689
*Der Manager der Kriegswirtschaft. Hans Kehrl: Ein Unternehmer in der Politik des
Dritten Reiches* (Essen, 1999)
'Nécrologie: René Carmille', *JSSP*, 86 (1945), pp. 145–148
Neebe, R., *Großindustrie, Staat und NSDAP 1930–1933. Paul Silverberg und der
Reichsverband der Deutschen Industrie in der Krise der Weimarer Republik*
(Göttingen, 1981)
Nerschmann, O., 'Die Englische Produktionserhebung von 1907', *ASA*, 8
(1914/1915), pp. 53–71
Neumann, F., *Behemoth. The Structure and Practice of National Socialism
1933–1944* (New York, 1963, reprint)
Nolan, M., *Visions of Modernity. American Business and the Modernization of
Germany* (Oxford, 1994)
Osterwald, E., *Die Entstehung des Stabilitätsgesetzes. Eine studie über Entscheldungs-
prozesse des politischen Systems* (Frankfurt, 1982)
Overy, R.J., *Goering The 'Iron Man'* (London, 1984)
War and Economy in the Third Reich (Oxford, 1994)
Why the Allies Won (London, 1995)
Patinkin, D., *Anticipations of the General Theory. And other Essays on Keynes*
(Chicago, 1982)
Patriarca, S., *Numbers and Nationhood: Writing Statistics in Nineteenth-Century
Italy* (Cambridge, 1996)
Peden, G.C., *Keynes, The Treasury and British Economic Policy* (London, 1988)
Perlman, M., 'Political Purpose and the National Accounts', in W. Alonson and
P. Starr (eds.), *The Politics of Numbers* (New York, 1987)
Perrot, J.-C. and Woolf, S.J., *State and Statistics in France, 1789–1915* (London,
1984)
Petzold, H., *Rechnende Maschinen. Eine historische Untersuchung ihrer Herstellung
und Anwendung vom Kaiserreich bis zur Bundesrepublik* (Düsseldorf, 1985)
Peukert, D., *Die Weimarer Republik. Krisenjahre der Klassischen Moderne* (Frank-
furt, 1987)
'Zur Erforschung der Sozialpolitik im Dritten Reich', in H.-U. Otto and
H. Sünker (eds.), *Soziale Arbeit und Faschismus* (Frankfurt, 1989)
'The Genesis of the "Final Solution" from the Spirit of Science', in
T. Childers and J. Caplan (eds.), *Reevaluating the Third Reich* (New York,
1993), pp. 234–252
Pietzsch, A. and Grünig, F., 'Grundlagen der Wirtschaftslenkung', in *Grund-
lagen, Aufbau und Wirtschaftsordnung des nationalsozialistischen Staates*
(Berlin, 1936), 3, Beitrag 45
Pigou, A.C., *Wealth and Welfare* (London, 1912)
Plenge, J., 'Zum "Tableau Economique"', *Weltwirtschaftliches Archiv*, 24 (1926),
pp. 109–129
Plumpe, G., 'Wirtschaftspolitik in der Weltwirtschaftskrise. Realität und Alter-
nativen', *GuG*, 11 (1985), pp. 326–357
Pohl, M., 'Gedanken zur Entstehung und Bedeutung der Grossen Bankarchive',
Bankhistorisches Archiv, Zeitschrift zur Bankgeschichte, 2 (1976), pp. 46–52

Porter, T.M., *Trust in Numbers. The Pursuit of Objectivity in Science and Public Life* (Princeton, 1995)

Pribram, K., 'Die Zukunft der amtlichen Statistik', *DSZ*, 9 (1917), pp. 129–138

'European Experiences and New Deal Statistics', *Journal of the American Statistical Association*, 30 (1935), pp. 227–236

Quante, P., 'Die Erfahrung mit elektrischen Zählmaschinen in Preußen bei der Volks- und Berufszählung vom 16. Juni 1925', *ASA*, 20 (1930), pp. 82–112

Radice, H., 'The National Economy: A Keynesian Myth?', *Capital and Class*, 22 (1984), pp. 111–140

Rassem, M. (ed.), *Statistik und Staatsbeschreibung in der Neuzeit* (Paderborn, 1980)

Rathenau, W., *Deutschlands Rohstoffversorgung* (Berlin, 1918)

Reichardt, W., 'Die Reichsstatistik', in *Die Statistik in Deutschland nach ihrem heutigen Stand. Ehrengabe für Friedrich Zahn*, ed. F. Burgdörfer (Berlin, 1940), 1, pp. 77–90

Reichsamt für wehrwirtschaftliche Planung, *Die Deutsche Industrie. Gesamtergebnisse der Amtlichen Produktionsstatistik* (Berlin, 1939)

Ritschl, A. and Spoerer, M., 'Das Bruttosozialprodukt in Deutschland nach den amtlichen Volkseinkommens- und Sozialproduktsstatistiken, 1901–1995', *Jahrbuch für Wirtschaftsgeschichte* (1997), pp. 27–54

Robertson, D.H., *A Study in Industrial Fluctuations* (London, 1915)

Roerkohl, A., *Hungerblockade und Heimatfront. Die kommunale Lebensmittelversorgung in Westfalen während des Ersten Weltkriegs* (Stuttgart, 1991)

Roseman, M., 'National Socialism and Modernization', in R. Bessel (ed.), *Fascist Italy and Nazi Germany. Comparisons and Contrasts* (Cambridge, 1996), pp. 197–229

Röske, U., 'Die amtliche Statistik des Deutschen Reichs 1872 bis 1939. Historische Entwicklung, Organisationsstruktur, Veröffentlichungen', *Jahrbuch für Wirtschaftsgeschichte*, 4 (1978), pp. 85–107

Ross, D., *The Origins of American Social Science* (Cambridge, 1991)

(ed.), *Modernist Impulses in the Human Sciences 1870–1930* (Baltimore, 1994)

'Rudolf Meerwarth zum Gedächtnis', *ASA*, 35 (1951), pp. 157–162

Rürup, R., *Probleme der Revolution in Deutschland 1918/19* (Wiesbaden, 1968)

Saenger, K., 'Das Preußische Statistische Landesamt 1805–1934. Ein Nachruf', *ASA*, 24 (1935/1936), pp. 445–460

Salais, R., Bavarez, N. and Reynaud, B., *L'invention du chômage* (Paris, 1986)

Schoenbaum, D., *Hitler's Social Revolution: Class and Status in Nazi Germany 1933–1939* (New York, 1966)

Scholz, R., 'Lohn und Beschäftigung als Indikatoren für die soziale Lage der Arbeiterschaft in der Inflation', in G.D. Feldman, C.-L. Holtfrerich, G.A. Ritter and P.-C. Witt (eds.), *Die Anpassung an die Inflation* (Berlin, 1986), pp. 278–322

Schröter, A., *Krieg – Staat – Monopol: 1914–1918. Die Zusammenhänge von imperialistischer Kriegswirtschaft, Militarisierung der Volkswirtschaft und staatsmonopolistischer Kapitalismus in Deutschland während des ersten Weltkrieges* (Berlin, 1965)

Schröter, A., and Bach, J., 'Zur Planung der wirtschaftlichen Mobilmachung durch den deutschen faschistischen Imperialismus vor dem Beginn des zweiten Weltkrieges', *Jahrbuch für Wirtschaftsgeschichte*, 1 (1978), pp. 31–47

Schubert, J., 'Die Amtsverschwiegenheit der Statistik. Eine statistisch-juristische Betrachtung', *ASA*, 23 (1934), pp. 610–618

Schulz, G., *Zwischen Demokratie und Diktatur. Verfassungspolitik und Reichsform in der Weimarer Republik*. Vol. I, *Die Periode der Konsolidierung und der Revision des Bismarckschen Reichsaufbaus 1919–1930* (Berlin, 1987, 2nd edn.); Vol. III, *Von Brüning von Hitler. Der Wandel des politischen Systems in Deutschland 1930–1933* (Berlin, 1992)

Schultz, G., Maurer, I. and Wengst, U. (eds.), *Politik and Wirtschaft in der Krise 1930–1932. Quellen zur Ära Brüning* (Düsseldorf, 1980)

Schumpeter, J.A., 'Das Sozialprodukt und die Reichenpfennige', *Archiv für Sozialwissenschaft und Sozialpolitik*, 44 (1918), pp. 627–715

Theorie der wirtschaftlichen Entwicklung (1931, Munich, 3rd edn.)

The Great Economists from Marx to Keynes (London, 1952)

'Die Wirtschaftstheorie der Gegenwart in Deutschland', in *Dogmenhistorische und Biographische Aufsätze* (Tübingen, 1954), pp. 255–284

History of Economic Analysis (New York, 1954)

Schwartz, P., 'Zur Frage der Anwendbarkeit der mechanischen Auszählung bei statistischen Erhebungen', *ASA*, 20 (1930), pp. 266–270

Scott, J.C., *Seeing Like a State. How Certain Schemes to Improve the Human Condition have Failed* (New Haven, 1998)

Skalweit, A., *Die Deutsche Kriegsernährungswirtschaft* (Stuttgart, 1927)

Skowronek, S., *Building a New American State. The Expansion of National Administrative Capacities, 1877–1920* (Cambridge, 1982)

Smolinski, L., 'Planning Without Theory 1917–1967', *Survey. A Journal of Soviet and East European Studies*, 64 (1967), pp. 108–128

Sombart, W., *Der moderne Kapitalismus* (Munich, 1927)

Die Deutsche Volkswirtschaft im neunzehnten Jahrhundert und im Anfang des 20. Jahrhunderts. Eine Einführung in die Nationalökonomie (Berlin, 1927, 7th edn.)

Spluber, N. (ed.), *Foundations of Soviet Strategy for Economic Growth. Selected Soviet Essays, 1924–1930* (Bloomington, 1964)

SRA, *Zahlen zur Geldentwertung in Deutschland 1914 bis 1923. Sonderheft 1 zu Wirtschaft und Statistik, Bd. 5* (Berlin, 1925)

Konzerne, Interessensgemeinschaften und ähnliche Zusammenschlüsse im Deutschen Reich Ende 1926. Einzelschriften zur Statistik des Deutschen Reichs Nr. 1 (Berlin, 1927)

Das deutsche Volkseinkommen vor und nach dem Kriege. Einzelschriften zur Statistik des Deutschen Reichs Nr. 24 (Berlin, 1932)

Öffentlicher Kredit und Wirtschaftskrise. Ergebnisse der Reichsschuldenstatistik 1929 bis 1932 und Zusammenstellung von Rechtsvorschriften über das öffentliche Schuldenwesen. Einzelschriften zur Statistik des Deutschen Reichs Nr. 27 (Berlin, 1933)

Staudinger, H., *Wirtschaftspolitik im Weimarer Staat. Lebenserinnerungen eines politischen Beamten im Reich und in Preußen 1889 bis 1934* (Bonn, 1982)

Stegmann, D., *Die Erben Bismarcks. Parteien und Verbände in der Spätphase des Wilhelminischen Deutschlands. Sammlungspolitik 1897–1918* (Cologne, 1970)

Steinmetz, G., *Regulating the Social. The Welfare State and Local Politics in Imperial Germany* (Princeton, 1993)

Stolleis, M., 'Gemeinschaft und Volksgemeinschaft. Zur juristischen Terminologie im Nationalsozialismus', *Vierteljahrshefte für Zeitgeschichte*, 20 (1972), pp. 16–38

Gemeinwohlformeln im nationalsozialistischen Recht (Berlin, 1974)

Studenski, P. *The Income of Nations*, I (New York, 1958, rev. edn.), pp. 171–153

Tammen, H., *Die IG Farben-Industrie AG (1925–1933). Ein Chemiekonzern in der Weimarer Republik* (Berlin, 1978)

Teichert, E., *Autarkie und Großraumwirtschaft in Deutschland 1930–1939. Außenwirtschaftliche Konzeptionen zwischen Wirtschaftskrise und Zweitem Weltkrieg* (Munich, 1984)

The Economist 1843–1943 (Oxford, 1943)

Thomä, K.E., *Auskunfts- und Betriebsprüfungsrecht der Verwaltung, seine rechtstaatlichen Grenzen* (Heidelberg, 1955)

Thomas, G., *Geschichte der deutschen Wehr- und Rüstungswirtschaft (1918–1943/45)*, ed. W. Birkenfeld (Boppard, 1966)

Tinbergen, J., 'Annual Survey: Suggestions on Quantitative Business Cycle Theory', *Econometrica*, 3 (1935), pp. 241–308

Tomlinson, J., *Democratic Socialism and Economic Policy. The Attlee years, 1945–1951* (Cambridge, 1997)

Tooze, J.A., 'Imagining National Economies: National and International Economic Statistics, 1900–1950', in G. Cubitt (ed.), *Imagining Nations* (Manchester, 1998)

'La connaissance de l'activité économique. Reflexions sur l'histoire de la statistique économique en France et en Allemagne, 1914–1950', in B. Zimmermann, C. Didry and P. Wagner (eds.), *Le Travail et la Nation. Histoire croisée de la France et de l'Allemagne* (Paris, 1999), pp. 55–80

Tribe, K., *Strategies of Economic Order. German Economic Discourse, 1750–1950* (Cambridge, 1995)

Tudor, H., *Marxism and Social Democracy. The Revisionist Debate 1896–1898* (Cambridge, 1988)

Vilk, R., *Von der Konjunkturtheorie zur Theorie der Konjunkturpolitik. Ein historischer Abriß 1930–1945* (Wiesbaden, 1992)

Vogelsang, M., 'Die deutsche Konzernstatistik. Ein geschichtlicher, kritischer und technischer Beitrag', *ASA*, 19 (1929), pp. 29–46

Volkmann, H.-E., 'Die NS-Wirtschaft in Vorbereitung des Krieges', in W. Deist, M. Messerschmidt, H.-E. Volkmann and W. Wette, *Ursachen und Voraussetzungen des Zweiten Weltkrieges* (Frankfurt, 1989, 2nd edn.)

von Krüdener, J. (ed.), *Economic Crisis and Political Collapse: The Weimar Republic 1924–1933* (Oxford, 1990)

von Roeder, E., 'Die industrielle Produktionsstatistik', in F. Burgdörfer (ed.), *Die Statistik in Deutschland nach ihrem heutigen Stand. Ehrengabe für Friedrich Zahn* (Berlin, 1940), 2, pp. 1012–1024

von Scheel, H., 'Die politische ökonomie als Wissenschaft', in G. von Schönberg (ed.), *Handbuch der Politischen Ökonomie* (Tübingen 1896, 4th edn.), I, pp. 77–118 von Valta, R., 'Das Arbeitsbuch in der Statistik', *ASA*, 27 (1937/1938), pp. 263–273

'Die erste Arbeitsbucherhebung vom 25. Juni 1938', *ASA*, 28 (1939), pp. 401–421

'Die Statistik des Arbeitseinsatzes', in F. Burgdörfer (ed.), *Die Statistik in Deutschland nach ihrem heutigen Stand. Ehrengabe für Friedrich Zahn* (Berlin, 1940), 2, pp. 663–675

Wagemann, E., *Allgemeine Geldlehre* (Berlin, 1923)

Konjunkturlehre. Eine Grundlegung zur Lehre von Rhythmus der Wirtschaft (Berlin, 1928)

Struktur und Rhythmus der Weltwirtschaft. Grundlagen einer Weltwirtschaftlichen Konjunkturlehre (Berlin, 1931)

Geld- und Kreditreform (Berlin, 1932)

Zwischenbilanz der Krisenpolitik (Berlin, 1935)

Wirtschaftspolitische Strategie (Hamburg, 1937)

Wagen, Wägen and Wirtschaften. Erprobte Faustregeln – Neue Wege (Hamburg, 1954), p. 72

Wagenführ, R., 'Die "Volkswirtschaftliche Bilanz" (II): Das "Schachbrett"', *Mitteilungen des wirtschaftswissenschaftlichen Instituts der Gewerkschaften* (1952), pp. 39–45

Mensch und Wirtschaft. Eine Nationalökonomie für Jedermann (Cologne, 1952)

Die deutsche Industrie im Kriege 1939–1945 (Berlin, 1963, 2nd edn.)

'Walter Grävell ist 65', *ASA*, 40 (1956), p. 176

'Walter Grävell', *ASA*, 46 (1962), pp. 81–83

Walters, W., 'The Discovery of "Unemployment": New Forms for the Government of Poverty', *Economy and Society*, 23 (1994), pp. 265–290

Walther, R., '. . . aber nach der Sündflut kommen wir und nur wir.' *'Zusammenbruchstheorie', Marxismus und politisches Defizit in der SPD, 1890–1914* (Frankfurt, 1981)

Wandel, E., *Hans Schäffer. Steuermann in wirtschaftlichen und politischen Krisen 1886–1967* (Stuttgart, 1974)

Webb, S.B., *Hyperinflation and Stabilization in Weimar Germany* (Oxford, 1989)

Weber, M., *Wirtschaft und Gesellschaft* (Tübingen, 1972, 5th edn.)

Weisbrod, B., *Schwerindustrie in der Weimarer Republik* (Wuppertal, 1978)

Welter, E., *Falsch und Richtig Planen* (Frankfurt, 1954)

Wilts, A., 'Changes in Dutch Economics in the 1930s', in P. Fontaine and A. Jolink (eds.), *Historical Perspectives on Macroeconomics. Sixty Years after the General Theory* (London, 1998), pp. 105–132

Winkler, H.A., *Von der Revolution zur Stabilisierung. Arbeiter und Arbeiterbewegung in der Weimarer Republik 1918 bis 1924* (Berlin, 1984)

Winter, J. and Robert, J.-L. (eds.), *Capital Cities at War: Paris, London, Berlin 1914–1919* (Cambridge, 1999)

Wirth, F., *Die Wirtschaftsteile Deutscher Zeitungen* (Leipzig, 1927)

Wissler, A., *Ernst Wagemann: Begründer der empirischen Konjunkturforschung in Deutschland* (Berlin 1954)

Witt, P.-C., *Die Finanzpolitik des Deutschen Reiches von 1903 bis 1913. Eine Studie zur Innenpolitik des Wilhelminischen Deutschland* (Lübeck, 1970)

'Bemerkungen zur Wirtschaftspolitik in der "Übergangswirtschaft" 1918/19, zur Entwicklung von Konjunkturbeobachtung und Konjunktursteuerung in Deutschland', in D. Stegmann, B.J. Wendt and P.-C. Witt (eds.), *Industrielle Gesellschaft und politisches System. Beiträge zur politischen Sozialgeschichte. Festschrift für F. Fischer zum 70. Geburtstag* (Bonn, 1978), pp. 79–96

'Staatliche Wirtschaftspolitik in Deutschland 1918–1923: Entwicklung und Zerstörung einer modernen wirtschaftspolitischen Strategie', in G.D. Feldman, C.-L. Holtfrerich, G.A. Ritter and P.-C. Witt (eds.), *The German Inflation Reconsidered. A Preliminary Balance* (Berlin, 1982), pp. 151–179

Wolff, H., 'Struktur und Konjunktur', *ASA*, 17 (1927/1928), pp. 205–235

Woolf, S.J., 'Statistics and the Modern State', *Comparative Studies in Society and History*, 31 (1989), pp. 588–604

Yates, J., *Control through Communication. The Rise of System in American Management* (Baltimore, 1989)

Zitelmann, R., *Hitler. Selbstverständnis eines Revolutionärs* (Stuttgart, 1990, 2nd edn.)

Zunkel, F., *Industrie und Staatssozialismus. Der Kampf um die Wirtschaftsordnung in Deutschland 1914–1918* (Düsseldorf, 1974)

Index